G000095632

WORLD INVESTMENT REPORT 2012

TOWARDS A NEW GENERATION OF INVESTMENT POLICIES

UNITED NATIONS

New York and Geneva, 2012

NOTE

The Division on Investment and Enterprise of UNCTAD is a global centre of excellence, dealing with issues related to investment and enterprise development in the United Nations System. It builds on three and a half decades of experience and international expertise in research and policy analysis, intergovernmental consensus-building, and provides technical assistance to developing countries.

The terms country/economy as used in this *Report* also refer, as appropriate, to territories or areas; the designations employed and the presentation of the material do not imply the expression of any opinion whatsoever on the part of the Secretariat of the United Nations concerning the legal status of any country, territory, city or area or of its authorities, or concerning the delimitation of its frontiers or boundaries. In addition, the designations of country groups are intended solely for statistical or analytical convenience and do not necessarily express a judgment about the stage of development reached by a particular country or area in the development process. The major country groupings used in this *Report* follow the classification of the United Nations Statistical Office. These are:

Developed countries: the member countries of the OECD (other than Chile, Mexico, the Republic of Korea and Turkey), plus the new European Union member countries which are not OECD members (Bulgaria, Cyprus, Latvia, Lithuania, Malta and Romania), plus Andorra, Bermuda, Liechtenstein, Monaco and San Marino.

Transition economies: South-East Europe and the Commonwealth of Independent States.

Developing economies: in general all economies not specified above. For statistical purposes, the data for China do not include those for Hong Kong Special Administrative Region (Hong Kong SAR), Macao Special Administrative Region (Macao SAR) and Taiwan Province of China.

Reference to companies and their activities should not be construed as an endorsement by UNCTAD of those companies or their activities.

The boundaries and names shown and designations used on the maps presented in this publication do not imply official endorsement or acceptance by the United Nations.

The following symbols have been used in the tables:
- Two dots (..) indicate that data are not available or are not separately reported. Rows in tables have been omitted in those cases where no data are available for any of the elements in the row;
- A dash (–) indicates that the item is equal to zero or its value is negligible;
- A blank in a table indicates that the item is not applicable, unless otherwise indicated;
- A slash (/) between dates representing years, e.g., 1994/95, indicates a financial year;
- Use of a dash (–) between dates representing years, e.g., 1994–1995, signifies the full period involved, including the beginning and end years;
- Reference to "dollars" ($) means United States dollars, unless otherwise indicated;
- Annual rates of growth or change, unless otherwise stated, refer to annual compound rates;

Details and percentages in tables do not necessarily add to totals because of rounding.

The material contained in this study may be freely quoted with appropriate acknowledgement.

UNITED NATIONS PUBLICATION
Sales No. E.12.II.D.3
ISBN 978-92-1-112843-7
e-ISBN 978-92-1-055375-9
Copyright © United Nations, 2012
All rights reserved
Printed in Switzerland

PREFACE

Prospects for foreign direct investment (FDI) continue to be fraught with risks and uncertainties. At $1.5 trillion, flows of global FDI exceeded pre-financial crisis levels in 2011, but the recovery is expected to level off in 2012 at an estimated $1.6 trillion. Despite record cash holdings, transnational corporations have yet to convert available cash into new and sustained FDI, and are unlikely to do so while instability remains in international financial markets. Even so, half of the global total will flow to developing and transition economies, underlining the important development role that FDI can play, including in least developed countries.

A broader development policy agenda is emerging that has inclusive and sustainable development goals at its core. For investment policy, this new paradigm poses specific challenges. At the national level they include integrating investment policy into development strategy, incorporating sustainable development objectives, and ensuring relevance and effectiveness. At the international level it is necessary to strengthen the development dimension of international investment agreements, manage their complexity, and balance the rights and obligations of States and investors.

Against this background, this year's World Investment Report unveils the UNCTAD Investment Policy Framework for Sustainable Development. Mobilizing investment for sustainable development is essential in this era of persistent crises and pressing social and environmental challenges. As we look ahead to the post-2015 development framework, I commend this important tool for the international investment community.

BAN Ki-moon
Secretary-General of the United Nations

ACKNOWLEDGEMENTS

The *World Investment Report 2012* (*WIR12*) was prepared by a team led by James Zhan. The team members included Richard Bolwijn, Quentin Dupriez, Kumi Endo, Masataka Fujita, Thomas van Giffen, Michael Hanni, Joachim Karl, Guoyong Liang, Anthony Miller, Hafiz Mirza, Nicole Moussa, Shin Ohinata, Sergey Ripinsky, Astrit Sulstarova, Elisabeth Tuerk and Jörg Weber. Wolfgang Alschner, Amare Bekele, Dolores Bentolila, Anna-Lisa Brahms, Joseph Clements, Hamed El Kady, Noelia Garcia Nebra, Ariel Ivanier, Elif Karakas, Abraham Negash, Faraz Rojid, Diana Rosert, Claudia Salgado, John Sasuya, Katharina Wortmann, Youngjun Yoo and intern Cree Jones also contributed to the Report.

WIR12 benefited from the advice of Lorraine Eden, Arvind Mayaram, Ted Moran, Rajneesh Narula, Karl Sauvant and Pierre Sauvé.

Bradley Boicourt and Lizanne Martinez provided research and statistical assistance. They were supported by Hector Dip and Ganu Subramanian. Production and dissemination of *WIR12* was supported by Elisabeth Anodeau-Mareschal, Severine Excoffier, Rosalina Goyena, Natalia Meramo-Bachayani and Katia Vieu.

The manuscript was copy-edited by Lise Lingo and typeset by Laurence Duchemin and Teresita Ventura. Sophie Combette designed the cover.

At various stages of preparation, in particular during the seminars organized to discuss earlier drafts of *WIR12*, the team benefited from comments and inputs received from Masato Abe, Michael Addo, Ken-ichi Ando, Yuki Arai, Nathalie Bernasconi, Michael Bratt, Jeremy Clegg, Zachary Douglas, Roberto Echandi, Wenjie Fan, Alejandro Faya, Stephen Gelb, Robert Howse, Christine Kaufmann, Anna Joubin-Bret, Jan Kleinheisterkamp, John Kline, Galina Kostyunina, Markus Krajewski, Padma Mallampally, Kate Miles, Peter Muchlinski, Marit Nilses, Federico Ortino, Joost Pauwelyn, Andrea Saldarriaga, Stephan Schill, Jorge Vinuales, Stephen Young and Zbigniew Zimny. Comments were also received from numerous UNCTAD colleagues, including Kiyoshi Adachi, Stephania Bonilla, Chantal Dupasquier, Fulvia Farinelli, Torbjörn Fredriksson, Kálmán Kalotay, Fiorina Mugione, Christoph Spennemann, Paul Wessendorp, Richard Kozul-Wright and colleagues from the Division on Globalization and Development Strategies and the Division on International Trade and Commodities.

Numerous officials of central banks, government agencies, international organizations and non-governmental organizations also contributed to *WIR12*. The financial support of the Governments of Finland, Norway, Sweden and Switzerland is gratefully acknowledged.

TABLE OF CONTENTS

Boxes

Box Tables

Box Figures

Figures

Tables

ABBREVIATIONS

ADR	alternative dispute resolution
ASEAN	Association of Southeast Asian Nations
BIT	bilateral investment treaty
BRIC	Brazil, Russian Federation, India and China
CIS	Commonwealth of Independent States
CSR	corporate social responsibility
EPF	Entrepreneurship Policy Framework
FDI	foreign direct investment
FET	fair and equitable treatment
FPS	full protection and security
FTA	free trade agreement
GATS	General Agreement on Trade in Services
GCC	Gulf Cooperation Council
GDP	gross domestic product
GSP	Generalized System of Preferences
GVC	global value chain
ICC	International Chamber of Commerce
ICSID	International Centre for Settlement of Investment Disputes
IIA	international investment agreement
IP	intellectual property
IPA	investment promotion agency
IPFSD	Investment Policy Framework for Sustainable Development
IPM	Investment Policy Monitor
IPR	Investment Policy Review
ISDS	investor–State dispute settlement
LDC	least developed countries
LLDC	landlocked developing countries
M&A	mergers and acquisitions
MFN	most-favoured-nation
MST-CIL	minimum standard of treatment – customary international law
NAFTA	North American Free Trade Agreement
NEM	non-equity mode
NGO	non-governmental organization
NT	national treatment
PPP	public-private partnership
PR	performance requirement
PRAI	Principles for Responsible Agricultural Investment
SD	sustainable development
SEZ	special economic zone
SDT	special and different treatment
SIDS	small island developing States
SME	small and medium-sized enterprise
SOE	State-owned enterprise
SPE	special-purpose entity
SWF	sovereign wealth fund
TNC	transnational corporation
TPP	Trans-Pacific Partnership
TRIMs	Trade-Related Investment Measures
UNCITRAL	United Nations Commission on International Trade Law
WIPS	World Investment Prospects Survey

KEY MESSAGES

FDI TRENDS AND PROSPECTS

Global foreign direct investment (FDI) flows exceeded the pre-crisis average in 2011, reaching $1.5 trillion despite turmoil in the global economy. However, they still remained some 23 per cent below their 2007 peak.

UNCTAD predicts slower FDI growth in 2012, with flows levelling off at about $1.6 trillion. Leading indicators – the value of cross-border mergers and acquisitions (M&As) and greenfield investments – retreated in the first five months of 2012 but fundamentals, high earnings and cash holdings support moderate growth. Longer-term projections show a moderate but steady rise, with global FDI reaching $1.8 trillion in 2013 and $1.9 trillion in 2014, barring any macroeconomic shocks.

FDI inflows increased across all major economic groupings in 2011. Flows to developed countries increased by 21 per cent, to $748 billion. In developing countries FDI increased by 11 per cent, reaching a record $684 billion. FDI in the transition economies increased by 25 per cent to $92 billion. Developing and transition economies respectively accounted for 45 per cent and 6 per cent of global FDI. UNCTAD's projections show these countries maintaining their high levels of investment over the next three years.

Africa and the least developed countries (LDCs) saw a third year of declining FDI inflows. But prospects in Africa are brightening. The 2011 decline in flows to the continent was due largely to divestments from North Africa. In contrast, inflows to sub-Saharan Africa recovered to $37 billion, close to their historic peak.

Sovereign wealth funds (SWFs) show significant potential for investment in development. FDI by SWFs is still relatively small. Their cumulative FDI reached an estimated $125 billion in 2011, with about a quarter in developing countries. SWFs can work in partnership with host-country governments, development finance institutions or other private sector investors to invest in infrastructure, agriculture and industrial development, including the build-up of green growth industries.

The international production of transnational corporations (TNCs) advanced, but they are still holding back from investing their record cash holdings. In 2011, foreign affiliates of TNCs employed an estimated 69 million workers, who generated $28 trillion in sales and $7 trillion in value added, some 9 per cent up from 2010. TNCs are holding record levels of cash, which so far have not translated into sustained growth in investment. The current cash "overhang" may fuel a future surge in FDI.

UNCTAD's new FDI Contribution Index shows relatively higher contributions by foreign affiliates to host economies in developing countries, especially Africa, in terms of value added, employment and wage generation, tax revenues, export generation and capital formation. The rankings also show countries with less than expected FDI contributions, confirming that policy matters for maximizing positive and minimizing negative effects of FDI.

INVESTMENT POLICY TRENDS

Many countries continued to liberalize and promote foreign investment in various industries to stimulate growth in 2011. At the same time, new regulatory and restrictive measures continued to be introduced, including for industrial policy reasons. They became manifest primarily in the adjustment of entry policies for foreign investors (in e.g. agriculture, pharmaceuticals); in extractive industries, including through nationalization and divestment requirements; and in a more critical approach towards outward FDI.

International investment policymaking is in flux. The annual number of new bilateral investment treaties (BITs) continues to decline, while regional investment policymaking is intensifying. Sustainable development is gaining prominence in international investment policymaking. Numerous ideas for reform of investor–State dispute settlement have emerged, but few have been put into action.

Suppliers need support for compliance with corporate social responsibility (CSR) codes. The CSR codes of TNCs often pose challenges for suppliers in developing countries (particularly small and medium-sized enterprises), which have to comply with and report under multiple, fragmented standards. Policymakers can alleviate these challenges and create new opportunities for suppliers by incorporating CSR into enterprise development and capacity-building programmes. TNCs can also harmonize standards and reporting requirements at the industry level.

UNCTAD'S INVESTMENT POLICY FRAMEWORK FOR SUSTAINABLE DEVELOPMENT

Mobilizing investment and ensuring that it contributes to sustainable development is a priority for all countries. A new generation of investment policies is emerging, as governments pursue a broader and more intricate development policy agenda, while building or maintaining a generally favourable investment climate.

"New generation" investment policies place inclusive growth and sustainable development at the heart of efforts to attract and benefit from investment. This leads to specific investment policy challenges at the national and international levels. At the national level, these include integrating investment policy into development strategy, incorporating sustainable development objectives in investment policy and ensuring investment policy relevance and effectiveness. At the international level, there is a need to strengthen the development dimension of international investment agreements (IIAs), balance the rights and obligations of States and investors, and manage the systemic complexity of the IIA regime.

To address these challenges, UNCTAD has formulated a comprehensive Investment Policy Framework for Sustainable Development (IPFSD), consisting of (i) Core Principles for investment policymaking, (ii) guidelines for national investment policies, and (iii) options for the design and use of IIAs.

UNCTAD's IPFSD can serve as a point of reference for policymakers in formulating national investment policies and in negotiating or reviewing IIAs. It provides a common language for discussion and cooperation on national and international investment policies. It has been designed as a "living document" and incorporates an online version that aims to establish an interactive, open-source platform, inviting the investment community to exchange views, suggestions and experiences related to the IPFSD for the inclusive and participative development of future investment policies.

OVERVIEW

FDI TRENDS AND PROSPECTS

Global FDI losing momentum in 2012

Global foreign direct investment (FDI) inflows rose 16 per cent in 2011, surpassing the 2005–2007 pre-crisis level for the first time, despite the continuing effects of the global financial and economic crisis of 2008–2009 and the ongoing sovereign debt crises. This increase occurred against a background of higher profits of transnational corporations (TNCs) and relatively high economic growth in developing countries during the year.

A resurgence in economic uncertainty and the possibility of lower growth rates in major emerging markets risks undercutting this favourable trend in 2012. UNCTAD predicts the growth rate of FDI will slow in 2012, with flows levelling off at about $1.6 trillion, the midpoint of a range. Leading indicators are suggestive of this trend, with the value of both cross-border mergers and acquisitions (M&As) and greenfield investments retreating in the first five months of 2012. Weak levels of M&A announcements also suggest sluggish FDI flows in the later part of the year.

Medium-term prospects cautiously optimistic

UNCTAD projections for the medium term based on macroeconomic fundamentals continue to show FDI flows increasing at a moderate but steady pace, reaching $1.8 trillion and $1.9 trillion in 2013 and 2014, respectively, barring any macroeconomic shocks. Investor uncertainty about the course of economic events for this period is still high. Results from UNCTAD's *World Investment Prospects Survey* (*WIPS*), which polls TNC executives on their investment plans, reveal that while respondents who are pessimistic about the global investment climate for 2012 outnumber those who are optimistic by 10 percentage points, the largest single group of respondents – roughly half – are either neutral or undecided. Responses for the medium term, after 2012, paint a gradually more optimistic picture. When asked about their planned future FDI expenditures, more than half of respondents foresee an increase between 2012 and 2014, compared with 2011 levels.

FDI inflows up across all major economic groupings

FDI flows to developed countries grew robustly in 2011, reaching $748 billion, up 21 per cent from 2010. Nevertheless, the level of their inflows was still a quarter below the level of the pre-crisis three-year average. Despite this increase, developing and transition economies together continued to account for more than half of global FDI (45 per cent and 6 per cent, respectively) for the year as their combined inflows reached a new record high, rising 12 per cent to $777 billion. Reaching high level of global FDI flows during the economic and financial crisis it speaks to the economic dynamism and strong role of these countries in future FDI flows that they maintained this share as developed economies rebounded in 2011.

Rising FDI to developing countries was driven by a 10 per cent increase in Asia and a 16 per cent increase in Latin America and the Caribbean. FDI to the transition economies increased by 25 per cent to $92 billion. Flows to Africa, in contrast, continued their downward trend for a third consecutive year, but the decline was marginal. The poorest countries remained in FDI recession, with flows to the least developed countries (LDCs) retreating 11 per cent to $15 billion.

Indications suggest that developing and transition economies will continue to keep up with the pace of growth in global FDI in the medium term. TNC executives responding to this year's WIPS ranked 6 developing and transition economies among their top 10 prospective destinations for the period ending in 2014, with Indonesia rising two places to enter the top five destinations for the first time.

The growth of FDI inflows in 2012 will be moderate in all three groups – developed, developing and transition economies. In developing regions, Africa is noteworthy as inflows are expected to recover. Growth in FDI is expected to be temperate in Asia (including East and South-East Asia, South Asia and West Asia) and Latin America. FDI flows to transition economies are expected to grow further in 2012 and exceed the 2007 peak in 2014.

Rising global FDI outflows driven by developed economies

FDI from developed countries rose sharply in 2011, by 25 per cent, to reach $1.24 trillion. While all three major developed-economy investor blocs – the European Union (EU), North America and Japan – contributed to this increase, the driving factors differed for each. FDI from the United States was driven by a record level of reinvested earnings (82 per cent of total FDI outflows), in part driven by TNCs building on their foreign cash holdings. The rise of FDI outflows from the EU was driven by cross-border M&As. An appreciating yen improved the purchasing power of Japanese TNCs, resulting in a doubling of their FDI outflows, with net M&A purchases in North America and Europe rising 132 per cent.

Outward FDI from developing economies declined by 4 per cent to $384 billion in 2011, although their share in global outflows remained high at 23 per cent. Flows from Latin America and the Caribbean fell 17 per cent, largely owing to the repatriation of capital to the region (counted as negative outflows) motivated in part by financial considerations (exchange rates, interest rate differentials). Flows from East and South-East Asia were largely stagnant (with an 9 per cent decline in those from East Asia), while outward FDI from West Asia increased significantly, to $25 billion.

M&As picking up but greenfield investment dominates

Cross-border M&As rose 53 per cent in 2011 to $526 billion, spurred by a rise in the number of megadeals (those with a value over $3 billion), to 62 in 2011, up from 44 in 2010. This reflects both the growing value of assets on stock markets and the increased financial capacity of buyers to carry out such operations. Greenfield investment projects, which had declined in value terms for two straight years, held steady in 2011 at $904 billion. Developing and transition economies continued to host more than two thirds of the total value of greenfield investments in 2011.

Although the growth in global FDI flows in 2011 was driven in large part by cross-border M&As, the total project value of greenfield investments remains significantly higher than that of cross-border M&As, as has been the case since the financial crisis.

Turnaround in primary and services-sector FDI

FDI flows rose in all three sectors of production (primary, manufacturing and services), according to FDI projects data (comprising cross-border M&As and greenfield investments). Services-sector FDI rebounded in 2011 after falling sharply in 2009 and 2010, to reach some $570 billion. Primary sector investment also reversed the negative trend of the previous two years, at $200 billion. The share of both sectors rose slightly at the expense of manufacturing. Overall, the top five industries contributing to the rise in FDI projects were extractive industries (mining, quarrying and petroleum), chemicals, utilities (electricity, gas and water), transportation and communications, and other services (largely driven by oil and gas field services).

SWFs show potential for investment in development

Compared with assets of nearly $5 trillion under management, FDI by sovereign wealth funds (SWFs) is still relatively small. By 2011, their cumulative FDI reached an estimated $125 billion, with more than a quarter of that in developing countries. However, with their long-term and strategically oriented investment outlook, SWFs appear well placed to invest in productive sectors in developing countries, particularly the LDCs. They offer the scale to be able to invest in infrastructure development and the upgrading of agricultural productivity – key to economic development in many LDCs – as well as in industrial development, including the build-up of green growth industries. To increase their investment in these areas, SWFs can work in partnership with host-country governments, development finance institutions or other private sector investors that can bring technical and managerial competencies to projects.

TNCs still hold back from investing record cash holdings

Foreign affiliates' economic activity rose in 2011 across all major indicators of international production. During the year, foreign affiliates employed an estimated 69 million workers, who generated $28 trillion in sales and $7 trillion in value added. Data from UNCTAD's annual survey of the largest 100 TNCs reflects the overall upward trend in international production, with the foreign sales and employment of these firms growing significantly faster than those in their home economy.

Despite the gradual advance of international production by TNCs, their record levels of cash have so far not translated into sustained growth in investment levels. UNCTAD estimates that these cash levels have reached more than $5 trillion, including earnings retained overseas. Data on the largest 100 TNCs show that during the global financial crisis they cut capital expenditures in productive assets and acquisitions (especially foreign acquisitions) in favour of holding cash. Cash levels for these 100 firms alone peaked in 2010 at $1.03 trillion, of which an estimated $166 billion was additional – above the levels suggested by average pre-crisis cash holdings. Although recent figures suggest that TNCs' capital expenditures in productive assets and acquisitions are picking up, rising 12 per cent in 2011, the additional cash they are holding – an estimated $105 billion in 2011 – is still not being fully deployed. Renewed instability in international financial markets will continue to encourage cash holding and other uses of cash such as paying dividends or reducing debt levels. Nevertheless, as conditions improve, the current cash "overhang" may fuel a future surge in FDI. Projecting the data for the top 100 TNCs over the estimated $5 trillion in total TNC cash holdings results in more than $500 billion in investable funds, or about one third of global FDI flows.

UNCTAD's FDI Attraction and Contribution Indices show developing countries moving up the ranks

The UNCTAD FDI Attraction Index, which measures the success of economies in attracting FDI (combining total FDI inflows and inflows relative to GDP), features 8 developing and transition economies in the top 10, compared with only 4 a decade ago. A 2011 newcomer in the top ranks is Mongolia. Just outside the top 10, a number of other countries saw significant improvements in their ranking, including Ghana (16), Mozambique (21) and Nigeria (23). Comparing the FDI Attraction Index with another UNCTAD index, the FDI Potential Index, shows that a number of developing and transition economies have managed to attract more FDI than expected, including Albania, Cambodia, Madagascar and Mongolia. Others have received less FDI than could be expected based on economic determinants, including Argentina, the Philippines, Slovenia and South Africa.

The UNCTAD FDI Contribution Index – introduced in *WIR12* – ranks economies on the basis of the significance of FDI and foreign affiliates in their economy, in terms of value added, employment, wages, tax receipts, exports, research and development (R&D) expenditures, and capital formation (e.g. the share of employment in foreign affiliates in total formal employment in each country, and so forth). These variables are among the most important indicators of the economic impact of FDI. According to the index, in 2011 the host economy with the largest contribution by FDI was Hungary followed by Belgium and the Czech Republic. The UNCTAD FDI Contribution Index shows relatively higher contributions of foreign affiliates to local economies in developing countries, especially Africa, in value added, employment, export generation and R&D expenditures.

Comparing the FDI Contribution Index with the weight of FDI stock in a country's GDP shows that a number of developing and transition economies get a higher economic development impact "per unit of FDI" than others, including Argentina, the Plurinational State of Bolivia and Colombia and, to a lesser degree, Brazil, China and Romania. In other cases, FDI appears to contribute less than could be expected by the volume of stock present in the country, as in Bulgaria, Chile and Jamaica. The latter group also includes a number of economies that attract significant investment largely because of their fiscal regime, but without the equivalent impact on the domestic economy.

RECENT TRENDS BY REGION

FDI to Africa continues to decline, but prospects are brightening

FDI inflows to Africa as a whole declined for the third successive year, to $42.7 billion. However, the decline in FDI inflows to the continent in 2011 was caused largely by the fall in North Africa; in particular, inflows to Egypt and Libya, which had been major recipients of FDI, came to a halt owing to their protracted political instability. In contrast, inflows to sub-Saharan Africa recovered from $29 billion in 2010 to $37 billion in 2011, a level comparable with the peak in 2008. A rebound of FDI to South Africa accentuated the recovery. The continuing rise in commodity prices and a relatively positive economic outlook for sub-Saharan Africa are among the factors contributing to the turnaround. In addition to traditional patterns of FDI to the extractive industries, the emergence of a middle class is fostering the growth of FDI in services such as banking, retail and telecommunications, as witnessed by an increase in the share of services FDI in 2011.

The overall fall in FDI to Africa was due principally to a reduction in flows from developed countries, leaving developing countries to increase their share in inward FDI to the continent (from 45 per cent in 2010 to 53 per cent in 2011 in greenfield investment projects).

South-East Asia is catching up with East Asia

In the developing regions of East Asia and South-East Asia, FDI inflows reached new records, with total inflows amounting to $336 billion, accounting for 22 per cent of global inflows. South-East Asia, with inflows of $117 billion, up 26 per cent, continued to experience faster FDI growth than East Asia, although the latter was still dominant at $219 billion, up 9 per cent. Four economies of the Association of South-East Asian Nations (ASEAN) – Brunei Darussalam, Indonesia, Malaysia and Singapore – saw a considerable rise.

FDI flows to China also reached a record level of $124 billion, and flows to the services sector surpassed those to manufacturing for the first time. China continued to be in the top spot as investors' preferred destination for FDI, according to UNCTAD's *WIPS*, but the rankings of South-East Asian economies such as Indonesia and Thailand have risen markedly. Overall, as China continues to experience rising wages and production costs, the relative competitiveness of ASEAN countries in manufacturing is increasing.

FDI outflows from East Asia dropped by 9 per cent to $180 billion, while those from South-East Asia rose 36 per cent to $60 billion. Outflows from China dropped by 5 per cent, while those from Hong Kong,

China, declined by 15 per cent. By contrast, outflows from Singapore registered a 19 per cent increase and outflows from Indonesia and Thailand surged.

Rising extractive industry M&As boost FDI in South Asia

In South Asia, FDI inflows have turned around after a slide in 2009–2010, reaching $39 billion, mainly as a result of rising inflows in India, which accounted for more than four fifths of the region's FDI. Cross-border M&A sales in extractive industries surged to $9 billion, while M&A sales in manufacturing declined by about two thirds, and those in services remained much below the annual amounts witnessed during 2006–2009.

Countries in the region face different challenges, such as political risks and obstacles to FDI, that need to be tackled in order to build an attractive investment climate. Nevertheless, recent developments such as the improving relationship between India and Pakistan have highlighted new opportunities.

FDI outflows from India rose by 12 per cent to $15 billion. A drop in cross-border M&As across all three sectors was compensated by a rise in overseas greenfield projects, particularly in extractive industries, metal and metal products, and business services.

Regional and global crises still weigh on FDI in West Asia

FDI inflows to West Asia declined for the third consecutive year, to $49 billion in 2011. Inflows to the Gulf Cooperation Council (GCC) countries continued to suffer from the effects of the cancellation of large-scale investment projects, especially in construction, when project finance dried up in the wake of the global financial crisis, and were further affected by the unrest across the region during 2011. Among non-GCC countries the growth of FDI flows was uneven. In Turkey they were driven by a more than three-fold increase in cross-border M&A sales. Spreading political and social unrest has directly and indirectly affected FDI inflows to the other countries in the region.

FDI outflows recovered in 2011 after reaching a five-year low in 2010, indicating a return to overseas acquisitions by investors based in the region (after a period of divestments). It was driven largely by an increase in overseas greenfield projects in the manufacturing sector.

Latin America and the Caribbean: shift towards industrial policy

FDI inflows to Latin America and the Caribbean increased by 16 per cent to $217 billion, driven mainly by higher flows to South America (up 34 per cent). Inflows to Central America and the Caribbean, excluding offshore financial centres, increased by 4 per cent, while those to the offshore financial centres registered a 4 per cent decrease. High FDI growth in South America was mainly due to its expanding consumer markets, high growth rates and natural-resource endowments.

Outflows from the region have become volatile since the beginning of the global financial crisis. They decreased by 17 per cent in 2011, after a 121 per cent increase in 2010, which followed a 44 per cent decline in 2009. This volatility is due to the growing importance of flows that are not necessarily related to investment in productive activity abroad, as reflected by the high share of offshore financial centres in total FDI from the region, and the increasing repatriation of intracompany loans by Brazilian outward investors ($21 billion in 2011).

A shift towards a greater use of industrial policy is occurring in some countries in the region, with a series of measures designed to build productive capacities and boost the manufacturing sector. These measures include higher tariff barriers, more stringent criteria for licenses and increased preference for domestic production in public procurement. These policies may induce "barrier hopping" FDI into the region and appear to have had an effect on firms' investment plans. TNCs in the automobile, computer and agriculture-machinery industries have announced investment plans in the region. These investments are by traditional European and North American investors in the region, as well as TNCs from developing countries and Japan.

FDI prospects for transition economies helped by the Russian Federation's WTO accession

In economies in transition in South-East Europe, the Commonwealth of Independent States (CIS) and Georgia, FDI recovered some lost ground after two years of stagnant flows, reaching $92 billion, driven in large part by cross-border M&A deals. In South-East Europe, manufacturing FDI increased, buoyed by competitive production costs and open access to EU markets. In the CIS, resource-based economies benefited from continued natural-resource-seeking FDI. The Russian Federation continued to account for the lion's share of inward FDI to the region and saw FDI flows grow to the third highest level ever. Developed countries, mainly EU members, remained the most important source of FDI, with the highest share of projects (comprising cross-border M&As and greenfield investments), although projects by investors from developing and transition economies gained importance.

The services sector still plays only a small part in inward FDI in the region, but its importance may increase with the accession to the World Trade Organization (WTO) of the Russian Federation. Through WTO accession the country has committed to reduce restrictions on foreign investment in a number of services industries (including banking, insurance, business services, telecommunications and distribution). The accession may also boost foreign investors' confidence and improve the overall investment environment.

UNCTAD projects continued growth of FDI flows to transition economies, reflecting a more investor-friendly environment, WTO accession by the Russian Federation and new privatization programmes in extractive industries, utilities, banking and telecommunications.

Developed countries: signs of slowdown in 2012

Inflows to developed countries, which bottomed out in 2009, accelerated their recovery in 2011 to reach $748 billion, up 21 per cent from the previous year. The recovery since 2010 has nonetheless made up only one fifth of the ground lost during the financial crisis in 2008–2009. Inflows remained at 77 per cent of the pre-crisis three-year average (2005–2007). Inflows to Europe, which had declined until 2010, showed a turnaround while robust recovery of flows to the United States continued. Australia and New Zealand attracted significant volumes. Japan saw a net divestment for the second successive year.

Developed countries rich in natural resources, notably Australia, Canada and the United States, attracted FDI in oil and gas, particularly for unconventional fossil fuels, and in minerals such as coal, copper and iron ore. Financial institutions continued offloading overseas assets to repay the State aid they received during the financial crisis and to strengthen their capital base so as to meet the requirements of Basel III.

The recovery of FDI in developed regions will be tested severely in 2012 by the eurozone crisis and the apparent fragility of the recovery in most major economies. M&A data indicate that cross-border acquisitions of firms in developed countries in the first three months of 2012 were down 45 per cent compared with the same period in 2011. Announcement-based greenfield data show the same tendency (down 24 per cent). While UNCTAD's 2012 projections suggest inflows holding steady in North America and managing a modest increase in Europe, there are significant downside risks to these forecasts.

LDCs in FDI recession for the third consecutive year

In the LDCs, large divestments and repayments of intracompany loans by investors in a single country, Angola, reduced total group inflows to the lowest level in five years, to $15 billion. More significantly, greenfield investments in the group as a whole declined, and large-scale FDI projects remain concentrated in a few resource-rich LDCs.

Investments in mining, quarrying and petroleum remained the dominant form of FDI in LDCs, although investments in the services sector are increasing, especially in utilities, transport and storage, and telecommunication. About half of greenfield investments came from other developing economies, although neither the share nor the value of investments from these and transition economies recovered to the levels of 2008–2009. India remained the largest investor in LDCs from developing and transition economies, followed by China and South Africa.

In landlocked developing countries (LLDCs), FDI grew to a record high of $34.8 billion. Kazakhstan continued to be the driving force of FDI inflows. In Mongolia, inflows more than doubled because of large-scale projects in extractive industries. The vast majority of inward flows continued to be greenfield investments in mining, quarrying and petroleum. The share of investments from transition economies soared owing to a single large-scale investment from the Russian Federation to Uzbekistan. Together with developing economies, their share in greenfield projects reached 60 per cent in 2011.

In small island developing States (SIDS), FDI inflows fell for the third year in a row and dipped to their lowest level in six years at $4.1 billion. The distribution of flows to the group remained highly skewed towards tax-friendly jurisdictions, with three economies (the Bahamas, Trinidad and Tobago, and Barbados) receiving the bulk. In the absence of megadeals in mining, quarrying and petroleum, the total value of cross-border M&A sales in SIDS dropped significantly in 2011. In contrast, total greenfield investments reached a record high, with South Africa becoming the largest source. Three quarters of greenfield projects originated in developing and transition economies.

INVESTMENT POLICY TRENDS

National policies: investment promotion intensifies in crisis

Against a backdrop of continued economic uncertainty, turmoil in financial markets and slow growth, countries worldwide continued to liberalize and promote foreign investment as a means to support economic growth and development. At the same time, regulatory activities with regard to FDI continued.

Investment policy measures undertaken in 2011 were generally favourable to foreign investors. Compared with 2010, the percentage of more restrictive policy measures showed a significant decrease, from approximately 32 per cent to 22 per cent. It would, however, be premature to interpret this decrease as an indication of a reversal of the trend towards a more stringent policy environment for investment that has been observed in previous years – also because the 2011 restrictive measures add to the stock accumulated in previous years. The share of measures introducing new restrictions or regulations was roughly equal between the developing and transition economies and the developed countries.

The overall policy trend towards investment liberalization and promotion appears more and more to be targeted at specific industries, in particular some services industries (e.g. electricity, gas and water supply; transport and communication). Several countries pursued privatization policies. Other important measures related to the facilitation of admission procedures for foreign investment.

As in previous years, extractive industries proved the main exception inasmuch as most policy measures related to this industry were less favourable. Agribusiness and financial services were the other two industries with a relatively high share of less favourable measures.

More State regulation became manifest primarily in two policy areas: (i) an adjustment of entry policies with regard to inward FDI by introducing new entry barriers or by reinforcing screening procedures (in e.g. agriculture, pharmaceuticals) and (ii) more regulatory policies in extractive industries, including nationalization, expropriation or divestment requirements as well as increases in corporate taxation rates, royalties and contract renegotiations. Both policy types were partly driven by industrial policy considerations.

In 2011–2012, several countries took a more critical approach towards outward FDI. In light of high domestic unemployment, concerns are rising that outward FDI may contribute to job exports and a weakening of the domestic industrial base. Other policy objectives include foreign exchange stability and an improved balance of payments. Policy measures undertaken included outward FDI restrictions and incentives to repatriate foreign investment.

IIAs: regionalism on the rise

By the end of 2011, the overall IIA universe consisted of 3,164 agreements, which include 2,833 bilateral investment treaties (BITs) and 331 "other IIAs", including, principally, free trade agreements (FTAs) with investment provisions, economic partnership agreements and regional agreements (*WIR12* no longer includes double taxation treaties among IIAs). With a total of 47 IIAs signed in 2011 (33 BITs and 14 other IIAs), compared with 69 in 2010, traditional investment treaty making continued to lose momentum. This may have several causes, including (i) a gradual shift towards regional treaty making, and (ii) the fact that IIAs are becoming increasingly controversial and politically sensitive.

In quantitative terms, bilateral agreements still dominate; however, in terms of economic significance, regionalism becomes more important. The increasing economic weight and impact of regional treaty making is evidenced by investment negotiations under way for the Trans-Pacific Partnership (TPP) Agreement; the conclusion of the 2012 trilateral investment agreement between China, Japan and the Republic of Korea; the Mexico–Central America FTA, which includes an investment chapter; the fact that at the EU level the European Commission now negotiates investment agreements on behalf of all EU member States; and developments in ASEAN.

In most cases, regional treaties are FTAs. By addressing comprehensively the trade and investment elements of international economic activities, such broader agreements often respond better to today's economic realities, in which international trade and investment are increasingly interconnected (see *WIR11*). While this shift can bring about the consolidation and harmonization of investment rules and represent a step towards multilateralism, where the new treaties do not entail the phase-out of the old ones, the result can also be the opposite. Instead of simplification and growing consistency, regionalization may lead to a multiplication of treaty layers, making the IIA network even more complex and prone to overlaps and inconsistencies.

Sustainable development: increasingly recognized

While some IIAs concluded in 2011 keep to the traditional treaty model that focuses on investment protection as the sole aim of the treaty, others include innovations. Some new IIAs include a number of features to ensure that the treaty does not interfere with, but instead contributes to countries' sustainable development strategies that focus on the environmental and social impact of investment.

A number of other recent developments also indicate increased attention to sustainable development considerations. They include the 2012 revision of the United States Model BIT; the 2012 Joint Statement by the European Union and the United States, issued under the auspices of the Transatlantic Economic Council; and the work by the Southern African Development Community (SADC) on its model BIT.

Finally, increased attention to sustainable development also manifested itself in other international policymaking related to investment, e.g. the adoption of and follow-up work on the 2011 UN Guiding Principles on Business and Human Rights; the implementation of the UNCTAD/FAO/World Bank/ IFAD Principles for Responsible Agricultural Investment; the 2011 Revision of the OECD Guidelines for Multinational Enterprises (1976); the 2012 Revision of the International Chamber of Commerce Guidelines for International Investment (1972); the Doha Mandate adopted at UNCTAD's XIII Ministerial Conference in 2012; and the Rio+20 Conference in 2012.

ISDS reform: unfinished agenda

In 2011, the number of known investor–State dispute settlement (ISDS) cases filed under IIAs grew by at least 46. This constitutes the highest number of known treaty-based disputes ever filed within one year. In some recent cases, investors challenged core public policies that had allegedly negatively affected their business prospects.

Some States have been expressing their concerns with today's ISDS system (e.g. Australia's trade-policy statement announcing that it would stop including ISDS clauses in its future IIAs; Venezuela's recent notification that it would withdraw from the ICSID Convention). These reflect, among others, deficiencies in the system (e.g. the expansive or contradictory interpretations of key IIA provisions by arbitration tribunals, inadequate enforcement and annulment procedures, concerns regarding the qualification of arbitrators, the lack of transparency and high costs of the proceeding, and the relationship between ISDS and State–State proceedings) and a broader public discourse about the usefulness and legitimacy of the ISDS mechanism.

Based on the perceived shortcomings of the ISDS system, a number of suggestions for reform are emerging. They aim at reigning in the growing number of ISDS cases, fostering the legitimacy and increasing the transparency of ISDS proceedings, dealing with inconsistent readings of key provisions in IIAs and poor treaty interpretation, improving the impartiality and quality of arbitrators, reducing the length and costs of proceedings, assisting developing countries in handling ISDS cases, and addressing overall concerns about the functioning of the system.

While some countries have already incorporated changes into their IIAs, many others continue with business as usual. A systematic assessment of individual reform options and their feasibility, potential effectiveness and implementation methods (e.g. at the level of IIAs, arbitral rules or institutions) remains to be done. A multilateral policy dialogue on ISDS could help to develop a consensus about the preferred course for reform and ways to put it into action.

Suppliers need support for CSR compliance

Since the early 2000s, there has been a significant proliferation of CSR codes in global supply chains, including both individual TNC codes and industry-level codes. It is now common across a broad range of industries for TNCs to set supplier codes of conduct detailing the social and environmental performance standards for their global supply chains. Furthermore, CSR codes and standards themselves are becoming more complex and their implementation more complicated.

CSR codes in global supply chains hold out the promise of promoting sustainable and inclusive development in host countries, transferring knowledge on addressing critical social and environmental issues, and opening new business opportunities for domestic suppliers meeting these standards. However, compliance with such codes also presents considerable challenges for many suppliers, especially small and medium-sized enterprises (SMEs) in developing countries. They include, inter alia, the use of international standards exceeding the current regulations and common market practices of host countries; the existence of diverging and sometimes conflicting requirements from different TNCs; the capacity constraints of suppliers to apply international standards in day-to-day operations and to deal with complex reporting requirements and multiple on-site inspections; consumer and civil society concerns; and competitiveness concerns for SMEs that bear the cost of fully complying with CSR standards relative to other SMEs that do not attempt to fully comply.

Meeting these challenges will require an upgrade of entrepreneurial and management skills. Governments, as well as TNCs, can assist domestic suppliers, in particular SMEs, through entrepreneurship-building and capacity-development programmes and by strengthening existing national institutions that promote compliance with labour and environmental laws. Policymakers can also support domestic suppliers by working with TNCs to harmonize standards at the industry level and to simplify compliance procedures.

UNCTAD'S INVESTMENT POLICY FRAMEWORK FOR SUSTAINABLE DEVELOPMENT

A new generation of investment policies emerges

Cross-border investment policy is made in a political and economic context that, at the global and regional levels, has been buffeted in recent years by a series of crises in finance, food security and the environment, and that faces persistent global imbalances and social challenges, especially with regard to poverty alleviation. These crises and challenges are having profound effects on the way policy is shaped at the global level. First, current crises have accentuated a longer-term shift in economic weight from developed countries to emerging markets. Second, the financial crisis in particular has boosted the role of governments in the economy, in both the developed and the developing world. Third, the nature of the challenges, which no country can address in isolation, makes better international coordination imperative. And fourth, the global political and economic context and the challenges that need to be addressed – with social and environmental concerns taking centre stage – are leading policymakers to reflect on an emerging new development paradigm that places inclusive and sustainable development goals on the same footing as economic growth. At a time of such persistent crises and pressing social and environmental challenges, mobilizing investment and ensuring that it contributes to sustainable development objectives is a priority for all countries.

Against this background, a new generation of foreign investment policies is emerging, with governments pursuing a broader and more intricate development policy agenda, while building or maintaining a generally favourable investment climate. This new generation of investment policies has been in the making for some time and is reflected in the dichotomy in policy directions over the last few years – with simultaneous moves to further liberalize investment regimes and promote foreign investment, on the one hand, and to regulate investment in pursuit of public policy objectives, on the other. It reflects the recognition that liberalization, if it is to generate sustainable development outcomes, has to be accompanied – if not preceded – by the establishment of proper regulatory and institutional frameworks.

"New generation" investment policies place inclusive growth and sustainable development at the heart of efforts to attract and benefit from investment. Although these concepts are not new in and by themselves, to date they have not been systematically integrated in mainstream investment policymaking. "New generation" investment policies aim to operationalize sustainable development in concrete measures and mechanisms at the national and international levels, and at the level of policymaking and implementation.

Broadly, "new generation" investment policies strive to:

- create synergies with wider economic development goals or industrial policies, and achieve seamless *integration in development strategies*;

- foster *responsible investor behaviour* and incorporate principles of CSR;

- ensure *policy effectiveness* in their design and implementation and in the institutional environment within which they operate.

New generation investment policies: new challenges

These three broad aspects of "new generation" foreign investment policies translate into specific investment policy challenges at the national and international levels (tables 1 and 2).

Table 1. National investment policy challenges	
Integrating investment policy in development strategy	• Channeling investment to areas key for the build-up of productive capacity and international competitiveness • Ensuring coherence with the host of policy areas geared towards overall development objectives
Incorporating sustainable development objectives in investment policy	• Maximizing positive and minimizing negative impacts of investment • Fostering responsible investor behaviour
Ensuring investment policy relevance and effectiveness	• Building stronger institutions to implement investment policy • Measuring the sustainable development impact of investment

Table 2. International investment policy challenges	
Strengthening the development dimension of IIAs	• Safeguarding policy space for sustainable development needs • Making investment promotion provisions more concrete and consistent with sustainable development objectives
Balancing rights and obligations of states and investors	• Reflecting investor responsibilities in IIAs • Learning from and building on CSR principles
Managing the systemic complexity of the IIA regime	• Dealing with gaps, overlaps and inconsistencies in IIA coverage and content and resolving institutional and dispute settlement issues • Ensuring effective interaction and coherence with other public policies (e.g. climate change, labour) and systems (e.g. trading, financial)

Addressing the challenges: UNCTAD's IPFSD

To address these challenges, UNCTAD has developed a comprehensive Investment Policy Framework for Sustainable Development (IPFSD), consisting of (i) a set of Core Principles for foreign investment policymaking, (ii) guidelines for investment policies at the national level and (iii) options for the design and use of IIAs (figure 1).

UNCTAD's IPFSD is meant to provide guidance on cross-border investment policies, with a particular focus on FDI, although many of the guidelines in the section on national investment policies could also have relevance for domestic investment. Policies covered include those with regard to the establishment, treatment and promotion of investment; in addition, a comprehensive framework needs to look beyond investment policies per se and include investment-related aspects of other policy areas. Investment policies

Figure 1. Structure and components of the IPFSD

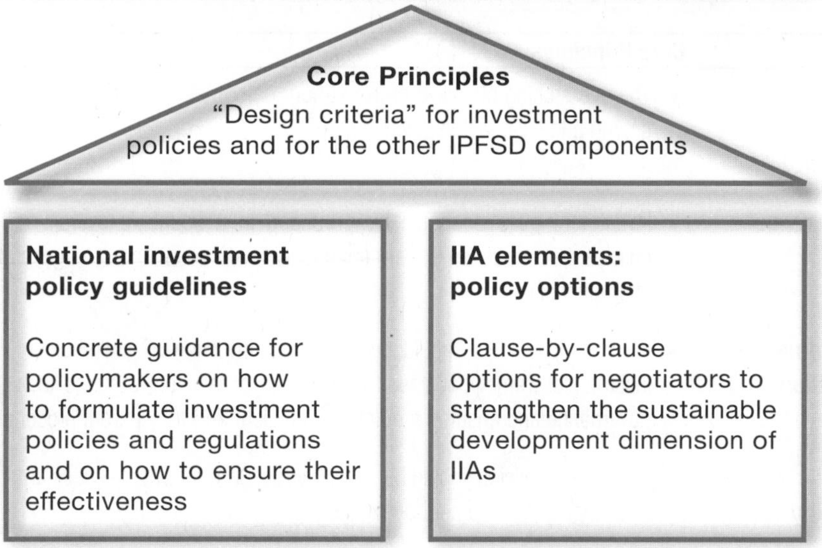

Core Principles
"Design criteria" for investment
policies and for the other IPFSD components

**National investment
policy guidelines**

Concrete guidance for
policymakers on how
to formulate investment
policies and regulations
and on how to ensure their
effectiveness

**IIA elements:
policy options**

Clause-by-clause
options for negotiators to
strengthen the sustainable
development dimension of
IIAs

covered comprise national and international policies, because coherence between the two is fundamental. The IPFSD focuses on direct investment in productive assets; portfolio investment is considered only where explicitly stated in the context of IIAs.

Although a number of existing international instruments provide guidance to investment policymakers, UNCTAD's IPFSD distinguishes itself in several ways. First, it is meant as a comprehensive instrument for dealing with all aspects of policymaking at the national and international levels. Second, it puts a particular emphasis on the relationship between foreign investment and sustainable development, advocating a balanced approach between the pursuit of purely economic growth objectives by means of investment liberalization and promotion, on the one hand, and the need to protect people and the environment, on the other hand. Third, it underscores the interests of developing countries in investment policymaking. Fourth, it is neither a legally binding text nor a voluntary undertaking between States, but expert guidance by an international organization, leaving policymakers free to "adapt and adopt" as appropriate, taking into account that one single policy framework cannot address the specific investment policy challenges of individual countries.

The IPFSD's Core Principles: "design criteria"

The Core Principles for investment policymaking aim to guide the development of national and international investment policies. To this end, they translate the policy challenges into a set of "design criteria" for investment policies (table 3). Overall, they aim to mainstream sustainable development in investment policymaking, while confirming the basic principles of sound development-oriented investment policies, in a balanced approach.

The Core Principles are not a set of rules per se. They are an integral part of the IPFSD, which attempts to convert them, collectively and individually, into concrete guidance for national investment policymakers and options for negotiators of IIAs. As such, they do not always follow the traditional policy areas of a national investment policy framework, nor the usual articles of IIAs. The overarching concept behind the principles is sustainable development; the principles should be read as a package, because interaction between them is fundamental to the IPFSD's balanced approach.

Table 3. Core Principles for investment policymaking for sustainable development	
Area	**Core Principles**
1 **Investment for sustainable development**	• The overarching objective of investment policymaking is to promote investment for inclusive growth and sustainable development.
2 **Policy coherence**	• Investment policies should be grounded in a country's overall development strategy. All policies that impact on investment should be coherent and synergetic at both the national and international levels.
3 **Public governance and institutions**	• Investment policies should be developed involving all stakeholders, and embedded in an institutional framework based on the rule of law that adheres to high standards of public governance and ensures predictable, efficient and transparent procedures for investors.
4 **Dynamic policymaking**	• Investment policies should be regularly reviewed for effectiveness and relevance and adapted to changing development dynamics.
5 **Balanced rights and obligations**	• Investment policies should be balanced in setting out rights and obligations of States and investors in the interest of development for all.
6 **Right to regulate**	• Each country has the sovereign right to establish entry and operational conditions for foreign investment, subject to international commitments, in the interest of the public good and to minimize potential negative effects.
7 **Openness to investment**	• In line with each country's development strategy, investment policy should establish open, stable and predictable entry conditions for investment.
8 **Investment protection and treatment**	• Investment policies should provide adequate protection to established investors. The treatment of established investors should be non-discriminatory.
9 **Investment promotion and facilitation**	• Policies for investment promotion and facilitation should be aligned with sustainable development goals and designed to minimize the risk of harmful competition for investment.
10 **Corporate governance and responsibility**	• Investment policies should promote and facilitate the adoption of and compliance with best international practices of corporate social responsibility and good corporate governance.
11 **International cooperation**	• The international community should cooperate to address shared investment-for-development policy challenges, particularly in least developed countries. Collective efforts should also be made to avoid investment protectionism.

The design of the Core Principles has been inspired by various sources of international law and politics. They can be traced back to a range of existing bodies of international law, treaties and declarations, including the UN Charter, the UN Millennium Development Goals, the "Monterrey Consensus", the UN Johannesburg Plan of Implementation and the Istanbul Programme of Action for the LDCs. Importantly, the 2012 UNCTAD XIII Conference recognized the role of FDI in the development process and called on countries to design policies aimed at enhancing the impact of foreign investment on sustainable development and inclusive growth, while underlining the importance of stable, predictable and enabling investment climates.

From Core Principles to national policy guidelines

The IPFSD's national investment policy guidelines translate the Core Principles for investment policymaking into numerous concrete and detailed guidelines that aim to address the "new generation" challenges for policymakers at the domestic level (see table 1 for the challenges). Table 4 provides an overview of (selected) distinguishing features of the IPFSD's national investment policy guidelines, with a specific focus on the sustainable development dimension.

Table 4. Sustainable development features of the National Investment Policy Guidelines	
Challenges	**IPFSD National Investment Policy Guidelines – *selected features***
Integrating investment policy in development strategy	• Dedicated section (section 1) on *strategic investment priorities* and investment policy *coherence for productive capacity building*, including sub-sections on investment and: - Human resource development - Infrastructure (including section on public-private partnerships) - Technology dissemination - Enterprise development (including promoting linkages) • Attention to investment policy options for the *protection of sensitive industries* (sub-section 2.1) • Sections on other policy areas geared towards overall sustainable development objectives to ensure *coherence* with investment policy (section 3)
Incorporating sustainable development objectives in investment policy	• Specific guidelines for the design of investment-specific policies and regulations (section 2), including not only establishment and operations, treatment and protection of investments, and investment promotion and facilitation, but also *investor responsibilities* (as well as a dedicated sub-section on corporate responsibility, sub-section 3.7) • Guidance on the encouragement of *responsible investment* and on guaranteeing compliance with *international core standards* (sub-section 2.3) • Guidance on investment promotion and use of incentives in the *interest of inclusive and sustainable development* (sub-section 2.4) • Specific guidelines aimed at *minimizing potential negative effects of investment*, such as: - Addressing tax avoidance (sub-section 3.2) - Preventing anti-competitive behaviour (sub-sections 3.4 and 3.9) - Guaranteeing core labour standards (sub-section 3.5) - Assessing and improving environmental impact (sub-section 3.8) • A sub-section on access to land, incorporating the *Principles for Responsible Agricultural Investment* (PRAI) (sub-section 3.6)
Ensuring investment policy relevance and effectiveness	• Dedicated section on *investment policy effectiveness* (section 4), including guidance on public governance and institutional capacity-building • Guidance on the measurement of policy *effectiveness* (sub-section 4.3) and the effectiveness of specific measures (e.g. incentives), with reference to: - Specific quantitative investment impact indicators - Dedicated UNCTAD tools (FDI Attraction and Contribution Indices)

The sustainable development features of the national policy guidelines imply that governments have the policy space to consider and adopt relevant measures. Such policy space may be restricted by international commitments. It is therefore essential to consider the IPFSD's national investment policy guidelines and its guidance for the design of IIAs as an integrated whole. Coherence between national and international investment policies is crucial, with a view to, among others, avoiding policy discrepancies and investor–State disputes.

The national investment policy guidelines argue for policy action at the *strategic, normative*, and *administrative levels*.

At the *strategic* level, the IPFSD's national investment policy guidelines suggest that policymakers should ground investment policy in a broad road map for economic growth and sustainable development – such as those set out in formal economic or industrial development strategies in many countries. These strategies necessarily vary by country, depending on its stage of development, domestic endowments and individual preferences.

Defining the role of public, private, domestic and especially foreign direct investment in development strategy is important. Mobilizing investment for sustainable development remains a major challenge for developing countries, particularly for LDCs. Given the often huge development financing gaps in these countries, foreign investment can provide a necessary complement to domestic investment, and it can be particularly beneficial when it interacts in a synergetic way with domestic public and private investment.

At this level it is also important to develop policies to harness investment for productive capacity-building and to enhance international competitiveness, especially where investment is intended to play a central role in industrial upgrading and structural transformation in developing economies. Critical elements of productive capacity-building include human resources and skills development, technology and know-how, infrastructure development, and enterprise development. It is crucial to ensure coherence between investment policies and other policy areas geared towards overall development objectives.

At the *normative* level, IPFSD's national investment policy guidelines propose that through the setting of rules and regulations, on investment and in a range of other policy areas, policymakers should promote and regulate investment that is geared towards sustainable development goals.

Positive development impacts of FDI do not always materialize automatically. And the effect of FDI can also be negative. Reaping the development benefits from investment requires not only an enabling policy framework that provides clear, unequivocal and transparent rules for the entry and operation of foreign investors, it also requires adequate regulation to minimize any risks associated with investment. Such regulations need to cover policy areas beyond investment policies per se, such as trade, taxation, intellectual property, competition, labour market regulation, environmental policies and access to land.

Although laws and regulations are the basis of investor responsibility, voluntary CSR initiatives and standards have proliferated in recent years, and they are increasingly influencing corporate practices, behaviour and investment decisions. Governments can build on them to complement the regulatory framework and maximize the development benefits of investment.

At the *administrative* level, the guidelines make the point that through appropriate implementation and institutional mechanisms, policymakers should ensure the continued relevance and effectiveness of investment policies. Policies to address implementation issues should be an integral part of the investment strategy and should strive to achieve both integrity across government and regulatory institutions and a service orientation where warranted.

Measuring policy effectiveness is a critical aspect of investment policymaking. Investment policy should be based on a set of explicitly formulated policy objectives with clear priorities and a time frame for achieving them. These objectives should be the principal yard-stick for measuring policy effectiveness. Assessment of progress in policy implementation and verification of the application of rules and regulations at all administrative levels is at least as important as the measurement of policy effectiveness.

Objectives of investment policy should ideally include a number of quantifiable goals for both the *attraction* of investment and its *development contribution*. UNCTAD has developed – and field-tested – a number of indicators that can be used by policymakers for this purpose. In addition, UNCTAD's Investment Contribution Index can also serve as a starting point (see figure 4 above). To measure policy effectiveness for the *attraction* of investment, UNCTAD's Investment Potential and Attraction Matrix can be a useful tool.

The IPFSD's guidance on IIAs: design options

The guidance on international investment policies set out in UNCTAD's IPFSD translates the Core Principles into options for policymakers, with an analysis of sustainable development implications. While national investment policymakers address these challenges through rules, regulations, institutions and initiatives, at the international policy level this is done through a complex web of IIAs (including, principally, BITs, FTAs with investment provisions, economic partnership agreements and regional integration agreements). The complexity of that web, which leads to gaps, overlaps and inconsistencies in the system of IIAs, is itself one of the challenges to be addressed. The others include the need to strengthen the development dimension of IIAs, balancing the rights and obligations of States and investors, ensuring sufficient policy space for sustainable development policies and making investment promotion provisions more concrete and aligned with sustainable development objectives.

International investment policy challenges must be addressed at three levels:

- When formulating their *strategic approach* to IIAs, policymakers need to embed international investment policymaking into their countries' development strategies. This involves managing the interaction between IIAs and national policies (e.g. ensuring that IIAs support industrial policies) and that between IIAs and other international policies or agreements (e.g. ensuring that IIAs do not contradict international environmental agreements or human rights obligations). The overall objective is to ensure coherence between IIAs and sustainable development needs.

- In the *detailed design of provisions in investment agreements* between countries, policymakers need to incorporate sustainable development considerations, addressing concerns related to policy space (e.g. through reservations and exceptions), balanced rights and obligations of States and investors (e.g. through encouraging compliance with CSR standards), and effective investment promotion (e.g. through home-country measures).

- *International dialogue on key and emerging investment policy issues*, in turn, can help address some of the systemic challenges stemming from the multilayered and multifaceted nature of IIAs, including the gaps, overlaps and inconsistencies amongst these agreements, their multiple dispute resolution mechanisms, and their piecemeal and erratic expansion.

Addressing sustainable development challenges through the detailed design of provisions in investment agreements principally implies four areas of evolution in treaty-making practice:

- *Incorporating concrete commitments to promote and facilitate investment for sustainable development*. Options to improve the investment promotion aspect of treaties include concrete facilitation mechanisms (information sharing, investment promotion forums), outward investment promotion schemes (insurance and guarantees), and technical assistance and capacity-building initiatives targeted at sustainable investment, supported by appropriate institutional arrangements for long-term cooperation.

- *Balancing State commitments with investor obligations and promoting responsible investment.* For example, IIAs could include a requirement for investors to comply with investment-related national laws of the host State when making and operating an investment, and even at the post-operations stage, provided that such laws conform to the host country's international obligations. Such an investor obligation could be the basis for further stipulating in the IIA the consequences of an investor's failure to comply with domestic laws, such as the right of host States to make a counter claim in dispute settlement proceedings. In addition, IIAs could refer to commonly recognized international standards (e.g. the UN Guidelines on Business and Human Rights) and support the spread of CSR standards – which are becoming an ever more important feature of the investment policy landscape.

- *Ensuring an appropriate balance between protection commitments and regulatory space for development.* Countries can safeguard policy space by carefully crafting the structure of IIAs, and by clarifying the scope and meaning of particularly vague treaty provisions such as the fair and equitable treatment standard and expropriation, as well as by using specific flexibility mechanisms such as general or national security exceptions and reservations. The right balance between protecting foreign investment and maintaining policy space for domestic regulation should flow from each country's development strategy.

- *Shielding host countries from unjustified liabilities and high procedural costs.* The strength of IIAs in granting protection to foreign investors has become increasingly evident through the number of ISDS cases brought over the last decade, most of which have been directed at developing countries. Shielding countries from unjustified liabilities and excessive procedural costs through treaty design involves looking at options both in ISDS provisions and in the scope and application of substantive clauses.

These areas of evolution are also relevant for "pre-establishment IIAs", i.e. agreements that – in addition to protecting established investors – contain binding rules regarding the establishment of new investments. As a growing number of countries opt for the pre-establishment approach, it is crucial to ensure that any market opening through IIAs is in line with host countries' development strategies. Relevant provisions include selective liberalization, exceptions and reservations designed to protect a country from overcommitting, and flexibilities in the relevant treaty obligations.

Operationalizing sustainable development objectives in IIAs principally involves three mechanisms (table 5):

- Adjusting existing provisions to make them more sustainable-development-friendly through clauses that safeguard policy space and limit State liability.

- Adding new provisions or new, stronger paragraphs within provisions for sustainable development purposes to balance investor rights and responsibilities, promote responsible investment and strengthen home-country support.

- Introducing Special and Differential Treatment for the less developed party – with effect on both existing and new provisions – to calibrate the level of obligations to the country's level of development.

Table 6. Policy options to operationalize sustainable development objectives in IIAs

	Mechanisms	Examples
Adjusting existing/ common provisions to make them more sustainable-development-friendly through clauses that: • safeguard policy space • limit State liability	Hortatory language	- *Preamble*: stating that attracting responsible foreign investment that fosters sustainable development is one of the key objectives of the treaty.
	Clarifications	- *Expropriation*: specifying that non-discriminatory good faith regulations pursuing public policy objectives do not constitute indirect expropriation. - *Fair and equitable treatment* (FET): including an exhaustive list of State obligations.
	Qualifications/ limitations	- *Scope and definition*: requiring covered investments to fulfil specific characteristics, e.g., positive development impact on the host country.
	Reservations/ carve-outs	- *Country-specific reservations* to national treatment (NT), most-favoured-nation (MFN) or pre-establishment obligations, carving out policy measures (e.g. subsidies), policy areas (e.g. policies on minorities, indigenous communities) or sectors (e.g. social services).
	Exclusions from coverage/exceptions	- *Scope and definition*: excluding portfolio, short-term or speculative investments from treaty coverage. - *General exception* for domestic regulatory measures that aim to pursue legitimate public policy objectives.
	Omissions	- Omit FET, umbrella clause.
Adding new provisions or new, stronger paragraphs within provisions for sustainable development purposes to: • balance investor rights and responsibilities • promote responsible investment • strengthen home-country support	Investor obligations and responsibilities	- Requirement that investors comply with host-State laws at both the entry and the operations stage of an investment. - Encouragement to investors to comply with universal principles or to observe applicable CSR standards.
	Institutional set-up for sustainable development impact	- Institutional set-up under which State parties cooperate to e.g. review the functioning of the IIA or issue interpretations of IIA clauses. - Call for cooperation between the parties to promote observance of applicable CSR standards.
	Home-country measures to promote responsible investment	- Encouragement to offer incentives for sustainable-development-friendly outward investment; investor compliance with applicable CSR standards may be an additional condition. - Technical assistance provisions to facilitate the implementation of the IIA and to maximize its sustainable development impact, including through capacity-building on investment promotion and facilitation.
Introducing Special and Differential Treatment for the less developed party – with effect on both existing and new provisions – to: • calibrate the level of obligations to the country's level of development	Lower levels of obligations	- Pre-establishment commitments that cover fewer economic activities.
	Development-focused exceptions from obligations/ commitments	- Reservations, carving out sensitive development-related areas, issues or measures.
	Best-endeavour commitments	- FET, NT commitments that are not legally binding.
	Asymmetric implementation timetables	- Phase-in of obligations, including pre-establishment, NT, MFN, performance requirements, transfer of funds and transparency.

Source: UNCTAD, *World Investment Report 2012*. Detailed guidelines are also available in the online version of the IPFSD at www.unctad.org/DIAE/IPFSD.

The IPFSD and the way forward

UNCTAD's IPFSD comes at a time when the development community is looking for a new development paradigm, of which cross-border investment is an essential part; when most countries are reviewing and adjusting their regulatory frameworks for such investment; when regional groupings are intensifying their cooperation on investment; and when policymakers and experts are seeking ways and means to factor sustainable development and inclusive growth into national investment regulations and international negotiations.

The IPFSD may serve as a key point of reference for policymakers in formulating national investment policies and in negotiating or reviewing IIAs. It may also serve as a reference for policymakers in areas as diverse as trade, competition, industrial policy, environmental policy or any other field where investment plays an important role. The IPFSD can also serve as the basis for capacity-building on investment policy. And it may come to act as a point of convergence for international cooperation on investment issues.

To foster such cooperation, UNCTAD will continue to provide a platform for consultation and discussion with all investment stakeholders and the international development community, including policymakers, investors, business associations, labour unions, and relevant NGOs and interest groups.

For this purpose, a new interactive, open-source platform has been created, inviting the investment and development community to exchange views, suggestions and experiences related to the IPFSD for the inclusive and participative development of future investment policies.

Geneva, June 2012

Supachai Panitchpakdi
Secretary-General of the UNCTAD

GLOBAL INVESTMENT TRENDS

CHAPTER I

Global foreign direct investment (FDI) flows exceeded the pre-crisis average in 2011, reaching $1.5 trillion despite turmoil in the global economy. However, they still remained some 23 per cent below their 2007 peak.

UNCTAD predicts slower FDI growth in 2012, with flows levelling off at about $1.6 trillion. Leading indicators – the value of cross-border mergers and acquisitions (M&As) and greenfield investments – retreated in the first five months of 2012. Longer-term projections show a moderate but steady rise, with global FDI reaching $1.8 trillion in 2013 and $1.9 trillion in 2014, barring any macroeconomic shocks.

FDI inflows increased across all major economic groupings in 2011. Flows to developed countries increased by 21 per cent, to $748 billion. In developing countries FDI increased by 11 per cent, reaching a record $684 billion. FDI in the transition economies increased by 25 per cent to $92 billion. Developing and transition economies respectively accounted for 45 per cent and 6 per cent of global FDI. UNCTAD's projections show these countries maintaining their high levels of investment over the next three years.

Sovereign wealth funds (SWFs) show significant potential for investment in development. FDI by SWFs is still relatively small. Their cumulative FDI reached an estimated $125 billion in 2011, with about a quarter in developing countries. SWFs can work in partnership with host-country governments, development finance institutions or other private sector investors to invest in infrastructure, agriculture and industrial development, including the build-up of green growth industries.

The international production of transnational corporations (TNCs) advanced, but they are still holding back from investing their record cash holdings. In 2011, foreign affiliates of TNCs employed an estimated 69 million workers, who generated $28 trillion in sales and $7 trillion in value added, some 9 per cent up from 2010. TNCs are holding record levels of cash, which so far have not translated into sustained growth in investment. The current cash "overhang" may fuel a future surge in FDI.

UNCTAD's new FDI Contribution Index shows relatively higher contributions by foreign affiliates to host economies in developing countries, especially Africa, in terms of value added, employment and wage generation, tax revenues, export generation and capital formation. The rankings also show countries with less than expected FDI contributions, confirming that policy matters for maximizing positive and minimizing negative effects of FDI.

A. GLOBAL FDI FLOWS

1. Overall trends

Global FDI inflows in 2011 surpassed their pre-crisis average despite turmoil in the global economy, but remained 23 per cent short of the 2007 peak.

Global foreign direct investment (FDI) inflows rose in 2011 by 16 per cent compared with 2010, reflecting the higher profits of TNCs and the relatively high economic growth in developing countries during the year. Global inward FDI stock rose by 3 per cent, reaching $20.4 trillion.

The rise was widespread, covering all three major groups of economies – developed, developing and transition – though the reasons for the increase differed across the globe. FDI flows to developing and transition economies saw a rise of 12 per cent, reaching a record level of $777 billion, mainly through a continuing increase in greenfield projects. FDI flows to developed countries also rose – by 21 per cent – but in their case the growth was due largely to cross-border M&As by foreign TNCs.

Among components and modes of entry, the rise of FDI flows displayed an uneven pattern. Cross-border M&As rebounded strongly, but greenfield projects – which still account for the majority of FDI – remained steady. Despite the strong rebound in cross-border M&As, equity investments – one of

the three components of FDI flows – remained at their lowest level in recent years, particularly so in developed countries. At the same time, difficulties with raising funds from third parties, such as commercial banks, obliged foreign affiliates to rely on intracompany loans from their parents to maintain their current operations.

On the basis of current prospects for underlying factors such as growth in gross domestic product (GDP), UNCTAD estimates that world FDI flows will rise moderately in 2012, to about $1.6 trillion, the midpoint of a range estimate. However, the fragility of the world economy, with growth tempered by the debt crisis and further financial market volatility, will have an impact on flows. Both cross-border M&As and greenfield investments slipped in the last quarter of 2011 and the first five months of 2012. The number of M&A announcements, although marginally up in the last quarter, continues to be weak, providing little support for growth in overall FDI flows in 2012, especially in developed countries. In the first quarter of 2012, the value of UNCTAD's Global FDI Quarterly Index declined slightly (figure I.1) – a decline within the range of normal first-quarter oscillations. But the high cash holdings of TNCs and continued strong overseas earnings – guaranteeing a high reinvested earnings component of FDI – support projections of further growth.

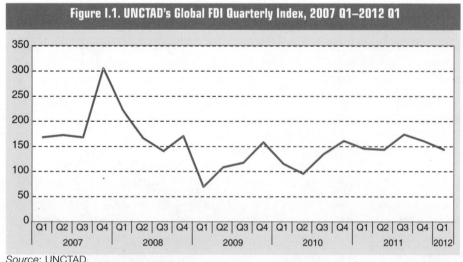

Figure I.1. UNCTAD's Global FDI Quarterly Index, 2007 Q1–2012 Q1

Source: UNCTAD.
Note: The Global FDI Quarterly Index is based on quarterly data on FDI inflows for 82 countries. The index has been calibrated so that the average of quarterly flows in 2005 is equivalent to 100.

a. FDI by geography

(i) FDI inflows

The rise of FDI flows in 2011 was widespread in all three major groups – developed, developing and transition economies. Developing economies continued to absorb nearly half of global FDI and transition economies another 6 per cent.

Amid uncertainties over the global economy, global FDI flows rose by 16 per cent in 2011 to $1,524 billion, up from $1,309 billion in 2010 (figure I.2). While the increase in developing and transition economies was driven mainly by robust greenfield investments, the growth in developed countries was due largely to cross-border M&As.

FDI flows to developed countries grew strongly in 2011, reaching $748 billion, up 21 per cent from 2010. FDI flows to Europe increased by 19 per cent, mainly owing to large cross-border M&A purchases by foreign TNCs (chapter II). The main factors driving such M&As include corporate restructuring, stabilization and rationalization of companies' operations, improvements in capital usage and reductions in costs. Ongoing and post-crisis corporate and industrial restructuring, and gradual exits by States from some nationalized financial and non-financial firms created new opportunities for FDI in developed countries. In addition, the growth of FDI was due to increased amounts of reinvested earnings, part of which was retained in foreign affiliates as cash reserves

(see section B). (Reinvested earnings can be transformed immediately in capital expenditures or retained as reserves on foreign affiliates' balance sheets for future investment. Both cases translate statistically into reinvested earnings, one of three components of FDI flows.) They reached one of the highest levels in recent years, in contrast to equity investment (figure I.3).

Developing countries continued to account for nearly half of global FDI in 2011 as their inflows reached a new record high of $684 billion. The rise in 2011 was driven mainly by investments in Asia and better than average growth in Latin America and the Caribbean (excluding financial centres). FDI flows to transition economies also continued to rise, to $92 billion, accounting for another 6 per cent of the global total. In contrast, Africa, the region with the highest number of LDCs, and West Asia continued to experience a decline in FDI.

- FDI inflows to Latin America and the Caribbean (excluding financial centres) rose an estimated 27 per cent in 2011, to $150 billion. Foreign investors continued to find appeal in South America's natural resources and were increasingly attracted by the region's expanding consumer markets.

- FDI inflows to developing Asia continued to grow, while South-East Asia and South Asia experienced faster FDI growth than East Asia. The two large emerging economies, China and India, saw inflows rise by nearly 8 per cent and

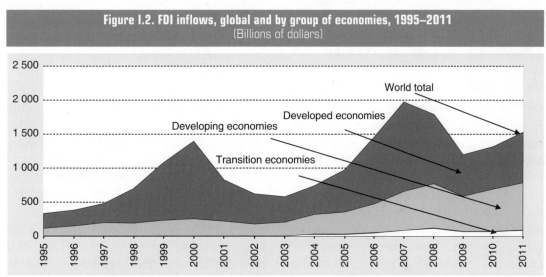

Figure I.2. FDI inflows, global and by group of economies, 1995–2011
(Billions of dollars)

Source: UNCTAD, based on annex table I.1 and the FDI/TNC database (www.unctad.org/fdistatistics).

Figure I.3. FDI inflows in developed countries by component, 2005–2011
(Billions of dollars)

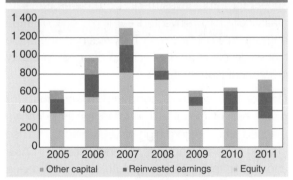

■ Other capital   ■ Reinvested earnings   Equity

Source: UNCTAD, based on data from FDI/TNC database (www.unctad.org/fdistatistics).

Note: Countries included Australia, Austria, Belgium, Bulgaria, Canada, Cyprus, the Czech Republic, Denmark, Estonia, Finland, France, Germany, Greece, Hungary, Ireland, Israel, Italy, Japan, Latvia, Lithuania, Luxembourg, Malta, the Netherlands, New Zealand, Norway, Poland, Portugal, Romania, Slovakia, Slovenia, Spain, Sweden, Switzerland, the United Kingdom and the United States.

by 31 per cent, respectively. Major recipient economies in the Association of South-East Asian Nations (ASEAN) subregion, including Indonesia, Malaysia and Singapore, also experienced a rise in inflows.

- West Asia witnessed a 16 per cent decline in FDI flows in 2011 despite the strong rise of FDI in Turkey. Some Gulf Cooperation Council (GCC) countries are still recovering from the suspension or cancellation of large-scale projects in previous years.

- The fall in FDI flows to Africa seen in 2009 and 2010 continued into 2011, though at a much slower rate. The 2011 decline in flows to the continent was due largely to divestments from North Africa. In contrast, inflows to sub-Saharan Africa recovered to $37 billion, close to their historic peak.

- FDI to the transition economies of South-East Europe, the Commonwealth of Independent States (CIS) and Georgia recovered strongly in 2011. In South-East Europe, competitive production costs and access to European Union (EU) markets drove FDI; in the CIS, large, resource-based economies benefited from continued natural-resource-seeking FDI and the continued strong growth of local consumer markets.

(ii) FDI outflows

Global FDI outflows rose by 17 per cent in 2011, compared with 2010. The rise was driven mainly by growth of outward FDI from developed countries. Outward FDI from developing economies fell slightly by 4 per cent, while FDI from the transition economies rose by 19 per cent (annex table I.1). As a result, the share of developing and transition economies in global FDI outflows declined from 32 per cent in 2010 to 27 per cent in 2011 (figure I.4). Nevertheless, outward FDI from developing and transition economies remained important, reaching the second highest level recorded.

Driven by developed-country TNCs, global FDI outflows also exceeded the pre-crisis average of 2005–2007. The growth in FDI outflows from developing economies seen in the past several years lost some momentum in 2011.

Figure I.4. FDI outflow shares by major economic groups, 2000–2011
(Per cent)

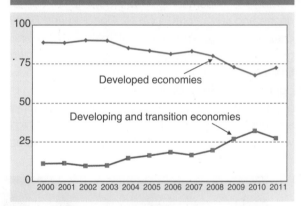

Developed economies

Developing and transition economies

Source: UNCTAD, based on annex table I.1 and the FDI/TNC database (www.unctad.org/fdistatistics).

Outward FDI from developed countries rose by 25 per cent, reaching $1.24 trillion, with the EU, North America and Japan all contributing to the growth. Outward FDI from the United States reached a record of $397 billion. Japan re-emerged as the second largest investor, helped by the appreciation of the Japanese yen, which increased the purchasing power of the country's TNCs in making foreign acquisitions. The rise of FDI outflows from the EU was driven by cross-border M&As.

Developed-country TNCs made acquisitions largely in other developed countries, resulting in a higher share of the group in total FDI projects (both cross-border M&A transactions and greenfield projects). FDI flows for greenfield projects alone, however, show that developed-country TNCs are continuing to shift capital expenditures to developing and transition economies for their stronger growth potential.

The growth in FDI outflows from developing economies seen in the past several years lost some momentum in 2011 owing to declines in outward FDI from Latin American and the Caribbean and a slowdown in the growth of investments from developing Asia. FDI outflows from developing countries fell by 4 per cent to $384 billion in that year. More specifically:

- Outward flows from Latin America and the Caribbean have become highly volatile in the aftermath of the global financial crisis. They decreased by 17 per cent in 2011, after a strong 121 per cent increase in 2010, which followed a large decline in 2009 (-44 per cent). This high volatility is due in part to the importance of the region's offshore financial centres such as the British Virgin Islands and Cayman Islands (which accounted for roughly 70 per cent of the outflows from Latin America and the Caribbean in 2011). Such centres can contribute to volatility in FDI flows, and they can distort patterns of FDI (box I.1). In South America, a healthy level of equity investments abroad was undercut by a large negative swing in intracompany loans as foreign affiliates of some Latin American TNCs provided or repaid loans to their home-country parent firms.

- FDI outflows from developing Asia (excluding West Asia) declined marginally in 2011, after a significant increase in the previous year. Outward FDI from East Asia decreased, while that from South Asia and South-East Asia rose markedly. FDI from Hong Kong, China, the region's largest source of FDI, declined by 14 per cent to $82 billion. FDI outflows from China also fell, to $65 billion, a 5 per cent decline from 2010. Cross-border M&As by Asian firms rose significantly in developed countries, but declined in developing countries.

- FDI from Africa accounts for a much smaller share of outward FDI from developing economies than do Latin America and the Caribbean, and developing Asia. It fell by half in 2011, to $3.5 billion, compared with $7.0 billion in 2010. The decline in outflows from Egypt and Libya, traditionally important sources of outward FDI from the region, weighed heavily in that fall. Divestments by TNCs from South Africa, another major outward investor, also pulled down the total.

- In contrast, West Asia witnessed a rebound of outward FDI, with flows rising by 54 per cent to $25 billion in 2011, after falling to a five-year low in 2010. The strong rise registered in oil prices since the end of 2010 increased the availability of funds for outward FDI from a number of oil-rich countries – the region's main outward investors.

FDI outflows from the transition economies also grew, by 19 per cent, reaching an all-time record of $73 billion. Natural-resource-based TNCs in transition economies (mainly in the Russian Federation), supported by high commodity prices and increasing stock market valuations, continued their expansion into emerging markets rich in natural resources.[1]

Many TNCs in developing and transition economies continued to invest in other emerging markets. For example, 65 per cent of FDI projects by value (comprising cross-border M&As and greenfield investments) from the BRIC countries (Brazil, the Russian Federation, India and China) were invested in developing and transition economies (table I.1), compared with 59 percent in the pre-crisis period.

A key policy concern related to the growth in FDI flows in 2011 is that it did not translate to an equivalent expansion of productive capacity. Much of it was due to cross-border acquisitions and the increased amount of cash reserves retained in foreign affiliates (rather than the much-needed direct investment in new productive assets through greenfield investment projects or capital expenditures in existing foreign affiliates). TNCs from the United States, for example, increased cash holdings in their foreign affiliates in the form of reinvested (retained) earnings.

Table I.1. Share of FDI projects by BRIC countries, by host region, average 2005–2007 (pre-crisis period) and 2011
(Per cent)

Partner region/economy	2005–2007 (average)	2011
World	**100**	**100**
Developed countries	**41**	**34**
European Union	18	14
United States	9	5
Developing economies	**49**	**57**
Africa	9	11
Asia	30	31
East and South-East Asia	13	22
South Asia	5	2
West Asia	11	7
Latin America and the Caribbean	10	15
Transition economies	**10**	**8**
Memorandum		
BRIC	8	11

Source: UNCTAD estimates based on cross-border M&A database for M&As, and information from the Financial Times Ltd, fDi Markets (www.fDimarkets.com) for greenfield projects.

Figure I.5. Value of cross-border M&As and greenfield FDI projects worldwide, 2007–2011

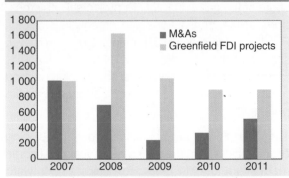

Source: UNCTAD, based on UNCTAD cross-border M&A database and information from Financial Times Ltd, fDi Markets (www.fDimarkets.com).

Note: Data for value of greenfield FDI projects refer to estimated amounts of capital investment. Values of all cross-border M&As and greenfield investments are not necessarily translated into the value of FDI.

b. FDI by mode of entry

Cross-border M&As and greenfield investments have shown diverging trends over the past three years, with M&As rising and greenfield projects in slow decline, although the value of greenfield investments is still significantly higher. Cross-border M&As rose 53 per cent in 2011 to $526 billion (figure I.5), as deals announced in late 2010 came to fruition, reflecting both the growing value of assets on stock markets and the increased financial capacity of buyers to carry out such operations. Rising M&A activity, especially in the form of megadeals in both developed countries and transition economies, served as the major driver for this increase. The total number of megadeals (those with a value over $3 billion) increased from 44 in 2010 to 62 in 2011 (annex table I.7). The extractive industry was targeted by a number of important deals in both of those regions, while in developed countries a sharp rise took place in M&As in pharmaceuticals. M&As in developing economies rose slightly in value. New deal activity worldwide began to falter in the middle part of the year as the number of announcements tumbled. Completed deals, which

follow announcements by roughly half a year, also started to slow down by year's end.

In contrast, greenfield investment projects remained flat in value terms, at $904 billion despite a strong performance in the first quarter. Because these projects are registered on an announcement basis,[2] their performance coincides with investor sentiment during a given period. Thus, their fall in value terms beginning in the second quarter of 2011 was strongly linked with rising concerns about the direction of the global economy and events in Europe. Greenfield investment projects in developing and transition economies rose slightly in 2011, accounting for more than two thirds of the total value of such projects.

Greenfield investment and M&A differ in their impacts on host economies, especially in the initial stages of investment (*WIR00*). In the short run, M&As clearly do not bring the same development benefits as greenfield investment projects, in terms of the creation of new productive capacity, additional value added, employment and so forth. The effect of M&As on, for example, host-country employment can even be negative, in cases of restructuring to achieve synergies. In special circumstances M&As can bring short-term benefits not dissimilar to greenfield investments; for example, where the alternative for acquired assets

Box I.1. The increasing importance of indirect FDI flows

The current geographical pattern of FDI in terms of home and host countries is influenced by several factors that are not, or not adequately, taken into account by current data on FDI. A significant proportion of global FDI flows is indirect. Various mechanisms are behind these indirect flows, including:

- *Tax-haven economies and offshore financial centres.* Tax-haven economies[a] account for a non-negligible and increasing share of global FDI flows, reaching more than 4 per cent in 2011. It is likely that those investment flows do not stay in the tax-haven economies and are redirected. At the regional or country level, the share of those economies in inward FDI can be as high as 30 per cent for certain Latin American countries (Brazil and Chile), Asian economies (Hong Kong, China) and the Russian Federation.

- *Special-purpose entities (SPEs).* Although many tax-haven economies are in developing countries, SPEs, including financial holding companies, are more prevalent in developed countries. Luxembourg and the Netherlands are typical of such countries (box table I.1.1). It is not known to what extent investment in SPEs is directed to activities in the host economy or in other countries.

Box table I.1.1. FDI stock in financial holding companies, 2009
(Per cent)

Economy	Share in total	
	Inward	Outward
Cyprus	33	31
Denmark	22	18
France	9	6
Luxembourg	93	90
Netherlands	79	75
Argentina	2	-
Hong Kong, China	66	73
Singapore	34	-

Source: UNCTAD, FDI/TNC database (www.unctad.org/fdistatistics).
Note: Data for Hong Kong, China, refer to FDI in investment holdings, real estate and various business activities.

FDI by SPEs and FDI from tax-haven economies are often indirect in the sense that the economies from which the investment takes place are not necessarily the home economies of the ultimate beneficiary owners. Such investments influence real patterns of FDI. Survey data on FDI stock in the United States allows a distinction by countries of the immediate and the ultimate owner. The data show that FDI through SPEs or originating in offshore financial centres is undertaken largely by foreign affiliates (e.g. as in Luxembourg) (box table I.1.2). By contrast, foreign assets of developing countries that are home to TNCs are underestimated in many cases (e.g. Brazil).

In general, whether or not through the use of tax havens and SPEs, investments made by foreign affiliates of TNCs represent an indirect flow of FDI from the TNC's home country and a direct flow of FDI from the country where the affiliate is located. The extent of this indirect FDI depends on various factors:

- *Corporate governance and structures.* A high degree of independence of foreign affiliates from parent firms induces indirect FDI. Affiliates given regional headquarters status often undertake FDI on their own account.

- *Tax.* Differences in corporate taxation standards lead to the channelling of FDI through affiliates, some established specifically for that purpose. For example, Mauritius has concluded a double-taxation treaty with India and has attracted foreign firms – many owned by non-resident Indians – that establish holding firms to invest in India. As a result, Mauritius has become one of the largest FDI sources for India.

- *Cultural factors.* Greater cultural proximity between intermediary home countries and the host region can lead to TNCs channeling investment through affiliates in such countries. Investment in Central and Eastern Europe by foreign affiliates in Austria is a typical case.

Investment can originate from any affiliate of a TNC system at any stage of the value chain. As TNCs operate more and more globally, and their corporate networks become more and more complex, investments by foreign affiliates will become more important.

Box I.1. The increasing importance of indirect FDI flows (concluded)

**Box table I.1.2. Inward FDI stock in the United States,
by immediate and ultimate source economy, 2000 and 2010**
(Millions of dollars)

Source economy	2000		2010	
	By immediate source economy	By economy of ultimate beneficial owner	By immediate source economy	By economy of ultimate beneficial owner
Australia	18 775	18 624	49 543	52 893
Bahamas	1 254	51	128	211
Bermuda	18 336	38 085	5 142	124 804
Brazil	882	1 655	1 093	15 476
Canada	114 309	127 941	206 139	238 070
France	125 740	126 256	184 762	209 695
Germany	122 412	131 936	212 915	257 222
Hong Kong, China	1 493	12 655	4 272	11 615
Japan	159 690	161 855	257 273	263 235
Korea, Republic of	3 110	3 224	15 213	16 610
Luxembourg	58 930	1 779	181 203	24 437
Mexico	7 462	9 854	12 591	33 995
Netherlands	138 894	111 514	217 050	118 012
Netherlands Antilles	3 807	1 195	3 680	12 424
Panama	3 819	377	1 485	761
Singapore	5 087	5 214	21 831	21 283
South Africa	704	1 662	687	2 190
Spain	5 068	6 352	40 723	44 237
Sweden	21 991	23 613	40 758	36 034
Switzerland	64 719	54 265	192 231	61 598
United Arab Emirates	64	1 592	591	13 319
United Kingdom	277 613	326 038	432 488	497 531
Venezuela, Bolivarian Republic of	792	4 032	2 857	3 111

Source: UNCTAD, based on information from the United States Department of Commerce, Bureau of Economic Analysis.

Source: UNCTAD.
[a]   As defined by OECD, includes Andorra, Gibraltar, the Isle of Man, Liechtenstein and Monaco in Europe; Bahrain, Liberia and Seychelles in Africa; and the Cook Islands, Maldives, the Marshall Islands, Nauru, Niue, Samoa, Tonga and Vanuatu in Asia; as well as economies in the Caribbean such as Anguilla, Antigua and Barbuda, Aruba, Barbados, Belize, the British Virgin Islands, the Cayman Islands, Dominica, Grenada, Montserrat, the Netherlands Antilles, Panama, Saint Kitts and Nevis, Saint Lucia, Saint Vincent and the Grenadines, the Turks and Caicos Islands and the United States Virgin Islands.

would be closure. Privatizations are another special case, where openness of the bidding process to foreign acquirers will enlarge the pool of bidders and increase the value of privatized assets to the State. In any case, over a longer period, M&As are often followed by sequential investments yielding benefits similar to greenfield investments. Also, in other investment impact areas, such as employment and technology dissemination, the differentiated impact of the two modes fades away over time.

c. FDI by sector and industry

In 2011, FDI flows rose in all three sectors of production (primary, manufacturing and services), and the rise was widespread across all major economic activities. This is confirmed by the increased value of FDI projects (cross-border M&As and greenfield investments) in various industries,

FDI in the services and primary sectors rebounded in 2011 after falling sharply in 2009 and 2010, with their shares rising at the expense of the manufacturing sector.

which may be considered indicative of the sectoral and industrial patterns of FDI flows, for which data become available only one or two years after the reference period. On the basis of the value of FDI projects, FDI in the services sector rebounded in 2011 to reach some $570 billion, after falling sharply in the previous two years. Investment in the primary sector also reversed the negative trend of the previous two years, reaching $200 billion. The share of both sectors rose slightly at the expense of the manufacturing sector (table I.2). Compared with the average value in the three years before the financial crisis (2005–2007), the value of FDI in manufacturing has recovered. The value of FDI in the primary sector now exceeds the pre-crisis average, while the value of FDI in services has remained lower, at some 70 per cent of its value in the earlier period.

During this period, FDI in the primary sector rose gradually, characterized by an increase in investment in mining, quarrying and petroleum. It now accounts for 14 per cent of total FDI projects (see table I.2). Investment in petroleum and natural gas rose, mainly in developed countries and transition economies, in the face of stronger final demand (after a fall in 2009, global use of energy resumed its long-term upward trend).[3] In the oil and gas industries, for example, foreign firms invested heavily in United States firms.[4]

The value of FDI projects in manufacturing rose by 7 per cent in 2011 (table I.3). The largest increases were observed in the food and chemicals industries, while FDI projects in coke, petroleum and nuclear fuel saw the biggest percentage decrease. The food, beverages and tobacco industry was among those least affected by the crisis because it produces mainly basic consumption goods. TNCs in the industry that had strong balance sheets took advantage of lower selling values and reduced competition to strengthen their competitive positions and consolidate their roles in the industry. For example, in the largest deal in the industry, SABMiller (United Kingdom) acquired Foster's Group (Australia) for $10.8 billion.

The chemicals industry saw a 65 per cent rise in FDI, mainly as a result of large investments in pharmaceuticals. Among the driving forces behind its growth is the dynamism of its final markets, especially in emerging economies, as well as the need to set up production capabilities for new health products and an ongoing restructuring trend throughout the industry. As a record number of popular drugs lose their patent protection, many companies are investing in developing countries, as illustrated by the $4.6 billion acquisition of Ranbaxy (India) by Daiichi Sankyo (Japan). The acquisition by Takeda (Japan) of Nycomed (Switzerland), a generic drug maker, for $13.7 billion was one the largest deals in 2011.

The automotive industry was strongly affected by the economic uncertainty in 2011. The value of FDI projects declined by 15 per cent. The decline was more pronounced in developed countries because of the effects of the financial and sovereign debt crises. Excess capacity in industries located in developed countries, which was already an issue before the crisis, was handled through shift reductions, temporary closures and shorter working hours, but there were no major structural capacity reductions, and thus divestments, in Europe.

FDI in the services sector rose by 15 per cent in 2011, reaching $570 billion. Non-financial services,

Year	Value			Share		
	Primary	Manufacturing	Services	Primary	Manufacturing	Services
Average 2005–2007	130	670	820	8	41	50
2008	230	980	1 130	10	42	48
2009	170	510	630	13	39	48
2010	140	620	490	11	50	39
2011	200	660	570	14	46	40

Table I.2. Sectoral distribution of FDI projects, 2005–2011
(Billions of dollars and per cent)

Source: UNCTAD estimates based on cross-border M&A database for M&As, and information from the Financial Times Ltd, fDi Markets (www.fDimarkets.com) for greenfield projects.

Table I.3. Distribution shares and growth rates of FDI project values, by sector/industry, 2011 (Per cent)			
		Growth rates	
Sector/industry	**Distribution shares**	**2011 compared with 2010**	**2011 compared with pre-crisis average (2005–2007)**
Total	**100**	**15**	**-12**
Primary	**14**	**46**	**50**
Mining, quarrying and petroleum	14	51	53
Manufacturing	**46**	**7**	**-1**
Food, beverages and tobacco	6	18	40
Coke, petroleum and nuclear fuel	4	-37	-30
Chemicals and chemical products	10	65	25
Electrical and electronic equipment	5	-8	-26
Motor vehicles and other transport equipment	6	-15	10
Services	**40**	**15**	**-31**
Electricity, gas and water	8	43	6
Transport, storage and communications	8	38	-31
Finance	6	13	-52
Business services	8	8	-33

Source: UNCTAD estimates based on cross-border M&A database for M&As, and information from the Financial Times Ltd, fDi Markets (www.fDimarkets.com) for greenfield projects.

which accounted for 85 per cent of the total, rose modestly, on the back of increases in FDI targeting electricity, gas and water as well as transportation and communications. A number of megadeals – including Vattenfall's acquisition of an additional 15 per cent stake, valued at $4.7 billion, in Nuon (Netherlands) and Hutchison Whampoa's $3.8 billion acquisition of the Northumbrian Water Group (United Kingdom) – increased the value of FDI projects in electricity, gas and water. FDI projects in the transportation and communication industry also rose, with the majority coming from greenfield investments in telecommunications. Latin America, in particular, hosted a number of important telecommunications investments from America Movil (Mexico), Sprint Nextel (United States), Telefonica (Spain) and Telecom Italia (Italy), which all announced projects that target the growing middle class in the region.

Financial services recorded a 13 per cent increase in the value of FDI projects, reaching $80 billion. However, they remained some 50 per cent below their pre-crisis average (see table I.3). The bulk of activity targeted the insurance industry, with the acquisition of AXA Asian Pacific (France) by AMP

(Australia) for $11.7 billion. FDI projects in banking remained subdued in the wake of the global financial crisis. European banks, which had been at the forefront of international expansion through FDI, were largely absent, with a number of them remaining under government control (*WIR11*: 71–73).

d. Investments by special funds

Investments by private equity funds and sovereign wealth funds (SWFs) have been affected quite differently by the crisis and its aftermath. Private equity funds have faced continuing financial difficulties and are declining considerably as sources of FDI. SWFs, by contrast, have continued to add to their assets and strengthen their potential as sources of FDI, especially in developing economies.

(i) Private equity funds and FDI

FDI by private equity funds[5] increased 18 per cent to $77 billion – measured by the net value of cross-border M&As (table I.4).[6] They once were emerging as a new and growing source of international investment but have lost momentum. Before the crisis, some private equity firms (e.g.

FDI by private equity funds rose in 2011 but remained far short of its pre-crisis average, with investments in the services sector outgrowing investments in both the primary and manufacturing sectors. Rising concerns relate to long-term sustainability, transparency and corporate governance.

Apollo Management, RHJ International and KKR) had listed their shares in stock markets and successfully raised funds for investments. Most of the money stemmed from institutional investors, such as banks, pension funds and insurance companies. Hence, the deterioration of the finance industry in the recent crisis has led to difficulties in the private equity fund industry and slowed the dynamic development of such funds' investment abroad. The supply of finance for their investments has shrunk. As a result, funds raised by private equity have fallen by more than 50 per cent since the peak in 2007, to about $180 billion in 2011. The scale of investment has also changed. In contrast to the period when large funds targeted big, publicly traded companies, private equity in recent years has been predominantly aimed at smaller firms.

While the private equity industry is still largely concentrated in the United States and the United Kingdom, its activity is expanding to developing and transition economies where funds have been established. Examples include Capital Asia (Hong Kong, China), Dubai International Capital (United Arab Emirates), and H&Q Asia Pacific (China). Asian companies with high growth potential have attracted the lion's share of spending in developing and transition regions, followed by Latin America and Africa. In 2009–2010, private equity activity expanded in Central and Eastern Europe (including both new EU member States such as Poland, the Czech Republic, Romania, Hungary and Bulgaria, in that order, and transition economies such as Ukraine). This activity was driven by venture and growth capital funds, which are becoming important in the financing of small and medium-sized enterprises in the region.[7]

The private equity market has traditionally been stronger in the United States than in other countries. The majority of private equity funds invest in their own countries or regions. But a growing proportion of investments now cross borders. Private equity funds compete in many cases with traditional TNCs in acquiring foreign companies and have joined with other funds to create several of the largest deals in the world.[8]

In terms of sectoral interest, private equity firms invest in various industries abroad but are predominantly represented in the services sector, with finance playing a significant part. However, the primary sector, which was not a significant target in the mid-2000s, has become an increasingly important sector in the past few years (figure I.6). Private equity has targeted mining companies and firms with a strong interest in the mining sector, such as Japanese transnational trading houses (sogo shosha).[9] Interest in manufacturing has also been increasing, particularly in 2011.

Differences have also emerged between the patterns of FDI by private equity firms in developing countries and in developed ones. In developing countries, they focus largely on services (finance and telecommunications) and mining. In developed countries, private equity firms invest in a wide range of industries, from food, beverages and tobacco in the manufacturing sector to business activities (including real estate) in the services sector.

The increasing activity of private equity funds in international investment differs from FDI by TNCs in terms of the strategic motivations of the investors, and this could have implications for the long-run growth and welfare of the host economies. On the upside, private equity can be used to start new firms or to put existing firms on a growth path. For example, it has been shown that firms that receive external private equity financing tend to have a greater start-up size and can therefore better exploit growth potential. In developing countries, where growth potential is high but perceived risks are equally high, traditional investors are often deterred or unfamiliar with the territory. Some private equity funds specialize in developing regions to leverage their region-specific knowledge and better risk perception. For example, Helios Investment Partners, a pan-African private equity group with a $1.7 billion investment fund, is one of the largest private equity firms specializing in the continent. BTG Pactual, Avent International

	Table I.4. Cross-border M&As by private equity firms, 1996–2011 (Number of deals and value)							
	Gross cross-border M&As				Net cross-border M&As			
	Number of deals		Value		Number of deals		Value	
Year	Number	Share in total (%)	$ billion	Share in total (%)	Number	Share in total (%)	$ billion	Share in total (%)
1996	932	16	42	16	464	13	19	14
1997	925	14	54	15	443	11	18	10
1998	1 089	14	79	11	528	11	38	9
1999	1 285	14	89	10	538	10	40	6
2000	1 340	13	92	7	525	8	45	5
2001	1 248	15	88	12	373	9	42	10
2002	1 248	19	85	18	413	13	28	11
2003	1 488	22	109	27	592	20	53	29
2004	1 622	22	157	28	622	17	76	33
2005	1 737	20	221	24	795	16	121	26
2006	1 698	18	271	24	786	14	128	20
2007	1 918	18	555	33	1 066	15	288	28
2008	1 785	18	322	25	1 080	17	204	29
2009	1 993	25	107	19	1 065	25	58	23
2010	2 103	22	131	18	1 147	21	65	19
2011	1 900	19	156	15	902	16	77	15

Source: UNCTAD, cross-border M&A database (www.unctad.org/fdistatistics).
Note: Value on a net basis takes into account divestments by private equity funds. Thus it is calculated as follows: Purchases of companies abroad by private equity funds (-) Sales of foreign affiliates owned by private equity funds. The table includes M&As by hedge and other funds (but not sovereign wealth funds). Private equity firms and hedge funds refer to acquirers as "investors not elsewhere classified". This classification is based on the Thomson Finance database on M&As.

and Vinci Partners, all based in Brazil, are major investors in Latin America, an $8 billion plus market for private equity funds.

On the downside, some concerns exist about the sustainability of high levels of FDI activity by private equity funds. First, the high prices that private equity funds paid for their investments in the past have made it increasingly difficult for them to find buyers, increasing further the pressure that private equity firms normally exert to focus on short-run profit targets, often leading to layoffs and restructuring of companies.[10] Second, acquiring stock-listed companies deviates from the private equity funds' former strategy of investing in alternative asset classes (e.g. venture capital, unlisted small firms with growth potential).

Furthermore, there are concerns related to transparency and corporate governance, because most funds are not traded on exchanges that have regulatory mechanisms and disclosure requirements. And there are differences in the investment horizons of private equity funds and traditional TNCs. Private equity funds, often driven by short-term performance targets, hold newly acquired firms on average for five to six years, a period which has declined in recent years. TNCs, which typically are engaged in expanding the production of their goods and services to locations abroad, have longer investment horizons.

Despite the implications of these differences for the host economy, many private equity firms have nevertheless demonstrated more awareness about long-term governance issues and disclosure; for example, environmental and social governance. According to a survey by the British Private Equity and Venture Capital Association (2011), more than half of private equity firms have implemented programmes on environmental and social governance in their investments.[11]

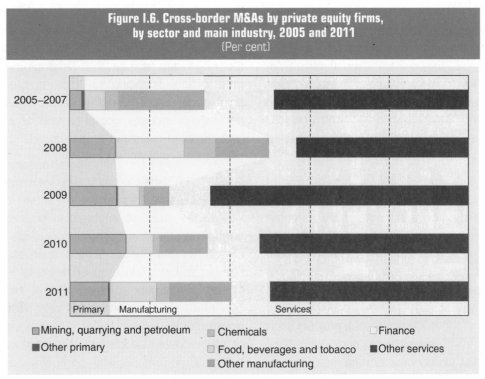

Figure I.6. Cross-border M&As by private equity firms, by sector and main industry, 2005 and 2011
(Per cent)

2005–2007
2008
2009
2010
2011

Primary   Manufacturing   Services

☐ Mining, quarrying and petroleum   ▨ Chemicals   ☐ Finance
■ Other primary   ☐ Food, beverages and tobacco   ■ Other services
                                     ▨ Other manufacturing

Source: UNCTAD, cross-border M&A database (www.unctad.org/fdistatistics).

(ii) FDI by sovereign wealth funds

Cumulative FDI by SWFs amounts to only $125 billion, on an asset base of nearly $5 trillion, suggesting significant potential for further investment in sustainable development.

With nearly $5 trillion in assets under management at the end of 2011, SWFs – funds set up by or on behalf of sovereign states – have become important actors in global financial markets.[12] The growth of SWFs has been impressive: even during 2007–2011, a period spanning the global financial crisis, and despite losses on individual holdings, the total cumulative value of SWF assets rose at an annual rate of 10 per cent, compared with a 4 per cent decline in the value of international banking assets.[13] That growth is likely to continue as the emerging-market owners of most funds keep outperforming the world economy, and as high commodity prices further inflate the revenue surpluses of countries with some of the largest SWFs.

SWFs are for the most part portfolio investors, with the bulk of their funds held in relatively liquid financial assets in mature market economies. Only a small proportion of their value (an estimated $125 billion) is in the form of FDI. FDI thus accounts for less than 5 per cent of SWF assets under management and less than 1 per cent of global FDI stock in 2011. However, evidence shows a clear growth trend since 2005 (figure I.7) – when SWFs invested a mere $7 billion – despite a steep decline in annual flows in 2010 in response to global economic conditions.

FDI by SWFs in developed countries has grown faster than that in developing countries (table I.5), also reflecting the availability of acquisition opportunities in North America and Europe during the crisis. However, SWF FDI in developing countries is rising steadily. Some countries in developing Asia that have more advanced capital markets are already significant recipients of investment by SWFs, but in forms other than FDI.

FDI by SWFs is concentrated on specific projects in a limited number of industries, finance, real estate and construction, and natural resources (table I.6). In part, this reflects the strategic aims of the relatively few SWFs active in FDI, such as Temasek (Singapore), China Investment Corporation, the

Qatar Investment Authority and Mubadala (United Arab Emirates). Even these four SWFs have devoted only a fraction of their total holdings to FDI. For example, Temasek is the most active SWF investor in developing countries, where it holds roughly 71 per cent of all its assets located abroad (S$131 billion or $102 billion in 2011). Yet, only $3 billion of those assets are FDI (acquisitions of more than 10 per cent equity).[14]

Despite SWFs' current focus on developed countries, and the concentration of their activities with their long-term and strategically oriented investment outlook, SWFs may be ideally well placed to invest in productive activities abroad, especially in developing countries, including in particular the LDCs that attract only modest FDI flows from other sources. The scale of their holdings enables SWFs to invest in large-scale projects such as infrastructure development and agricultural production – key to economic development in many LDCs – as well as industrial development, including the build-up of green growth industries.

For both developing and developed countries, investment by foreign State-owned entities in

strategic assets such as agricultural land, natural resources or key infrastructure assets can lead to legitimate policy concerns. Nonetheless, given the huge gap across the developing world in development financing for the improvement of agricultural output, construction of infrastructure, provision of industry goods as well as jobs, and generation of sustainable growth, FDI by SWFs presents a significant opportunity.

As SWFs become more active in direct investments in infrastructure, agriculture or other industries vital to the strategic interests of host countries, controlling stakes in investment projects may not always be imperative. Where such stakes are needed to bring the required financial resources to an investment project, SWFs may have options to work in partnership with host-country governments, development finance institutions or other private sector investors that can bring technical and managerial competencies to the project – acting, to some extent, as management intermediaries.

SWFs may set up, alone or in cooperation with others, their own general partnerships dedicated

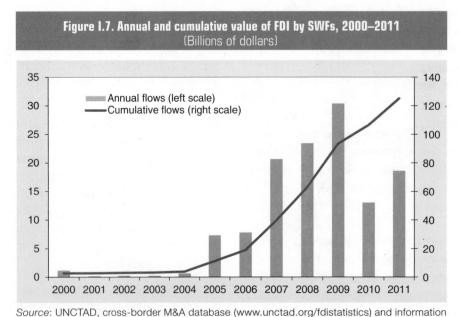

Figure I.7. Annual and cumulative value of FDI by SWFs, 2000–2011
(Billions of dollars)

Source: UNCTAD, cross-border M&A database (www.unctad.org/fdistatistics) and information obtained from Financial Times Ltd, fDi Markets (www.fDimarkets.com).
Note: Data include value of flows for both cross-border M&As and greenfield FDI projects and only investments by SWFs which are the sole and immediate investors. Data do not include investments made by entities established by SWFs or those made jointly with other investors. In 2003–2011, cross-border M&As accounted for 85 per cent of the total.

Table I.5. FDI by SWFs by host region/country, cumulative flows, 2005–2011
(Millions of dollars)

Target economy	2005	2006	2007	2008	2009	2010	2011
World	**11 186**	**19 005**	**39 673**	**63 085**	**93 476**	**106 534**	**125 152**
Developed economies	**5 738**	**12 582**	**26 573**	**38 354**	**62 016**	**71 722**	**84 346**
Europe	4 394	9 438	17 775	23 429	39 078	42 148	53 143
European Union	4 394	9 438	17 746	23 399	39 049	42 118	53 113
United States	125	1 925	5 792	10 210	10 335	12 007	14 029
Developing economies	**5 449**	**6 423**	**12 926**	**23 544**	**29 277**	**31 210**	**35 868**
Africa	900	900	1 304	7 560	7 560	8 973	11 418
Latin America and the Caribbean	228	228	1 149	1 216	1 291	1 696	3 118
East and South-East Asia	4 278	5 040	5 270	7 366	9 845	9 930	10 721
South Asia	43	143	1 092	1 209	1 239	1 268	1 268
West Asia	-	112	4 112	6 193	9 343	9 343	9 343
Transition economies	**-**	**-**	**174**	**1 187**	**2 183**	**3 602**	**3 938**

Source: UNCTAD, cross-border M&A database (www.unctad.org/fdistatistics) and information from the Financial Times Ltd, fDi Markets (www.fDimarkets.com).

Note: Data refer to net M&A cumulative flows since 1992 and greenfield cumulative flows since 2003. Only data on investments by SWFs that are the sole and immediate investors are included, not those made by entities established by SWFs or those made jointly with other investors.

Table I.6. FDI by SWFs by sector/industry, cumulative flows, 2005–2011
(Millions of dollars)

Target industy	2005	2006	2007	2008	2009	2010	2011
Total industry	**11 186**	**19 005**	**39 673**	**63 085**	**93 476**	**106 534**	**125 152**
Primary	**1 170**	**1 512**	**1 682**	**3 055**	**9 645**	**10 945**	**11 899**
Agriculture, hunting, forestry and fisheries	-	-	170	170	170	170	170
Mining, quarrying and petroleum	1 170	1 512	1 512	2 885	9 475	10 775	11 729
Manufacturing	**3 114**	**4 369**	**10 675**	**16 357**	**30 122**	**31 470**	**31 594**
Publishing and printing	-	-	-	248	248	248	248
Coke, petroleum and nuclear fuel	-	-	5 146	10 253	13 449	13 457	13 457
Chemicals and chemical products	2 800	2 800	2 800	2 800	3 301	4 641	4 765
Rubber and plastic products	-	-	1 160	1 160	1 160	1 160	1 160
Non-metallic mineral products	-	-	-	-	150	150	150
Metals and metal products	47	47	47	374	374	374	374
Machinery and equipment	15	15	15	15	15	15	15
Electrical and electronic equipment	-	15	15	15	364	364	364
Motor vehicles and other transport equipment	251	1 492	1 492	1 492	11 061	11 061	11 061
Services	**6 903**	**13 124**	**27 316**	**43 673**	**53 709**	**64 120**	**81 659**
Electricity, gas and water	1 396	1 396	2 317	2 317	2 532	4 112	8 789
Construction	19	19	19	2 738	3 994	5 227	13 081
Hotels and restaurants	508	2 300	3 132	4 174	4 249	4 337	4 997
Trade	20	320	2 125	2 125	3 011	5 309	5 380
Transport, storage and communications	14	303	3 197	3 499	3 652	4 532	6 280
Finance	754	1 296	4 171	14 878	15 199	18 667	19 596
Business services	2 697	5 994	9 282	10 385	12 413	12 698	14 299
Real estate	2 697	5 994	8 872	9 975	12 002	12 287	13 889
Health and social services	-	-	1 578	2 062	2 062	2 062	2 062
Community, social and personal service activities	1 495	1 495	1 495	1 495	6 598	7 174	7 174

Source: UNCTAD, cross-border M&A database (www.unctad.org/fdistatistics) and information from the Financial Times Ltd, fDi Markets (www.fDimarkets.com).

Note: Data refer to net cumulative flows through cross-border M&As since 1992 and cumulative flows through greenfield projects since 2003. Only data on investments by SWFs that are the sole and immediate investors are included, not those made by entities established by SWFs or those made jointly with other investors.

to particular investment themes – for example, infrastructure, renewable energy or natural resources. In 2010, Qatar Holding, the investment arm of the Qatar Investment Authority, set up a $1 billion Indonesian fund to invest in infrastructure and natural resources in Indonesia. In the same year, the International Finance Corporation (IFC) committed up to $200 million as a limited partner in the IFC African, Latin American and Caribbean Fund, in which the anchor investors, with total commitments of up to $600 million, include SWFs such as the Korea Investment Corporation and the State Oil Fund of the Republic of Azerbaijan, as well as investors from Saudi Arabia. In 2011, Morocco's Tourism Investment Authority established Wissal Capital, a fund that aims to develop tourism in the country, through a partnership with the sovereign funds of Qatar, the United Arab Emirates and Kuwait, with investment funds of $2.5–4 billion.

Where SWFs do take on the direct ownership and management of projects, investments could focus on sectors that are particularly beneficial for inclusive and sustainable development, including the sectors mentioned above – agriculture, infrastructure and the green economy – while adhering to principles of responsible investment, such as the *Principles for Responsible Agricultural Investment*, which protect the rights of smallholders and local stakeholders.[15] Expanding the role of SWFs in FDI can provide significant opportunities for sustainable development, especially in less developed countries. Overcoming the challenges of unlocking more capital in the form of FDI from this investment source should be a priority for the international community.

2. Prospects

The growth rate of FDI will slow in 2012, with flows levelling off at about $1.6 trillion. Medium-term flows are expected to rise at a moderate but steady pace, barring macroeconomic shocks.

Prospects for FDI flows have continued to improve since the depth of the 2008–2009 crisis, but they remain constrained by global macroeconomic and financial conditions. At the macroeconomic level, the prospects for the world economy continue to be challenging. After a marked slowdown in 2011, global economic growth will likely remain tepid in

2012, with most regions, especially developed economies, expanding at a pace below potential and with subdued growth (United Nations et al., 2012). Sluggish import demand from developed economies is also weighing on trade growth, which is projected to slow further. Oil prices rose in 2011 and are projected to remain relatively elevated in 2012 and 2013, compared with the levels of 2010 (although recently there has been downward pressure on prices). The global outlook could deteriorate further. The eurozone crisis remains the biggest threat to the world economy, but a continued rise in global energy prices may also stifle growth.

The global economic outlook has had a direct effect on the willingness of TNCs to invest. After two years of slump, profits of TNCs picked up significantly in 2010 and continued to rise in 2011 (figure I.8). However, the perception among TNC managers of risks in the global investment climate continues to act as a brake on capital expenditures, even though firms have record levels of cash holdings.

In the first months of 2012 cross-border M&As and greenfield investments slipped in value. Cross-border M&As, which were the driving force for the growth in 2011, are likely to stay weak in the remainder of 2012, judging from their announcement data, although announcements increased slightly in the last quarter. These factors indicate that the risks to further FDI growth in 2012 remain in place.

UNCTAD scenarios for future FDI growth (figure I.9) are based on the results of leading indicators and an econometric model forecasting FDI inflows (table I.7). UNCTAD's *World Investment Prospects Survey 2012–2014* (WIPS), data for the first quarter of 2012 on FDI flows and data for the first four to five months of 2012 on the values of cross-border M&As and greenfield investment complement the picture. On the basis of the forecasting model, the recovery in 2012 is likely to be marginal. FDI flows are expected to come in between $1.5 trillion and $1.7 trillion, with a midpoint at about $1.6 trillion. WIPS data, strong earnings data (driving reinvested earnings) and first-quarter FDI data support this estimate. In the medium term, FDI flows are expected to increase at a moderate but steady pace, reaching $1.8 trillion in 2013 and $1.9 trillion in 2014 (baseline scenario).This trend also reflects

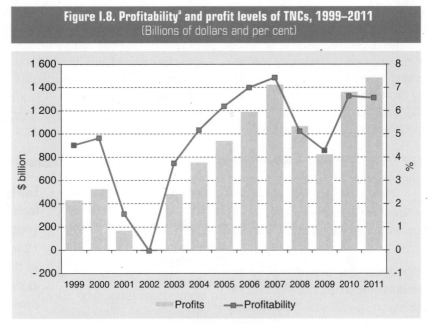

Figure I.8. Profitability[a] and profit levels of TNCs, 1999–2011
(Billions of dollars and per cent)

Source: UNCTAD, based on data from Thomson One Banker.
[a] Profitability is calculated as the ratio of net income to total sales.
Note: The number of TNCs covered in the calculations is 2,498.

opportunities arising not only from corporate and industry restructuring, including privatization or re-privatization, particularly in the crisis-hit countries, but also from continued investment in crisis-resilient industries related to climate change and the green economy such as foods and the energy sector.[16]

The baseline scenario, however, does not take into account the potential for negative macroeconomic shocks. It is also possible that the fragility of the world economy, the volatility of the business environment, uncertainties related to the sovereign debt crisis and apparent signs of lower economic growth in major emerging-market economies will negatively impact FDI flows in the medium term, including causing them to decline in absolute terms (scenario based on macroeconomic shocks).

The growth of FDI inflows in 2012 will be moderate in all three groups – developed, developing and transition economies (figure I.10; table I.7). All these groups are expected to experience further growth in the medium term (2013–2014).

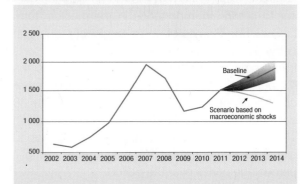

Figure I.9. Global FDI flows, 2002–2011, and projection for 2012–2014
(Billions of dollars)

Source: UNCTAD.

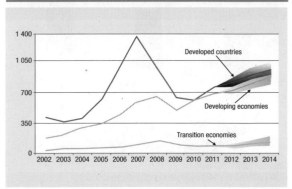

Figure I.10. FDI flows by group of economies, 2002–2011, and projection for 2012–2014
(Billions of dollars)

Source: UNCTAD.

There are some regional differences. In developing regions, inflows to Africa are expected to recover as a result of stronger economic growth, ongoing economic reforms and high commodity prices, as well as improving investor perceptions of the continent, mainly from other emerging markets (chapter II). In contrast, growth of FDI flows is expected to be moderate in Asia (including East and South-East Asia, South Asia and West Asia) and Latin America. FDI flows to transition economies are expected to grow further in 2012 and exceed the 2007 peak in 2014, in part because of the accession of the Russian Federation to the World Trade Organization and a new round of privatization in the region.

These regional forecasts are based mainly on economic fundamentals and do not necessarily take into account region-specific risk factors such as intensifying financial tensions in the eurozone or policy measures such as expropriations and capital controls that may significantly affect investor sentiment. (For a detailed discussion of the econometric model, see box I.3 in *WIR11*.)

Responses to this year's *WIPS* (box I.2) revealed that firms are cautious in their reading of the current global investment environment. Investor uncertainty appears to be high, with roughly half of respondents stating that they were neutral or undecided about the state of the international investment climate for 2012. However, although respondents who were pessimistic about the global investment outlook

for 2012 outnumbered those who were optimistic by 10 percentage points, medium-term prospects continued to hold relatively stable (figure I.11). Also, the uncertainty among investors does not necessarily translate to declining FDI plans. When asked about their intended FDI expenditures, half of the respondents forecast an increase in each year of the 2012–2014 period over 2011 levels.

a. By mode of entry

Among the ways TNCs enter foreign markets, equity modes (including M&As and greenfield/brownfield investments) are set to grow in importance, according to responses to this year's **Equity and non-equity forms of investment will grow in importance for TNCs in the medium term, as the importance of exports from TNCs' home economies declines.**

WIPS. Roughly 40 to 50 per cent of respondents remarked that these modes will be "very" or "extremely" important for them in 2014 (figure I.12). In the case of M&As, this reflects in part the increasing availability of potential targets around the world, especially in developing and transition economies. This trend is likely to drive M&As in these economies in the medium term as TNCs from both developed and developing economies seek to fulfil their internationalization plans. Nevertheless, M&A activity will be heavily contingent on the health of global financial markets, which could hamper any increase in activity in the short term.

International production by TNCs through equity modes is growing in importance, as are, to a lesser extent, non-equity modes, which nearly one third of respondents stated would be highly important in 2014 (up from one quarter saying so for 2012). In contrast, exports from TNCs' home countries are set to decline in importance in the medium term (figure I.12). The rise of complex global production networks has reduced the importance of exports from home by TNCs (Epilogue, *WIR10*). Whereas 43 per cent of survey respondents gave home-country exports high importance in 2012, only 38 per cent did so for 2014. Among manufacturing TNCs, which often operate highly developed global networks, the decline was greater, falling 7 percentage points over the period.

Figure I.11. TNCs' perception of the global investment climate, 2012–2014
(Percentage of respondents)

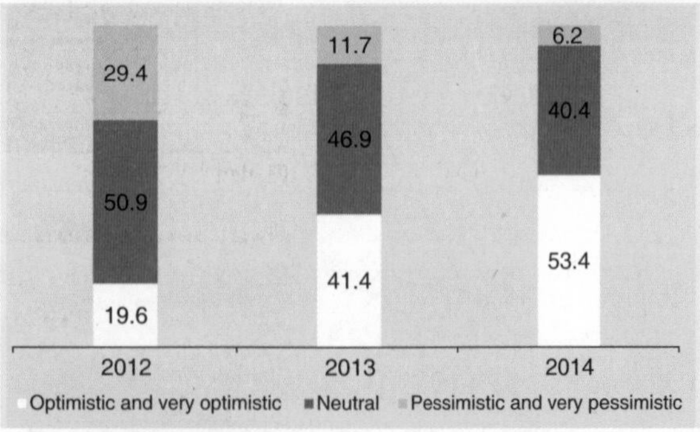

	2012	2013	2014
Pessimistic and very pessimistic	29.4	11.7	6.2
Neutral	50.9	46.9	40.4
Optimistic and very optimistic	19.6	41.4	53.4

Optimistic and very optimistic ■ Neutral Pessimistic and very pessimistic

Source: UNCTAD survey.
Note: Based on 174 validated company responses.

Table I.7. Summary of econometric results of medium-term baseline scenarios of FDI flows, by region
(Billions of dollars)

Host region	Averages		2009	2010	2011	Projections		
	2005–2007	2009–2011				2012	2013	2014
Global FDI flows	**1 473**	**1 344**	**1 198**	**1 309**	**1 524**	**1 495–1 695**	**1 630–1 925**	**1 700–2 110**
Developed countries	**972**	**658**	**606**	**619**	**748**	**735–825**	**810–940**	**840–1 020**
European Union	646	365	357	318	421	410–450	430–510	440–550
North America	253	218	165	221	268	255–285	280–310	290–340
Developing countries	**443**	**607**	**519**	**617**	**684**	**670–760**	**720–855**	**755–930**
Africa	40	46	53	43	43	55–65	70–85	75–100
Latin America and the Caribbean	116	185	149	187	217	195–225	215–265	200–250
Asia	286	374	315	384	423	420–470	440–520	460–570
Transition economies	**59**	**79**	**72**	**74**	**92**	**90–110**	**100–130**	**110–150**

Source: UNCTAD estimates, based on UNCTAD (for FDI inflows), IMF (G20 growth, GDP and openness) and United Nations (oil price) from the Link project.

Note: The variables employed in the model include: market growth of G-20 countries (G-20 growth rate), market size (GDP of each individual country), price of oil and trade openness (the share of exports plus imports over GDP). The following model, $FDI_{jt} = \alpha_0 + \alpha_1 * G20_t + \alpha_2 * GDP_{jt-1} + \alpha_3 * Openness_{jt} + \alpha_4 * Oil\_price_{jt-1} + \alpha_5 * FDI_{jt-1} + \varepsilon_{jt}$, is estimated with fixed effect panel regression using estimated generalized least squares with cross-section weights. Coefficients computed by using White's hereroscedasticity-consistent standard errors.

Box I.2. *World Investment Prospects Survey 2012–2014*: methodology and results

The aim of the *WIPS* is to provide insights into the medium-term prospects for FDI flows. This year's survey was directed to executives in the largest 5,000 non-financial TNCs and professionals working in 245 national and sub-national IPAs.[a] Questions for TNC executives were designed to capture their views on the global investment climate, their company's expected changes in FDI expenditures and internationalization levels, and the importance their company gives to various regions and countries. IPAs were asked about their views on the global investment climate and which investor countries and industries were most promising in terms of inward FDI.

This year's survey results are based on 174 validated responses by TNCs and 62 responses by IPAs collected by e-mail and through a dedicated website between February and May 2012. TNCs in developed economies accounted for 77 per cent of responses (Europe, 44 per cent; other developed economies – mainly Japan – 27 per cent; and North America, 6 per cent). TNCs in developing and transition economies accounted for 23 per cent of responses (Asia, 12 per cent; Africa, 6 per cent; Latin America and the Caribbean, 4 per cent; and transition economies, 1 per cent). In terms of sectoral distribution, 57 per cent of respondent TNCs were classified as operating in the manufacturing sector, 36 per cent in the services sector and 7 per cent in the primary sector. For IPAs, 74 per cent of respondents were located in developing or transition economies and 26 per cent were located in developed economies.

Source: UNCTAD.
[a] The past surveys are available at www.unctad.org/wips.

b. By industry

Although FDI expenditures are set to increase, short-term concerns about the global investment climate are shared across industries; primary sector TNCs may temper their investment plans in the medium term.

Reflecting the general trend, TNCs across all major sectors are similarly cautious about the international investment climate in 2012; however, medium-term prospects appear stronger across sectors.

Short-term FDI plans vary across sectors, according to the survey results. Manufacturing TNCs were the most bullish about their foreign investments in 2012, with roughly 60 per cent of respondents indicating that they will be increasing their FDI expenditures over 2011 levels. In contrast, only 45 per cent of TNCs in the primary sector and 43 per cent of those in services expected an increase. For 2014, however, more than half of TNCs in all three major sectors foresaw an increase in their FDI budgets, in line with their rising optimism about the global investment environment.

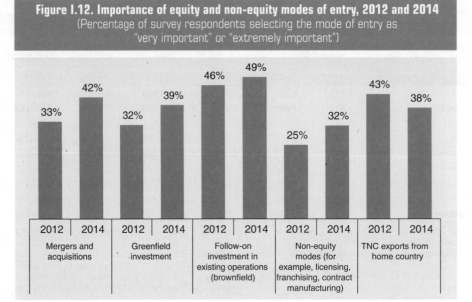

Figure I.12. Importance of equity and non-equity modes of entry, 2012 and 2014
(Percentage of survey respondents selecting the mode of entry as
"very important" or "extremely important")

Source: UNCTAD survey.
Note: Based on 174 validated company responses.

Overall trends, however, reflect a more complex spectrum of FDI prospects by sector. In the primary sector nearly 40 per cent of respondents forecast cuts in their FDI expenditures in 2013, with 30 per cent indicating this intention for 2014 as well. These percentages are much higher than those in other sectors, suggesting that the growth of FDI activity in the primary sector may slow in the medium term as TNCs consolidate the numerous acquisitions they have made in recent years. Notably, in the services sector a relatively high level of respondents (roughly 4 in 10) reported no expected change in FDI expenditures over the period.

At the receiving end of FDI projects, IPAs' views appear to be highly split by major region. IPAs in developed economies gave high marks to the prospects for FDI in high-tech industries – such as scientific research and development (R&D), as well as computer programming and consultancy – which they view as the most promising for attracting FDI to their countries. IPAs in developing and transition economies had a more expansive view, noting as promising for inward FDI activities in a variety of industries across sectors, including manufacture of food products, accommodation, mining of metal ores, extraction of crude petroleum and natural gas, and real estate activities.

c. By home region

This year's survey reveals a significant shift in opinions on the global investment climate held by TNCs in developed economies and by TNCs in developing and transition economies. While the latter have historically been more optimistic, results from the survey show that only 14 per cent were optimistic for 2012, compared with 21 per cent of the former. Strikingly, TNCs in developed economies were also less pessimistic than their peers in developing and transition economies about the global investment climate in 2013 and 2014 (9 per cent in 2013 and 4 per cent in 2014, compared with 20 per cent and 14 per cent). Yet, the inescapable undertone of this year's survey results is that investor uncertainty remains high, with 57 per cent of respondents from developing and transition economies either neutral or undecided about the investment climate in 2012.

Despite the uncertainty that TNCs, regardless of their region of origin, foresee an increase in their FDI expenditures in 2012 and beyond. For 2012,

FDI budgets are set to expand across home regions, though developing-country TNCs may rationalize their expenditures in the medium term.

more than half of the respondents across all groups of economies forecast an increase in their FDI over 2011 levels. Differences begin to appear when comparing medium-term prospects. Reflecting their greater pessimism about the medium term, nearly one quarter of respondents in developing and transition economies foresaw a decline in their FDI budgets in 2013 and 2014. This is in marked contrast to their developed-country peers, of which only 1 in 10 forecast a cut. In part this reflects the differing trends in outward FDI from these regions. TNCs from developing and transition economies, which continued to invest at near record levels during the crisis, may focus on rationalizing their investments in the medium term, consolidating their purchases and pursuing organic growth. TNCs from developed countries, in contrast, may just be entering new cycle of FDI expenditures after cutting back dramatically during the crisis. These dynamics may yield an increase in the share of global outward FDI originating in developed economies in the medium term, even though the long-term trend is likely to be one of greater participation by TNCs from developed and transition economies.

Reflecting these trends, IPAs largely saw developed-country TNCs as the most promising sources of FDI in the medium term (figure I.13). Only four developing economies were ranked as the most promising over the period by 10 per cent or more of the IPA respondents. China led the list, with more than 60 per cent of respondents selecting it, thanks largely to the rapid increase of its outward FDI in recent years. Chinese TNCs have raised awareness of their home country as a source of investment through their active role in a number of industries and the wide spread of their FDI projects over a large number of host economies. The United States, Germany and the United Kingdom ranked as the most promising developed-economy investors, underscoring their continuing role in global FDI flows despite the fallout of the global financial and economic crisis.

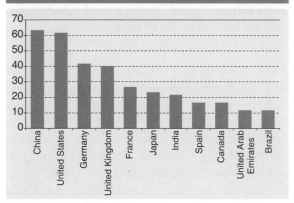

Figure I.13. IPAs' selection of most promising investor home economies for FDI in 2012–2014
(Percentage of IPA respondents selecting economy as a top source of FDI)

Source: UNCTAD survey.
Note: Based on 62 IPA responses.

d. By host region

IPAs, like TNCs, were also cautious about the global investment situation in 2012. Only one third of respondents in both developed economies and developing and transition economies were optimistic about FDI flows for the year.

> **Developing and transition economies will continue to experience strong FDI inflows in the medium term, becoming increasingly important for TNCs worldwide.**

Low optimism about the global situation did not, however, translate to expectations about inflows, with nearly 60 per cent of respondents in both groups of economies expressing optimism in that regard. For the medium term, IPAs – regardless of location – exhibited a rising optimism, although those in developing and transition economies were clearly the most optimistic when it came to their own countries' prospects for FDI inflows in 2014.

This optimism is not unwarranted. TNCs that respond to the survey have increasingly ranked developing-country host regions as highly important. Developing Asia scores particularly well, with 64 per cent of respondents rating East and

South-East Asia as "very" or "extremely" important and 43 per cent giving the same rating to South Asia. The rising importance of these regions as destinations for FDI does not come at the expense of developed regions. The survey results suggest that the EU and North America remain among the most important regions for FDI by TNCs.

The importance of developing regions to TNCs as locations for international production is also evident in the economies they selected as the most likely destinations for their FDI in the medium term. Among the top five, four are developing economies (figure I.14). Indonesia rose into the top five in this year's survey, displacing Brazil in fourth place. South Africa entered the list of top prospective economies, ranking 14th with the Netherlands and Poland. Among developed countries, Australia and the United Kingdom moved up from their positions in last year's survey, while Germany maintained its position.

Figure I.14. TNCs' top prospective host economies for 2012–2014
(Percentage of respondents selecting economy as a top destination)

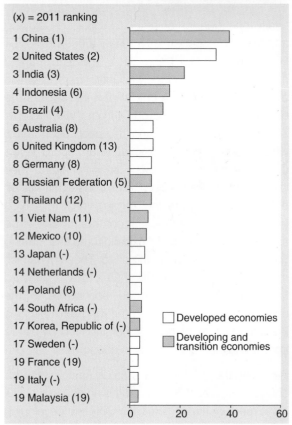

Source: UNCTAD survey.
Note: Based on 174 validated company responses.

B. INTERNATIONAL PRODUCTION AND THE LARGEST TNCs

1. International production

Foreign affiliates posted strong employment growth in 2011, as international production gathered strength, even as developed economies struggled to return to sustainable growth.

International production gathered strength across all major indicators (sales, value added, assets, exports and employment), in 2011 (table I.8). The underlying factors for this increase were two-fold. First, the relatively favourable economic conditions during the year, especially in emerging markets but also in some developed countries like the United States, increased demand for the goods and services produced by foreign affiliates representing the breadth of FDI stock. Second, that stock continued to be augmented by new FDI flows during the year, as TNCs increased their internationalization.

Employment in foreign affiliates rose noticeably during the year, as TNCs continued to expand their production abroad in response to the rise in market opportunities in emerging markets. Globally, foreign affiliates accounted for 69 million jobs in 2011, an 8 per cent increase over the previous year. This stands in stark contrast to the 2 per cent increase in employment projected globally for 2011 (ILO, 2012). Developing and transition economies increasingly account for the majority of employment in foreign affiliates. China alone, for example, accounted for 18.2 million, or 28 per cent, of the total in 2010 (China National Bureau of Statistics, 2012). This trend continued to be driven by increased FDI generated by both efficiency- and market-seeking motivations, with much of the recent momentum being driven by the latter. A rapidly expanding middle class has attracted FDI in both the manufacturing and the services sectors as TNC executives seek to go "local" and improve their positions in emerging markets (PWC, 2012).

Foreign affiliates' sales and value added also rose in 2011, continuing their recovery from the lows during the crisis. After dipping in 2009, sales generated by foreign affiliates rebounded in 2010 (table I.8). This trend continued into 2011, with sales rising 9 per cent over the previous year, hitting a record $28 trillion. Likewise, value added increased, reaching $7 trillion, or roughly 10 per cent of global GDP. Although M&As, especially in developed economies, have driven sales and value added figures in the past, the strong recent growth in international production originating in emerging markets has come largely from TNCs pursuing the organic growth of their own facilities and joint ventures with local companies (Deloitte, 2011). As noted in section A.1.b, in developing and transition economies rising international production is often generated from new production capacity, through greenfield investment, rather than through a change in ownership of existing assets.

The financial performance of foreign affiliates also improved in 2011. The rate of return on outward FDI rose 0.9 percentage points to 7.3 per cent (table I.8). Although this increase brings it near its 2005 high of 7.6 per cent, it remains below the more than 10 per cent returns of the early 1980s. This long-term structural decline in performance is likely to be the result of the changing industry composition of FDI stock over time, with a shift from capital-intensive, high-return activities in the primary sector to services-related activities with relatively lower returns.

Results from UNCTAD's annual survey of the internationalization levels of the world's largest TNCs reflect these global trends in international production, though they also suggest that the top 100 TNCs, mostly from developed economies, continue to struggle in their activities at home. Foreign sales of the largest 100 TNCs in the world increased almost 20 per cent in 2011, while their domestic sales – largely in developed economies – rose 13 per cent (table I.9). Foreign employment likewise expanded, rising 4 per cent for the year, while domestic employment slumped, falling 3 per cent. Although some of this differential represents the easier expansion of sales and employment in emerging markets than in mature markets, it also highlights the sluggish recovery of developed economies in the aftermath of the crisis. These trends in sales and employment are likely to be reinforced by the increasing impact of austerity

Table I.8. Selected indicators of FDI and international production, 1990–2011
(Billions of dollars, value at current prices)

Item	1990	2005–2007 pre-crisis average	2009	2010	2011
FDI inflows	207	1 473	1 198	1 309	1 524
FDI outflows	241	1 501	1 175	1 451	1 694
FDI inward stock	2 081	14 588	18 041	19 907	20 438
FDI outward stock	2 093	15 812	19 326	20 865	21 168
Income on inward FDI [a]	75	1 020	960	1 178	1 359
Rate of return on inward FDI [b]	*4.2*	*7.3*	*5.6*	*6.3*	*7.1*
Income on outward FDI [a]	122	1 100	1 049	1 278	1 470
Rate of return on outward FDI [b]	*6.1*	*7.2*	*5.6*	*6.4*	*7.3*
Cross-border M&As	99	703	250	344	526
Sales of foreign affiliates	5 102	20 656	23 866	25 622 [c]	27 877 [c]
Value added (product) of foreign affiliates	1 018	4 949	6 392	6 560 [c]	7 183 [c]
Total assets of foreign affiliates	4 599	43 623	74 910	75 609 [c]	82 131 [c]
Exports of foreign affiliates	1 498	5 003	5 060	6 267 [d]	7 358 [d]
Employment by foreign affiliates (thousands)	21 458	51 593	59 877	63 903 [c]	69 065 [c]
Memorandum:					
GDP	22 206	50 411	57 920	63 075 [e]	69 660 [e]
Gross fixed capital formation	5 109	11 208	12 735	13 940	15 770
Royalties and licence fee receipts	29	156	200	218	242
Exports of goods and non-factor services	4 382	15 008	15 196	18 821 [e]	22 095 [e]

Source: UNCTAD.

[a] Based on data from 168 countries for income on inward FDI and 136 countries for income on outward FDI in 2011, in both cases representing more than 90 per cent of global inward and outward stocks.

[b] Calculated only for countries with both FDI income and stock data.

[c] Data for 2010 and 2011 are estimated based on a fixed effects panel regression of each variable against outward stock and a lagged dependent variable for the period 1980–2009.

[d] Data for 1995–1997 are based on a linear regression of exports of foreign affiliates against inward FDI stock for the period 1982–1994. For 1998–2011, the share of exports of foreign affiliates in world export in 1998 (33.3 per cent) was applied to obtain values.

[e] Data from IMF, *World Economic Outlook*, April 2012.

Note: Not included in this table are the value of worldwide sales by foreign affiliates associated with their parent firms through non-equity relationships and of the sales of the parent firms themselves. Worldwide sales, gross product, total assets, exports and employment of foreign affiliates are estimated by extrapolating the worldwide data of foreign affiliates of TNCs from Australia, Austria, Belgium, Canada, the Czech Republic, Finland, France, Germany, Greece, Israel, Italy, Japan, Latvia, Lithuania, Luxembourg, Portugal, Slovenia, Sweden, and the United States for sales; those from the Czech Republic, France, Israel, Japan, Portugal, Slovenia, Sweden, and the United States for value added (product); those from Austria, Germany, Japan and the United States for assets; those from the Czech Republic, Japan, Portugal, Slovenia, Sweden, and the United States for exports; and those from Australia, Austria, Belgium, Canada, the Czech Republic, Finland, France, Germany, Italy, Japan, Latvia, Lithuania, Luxembourg, Macao (China), Portugal, Slovenia, Sweden, Switzerland and the United States for employment, on the basis of the shares of those countries in worldwide outward FDI stock.

policies, particularly in Europe, and a possible return to recession in many developed economies in 2012.

In contrast, data on internationalization indicators for the largest 100 TNCs domiciled in developing and transition economies, reveal the relative strength of their home economies. While foreign assets of those economies rose 7 per cent in 2010, a rate faster than that of the largest 100 TNCs, the rise could not keep up with the remarkable 23 per cent increase in domestic assets (table I.9). Sales at home also outpaced foreign sales in terms of growth, though both easily surpassed growth rates seen among developed-economy TNCs.

The only area where this trend did not hold was in employment, where the growth of foreign jobs outpaced that of domestic jobs in 2010.

For both groups of TNCs, however, their investment behaviour is indicative of their intention to follow through with their proactive internationalization plans. The top 100 TNCs undertook FDI projects worth $374 billion in 2011, largely driven by a minority of the group's members (figure I.15.a). During the year, the group concluded $194 billion in gross cross-border deals, representing 20 per cent of M&A purchases in the world by value. The share of cross-border deals in their total deals, both domestic and foreign, reached 72 per cent

Table I.9. Internationalization statistics of the 100 largest non-financial TNCs worldwide and from developing and transition economies
(Billions of dollars, thousands of employees and per cent)

Variable	100 largest TNCs worldwide					100 largest TNCs from developing and transition economies		
	2009	2010[a]	2009–2010 % Change	2011[b]	2010–2011 % Change	2009	2010	% Change
Assets								
Foreign	7 147	7 495	4.9	7 776	3.7	997	1 068	7.1
Domestic	4 396	4 417	0.5	4 584	3.8	2 154	2 642	22.6
Total	11 543	11 912	3.2	12 360	3.8	3 152	3 710	17.7
Foreign as % of total	62	63	1.0 [c]	63	0.0 [c]	32	29	-2.9 [c]
Sales								
Foreign	4 602	4 870	5.8	5 696	17.0	911	1 113	22.1
Domestic	2 377	2 721	14.5	3 077	13.1	1 003	1 311	30.7
Total	6 979	7 590	8.8	8 774	15.6	1 914	2 424	26.6
Foreign as % of total	66	64	-1.8 [c]	65	0.8 [c]	48	46	-1.7 [c]
Employment								
Foreign	8 568	8 684	1.4	9 059	4.3	3 399	3 726	9.6
Domestic	6 576	6 502	-1.1	6 321	-2.8	4 860	5 112	5.2
Total	15 144	15 186	0.3	15 380	1.3	8 259	8 837	7.0
Foreign as % of total	57	57	0.6 [c]	59	1.7 [c]	41	42	1.0 [c]

Source: UNCTAD.
[a] Revised results.
[b] Preliminary results.
[c] In percentage points.
Note: From 2009 onwards, data refer to fiscal year results reported between 1 April of the base year and 31 March of the following year. Complete 2011 data for the 100 largest TNCs from developing and transition economies are not yet available.

Figure I.15. Top investors among the largest TNCs, 2011
(Billions of dollars of completed cross-border M&As[a] and greenfield investments)

(a) Largest 100 TNCs worldwide

(b) Largest 100 TNCs from developing and transition economies

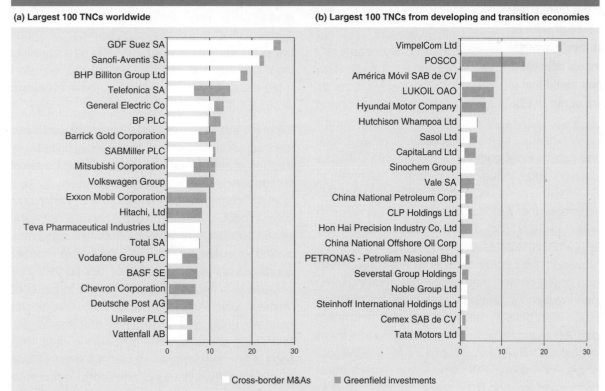

Cross-border M&As ☐   Greenfield investments ■

Source: UNCTAD, based on data from Thomson ONE and fDi Markets.
[a] Value is on a gross basis, not net value as in other M&A tables in this chapter.

in 2011, a level significantly higher than that of the preceding two years (roughly 50 per cent). Greenfield investments fell slightly to $180 billion in 2011, though this amount still represented 20 per cent of all greenfield investment projects.

FDI activity by the largest 100 TNCs from developing and transition economies slowed in 2011, after nearly doubling in 2010. As a group, these TNCs completed $119 billion of FDI projects in 2011 ($109 billion, excluding TNCs that are also members of the top 100 TNCs worldwide). Greenfield investments reached $66 billion, or 55 per cent of their total FDI projects, accounting for roughly 7 per cent of total projects around the world. The value of gross cross-border M&As completed by the group in 2011 jumped 42 per cent to $53 billion, or roughly 5.5 per cent of all deals. VimpelCom Ltd (Russian Federation) was the primary driver of this increase, completing $23 billion in deals during the year (figure I.15.b).

2. Disconnect between cash holdings and investment levels of the largest TNCs

TNCs' record cash levels have so far not translated into sustained growth in investment levels, though improved economic conditions could fuel a future surge in FDI.

In the aftermath of the recent global crisis, a lack of business investment stymied economic recovery, especially in developed economies. This occurred at the same time as many corporations around the world were posting record cash holdings. In the United States, for example, the non-financial corporations in the S&P 500 had cash holdings, including short-term investments, of $1.24 trillion at the end of 2011.[17] Globally UNCTAD estimates that TNCs had cash holdings of $4–5 trillion in 2011, including a significant share held as earnings retained overseas (UNCTAD, 2011a). However, it is unclear to what extent corporations can or will convert their sizable cash holdings into new investment. This section analyses this seeming disconnect between cash holdings and investment through an examination of the annual reports of the largest 100 TNCs, which account for a significant share of global FDI flows and international production (section B.1), with a particular view to their FDI expenditures.

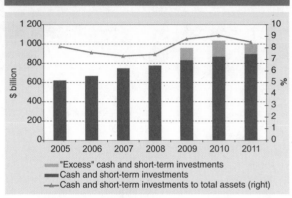

Figure I.16. Top 100 TNCs: cash holdings, 2005–2011
(Billions of dollars and per cent)

Source: UNCTAD, based on data from Thomson ONE.
Note: "Excess" cash and short-term investments are those above the cash level implied by the 2005–2008 average cash-to-assets ratio.

Following the general trend observed globally, the largest 100 TNCs also sharply increased their cash holdings (figure I.16). Compared with their 2008 levels, cash and short-term investments rose by one third, to reach a peak of $1.03 trillion in 2010. Concomitantly, the ratio of their cash to total assets jumped nearly 1.5 percentage points, from an average of 7.6 per cent in 2005–2008 to 9.1 per cent in 2010. This seemingly small change marks a sharp change in their cash-holding behaviour. Using the immediate pre-crisis ratio as a baseline, the largest 100 TNCs held an estimated $166 billion more in cash in 2010 than their pre-crisis behaviour would suggest.

Although this is a substantial sum, "excess" cash holdings are a symptom of the financial uncertainty that TNCs were faced with, rather than a cause of the decline in their investment activities. Today's "excess" cash must be contrasted with yesterday's surge in debt. In the run-up to the financial crisis, the largest 100 TNCs, and corporations more generally, availed themselves of the favourable market conditions of the time to open or expand their lines of credit with financial institutions and to tap debt markets. UNCTAD's analysis of corporate reports between 2006 and 2008 finds that the largest 100 TNCs added a net $709 billion in debt. This flood of borrowed money allowed the largest TNCs to maintain their dividend payments, repurchase shares and expand their investment expenditures, all at the same time (figure I.17).

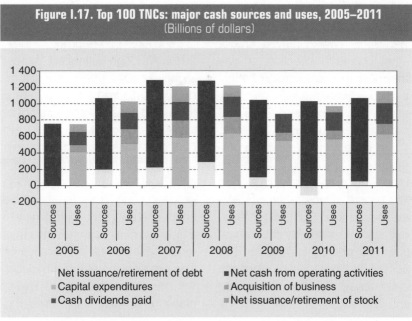

Figure I.17. Top 100 TNCs: major cash sources and uses, 2005–2011
(Billions of dollars)

Net issuance/retirement of debt   ■ Net cash from operating activities
Capital expenditures   ■ Acquisition of business
■ Cash dividends paid   ■ Net issuance/retirement of stock

Source: UNCTAD, based on data from Thomson ONE.

With the outbreak of the global financial crisis, this flood of available finance became a trickle seemingly overnight. Over the next two years, the top 100 TNCs faced a roughly $400 billion hole in their cash flows as net issuance of debt fell from $289 billion in 2008 to a net repayment of $125 billion in 2010, as debt markets froze and lenders refused to roll over maturing debt. The need to compensate for reduced credit issuance and to spend cash on debt repayments required a significant build-up of liquidity levels. Fiat (Italy) is a prime example of this behaviour, nearly quadrupling its cash holdings between 2008 and 2009 in an effort to create sufficient liquidity to cover its looming financial liabilities.[18]

The top 100 TNCs were forced to make difficult decisions on how to bring their expenditures in line with the cash generated from their operations. These measures, including layoffs and the shuttering of plants, were widely reported in the media and noted in the *World Investment Report 2009* (*WIR09*: 21–22), but they cut costs only marginally. To close the gap, TNCs were forced to contemplate cutting dividends or investment expenditures. Given companies' extreme reluctance to cut their dividends for fear of seeing their stock price punished by the market, most TNCs decided to slash their investment budgets. Capital expenditures and acquisitions

experienced a 23 per cent retrenchment between 2008 and 2009, despite a fall of only 5 per cent in cash from operating activities. In contrast, cash dividends retreated only 8 per cent, largely in line with the fall in cash from operations.

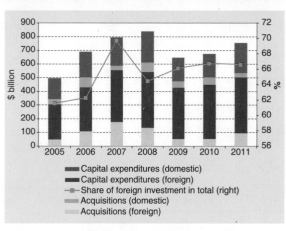

Figure I.18. Top 100 TNCs: capital expenditures and acquisitions, 2005–2011
(Billions of dollars and per cent)

■ Capital expenditures (domestic)
■ Capital expenditures (foreign)
─■─ Share of foreign investment in total (right)
Acquisitions (domestic)
Acquisitions (foreign)

Source: UNCTAD, based on data from Thomson ONE.
Note: Domestic versus foreign split of acquisitions calculated using data on the top 100 TNCs from UNCTAD's M&A database. Domestic versus foreign split of capital expenditures calculated using available data from annual reports of the top 100 TNCs over the period (on average, data for 39 firms per year).

While investment expenditures fell in general, not all types of investment were affected equally (figure I.18). Capital expenditures, which play a crucial role in shaping the long-term direction of any company, were the most resilient. Foreign capital expenditures, in particular, were the least affected, with only an 8 per cent decline between 2008 and 2009. Domestic capital expenditures, however, experienced a 25 per cent cut, reflecting the relatively weaker economic conditions in the home economies of the top 100 TNCs – mainly developed countries. Acquisitions were reduced sharply, falling 50 per cent over the period. Domestic M&As, normally a relatively small expense for the largest 100 TNCs, dropped 33 per cent in value. The investment component that bore the brunt of the decline was cross-border acquisitions, which were cut by 60 per cent. This largely is in line with the general global trends in cross-border M&As, which also fell sharply over the period (*WIR11*: 11).

The latest data from 2011 suggest that the investment drought of recent years – especially in cross-border acquisitions – may be subsiding. FDI expenditures by the top 100 TNCs, as estimated by UNCTAD, rose 12 per cent to $503 billion in 2011, compared with 2010. They remained, nevertheless, 10 per cent below their 2008 high. Of the major investment components, only foreign capital expenditures had returned to their 2008 levels as of 2011. Although estimated "excess" cash levels fell slightly in 2011, they were still far from being fully deployed (figure I.16). The data also suggest that these additional holdings are not necessarily waiting to be used for FDI. Shut out of the easy financing of the pre-crisis era, TNCs may also choose to use this cash for other purposes, including holding additional cash to insure liquidity, paying off debt or distributing cash to shareholders. The recent announcement that Apple (United States) would use $10 billion of its cash holdings to pay dividends and repurchase shares is indicative of this possibility.[19] The precarious state of the global financial system will also limit the ability of TNCs to translate into new investments their remaining $105 billion in "excess" cash – an amount that, if used completely, would equate to roughly one fifth of their estimated 2011 FDI expenditures. Nevertheless, as conditions improve the current cash "overhang" may fuel a future surge in FDI. Projecting the amount for the top 100 TNCs over the estimated $5 trillion in total TNC cash holdings results in more than $500 billion in investable funds, or about one third of global FDI flows.

C. FDI ATTRACTION, POTENTIAL AND CONTRIBUTION INDICES

1. Inward FDI Attraction and Potential Indices

The UNCTAD FDI Attraction Index features 8 developing and transition economies in the top 10, compared with only 4 a decade ago.

The ranking of economies in UNCTAD's FDI Attraction Index, which measures countries' success in attracting FDI over a rolling three-year period (box I.3), has seen some significant changes in 2011. The top 10 (figure I.19) contains newcomers including Ireland (5th, previously 13th) and Mongolia (8th, previously 20th) and Congo (10th, previously 11th). Saudi Arabia dropped out of the top 10 during the year, falling to 12th place.[20]

The top performers – Hong Kong, China; Belgium; Singapore; and Luxembourg – are fixed features at the top of the list, with high absolute inflows because of their attractive investment climates and the important "hinterlands" for which they act as gateways, and with outsized inflows relative to the size of their economies. A number of resource-rich countries also feature in the higher ranks of the

index, as resource-seeking FDI essentially ignores host-country size (as well as other determinants of FDI). In the top 10, these are Chile, Kazakhstan, Mongolia, Turkmenistan and Congo; immediately below the top 10, examples include Saudi Arabia (12th), Chad (14th) and Ghana (16th).

A number of countries have made significant jumps in the table. They include Portugal (moving from 116th to 68th place), Belarus (from 86th to 38th place), and Brunei Darussalam (from 121st to 80th place). In some cases these jumps can be mostly explained by a few large investments or deals; for example, in Equatorial Guinea (up 43 places), Zimbabwe (up 32) and Gabon (up 24). In other cases, improvements signal longer-term changes in the investment climate; examples include Peru and Ghana, which have improved their rankings in each of the last six years.

Comparing performance in attracting FDI over the past three years with the UNCTAD FDI Potential Index (figure I.20) yields two groups of economies that have attracted significantly more – or

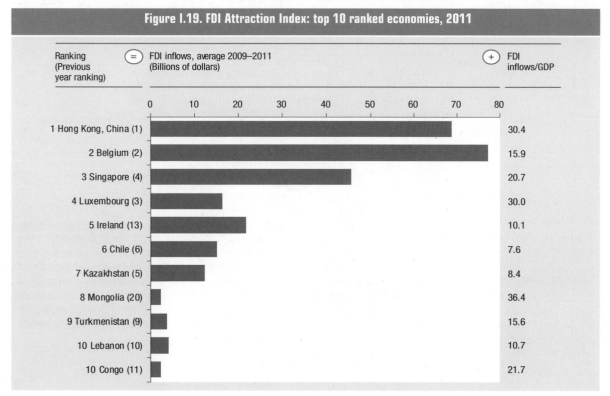

Figure I.19. FDI Attraction Index: top 10 ranked economies, 2011

Ranking (Previous year ranking)	FDI inflows, average 2009–2011 (Billions of dollars)	FDI inflows/GDP
1 Hong Kong, China (1)		30.4
2 Belgium (2)		15.9
3 Singapore (4)		20.7
4 Luxembourg (3)		30.0
5 Ireland (13)		10.1
6 Chile (6)		7.6
7 Kazakhstan (5)		8.4
8 Mongolia (20)		36.4
9 Turkmenistan (9)		15.6
10 Lebanon (10)		10.7
10 Congo (11)		21.7

Source: UNCTAD.

Box I.3. UNCTAD's FDI Attraction, Potential and Contribution Indices

Assessment Tools for Policymakers

UNCTAD has regularly published its FDI Attraction and Potential Indices in its annual *World Investment Report* since 2002. These indices have largely stayed the same over these 10 years. This year's report proposes a number of changes in the Indices[a] to strengthen their potential use as tools for policymakers and adds a new index to measure the extent to which FDI contributes to economic development in host countries.

Attraction Index

The Inward FDI Attraction Index ranks countries by the FDI they receive in absolute terms and relative to their economic size. It is the average of a country's rankings in FDI inflows and in FDI inflows as a share of GDP. The Attraction Index can be calculated using FDI flows, to measure success in attracting FDI in a given year, or using FDI stocks (or average flows over a certain period) to look at a longer time frame. For policymakers, looking at a longer time frame is more relevant because (i) FDI flows can fluctuate significantly year on year, (ii) direct investment decisions can span more than one year and imply long-term commitments, and (iii) policy initiatives and tools to improve FDI attraction generally take time to have an effect. This year's *WIR* therefore looks at FDI flows over the 2009–2011 period; data to generate alternative approaches can be found at www.unctad.org/wir.

Potential Index

The Inward FDI Potential Index captures four key economic determinants of the attractiveness of an economy for foreign direct investors (for a full discussion of FDI determinants, see *WIR98*). They are the attractiveness of the market (for market-seeking FDI), the availability of low-cost labour and skills (to capture efficiency-seeking FDI), the presence of natural resources (resource-seeking FDI), and the presence of FDI-enabling infrastructure. Countries can be ranked according to their attractiveness for FDI on each of these broad determinants using a range of proxy indicators, as summarized in box table I.3.1. The index purposely includes only economic determinants and indicators in order to facilitate its use as a tool for measuring policy effectiveness.

Box table I.3.1. Measuring FDI Potential: FDI determinants and proxy indicators

Market attractiveness	• Size of the market (GDP (purchasing power parity))
	• Spending power (per capita GDP (purchasing power parity))
	• Growth potential of the market (real GDP growth rate)
Availability of low-cost labour and skills	• Unit labour cost (hourly compensation and labour productivity)
	• Size of manufacturing workforce (existing skill base)
Presence of natural resources	• Exploitation of resources (value of fuels and ores exports)
	• Agricultural potential (availability of arable land)
Enabling infrastructure	• Transport infrastructure
	- (road density: km of road per 100 km^2 of land area)
	- (percentage of paved roads in total)
	- (rail lines total route-km)
	- (liner shipping connectivity index)
	• Energy infrastructure
	- (electric power consumption)
	• Telecom infrastructure
	- (telephone lines/100 inhabitants)
	- (mobile cellular subscriptions/100 inhabitants)
	- (fixed broadband Internet subscribers/100 inhabitants)

Source: UNCTAD.

For the purpose of this year's *WIR,* countries have been categorized in homogeneous groups (quartiles) with similar levels of attractiveness for each determinant. An overall FDI Potential Index is obtained by combining the score on all four determinants, using equal weights. For countries to be included in the ranking on individual determinants, at least three indicators must be available per determinant – sufficient data for an overall ranking are currently available for some 177 countries. Raw data used in the calculations can be found at the UNCTAD website. The list of proxy indicators cannot be exhaustive – UNCTAD's choices are based on relevance for developing countries, especially LDCs, leading to the exclusion of indicators such as R&D expenditures or patents. The website provides alternative calculation options and additional indicators.

/...

Box I.3. UNCTAD's FDI Attraction, Potential and Contribution Indices (Concluded)

Contribution Index

The Inward FDI Contribution Index aims to measure the development impact of FDI in the host economy. It looks at the contribution of foreign affiliates to GDP (value added), employment, wages and salaries, exports, R&D expenditures, capital formation and tax payments, as a share of the host-country total (e.g. employment by foreign affiliates as a percentage of total employment). These seven variables are among those recommended by the *Manual on Statistics of International Trade in Services* (2010) for inclusion in the collection of foreign affiliate statistics. A number of these variables are also proposed by the G-20 in its work on indicators for measuring and maximizing economic value added and job creation arising from private sector investment in value chains.[b]

Data on the impact of foreign affiliates in each area of contribution are not readily available for most countries. Where they are not, FDI contributions can be estimated by applying the ratios of each indicator in foreign affiliates of countries that collect data on their overseas investors (Finland, Germany, Japan, Sweden, Switzerland and the United States for employment; the United States alone for the other variables) to the inward stock of these countries in the total inward stock of host economies.

As in the case of the FDI Potential Index, countries have been categorized in homogeneous groups (quartiles) with similar levels of contribution for each type of impact. The ranking of an economy in the FDI Contribution Index is calculated based on the simple average of the percentile rankings for each of the impact types, using equal weights. An economy is ranked only if it has at least four data points. Currently, sufficient data are available for 79 countries.

Using the Indices as Policy Tools

FDI policy generally aims to set the conditions and create a climate conducive to the *attraction* of FDI and to maximize the *development contribution* of FDI. The Indices can help policymakers assess the effectiveness of their policy frameworks by plotting their countries' performance against potential and by measuring the contribution of FDI, making comparisons with peer countries or within regional groupings, and tracking changes in performance over time. Although the Indices can provide only rough guidance, because they necessarily exclude country-specific factors, they can be a useful starting point for the assessment of policy effectiveness, which is an integral part of UNCTAD's Investment Policy Framework for Sustainable Development (see chapter IV).

Source: UNCTAD.

[a] Numerous suggestions have been made over the past 10 years to improve the assessment of countries' potential for the attraction of investment. See, inter alia, Rodríguez et al. (2009).

[b] UNCTAD's work with the G-20 in the area of investment can be found at www.unctad.org/DIAE/G-20.

---

significantly less – FDI than could be expected on the basis of their economic determinants alone.

The "above-potential" economies include, again, resource-rich countries that – even though the Potential Index takes into account the presence of natural resources – exceeded expectations. They also include small economies, such as small island developing States, where single large investments can make a big impact on performance in attracting FDI (and, more importantly, on their economies) or that have created specific locational advantages, either in the investment or tax regime or by providing access to larger markets (e.g. through Djibouti's sea port). This group also includes a number of countries such as Albania, which are in a "catch-up phase" for FDI, having embarked on a course to improve their investment climates. Because the FDI Attraction Index captures the most recent investment performance, they receive a premium.

The "below-potential" group includes a number of economies that have traditionally not relied much on foreign investment for capital formation, such as Japan and the Republic of Korea, or that are traditionally low recipients of FDI, such as Italy. A number of countries have significant potential from the perspective of economic determinants but either are closed to FDI or maintain a policy climate that is unattractive to investors. A group of developing countries with emerging market status and with growing investment potential nevertheless is currently receiving FDI flows below expectations, including the Philippines and South Africa and, to a lesser extent, countries such as India, Indonesia and Mexico (although these countries may be successful in attracting NEM operations). To realize the investment flows that their economic determinants alone indicate, these countries may wish to explore policy options and innovations in comparable economies.

Figure I.20. FDI Attraction Index vs FDI Potential Index Matrix, 2011 (Quartiles)			
Above expectations	**In line with expectations**		**Below expectations**

	4th quartile	**3rd quartile**	**2nd quartile**	**1st quartile**
High **1st quartile**	Chad, Liberia, Madagascar, Niger	Albania, Bahamas, Congo, Congo (Democratic Republic of), Equatorial Guinea, Jordan, Lebanon, Luxembourg, Mongolia, Mozambique, Zambia	Bulgaria, Ghana, Ireland, Israel, Nigeria, Norway, Panama, Turkmenistan, Uruguay	Australia, Belarus, Belgium, Brazil, Chile, China, Colombia, Hong Kong (China), Kazakhstan, Malaysia, Peru, Poland, Russian Federation, Saudi Arabia, Singapore, Switzerland, Ukraine, United Kingdom, Viet Nam
2nd quartile	Armenia, Cambodia, Guinea, Nicaragua, Saint Vincent and the Grenadines, Solomon Islands	Costa Rica, Georgia, Honduras, Kyrgyzstan, Libya, Maldives, Malta, Namibia, Seychelles, Sudan, United Republic of Tanzania	Brunei Darussalam, Croatia, Dominican Republic, Egypt, Estonia, Iraq, Portugal, Qatar, Serbia, Tunisia, Uzbekistan	Austria, Canada, Czech Republic, France, Germany, Hungary, India, Indonesia, Mexico, Netherlands, Romania, Spain, Thailand, Turkey, United Arab Emirates, United States
3rd quartile	Antigua and Barbuda, Belize, Cape Verde, Central African Republic, Djibouti, Dominica, Fiji, Grenada, Guyana, Mali, São Tomé and Principe, Vanuatu	Barbados, Botswana, Cameroon, Lao People's Democratic Republic, the former Yugoslav Republic of Macedonia, Mauritius, the Republic of Moldova, Myanmar, Uganda, Zimbabwe	Algeria, Azerbaijan, Bolivia (Plurinational State of), Denmark, Gabon, Guatemala, Iceland, Jamaica, Latvia, Morocco, Oman, Pakistan, Syrian Arab Republic, Trinidad and Tobago	Argentina, Finland, Iran (Islamic Republic of), Italy, Japan, Korea (Republic of), South Africa, Sweden
4th quartile **Low**	Afghanistan, Benin, Bhutan, Burkina Faso, Burundi, Comoros, Côte d'Ivoire, Eritrea, Gambia, Guinea-Bissau, Haiti, Kiribati, Lesotho, Malawi, Mauritania, Nepal, Rwanda, Samoa, Sierra Leone, Suriname, Swaziland, Togo, Tonga	Angola, Bangladesh, Bosnia and Herzegovina, El Salvador, Ethiopia, Kenya, Papua New Guinea, Paraguay, Senegal, Tajikistan, Yemen	Bahrain, Ecuador, Greece, Kuwait, Lithuania, New Zealand, Philippines, Slovakia, Slovenia, Sri Lanka	Venezuela (Bolivarian Republic of)

FDI Attraction Index

Low ← **FDI Potential Index** → High

Source: UNCTAD.

2. Inward FDI Contribution Index

The UNCTAD FDI Contribution Index shows relatively higher contributions of foreign affiliates to local economies in developing countries, especially in Africa, in value added, employment and wage generation, tax revenues and export generation.

The UNCTAD FDI Contribution Index ranks economies on the basis of the significance of FDI – foreign affiliates – in their economy, in terms of value added, employment, wages, tax receipts, exports, R&D expenditures and capital formation (overall ranking in annex table I.10; methodology in box I.3). According to this year's index – the first of its kind – the host economy with the largest contribution by FDI is Hungary, followed by Belgium and the Czech Republic.

Looking at regional patterns in the Contribution Index shows that there are more host countries with higher index values in the developing regions (table I.10). Africa is the region where TNCs contribute most to the economy in terms of value added (tied with transition economies) and wages. In general, the index is higher for developing than developed countries and transition economies (with more indicators balanced in favour of developing economies): the role of TNCs relative to the size of the economy is larger. The higher ratio for employment compared to value added for developing countries reflects the fact that the labour-intensity of production there is higher than in developed countries. Similarly, the higher ratio for wages in developing countries compared with that for developed countries means that TNC affiliates in developing countries pay a higher wage premium over local wages than do those in developed countries. It also means that foreign affiliates there are likely to use more capital-intensive techniques (also reflected in lower ratios for capital expenditures for some regions).

The export ratio is higher in some developing regions, especially East and South-East Asia, where export-oriented industries have been built up with significant involvement of foreign affiliates of TNCs. The higher tax ratio compared with the value added ratio in Latin America and the Caribbean shows that TNCs can contribute to higher fiscal revenues for host states and to the process of formalizing the economy. The share of TNC foreign affiliates in total R&D expenditures in host countries is similar in developing than in developed countries, with high shares in Africa and Latin America.

Looking at individual countries shows significant variation in individual indicators. The export and employment quartile rankings vary from country to country depending on the predominant types of investment. Where efficiency-seeking FDI is high (e.g. China, Mexico), these indicators tend to have higher rankings than other indicators. The employment quartile ranking is clearly dependent on local labour costs and the consequent predominant industries in which TNCs operate in host countries, with common offshoring destinations such as China, India, Taiwan Province of China and Mexico all showing higher quartile rankings for employment

compared with the rankings for value added. The ranking for tax payments differs from that for value added in many countries, depending on the level of formalization of local economies (especially in poorer countries) on the one hand, and on the fiscal treatment of foreign investors on the other.

The "high contribution" (top quartile) countries show impact values significantly above the values given in table I.10. TNC foreign affiliates contribute about half of their GDP (in value added) and exports, about one fifth of employment and significantly higher values for three indicators: wages (with TNCs accounting for a large share of formal employment and paying higher wages than local firms), R&D spending (with TNCs accounting for nearly 70 per cent of some countries' registered R&D), and capital expenditures (in total gross fixed capital formation) (table I.11).

The contribution of foreign investors to host economies is first and foremost a function of the share of FDI stock to GDP (table I.11). However, for numerous economies the FDI contribution is either significantly above or below what could be expected on the basis of the presence of foreign investment. Comparing the FDI Contribution Index with the presence of FDI in each economy highlights those that have the greatest positive and negative differentials between FDI contribution to local economies and expected contribution levels based on FDI stock (figure I.21).

Table I.10. UNCTAD's FDI Contribution Index, by host region, 2009[a] (Percentage shares in each variable's total for the region)							
Region/economy	Value added	Employment	Exports	Tax revenue	Wages and salaries	R&D expenditures	Capital expenditures
Total world							
Developed countries	**12.7**	**7.5**	**19.3**	**13.9**	**14.6**	**24.2**	**10.5**
Developing economies	**12.2**	**7.9**	**17.3**	**14.6**	**15.4**	**24.1**	**11.6**
Africa	21.7	7.3	..	..	21.7	37.2	18.4
East and South-East Asia	10.5	9.9	30.9	7.7	8.9	22.5	6.2
South Asia	10.3	6.1	..	..	16.0	..	3.8
West Asia	16.8	5.5	1.9	..	15.0	..	3.8
Latin America and the Caribbean	15.9	6.0	17.9	18.9	16.0	35.0	14.8
Transition economies	**21.7**	**3.0**	**..**	**..**	**11.2**	**15.4**	**25.7**

Source: UNCTAD; for further information on data and methodology, see www.unctad.org/wir.
[a] Or latest year available.

Note: Data from economies not listed in the FDI Contribution Index (because they do not cover at least four of the seven variables), are included in these calculations.

	Table I.11. FDI Contribution Index median values, by indicator							
	(Per cent of economy totals)							
	FDI Contribution Index indicators							**Memorandum item:**
Quartiles	Value added	Employment	Exports	Tax revenue	Wages and salaries	R&D expenditures	Capital expenditures	FDI inward stock/GDP
1	41.1	22.2	47.2	64.5	37.0	62.7	37.9	75.4
2	24.6	12.0	20.0	28.3	22.8	34.0	17.6	42.8
3	16.5	4.6	7.6	12.7	12.0	19.6	7.3	31.2
4	5.5	0.9	2.3	4.9	5.0	7.8	2.1	13.3

Source: UNCTAD; for further information on data and methodology, see www.unctad.org/wir.

A number of major emerging markets – Argentina, Brazil, China, Indonesia and South Africa – appear to get a higher contribution to their economies "per unit of FDI" than average, with high quartile rankings in exports, employment, wages and R&D (more than in value added or capital formation). In some cases this may be due to active investment policymaking; for example, channeling investment to specific higher-impact industries. Other countries in this group, such as Germany or Italy, have traditionally low shares of FDI stock compared with the size of local economies but appear to get relatively high contributions, in some cases on individual indicator ratios (e.g. tax, wages and R&D expenditures in the case of Italy). A number of developing countries receive above-average contributions on some indicators but lag on others – with policy opportunities to improve impact. An example is Colombia, which has significant FDI stock that is contributing above-average value added but relatively little employment.

At the other end of the scale, a group of economies with a significant presence of TNCs (i.e. a high ratio of FDI stock to GDP) receives a below-average contribution of FDI in terms of the Index indicators. This group includes a number of economies that attract investment largely owing to their fiscal or corporate governance regimes (including tax havens and countries that allow special-purpose vehicles or other corporate governance structures favoured by investors, such as Luxembourg and the Netherlands). Such regimes obviously lead to investment that has little impact in terms of local value added or employment. This group also contains countries with a high share of resource-seeking FDI, such as Chile and Saudi Arabia, confirming concerns about the relatively low impact

of this type of investment in terms of, for example, local employment. (The poorest resource-rich countries are absent from the current list owing to the lack of data.)

Although the FDI Contribution Index provides valuable insights, it cannot fully capture FDI's contribution to development, which is multifaceted, with impacts – both positive and negative – that cannot be easily quantified. For example, it does not take into account impacts across the spectrum of labour, social, environmental and development issues. Its coverage of economic impacts is also limited, largely because of the paucity of data. The FDI Contribution Index also does not measure the full range of TNCs' involvement in a host economy. For example, non-equity modes of international production, an increasing phenomenon, play an important role in a number of developing economies, but their impact is not captured in their entirety in any of the indices presented in this section.

Even with these limitations, the rankings of the FDI Contribution Index underscore that FDI is not homogenous and that its economic contribution can differ markedly between countries, even those that have similar levels of FDI. This confirms that policy plays a critical role in maximizing positive and minimizing negative effects of FDI. UNCTAD's Investment Policy Framework for Sustainable Development may serve as a starting point for policymakers of those countries where performance does not match potential or where the economic contribution of FDI is lower than expected (see chapter IV).

The FDI Contribution Index is the very first attempt at a systematic comparative analysis of the contribution of FDI to economic development,

Figure I.21. FDI Contribution Index vs FDI presence, 2011
(Quartiles)

	Above expectations	In line with expectations		Below expectations
1st quartile (High)		Bolivia (Plurinational State of), Colombia, Finland, South Africa	Cambodia, Malaysia, Poland, Romania, Thailand, United Kingdom	Belgium, Czech Republic, Estonia, Hong Kong (China), Hungary, Ireland, Panama, Singapore, Sweden, Switzerland
2nd quartile	Argentina, Germany, Italy	Brazil, Dominican Republic, France, Slovenia	Bosnia and Herzegovina, Costa Rica, Croatia, Denmark, Honduras, Kazakhstan, Morocco, Norway, Portugal	Cyprus, Netherlands, Trinidad and Tobago
3rd quartile	China, Ecuador, Guatemala, Indonesia, Sri Lanka	Australia, Austria, Canada, Egypt, Lithuania, Peru, United Arab Emirates, Uruguay	Latvia, New Zealand, Spain, Ukraine	Bulgaria, Chile, Jamaica
4th quartile (Low)	Algeria, Greece, India, Japan, Kenya, Korea (Republic of), Paraguay, Philippines, Taiwan Province of China, Turkey, United States, Venezuela (Bolivarian Republic of)	Israel, Mexico, Russian Federation, Saudi Arabia		Bahamas, Barbados, Bermuda Luxembourg
	4th quartile (Low)	3rd quartile	2nd quartile	1st quartile (High)

FDI Contribution Index (vertical axis)

FDI inward stock/GDP (horizontal axis)

Source: UNCTAD.

a field in which data are extremely sparse and difficult to interpret because of widely varying national statistical methods. UNCTAD will continue to conduct research on the impact of investment and seek to improve on data and methodology for the index. UNCTAD is ready to engage with policymakers in the interpretation of the results of the index, and in helping countries to improve its statistical basis through national data collection efforts.

Notes

1. For example, TNK-BP (Russian Federation) entered the Brazilian oil industry in 2011 with a $1 billion acquisition of a 45 per cent stake in 21 oil blocks located in the Solimoes Basin.

2. The value of these projects on an announcement basis is eventually replaced in the database with the actual amount of funds invested.

3. International Energy Agency (2011) "World Energy Outlook 2011".

4. Examples include investments by Sinopec (China) in the oil and gas fields in Devon for $2.2 billion, and the acquisition of a minority stake by Total (France) in the oil and gas firm Chesapeake Energy (United States) for $2.3 billion, as well as the purchase by Repsol (Spain) of a $1 billion minority share in fields being developed by Sand Hill Energy (United States).

5. A number of types of private investment funds are involved in FDI. Because of data constraints, the following analysis concentrates on the activities of private equity funds, which are still the most active in the business. Unlike other funds (e.g. hedge funds), private equity funds typically obtain a majority stake or all of the shares, to control and manage the companies they buy, and they stay longer in that position than other funds. But the different kinds of funds increasingly act together and the boundaries between private equity funds, hedge funds, other collective investment funds and even investment banks are beginning to fade away.

6. This figure is based on the assumption that all the funds used in cross-border M&As are recorded as FDI flows.

7. European Private Equity and Venture Capital Association, "CEE private equity shows robust growth in fundraising and exits in 2010", 7 July 2011.

8. For example, Global Infrastructure Partners (United States), a joint venture between Credit Suisse Group and GE Infrastructure Inc., acquired London Gatwick Airport Ltd from Grupo Ferrovial (Spain) for $2.5 billion in 2009.

[9] KKR and Itochu Corp, for example, jointly invested $7 billion to buy assets of Samson Investment Company (United States), an oil and gas group, in 2011.

[10] For example, in the Republic of Korea, several cases provoked anger from the public towards such firms (e.g. Newbridge Capital and Lone-Star (United States), both private equity firms, when the former sold Korea First Bank in 2005 and the latter sold Korean Exchange Bank in 2006). Similar examples also were observed in developed countries (e.g. Japan) in the 1990s when, after the collapse of the bubble economy, nationalized Japanese banks were acquired by foreign private equity investors. In major EU countries where private equity business is more active, concerns about private equity business are also widespread.

[11] This survey, based on 79 private equity firms, found that 63 per cent of respondent firms had substantially implemented environmental and social policies in their investments, compared with only 24 per cent in 2009. For example, KKR (United States) has implemented such programmes in a quarter of its portfolio (Private Equity International, "Study: PE firms adjusting to ESG", 22 November 2011).

[12] There is considerable variation in estimates of assets under the management of SWFs because the definition of SWFs varies between sources and because not all SWFs release data on their assets.

[13] BIS, *Quarterly Review*, various issues. Data refer to the international position with respect to total assets of banks in all reporting countries taken together.

[14] Based on UNCTAD, cross-border M&A database (www.unctad.org/fdistatistics) and information from Financial Times Ltd and fDi Markets (www.fDimarkets.com).

[15] FAO, IFAD, UNCTAD and World Bank, *Principles for Responsible Agricultural Investment that Respects Rights, Livelihoods and Resources* (see www.unctad.org/en/Pages/DIAE/G-20/PRAI.aspx).

[16] For example, worldwide total investment in the renewable energy sector continued to grow (except in 2009) even during the financial crisis, to reach a record $257 billion in 2011 (UNEP and Frankfurt School of Finance & Management, 2012).

[17] See www.moodys.com/research/Moodys-US-Corporate-Cash-Pile-At-124-Trillion-Over-Half--PR_240419.

[18] Fiat SpA, *2009 Annual Report*, p. 65.

[19] *New York Times*, "Flush With Cash, Apple Plans Buyback and Dividend", 19 March 2012.

[20] Ranking comparisons are based on a time series of the FDI Attraction Index calculated for this *WIR*.

REGIONAL TRENDS IN FDI

CHAPTER II

Salient features of 2011 FDI trends by region include the following:

- Sub-Saharan Africa drew FDI not only to its natural resources, but also to its emerging consumer markets as the growth outlook remained positive. Political uncertainty in North Africa deterred investment in that region.

- FDI inflows reached new record levels in both East Asia and South-East Asia, while the latter is catching up with the former through higher FDI growth.

- FDI inflows to South Asia turned around as a result of higher inflows to India, the dominant FDI recipient in the region.

- Regional and global crises still weigh on FDI in West Asia, and prospects remain unclear.

- South America was the main driver of FDI growth in Latin America and the Caribbean. The pattern of investment by traditional investors – Europe and the United States – is changing, while there has been an advance in FDI from developing countries and Japan. A recent shift towards industrial policy in major countries may lead to investment flows to targeted industries.

- FDI flows to economies in transition recovered strongly. They are expected to grow further, partly because of the accession of the Russian Federation to the World Trade Organization (WTO).

- The search for energy and mineral resources resulted in cross-border megadeals in developed countries, but the eurozone crisis and a generally weak outlook still cloud investor sentiment.

- FDI inflows to the structurally weak, vulnerable and small economies were mixed. While FDI to landlocked developing countries (LLDCs) grew strongly, inflows to least developed countries (LDCs) and small island developing States (SIDS) continued to fall.

INTRODUCTION

In 2011, FDI inflows increased in all major economic groups – developed, developing and transition economies (table II.1). Developing countries accounted for 45 per cent of global FDI inflows in 2011. The increase was driven by East and South-East Asia and Latin America. East and South-East Asia still accounted for almost half of FDI in developing economies. Inflows to the transition economies of South-East Europe, the Commonwealth of Independent States (CIS) and Georgia accounted for another 6 per cent of the global total.

The rise in FDI outflows was driven mainly by the growth of FDI from developed countries.

The growth in outflows from developing economies seen in the past several years appeared to lose some momentum in 2011 because of significant declines in flows from Latin America and the Caribbean and a slowdown in the growth of investments from developing Asia (excluding West Asia).

FDI inflows to the structurally weak, vulnerable and small economies bounced back from $42.2 billion in 2010 to $46.7 billion in 2011, owing to the strong growth in FDI to LLDCs (table II.1). However, the improvement in their share was hardly visible, as FDI inflows to both LDCs and SIDS continued to fall.

Table II.1. FDI flows, by region, 2009–2011
(Billions of dollars and per cent)

Region	FDI inflows			FDI outflows		
	2009	2010	2011	2009	2010	2011
World	**1 197.8**	**1 309.0**	**1 524.4**	**1 175.1**	**1 451.4**	**1 694.4**
Developed economies	606.2	618.6	747.9	857.8	989.6	1 237.5
Developing economies	519.2	616.7	684.4	268.5	400.1	383.8
Africa	52.6	43.1	42.7	3.2	7.0	3.5
East and South-East Asia	206.6	294.1	335.5	176.6	243.0	239.9
South Asia	42.4	31.7	38.9	16.4	13.6	15.2
West Asia	66.3	58.2	48.7	17.9	16.4	25.4
Latin America and the Caribbean	149.4	187.4	217.0	54.3	119.9	99.7
Transition economies	72.4	73.8	92.2	48.8	61.6	73.1
Structurally weak, vulnerable and small economies[a]	**45.2**	**42.2**	**46.7**	**5.0**	**11.5**	**9.2**
LDCs	18.3	16.9	15.0	1.1	3.1	3.3
LLDCs	28.0	28.2	34.8	4.0	9.3	6.5
SIDS	4.4	4.2	4.1	0.3	0.3	0.6
Memorandum: percentage share in world FDI flows						
Developed economies	50.6	47.3	49.1	73.0	68.2	73.0
Developing economies	43.3	47.1	44.9	22.8	27.6	22.6
Africa	4.4	3.3	2.8	0.3	0.5	0.2
East and South-East Asia	17.2	22.5	22.0	15.0	16.7	14.2
South Asia	3.5	2.4	2.6	1.4	0.9	0.9
West Asia	5.5	4.4	3.2	1.5	1.1	1.5
Latin America and the Caribbean	12.5	14.3	14.2	4.6	8.3	5.9
Transition economies	6.0	5.6	6.0	4.2	4.2	4.3
Structurally weak, vulnerable and small economies[a]	**3.8**	**3.2**	**3.1**	**0.4**	**0.8**	**0.5**
LDCs	1.5	1.3	1.0	0.1	0.2	0.2
LLDCs	2.3	2.2	2.3	0.3	0.6	0.4
SIDS	0.4	0.3	0.3	0.0	0.0	0.0

Source: UNCTAD, FDI/TNC database (www.unctad.org/fdistatistics).
[a] Without double counting.

A. REGIONAL TRENDS

1. Africa

Table A. Distribution of FDI flows among economies, by range,[a] 2011

Range	Inflows	Outflows
Above $3.0 billion	Nigeria, South Africa and Ghana	..
$2.0 to $2.9 billion	Congo, Algeria, Morocco, Mozambique, Zambia	..
$1.0 to $1.9 billion	Sudan, Chad, Democratic Republic of the Congo, Guinea, Tunisia, United Republic of Tanzania, Niger	Angola, Zambia
$0.5 to $0.9 billion	Madagascar, Namibia, Uganda, Equatorial Guinea, Gabon, Botswana, Liberia	Egypt, Algeria
$0.1 to $0.4 billion	Zimbabwe, Cameroon, Côte d'Ivoire, Kenya, Senegal, Mauritius, Ethiopia, Mali, Seychelles, Benin, Central African Republic, Rwanda, Somalia	Liberia, Morocco, Libya
Below $0.1 billion	Swaziland, Cape Verde, Djibouti, Malawi, Togo, Lesotho, Sierra Leone, Mauritania, Gambia, Guinea-Bissau, Eritrea, São Tomé and Principe, Burkina Faso, Comoros, Burundi, Egypt, Angola	Democratic Republic of the Congo, Mauritius, Gabon, Sudan, Senegal, Niger, Tunisia, Togo, Zimbabwe, Kenya, Côte d'Ivoire, Seychelles, Ghana, Guinea, Swaziland, Mauritania, Burkina Faso, Botswana, Benin, Mali, Guinea-Bissau, São Tomé and Principe, Cape Verde, Namibia, Mozambique, Cameroon, South Africa, Nigeria

[a] Economies are listed according to the magnitude of their FDI flows.

Figure A. FDI flows, top 5 host and home economies, 2010–2011
(Billions of dollars)

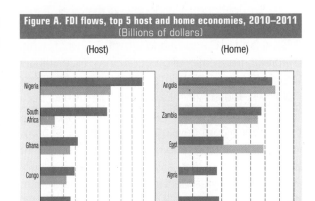

Figure B. FDI inflows, 2005–2011
(Billions of dollars)

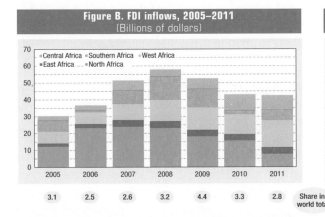

Share in world total: 3.1 | 2.5 | 2.6 | 3.2 | 4.4 | 3.3 | 2.8

Figure C. FDI outflows, 2005–2011
(Billions of dollars)

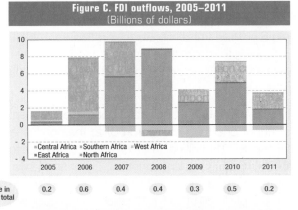

Share in world total: 0.2 | 0.6 | 0.4 | 0.4 | 0.3 | 0.5 | 0.2

Table B. Cross-border M&As by industry, 2010–2011
(Millions of dollars)

Sector/industry	Sales		Purchases	
	2010	2011	2010	2011
Total	**8 072**	**7 205**	**3 309**	**4 812**
Primary	**2 516**	**1 664**	**- 28**	**- 22**
Mining, quarrying and petroleum	2 516	1 595	- 28	- 22
Manufacturing	**303**	**1 922**	**404**	**4 393**
Food, beverages and tobacco	263	1 026	2	15
Chemicals and chemical products	5	155	- 15	810
Metals and metal products	32	286	-	-
Electrical and electronic equipment	- 9	470	-	-
Services	**5 253**	**3 619**	**2 933**	**441**
Trade	84	2 161	- 49	- 181
Transport, storage and communications	1 912	489	-	- 10
Finance	134	910	2 547	674
Business services	2 994	149	436	37

Table C. Cross-border M&As by region/country, 2010–2011
(Millions of dollars)

Region/country	Sales		Purchases	
	2010	2011	2010	2011
World	**8 072**	**7 205**	**3 309**	**4 812**
Developed economies	**6 722**	**4 308**	**1 371**	**4 265**
European Union	1 838	2 528	1 240	1 987
United States	1 931	1 408	45	41
Japan	3 199	649	-	-
Other developed countries	- 246	- 278	86	2 236
Developing economies	**1 048**	**2 865**	**1 550**	**547**
Africa	365	408	365	408
East and South-East Asia	499	1 679	257	- 78
South Asia	10 922	318	38	217
West Asia	- 10 653	464	965	-
Latin America and the Caribbean	- 84	- 5	- 75	-
Transition economies	**51**	**- 130**	**388**	**-**

Table D. Greenfield FDI projects by industry, 2010–2011
(Millions of dollars)

Sector/industry	Africa as destination		Africa as investors	
	2010	2011	2010	2011
Total	**88 918**	**82 315**	**16 662**	**16 551**
Primary	**20 237**	**22 824**	**1 246**	**4 640**
Mining, quarrying and petroleum	20 237	22 824	1 246	4 640
Manufacturing	**39 506**	**31 205**	**7 506**	**4 798**
Food, beverages and tobacco	1 888	5 185	175	628
Coke, petroleum and nuclear fuel	23 235	9 793	5 684	2 212
Metals and metal products	2 093	5 185	429	9
Motor vehicles and other transport equipment	2 568	3 118	99	-
Services	**29 175**	**28 286**	**7 910**	**7 113**
Electricity, gas and water	5 432	10 477	899	1 441
Construction	7 630	3 303	-	1 223
Transport, storage and communications	6 381	5 345	2 627	68
Business services	5 429	5 619	1 274	2 282

Table E. Greenfield FDI projects by region/country, 2010–2011
(Millions of dollars)

Partner region/economy	Africa as destination		Africa as investors	
	2010	2011	2010	2011
World	**88 918**	**82 315**	**16 662**	**16 551**
Developed economies	**48 554**	**38 939**	**1 192**	**487**
European Union	32 095	23 633	373	182
United States	5 507	6 627	49	259
Japan	473	1 299	-	-
Other developed countries	10 479	7 380	769	45
Developing economies	**37 752**	**42 649**	**15 462**	**16 064**
Africa	12 226	10 368	12 226	10 368
East and South-East Asia	9 929	12 357	141	400
South Asia	4 890	11 113	75	980
West Asia	9 897	7 038	2 517	150
Latin America and the Caribbean	809	1 774	503	1 167
Transition economies	**2 612**	**727**	**8**	**-**

Continued fall in FDI inflows to Africa but some cause for optimism. FDI flows to Africa were at $42.7 billion in 2011, marking a third successive year of decline, although the decline is marginal (figure B). Both cross-border mergers and acquisitions (M&As) (tables B and C) and greenfield investments by foreign transnational corporations (TNCs) (tables D and E) decreased. In terms of share in global FDI flows, the continent's position diminished from 3.3 per cent in 2010 to 2.8 per cent in 2011 (figure B). FDI to Africa from developed countries fell sharply, leaving developing and transition economies to increase their share in inward FDI to the continent (in the case of greenfield investment projects, from 45 per cent in 2010 to 53 per cent in 2011; table E).

However, this picture of an overall declining trend in FDI does not reflect the situation across all parts of the continent. The negative growth for the continent as a whole was driven in large part by reduced flows to North Africa caused by political unrest and by a small number of other exceptions to a generally more positive trend. Inflows to sub-Saharan Africa[1] recovered from $29.5 billion in 2010 to $36.9 billion in 2011, a level comparable with the peak in 2008 ($37.3 billion).

North Africa has traditionally been the recipient of about one third of inward FDI to the continent. Inflows in 2011 halved, to $7.69 billion, and those to the two major recipient countries, Egypt and Libya, were negligible. Outward FDI from North Africa also fell sharply in 2011 to $1.75 billion, compared with $4.85 billion in 2010. These figures are in stark contrast with the peak of 2008 when the outward FDI of North African countries reached $8.75 billion.

Flows to West Africa were destined primarily for Ghana and Nigeria, which together accounted for some three quarters of the subregion's inflows. Guinea emerged with one of the strongest gains in FDI growth in 2011, a trend that is likely to continue in the next few years in view of the $6 billion that State-owned China Power Investment Corporation plans to invest in bauxite and alumina projects. Overall, inward FDI flows to West Africa expanded by 36 per cent, to $16.1 billion.

The bulk of FDI in Central Africa goes to three commodity-rich countries: the primarily oil-exporting Congo and Equatorial Guinea and the mineral-exporting Democratic Republic of the Congo.

Although inward FDI flows to Congo grew strongly in 2011, weak inflows to the Democratic Republic of the Congo affected the region as a whole and resulted in inward investment flows to Central Africa falling by 10.2 per cent overall to $8.53 billion.

Inward FDI to Southern Africa, recovered from a 78 per cent decline in 2010, more than doubling its total to $6.37 billion. This reversal was precipitated primarily by the sharp rebound of flows to South Africa, the region's largest FDI recipient. Inflows to Angola, however, declined by over $2 billion.

East Africa, with historically the lowest FDI inflows in sub-Saharan Africa, reversed the downward trend of 2009–2010 to reach $3.96 billion, a level just 5 per cent below the peak of 2008. As most countries in this subregion have not been considered rich in natural resources, they have not traditionally attracted large investments into export-oriented production in the primary sector, except in agriculture. However, the discovery of gas fields is likely to change this pattern significantly.

New oil- and gas-producing countries are emerging as major recipients of FDI. Oil production in sub-Saharan Africa has been dominated by the two principal producer countries, Angola and Nigeria. Nigeria was Africa's largest recipient of FDI flows ($8.92 billion) in 2011, accounting for over one fifth of all flows to the continent. In gross terms, Angola attracted FDI inflows worth $10.5 billion, although in net terms, divestments and repatriated income left its inflows at -$5.59 billion.

Aside from these major oil-producing countries, investors are looking farther afield in search of oil and gas reserves. Ghana, in particular, benefited from FDI in the newly developed Jubilee oil field, where commercial production started in December 2010. Elsewhere, Tullow Oil (United Kingdom) announced its plan to invest $2.0 billion to establish an oil refinery in Uganda. Noble Energy (United States) also announced plans to invest $1.6 billion to set up production wells and a processing platform in Equatorial Guinea. Inward FDI flows to Uganda and Equatorial Guinea were $792 million and $737 million respectively in 2011, but announced greenfield projects show future investments of $6.1 billion in Uganda and $4.8 billion in Equatorial Guinea, indicating strong FDI growth in these countries.

If oil reserves off the Atlantic coast of Africa have drawn significant FDI to that region, natural gas reserves in East Africa, especially the offshore fields of Mozambique and the United Republic of Tanzania, hold equal promise. In 2011, inflows of FDI to Mozambique doubled from the previous year, to $2.09 billion. New discoveries of large-scale gas reserves continue to be made in 2012. Development of gas fields and the liquefied natural gas (LNG) industry will require huge upfront investments and presents considerable technological challenges. FDI is certain to play a large role in developing this industry in the region, as exemplified by the plans announced by Eni (Italy) to invest $50 billion to develop the gas fields recently discovered in Mozambique.

Sectoral shift emerging, especially towards services. The limited volume of FDI to Africa tends to make inflows vary widely from year to year. Nevertheless, viewed over a longer time period, a discernible sectoral shift is taking place in FDI to Africa. Data on greenfield projects by three-year periods show that, contrary to popular perceptions, the relative importance of the primary sector is declining, although the total value of projects is holding steady (figure II.1).

The data on projects in services in the period 2006–2008 are inflated by the announcements of no fewer than 13 construction projects worth more than $3 billion each, which take many years to complete. Still, a general ascendancy of the services sector is clear. Aside from the construction industry, projects are drawn into industries such as electric, gas and water distribution, and transport, storage and communications in the services sector and industries such as coke, petroleum products and nuclear fuel in the manufacturing sector.

This shift is more about diversification of natural-resource-related activities than a decline of the extractive industry. Many of the projects in manufacturing and services are premised on the availability of natural resources or play a supporting role for the extractive industry. Such projects include a $15 billion project by Western Goldfields (Canada) to construct a coal-fired power station in Nigeria and an $8 billion project by Klesch & Company (United Kingdom) to build an oil refinery in Libya, both announced in 2008.

Better prospects for 2012. The region's prospects for FDI in 2012 are promising, as strong economic growth, ongoing economic reforms and high commodity prices have improved investor perceptions of the continent. Relatively high profitability of FDI in the continent is another factor. Data on the profitability of United States FDI (FDI income as a share of FDI stock) show a 20 per cent return in Africa in 2010, compared with 14 per cent in Latin America and the Caribbean and 15 per cent in Asia (United States Department of Commerce, 2011: 51). In addition to traditional patterns of FDI to the extractive industries, the emergence of a middle class is fostering the growth of FDI in services such as banking, retail and telecommunications. UNCTAD's forecast of FDI inflows also points to this pattern (figure I.10). It is especially likely if investor confidence begins to return to North Africa and compensates for the recent declines in this region.

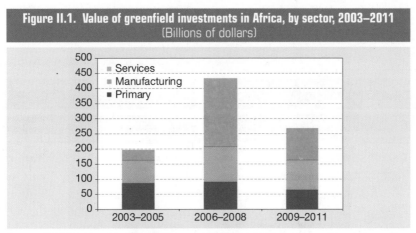

Figure II.1. Value of greenfield investments in Africa, by sector, 2003–2011
(Billions of dollars)

Source: UNCTAD, based on data from Financial Times Ltd, fDi Markets (www.fDimarkets.com).

2. East and South-East Asia

Table A. Distribution of FDI flows among economies, by range,[a] 2011

Range	Inflows	Outflows
Above $50 billion	China, Hong Kong (China), Singapore	Hong Kong (China), China
$10 to $49 billion	Indonesia, Malaysia	Singapore, Republic of Korea, Malaysia, Taiwan Province of China, Thailand
$1.0 to $9.9 billion	Viet Nam, Thailand, Mongolia, Republic of Korea, Macao (China), Philippines, Brunei Darussalam	Indonesia, Viet Nam
$0.1 to $0.9 billion	Cambodia, Myanmar, Lao People's Democratic Republic	..
Below $0.1 billion	Democratic People's Republic of Korea, Timor-Leste, Taiwan Province of China	Mongolia, Macao (China), Cambodia, Brunei Darussalam, Philippines, Lao People's Democratic Republic

[a] Economies are listed according to the magnitude of their FDI flows.

Figure A. FDI flows, top 5 host and home economies, 2010–2011
(Billions of dollars)

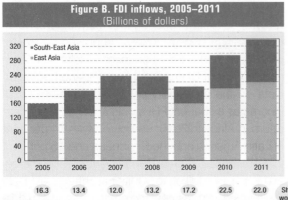

Figure B. FDI inflows, 2005–2011
(Billions of dollars)

	2005	2006	2007	2008	2009	2010	2011
Share in world total	16.3	13.4	12.0	13.2	17.2	22.5	22.0

Figure C. FDI outflows, 2005–2011
(Billions of dollars)

	2005	2006	2007	2008	2009	2010	2011
Share in world total	7.9	8.1	7.9	8.4	15.0	16.7	14.2

Table B. Cross-border M&As by industry, 2010–2011
(Millions of dollars)

Sector/industry	Sales 2010	Sales 2011	Purchases 2010	Purchases 2011
Total	**26 417**	**32 715**	**67 609**	**67 966**
Primary	**- 427**	**5 214**	**18 844**	**19 301**
Mining, quarrying and petroleum	- 607	4 780	18 932	19 695
Manufacturing	**11 423**	**10 253**	**6 994**	**12 609**
Food, beverages and tobacco	2 383	3 078	3 714	961
Chemicals and chemical products	1 796	1 159	2 396	6 596
Electrical and electronic equipment	864	3 279	- 331	1 794
Precision instruments	78	806	3	684
Services	**15 421**	**17 248**	**41 771**	**36 056**
Electricity, gas and water	796	2 280	1 345	3 855
Trade	194	1 704	1 912	1 752
Finance	952	6 484	33 111	31 215
Business services	5 642	4 365	- 483	- 1 273

Table C. Cross-border M&As by region/country, 2010–2011
(Millions of dollars)

Region/country	Sales 2010	Sales 2011	Purchases 2010	Purchases 2011
World	**26 417**	**32 715**	**67 609**	**67 966**
Developed economies	**7 439**	**15 007**	**34 985**	**45 773**
European Union	1 288	4 548	17 977	13 906
United States	673	2 086	4 849	12 369
Japan	3 229	6 760	647	1 084
Other developed countries	2 249	1 613	11 511	18 414
Developing economies	**18 087**	**15 346**	**32 604**	**21 814**
Africa	257	- 78	499	1 679
East and South-East Asia	18 870	12 968	18 870	12 968
South Asia	1 201	539	- 1 731	- 2 417
West Asia	- 2 320	1 758	127	253
Latin America and the Caribbean	79	159	14 664	9 311
Transition economies	**-**	**1 531**	**20**	**379**

Table D. Greenfield FDI projects by industry, 2010–2011
(Millions of dollars)

Sector/industry	East and South-East Asia as destination 2010	East and South-East Asia as destination 2011	East and South-East Asia as investors 2010	East and South-East Asia as investors 2011
Total	**213 770**	**206 924**	**143 094**	**125 466**
Primary	**3 658**	**4 444**	**4 262**	**5 158**
Mining, quarrying and petroleum	3 647	4 444	4 262	5 158
Manufacturing	**129 489**	**131 800**	**104 303**	**85 119**
Chemicals and chemical products	16 410	25 582	7 980	6 480
Metals and metal products	14 856	16 735	16 028	24 522
Electrical and electronic equipment	34 930	21 578	26 528	11 376
Motor vehicles and other transport equipment	28 559	17 921	10 523	9 084
Services	**80 623**	**70 681**	**34 530**	**35 189**
Construction	4 601	7 021	5 030	3 840
Transport, storage and communications	13 226	19 141	5 943	6 745
Finance	15 900	16 451	4 777	5 250
Business services	13 471	10 255	4 200	1 682

Table E. Greenfield FDI projects by region/country, 2010–2011
(Millions of dollars)

Partner region/economy	East and South-East Asia as destination 2010	East and South-East Asia as destination 2011	East and South-East Asia as investors 2010	East and South-East Asia as investors 2011
World	**213 770**	**206 924**	**143 094**	**125 466**
Developed economies	**136 798**	**133 339**	**32 559**	**16 470**
European Union	44 341	57 936	5 567	7 123
United States	44 237	33 515	8 093	5 961
Japan	36 353	30 198	362	510
Other developed countries	11 866	11 690	18 537	2 877
Developing economies	**71 324**	**72 353**	**105 283**	**102 434**
Africa	141	400	9 929	12 357
East and South-East Asia	63 779	56 138	63 779	56 138
South Asia	1 955	10 973	18 556	19 050
West Asia	2 910	3 965	2 541	5 930
Latin America and the Caribbean	2 531	675	9 556	8 950
Transition economies	**5 648**	**1 232**	**5 253**	**6 563**

South-East Asia is catching up. Registering a 14 per cent increase, total FDI inflows to East and South-East Asia amounted to $336 billion in 2011 (figure B). The region accounted for 22 per cent of total global FDI flows, up from about 12 per cent before the global financial crisis. FDI inflows reached new records in both subregions, as well as in the major economies, such as China; Hong Kong, China; Singapore and Indonesia (figure A).

South-East Asia continued to outperform East Asia in FDI growth. Inflows to the former reached $117 billion, up 26 per cent, compared with $219 billion, up 9 per cent, in the latter, narrowing the gap between the two subregions (figure B, annex table I.1).

Among the economies of the Association of Southeast Asian Nations (ASEAN), four – Brunei Darussalam, Indonesia, Malaysia and Singapore – saw a considerable rise in their FDI inflows. The performance of the relatively low-income countries, namely Cambodia, the Lao People's Democratic Republic and Myanmar was generally good as well, though Viet Nam declined slightly. Although natural disaster in Thailand disrupted production by foreign affiliates in the country, particularly in the automobile and electronic industries, and exposed a weakness of the current supply-chain management systems, FDI inflows to the country remained at a high level of nearly $10 billion, only marginally lower than that of 2010. Overall, as East Asian countries, particularly China, have continued to experience rising wages and production costs, the relative competitiveness of ASEAN in manufacturing has been enhanced. Accordingly, some foreign affiliates in China's coastal regions are relocating to South-East Asia,[2] while others are moving their production facilities to inland China.

The performance of East Asian economies showed a mixed picture. FDI flows to China reached a historically high level of $124 billion in 2011. The second largest recipient in the subregion, Hong Kong, China, saw its inflows increase to $83 billion (figure A), a historic high as well. By contrast, inflows to the Republic of Korea and Taiwan Province of China declined to $4.7 billion and -$2 billion, respectively.

Japan gains ground as investor in the region. Partly as a result of the significant appreciation of the Japanese yen in 2011, TNCs from Japan have strengthened their efforts in investing abroad (section A.7), particularly in low-cost production locations in South-East Asia. For instance, in 2011, attracted by low labour costs and good growth prospects, Japanese companies pledged to invest about $1.8 billion in Viet Nam.[3] In China, FDI from Japan rose from $4 billion (4 per cent of total inflows) in 2010 to $6 billion (9 per cent of total inflows) in 2011. In Mongolia, large projects in extractive industries, including the Tavan Tolgoi coal mine, are being implemented or negotiated, some with Japanese investors. In addition, negotiation of the Economic Partnership Agreement with Japan may bring in more FDI to Mongolia.

Owing to the worsening sovereign debt crisis and related liquidity problems at home, TNCs from Europe have slowed their pace of expansion in East and South-East Asia since late 2011. In particular, some European banks have undertaken divestments from the region, selling their Asian operations to regional players, a trend which may continue this year with banks such as HSBC and Royal Bank of Scotland selling assets in Hong Kong, China; Thailand; and Malaysia. The actions of TNCs from the United States were mixed: some in industries such as home appliances have been relocating production facilities to their home countries,[4] while others in industries such as automotives have continued to expand in Asia.[5]

Greenfield investment dominates, but M&As are on the rise. Greenfield investment is the dominant mode of entry in East and South-East Asia, although the total amount of investment decreased slightly in 2011 to about $207 billion. In contrast, cross-border M&As sales in the region increased by about 24 per cent to $33 billion, driven by a surge in South-East Asia, where total M&A sales more than doubled, reaching $20 billion. Sales in East Asia dropped by one fourth, with a rise in M&As in China (up 77 per cent to $11 billion) cancelled out by a fall in those in Hong Kong, China (down 92 per cent to $1 billion).

In manufacturing, the major industries in which greenfield investment took place were chemical products, electronics, automotive and metal and metal products in that order, while those most targeted for cross-border M&As were electronics and food and beverages. M&A sales also increased in services, contributing to a longer-term shift. In China, for example, FDI flows to services surpassed those to manufacturing for the first time as the result of a rise in flows to non-financial services and a slowdown of flows to manufacturing. FDI in finance is expected to grow as the country continues to open its financial markets,[6] and as foreign banks, including HSBC (United Kingdom) and Citigroup (United States), expand their presence through both M&As and organic growth.[7]

Outward FDI: East Asia slows down while South-East Asia sets a new record. FDI outflows from East and South-East Asia as a whole remained more or less stable after the significant increase in 2010 (figure C). FDI outflows from East Asia dropped by 9 per cent to $180 billion, the first decline since 2005, while those from South-East Asia rose 36 per cent to $60 billion, a record high.

FDI outflows from Hong Kong, China, the region's financial centre and largest source of FDI, declined in 2011 by 14.5 per cent to $82 billion, but increased in the last quarter of the year. FDI outflows from China dropped by 5.4 per cent to $65 billion. In contrast, outflows from Singapore, the leading source of FDI in South-East Asia, registered a 19 per cent growth, reaching $25 billion. Outflows from Thailand and Indonesia surged, reaching $11 billion and $8 billion. The boom was driven mainly by cross-border M&As in the case of Thailand and by greenfield investments in the case of Indonesia.

Diverging patterns in overseas M&As. TNCs from East and South-East Asia continued to expand globally by actively acquiring overseas assets. Their M&A purchases worldwide amounted to $68 billion in 2011, marginally higher than the previous record set in 2010. Their cross-border M&A activities demonstrated diverging trends: total purchases in developed countries increased by 31 per cent to $46 billion, while those in developing countries declined by 33 per cent to $22 billion (table C). The rise in their M&As in developed countries as a whole was driven mainly by increases in Australia (up 20 per cent to $8 billion), Canada (up 99 per cent to $9 billion) and the United States (up 155 per cent to $12 billion), while the value of total purchases in Europe decreased by 8 per cent to $17 billion. The rise in M&A purchases in the developed

world corresponded to an increase in M&As in manufacturing, to $13 billion (table B). Greenfield investment by TNCs from East and South-East Asia dropped, in both number and value (tables D and E). The number of recorded greenfield projects undertaken by firms based in East and South-East Asia was about 1,200. The value of investments dropped by 12 per cent to about $125 billion.

In manufacturing, East and South-East Asian TNCs in industries such as metals and metal products as well as food and beverages have been investing more frequently through greenfield investment. In services, companies from East Asia in particular continued to be active players in the M&A markets in both developed and developing countries.

Short-term prospects: slowing growth. FDI growth in the region has slowed since late 2011 because of growing uncertainties in the global economy. FDI to manufacturing stagnated in China, but the country is increasingly attracting market-seeking FDI, especially in services. According to the annual *World Investment Prospects Survey* (*WIPS*) undertaken by UNCTAD this year, China continues to be the most favoured destination of FDI inflows. FDI prospects in South-East Asia remain promising, as the rankings of ASEAN economies, such as Indonesia and Thailand, have risen markedly in the survey.

3. South Asia

Table A. Distribution of FDI flows among economies, by range,[a] 2011

Range	Inflows	Outflows
Above $10 billion	India	India
$1.0 to $9.9 billion	Islamic Republic of Iran, Pakistan, Bangladesh	..
$0.1 to $0.9 billion	Sri Lanka, Maldives	Islamic Republic of Iran
Below $0.1 billion	Nepal, Afghanistan, Bhutan	Pakistan, Sri Lanka, Bangladesh

[a] Economies are listed according to the magnitude of their FDI flows.

Figure A. FDI flows, top 5 host and home economies, 2010–2011
(Billions of dollars)

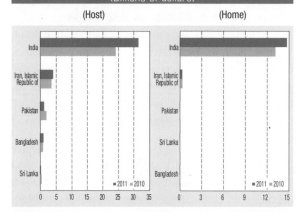

Figure B. FDI inflows, 2005–2011
(Billions of dollars)

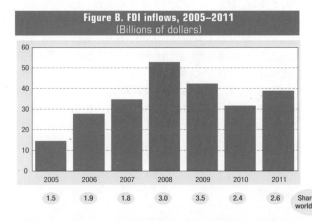

1.5	1.9	1.8	3.0	3.5	2.4	2.6	Share in world total

Figure C. FDI outflows, 2005–2011
(Billions of dollars)

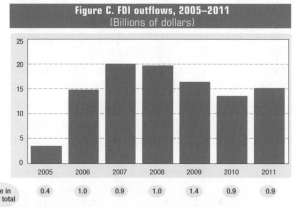

0.4	1.0	0.9	1.0	1.4	0.9	0.9

Table B. Cross-border M&As by industry, 2010–2011
(Millions of dollars)

Sector/industry	Sales		Purchases	
	2010	2011	2010	2011
Total	**5 569**	**12 875**	**26 682**	**6 078**
Primary	**18**	**8 997**	**5 240**	**111**
Mining, quarrying and petroleum	18	8 997	5 240	111
Manufacturing	**5 960**	**1 940**	**2 499**	**1 489**
Wood and wood products	-	435	-	6
Chemicals and chemical products	4 194	85	174	1 370
Non-metallic mineral products	3	152	393	24
Motor vehicles and other transport equipment	4	977	- 14	470
Services	**- 409**	**1 937**	**18 943**	**4 478**
Electricity, gas and water	-	310	95	1 636
Trade	53	341	29	-
Finance	275	701	5 745	1 461
Business services	- 602	291	424	96

Table C. Cross-border M&As by region/country, 2010–2011
(Millions of dollars)

Region/country	Sales		Purchases	
	2010	2011	2010	2011
World	**5 569**	**12 875**	**26 682**	**6 078**
Developed economies	**7 439**	**14 870**	**7 836**	**5 239**
European Union	153	12 450	971	1 094
United States	5 319	1 576	3 343	23
Japan	1 372	986	-	40
Other developed countries	596	- 142	3 522	4 082
Developing economies	**- 1 910**	**- 2 017**	**18 823**	**1 083**
Africa	38	217	10 922	318
East and South-East Asia	- 1 731	- 2 417	1 201	539
South Asia	342	46	342	46
West Asia	177	133	898	-
Latin America and the Caribbean	- 735	3	5 460	180
Transition economies	**-**	**-**	**24**	**- 245**

Table D. Greenfield FDI projects by industry, 2010–2011
(Millions of dollars)

Sector/industry	South Asia as destination		South Asia as investors	
	2010	2011	2010	2011
Total	**62 899**	**68 019**	**20 777**	**35 593**
Primary	**1 080**	**-**	**679**	**4 165**
Mining, quarrying and petroleum	1 080	-	679	4 165
Manufacturing	**43 943**	**47 649**	**12 446**	**19 435**
Chemicals and chemical products	4 224	4 567	3 905	1 370
Metals and metal products	13 635	19 223	3 740	8 287
Machinery and equipment	2 809	3 157	404	132
Motor vehicles and other transport equipment	9 483	11 466	2 349	2 628
Services	**17 876**	**20 369**	**7 653**	**11 993**
Construction	1 554	2 640	511	776
Transport, storage and communications	4 554	3 675	501	345
Finance	2 108	2 552	1 823	1 710
Business services	2 722	5 879	1 785	3 228

Table E. Greenfield FDI projects by region/country, 2010–2011
(Millions of dollars)

Partner region/economy	South Asia as destination		South Asia as investors	
	2010	2011	2010	2011
World	**62 899**	**68 019**	**20 777**	**35 593**
Developed economies	**38 423**	**41 532**	**6 368**	**4 503**
European Union	18 858	16 008	3 619	2 512
United States	11 169	14 024	728	1 497
Japan	6 258	8 366	8	8
Other developed countries	2 138	3 135	2 012	485
Developing economies	**23 900**	**26 097**	**13 341**	**30 266**
Africa	75	980	4 890	11 113
East and South-East Asia	18 556	19 050	1 955	10 973
South Asia	2 177	1 910	2 177	1 910
West Asia	2 266	4 093	3 752	5 672
Latin America and the Caribbean	826	64	566	598
Transition economies	**576**	**389**	**1 069**	**824**

FDI inflows to South Asia have turned around. Inflows rose by 23 per cent to $39 billion in 2011 (2.6 per cent of global FDI flows) after a slide in 2009–2010 (figure B). The recovery derived mainly from the inflows of $32 billion to India, the dominant FDI recipient in South Asia. Inflows to the Islamic Republic of Iran and Pakistan, recipients of the second and third largest FDI flows, amounted to $4.2 billion and $1.3 billion (figure A). Bangladesh has also emerged as an important recipient, with inflows increasing to a record high of $1.1 billion.

In 2011, about 145 cross-border M&As and 1,045 greenfield FDI projects by foreign TNCs were recorded in South Asia (annex tables I.4 and I.9). Cross-border M&As rose by about 131 per cent in value, and the total reached $13 billion (tables B and C), surpassing the previous record set in 2008. The significant increase was driven mainly by a number of large transactions in extractive industries undertaken by acquirers from the European Union (EU), as well as from developing Asia. By contrast, cross-border M&A sales in manufacturing declined by about two thirds, to a level below $2 billion (table B). Sales in services amounted to $2 billion as well but were still much below the annual amounts during 2006–2009. Within manufacturing, the automotive industry ($1 billion) was the main target of investors, while in services, finance ($700 million) was the main target.

FDI outflows from South Asia picked up as well. In 2011, outflows from the region rose by 12 per cent to $15 billion, after a decline of three years. Outflows from India, the dominant source of FDI from the region, increased from $13.2 billion in 2010 to $14.8 billion in 2011 (figure A). However, Indian TNCs became less active in acquiring overseas assets. The amount of total cross-border M&A purchases decreased significantly in all three sectors: from $5.2 billion to $111 million in the primary sector, from $2.5 billion to $1.5 billion in manufacturing, and from $19.0 billion to $4.5 billion in services. The drop was compensated largely by a rise in overseas greenfield projects, particularly in extractive industries, metal and metal products, and business services (table D).

Indian companies in information technology services have long been active players in global markets. In recent years, firms in service industries such as banking and food services have also become increasingly active in overseas markets, particularly in developed countries and especially in the United Kingdom. In early 2012, the State Bank of India started offering mortgages in the United Kingdom. India Hospitality Corp. acquired Adelie Food Holding, based in the United Kingdom, for $350 million, to capture growth opportunities in the Indian fast food market.

Cautiously optimistic prospects. Countries in the region face various challenges, which need to be tackled in order to build an attractive investment climate for enhancing development. Recent developments have highlighted new opportunities (box II.1). The growth of inflows so far appears likely to keep its momentum in 2012. As economic growth in India has slowed, however, concerns have arisen about short-term prospects for FDI inflows to South Asia. Whether countries in the region can overcome old challenges and grasp new opportunities to attract investment will depend to a large extent on Governments' efforts to further open their economies and deepen regional economic integration.

Box II.1. Attracting investment for development: old challenges and new opportunities for South Asia

South Asian countries face different challenges in building a conducive business environment and an attractive investment climate, which are crucial for promoting economic development. These challenges include, for instance, stabilization in Afghanistan, security concerns in the Islamic Republic of Iran and Pakistan, and macroeconomic as well as political issues in India. Two issues stand out as major concerns: political risks and obstacles at the country level and weak integration processes at the regional level.

At the country level, high political risks and obstacles have been an important factor deterring FDI inflows. Countries in the region rank high in the country risk guides of political-risk assessment services, and political restrictions on both FDI and business links between countries in the region have long existed. This has deterred FDI inflows and negatively affected the countries' FDI performance.

However, recent developments have highlighted new opportunities. For instance, the political relationship between India and Pakistan, the two major economies on the subcontinent, has been moving towards greater cooperation, with Pakistan granting India most-favoured-nation status in November 2011 and India recently announcing that it will allow FDI from Pakistan. In Afghanistan, some FDI has started to flow into extractive industries.

At the regional level, progress in economic integration (with the South Asian Association for Regional Cooperation as the key architect) has been slow, and the trade barriers between neighbouring countries in the region are among the highest in the world. South Asia is perhaps one of the least integrated developing regions: intraregional trade accounts for about 2 per cent of total gross domestic product (GDP), compared with more than 20 per cent in East Asia. In addition, investment issues have not yet been included in the regional integration process. As a result, the region has not been able to realize its potential for attracting FDI inflows, especially in promoting intraregional FDI flows. In 2011, intraregional greenfield investment accounted for merely 3 per cent of the regional total, compared with 27 per cent in East and South-East Asia.

Nevertheless, high economic growth in major economies in the subregion has created a momentum for regional integration in recent years, and South Asian countries have increasingly realized that regional integration can help them improve the climate for investment and business. The inclusion of an investment agenda in the regional integration process and in particular the creation of a regional investment area can play an important role in this regard.

Source: UNCTAD and UNESCAP.

4. West Asia

Table A. Distribution of FDI flows among economies, by range,[a] 2011

Range	Inflows	Outflows
Above $10 billion	Saudi Arabia, Turkey	..
$5.0 to $9.9 billion	United Arab Emirates	Kuwait, Qatar
$1.0 to $4.9 billion	Lebanon, Iraq, Jordan, Syrian Arab Republic	Saudi Arabia, Turkey, United Arab Emirates
Below $1.0 billion	Oman, Bahrain, Kuwait, Palestinian Territory, Qatar, Yemen	Lebanon, Bahrain, Oman, Iraq, Yemen, Jordan, Syrian Arab Republic, Palestinian Territory

[a] Economies are listed according to the magnitude of their FDI flows.

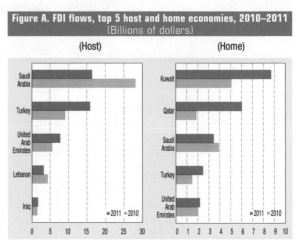

Figure A. FDI flows, top 5 host and home economies, 2010–2011
(Billions of dollars)

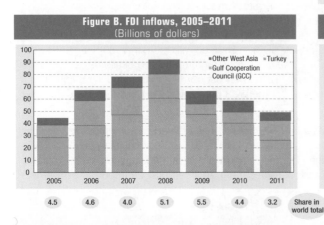

Figure B. FDI inflows, 2005–2011
(Billions of dollars)

Share in world total: 4.5 4.6 4.0 5.1 5.5 4.4 3.2

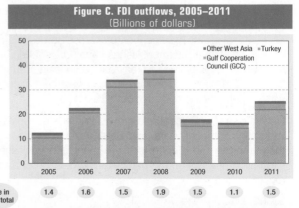

Figure C. FDI outflows, 2005–2011
(Billions of dollars)

Share in world total: 1.4 1.6 1.5 1.9 1.5 1.1 1.5

Table B. Cross-border M&As by industry, 2010–2011
(Millions of dollars)

Sector/industry	Sales 2010	Sales 2011	Purchases 2010	Purchases 2011
Total	**4 887**	**9 713**	**- 15 278**	**6 136**
Primary	**170**	**2 730**	**1 484**	**37**
Mining, quarrying and petroleum	170	2 682	1 484	37
Manufacturing	**2 416**	**665**	**18**	**780**
Wood and wood products	10	37	16	-
Chemicals and chemical products	19	180	- 19	- 89
Metals and metal products	410	174	-	- 2
Machinery and equipment	-	310	-	3
Services	**2 301**	**6 317**	**- 16 780**	**5 319**
Electricity, gas and water	- 59	555	400	190
Transport, storage and communications	100	338	- 10 721	- 2 568
Finance	1 611	4 128	- 4 163	7 954
Business services	172	895	281	314

Table C. Cross-border M&As by region/country, 2010–2011
(Millions of dollars)

Region/country	Sales 2010	Sales 2011	Purchases 2010	Purchases 2011
World	**4 887**	**9 713**	**- 15 278**	**6 136**
Developed economies	**2 257**	**8 222**	**- 2 555**	**2 599**
European Union	1 472	9 412	- 683	5 083
United States	112	- 1 579	- 2 333	- 1 110
Japan	343	33	-	-
Other developed countries	331	356	461	- 1 374
Developing economies	**2 062**	**1 187**	**- 12 724**	**3 420**
Africa	965	-	- 10 653	464
East and South-East Asia	127	253	- 2 320	1 758
South Asia	898	-	177	133
West Asia	72	916	72	916
Latin America and the Caribbean	-	18	-	147
Transition economies	**21**	**5**	**-**	**117**

Table D. Greenfield FDI projects by industry, 2010–2011
(Millions of dollars)

Sector/industry	West Asia as destination 2010	West Asia as destination 2011	West Asia as investors 2010	West Asia as investors 2011
Total	**60 011**	**69 151**	**37 190**	**44 194**
Primary	**1 631**	**915**	**-**	**503**
Mining, quarrying and petroleum	1 631	915	-	503
Manufacturing	**23 395**	**39 640**	**7 538**	**19 444**
Food, beverages and tobacco	1 443	3 783	1 110	2 414
Coke, petroleum and nuclear fuel	1 165	4 472	2 122	7 633
Chemicals and chemical products	8 977	13 877	1 771	3 372
Metals and metal products	3 155	8 260	737	3 088
Services	**34 985**	**28 595**	**29 652**	**24 247**
Electricity, gas and water	6 004	6 744	570	2 611
Construction	11 231	6 620	13 630	12 603
Hotels and restaurants	5 431	4 686	2 921	1 920
Business services	3 976	3 199	4 805	921

Table E. Greenfield FDI projects by region/country, 2010–2011
(Millions of dollars)

Partner region/economy	West Asia as destination 2010	West Asia as destination 2011	West Asia as investors 2010	West Asia as investors 2011
World	**60 011**	**69 151**	**37 190**	**44 194**
Developed economies	**36 532**	**38 990**	**3 769**	**9 687**
European Union	23 370	14 911	3 454	7 481
United States	8 219	18 121	123	1 937
Japan	1 162	2 896	-	-
Other developed countries	3 782	3 062	192	269
Developing economies	**21 726**	**29 466**	**28 313**	**33 371**
Africa	2 517	150	9 897	7 038
East and South-East Asia	2 541	5 930	2 910	3 965
South Asia	3 752	5 672	2 266	4 093
West Asia	12 403	17 535	12 403	17 535
Latin America and the Caribbean	513	178	836	699
Transition economies	**1 753**	**695**	**5 108**	**1 135**

Inflows to West Asia declined for a third year. They decreased by 16 per cent to $49 billion in 2011, affected by both the continuing political instability and the deterioration of global economic prospects in the second half of 2011. The level is the lowest since 2005 – when FDI flows stood at about $44 billion – and far below the record high of about $92 billion registered in 2008 (figure B).

Gulf Cooperation Council (GCC) countries are still recovering from the suspension or cancellation of large-scale projects in previous years. They registered a drop of 35 per cent in FDI inflows, which brought their share in the region's total from 69 per cent in 2010 to 53 per cent in 2011. Saudi Arabia – the region's biggest recipient – saw a 42 per cent fall in 2011 to $16 billion, which largely explains the overall decline. FDI flows to Oman and Qatar also decreased – reaching negative values in the latter – but those to Bahrain, Kuwait and the United Arab Emirates rebounded from relatively low values (figure A and annex table I.1).

Some of the big and expensive projects that had prospered in these countries during the pre-crisis period had to be suspended or cancelled when project finance dried up in the wake of the global financial crisis. After a period of calm and consolidation, projects started slowly coming back on line in 2010 but soon faced delays caused by the Arab uprising across the region during 2011, and by new uncertainties about global economic prospects. Some big projects with strong sponsors have managed to secure financing, sometimes with greater use of export credit agencies, in particular from Japan and the Republic of Korea, and highly liquid regional bank lenders.[8]

As of October 2011, the cancelled or suspended construction projects in the Middle East and North African market were estimated at $1.74 trillion, with $958 billion in the United Arab Emirates alone and $354 billion in Saudi Arabia.[9] Construction was one of the most important areas for investment to have emerged in the last oil boom, and the pace of its activity is among the key indicators of investment behaviour in housing, tourism, infrastructure, refineries, petrochemicals and real estate, where foreign investment prospered during the boom years.

Strong recovery of FDI into Turkey. Turkey stood as an exception to regional trends, with inflows registering a 76 per cent increase to $16 billion (figure A), maintaining the country's position as the region's second largest FDI recipient and increasing its share in the region's total from 16 to 33 per cent. The increase in inflows was mainly the result of a more than three-fold increase in cross-border M&A sales (annex table I.3), with two big deals making up most of the total.[10] In addition, Turkey's FDI promotion policy has been shifting towards a more sector-specific approach, aiming directly at high value added, high-tech and export-oriented projects. Investments in automotive and petrochemical industries have been designated primary objectives by the Investment Support and Promotion Agency, and the mining sector will soon be added as well.[11]

Political and social unrest has halted FDI to non-GCC Arab countries. Flows to this group of countries – which represented 14 per cent of the region's total – declined by 26 per cent in 2011 to $7 billion. Spreading political and social unrest has halted FDI inflows in the Syrian Arab Republic and Yemen. Flows to Lebanon were affected by the slowdown in the real estate sector – the most important recipient of FDI – as a consequence of adverse spillovers of both the global financial crisis and the regional unrest.

Increased oil revenues helped boost FDI outflows. FDI outflows from West Asia rebounded by 54 per cent in 2011 after bottoming out at a five-year low in 2010 (figure C). The rise in oil prices since the end of 2010 made more funds available for outward FDI from the GCC countries. In addition to these countries – the region's main outward-investing economies – Turkey registered a 68 per cent increase in outward FDI flows. This is reflected in the recovery of both cross-border M&A purchases and greenfield projects abroad by Turkish investors, with a strong shift of greenfield FDI projects from developed and transition economies to neighbouring developing regions and countries.

FDI prospects are still negative for inward FDI to the region. UNCTAD projects that FDI inflows will continue declining in 2012, judging by preliminary data on cross-border M&A sales and greenfield investment for the first five months of 2012, as uncertainties at the global and regional levels are likely to cause foreign investors to remain cautious about their investment plans in the region.

In the longer term, however, the concentration of oil wealth in the region and the strategic need to further reduce economic dependence on the oil and gas sectors through economic diversification will create additional business opportunities, and revive the region's attractiveness for foreign investors (see box II.2).

Box II.2. Economic diversification and FDI in the GCC countries

Economic diversification has recently taken high political priority in West Asia, as the lack of job prospects for a rapidly growing, educated and young population was a key trigger of political unrest. The oil-rich countries saw in the surge of oil prices in the early 2000s an opportunity for change. In 2001, the six GCC members signed an economic agreement aiming to boost their diversification efforts by encouraging the private sector, including foreign investors, to play a more active role and implementing liberalization measures to this end.

The new policy framework opened a wider range of activities to FDI. Together with new opportunities offered by the surge in oil revenues, this has increased annual inflows from a relatively modest $1 billion on average during 1990–2000 to $28 billion during 2001–2011, reaching a record $60 billion in 2008, and targeting mainly services. Stock data from three countries show that in 2010, services accounted for 59 per cent of inward FDI, manufacturing for 27 per cent and the primary sector – mainly the oil and gas upstream industry where restrictions on FDI participation remain – for 14 per cent (box figure II.2.1). Services was also dominant in greenfield FDI projects, attracting 51 per cent of estimated investments during 2003–2011; 44 per cent targeted manufacturing and 5 per cent went to the primary sector.

Box figure II.2.1. Accumulated inward FDI stock in Oman, Qatar and Saudi Arabia,[a] by sector, 2010

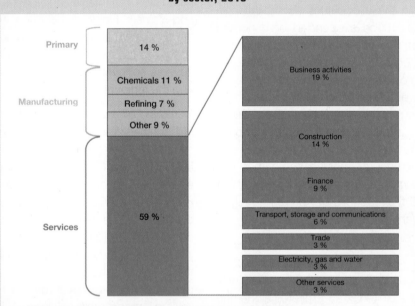

Source: UNCTAD, FDI/TNC database (www.unctad.org/fdistatistics).
[a] These three countries accounted for 69 per cent of GCC countries' inward FDI stocks in 2010. Sectoral data for Bahrain, Kuwait and the United Arab Emirates are not available.

Active industrial policies have targeted FDI in specific activities, using oil revenues to establish projects and encouraging foreign investors to participate – for example, in petrochemicals and petroleum refining, and the building of economic zones and new cities.

/...

Box II.2. Economic diversification and FDI in the GCC countries (concluded)

The soaring oil prices and increasing refining margins in the 2000s encouraged Gulf countries to establish refinery/ petrochemical complexes to produce products with higher value added. They also opened the door wider to international oil companies, as providers of technologies and market experience. Several projects have been built or are under way, through joint ventures or non-equity agreements with foreign TNCs. Several are hosted in Saudi Arabia, such as Petro Rabigh (with Sumitomo Chemical (Japan)), Al Jubail (with Total (France)), and Fujian (with ExxonMobil (United States) and Sinopec (China)), among others. Similar projects also took place in the United Arab Emirates, Qatar and Oman.

Building economic zones and cities has generally consisted of providing advanced information and communications technology, infrastructure and services to attract leading tenants to help establish new, globally competitive industries, especially service-based ones. More than 55 such cities or zones have been established or are under way, generally targeting knowledge-intensive industries.

GCC countries clearly experienced higher growth in their non-oil sectors during the 2000s (IMF, 2011), and the shift in their FDI policy allowed foreign direct investors to participate. Progress in equal treatment of GCC-country citizens – in freedom of movement, work, residence, economic engagement, capital movement and real estate ownership – has spurred intra-GCC FDI, which has helped develop services activities.

Despite this progress, hydrocarbons still dominate real GDP and export revenues, and the expansion of the non-oil sectors has not meant a decline in dependence on oil.[a] High growth rates in non-oil activities have created relatively few job opportunities for national workforce to assuage the high unemployment rates and reliance on government posts.[b] This might indicate a mismatch between career aspirations and available opportunities, on the one hand, and between the skills required by the private sector and those available in the workforce, on the other. This introduces the risk of the consolidation of a dual system, where modern enclaves with expatriate management and workforces are disconnected from the skills of the national workforce which relies mostly on government jobs.

GCC countries face common challenges. The scale of diversification plans will require both private and public funding, as well as cooperation and coordination between public and private sectors, which will continue to provide investment opportunities for TNCs.

Source: UNCTAD.

[a] Oil revenues represented 60–88 per cent on average of government revenues during 2005–2009, and its share in export revenues was 76–95 per cent in 2008, except in the United Arab Emirates, where it was 43 per cent (Samba, 2010).

[b] In 2008, national unemployment was estimated at close to 13 per cent in Saudi Arabia, 14 per cent in the United Arab Emirates and 15 per cent in both Bahrain and Oman. The majority of those employed worked in government; 88 per cent of nationals in Qatar, 86 per cent in Kuwait, 72 per cent in Saudi Arabia and 47 per cent in Oman. In 2007–2008, the share of migrants in total employment was estimated at 74 per cent in Bahrain, 77 per cent in Oman, 92 per cent in Qatar and 87 per cent in Saudi Arabia (Baldwin-Edwards, 2011).

5. Latin America and the Caribbean

Table A. Distribution of FDI flows among economies, by range,[a] 2011

Range	Inflows	Outflows
Above $10 billion	Brazil, British Virgin Islands, Mexico, Chile, Colombia	British Virgin Islands, Chile
$5.0 to $9.9 billion	Peru, Cayman Islands, Argentina, Bolivarian Republic of Venezuela	Mexico, Colombia
$1.0 to $4.9 billion	Panama, Dominican Republic, Uruguay, Costa Rica, Bahamas, Honduras, Guatemala, Nicaragua	Cayman Islands, Panama, Argentina
$0.1 to $0.9 billion	Plurinational State of Bolivia, Trinidad, Tobago, Ecuador, Aruba, El Salvador, Barbados, Paraguay, Jamaica, Haiti, Guyana, Saint Kitts, Nevis, Saint Vincent and the Grenadines, Cuba	Bahamas, Bolivarian Republic of Venezuela, Peru
Less than $0.1 billion	Turks and Caicos Islands, Belize, Saint Lucia, Curaçao, Antigua and Barbuda, Grenada, Dominica, Anguilla, Montserrat, Sint Maarten, Suriname	Jamaica, Costa Rica, Ecuador, Guatemala, Nicaragua, Curaçao, Turks and Caicos Islands, Aruba, Belize, Sint Maarten, Honduras, Suriname, Uruguay, Dominican Republic, Barbados, Brazil

[a] Economies are listed according to the magnitude of their FDI flows.

Figure A. FDI flows, top 5 host and home economies, 2010–2011
(Billions of dollars)

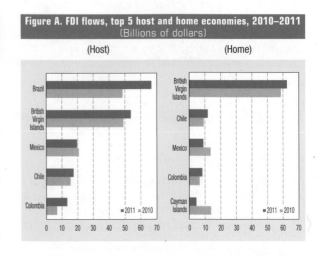

Figure B. FDI inflows, 2005–2011
(Billions of dollars)

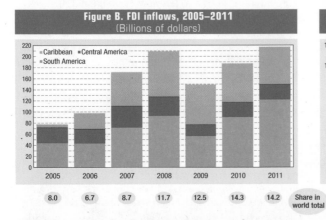

Share in world total: 8.0 6.7 8.7 11.7 12.5 14.3 14.2

Figure C. FDI outflows, 2005–2011
(Billions of dollars)

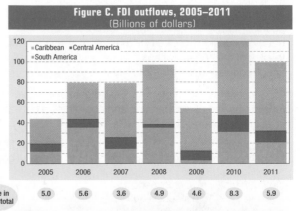

Share in world total: 5.0 5.6 3.6 4.9 4.6 8.3 5.9

Table B. Cross-border M&As by industry, 2010–2011
(Millions of dollars)

Sector/industry	Sales		Purchases	
	2010	2011	2010	2011
Total	**28 414**	**20 689**	**15 831**	**18 659**
Primary	**12 376**	**6 409**	**2 077**	**- 650**
Mining, quarrying and petroleum	11 898	6 249	1 981	- 745
Manufacturing	**7 398**	**2 766**	**4 700**	**6 035**
Food, beverages and tobacco	5 878	7 638	2 825	2 213
Textiles, clothing and leather	50	119	- 598	425
Wood and wood products	84	216	69	122
Electrical and electronic equipment	1 742	683	-	16
Services	**8 640**	**11 514**	**9 055**	**13 274**
Construction	18	1 417	49	826
Transport, storage and communications	2 409	3 523	263	6 123
Business services	2 438	1 415	1 070	- 272
Community, social and personal service activities	217	2 565	1 220	4

Table C. Cross-border M&As by region/country, 2010–2011
(Millions of dollars)

Region/country	Sales		Purchases	
	2010	2011	2010	2011
World	**28 414**	**20 689**	**15 831**	**18 659**
Developed economies	**2 744**	**908**	**12 036**	**9 173**
European Union	- 285	- 12 191	2 905	1 752
United States	- 395	- 3 497	4 719	5 402
Japan	4 907	10 946	125	-
Other developed countries	- 1 483	5 649	4 287	2 019
Developing economies	**24 741**	**17 585**	**3 951**	**8 157**
Africa	- 75	-	- 84	- 5
East and South-East Asia	14 664	9 311	79	159
South Asia	5 460	180	- 735	3
West Asia	-	147	-	18
Latin America and the Caribbean	4 692	7 983	4 692	7 983
Transition economies	**- 3**	**2 119**	**- 156**	**1 329**

Table D. Greenfield FDI projects by industry, 2010–2011
(Millions of dollars)

Sector/industry	LAC as destination		LAC as investors	
	2010	2011	2010	2011
Total	**120 113**	**138 680**	**21 754**	**20 655**
Primary	**17 234**	**21 481**	**7 429**	**2 300**
Mining, quarrying and petroleum	17 234	21 446	7 418	2 300
Manufacturing	**68 900**	**59 166**	**8 373**	**7 674**
Food, beverages and tobacco	6 258	10 632	2 038	1 197
Rubber and plastic products	4 541	3 424	3 050	170
Metals and metal products	20 242	15 233	678	1 769
Motor vehicles and other transport equipment	14 774	15 977	360	250
Services	**33 979**	**58 034**	**5 952**	**10 681**
Electricity, gas and water	9 518	11 989	1 688	156
Transport, storage and communications	9 916	20 643	1 424	3 678
Finance	2 892	2 786	1 392	1 290
Business services	7 291	20 557	410	5 117

Table E. Greenfield FDI projects by region/country, 2010–2011
(Millions of dollars)

Partner region/economy	LAC as destination		LAC as investors	
	2010	2011	2010	2011
World	**120 113**	**138 680**	**21 754**	**20 655**
Developed economies	**94 771**	**112 431**	**5 200**	**3 499**
European Union	50 871	57 462	1 132	1 319
United States	21 217	29 109	566	2 038
Japan	6 585	9 945	46	93
Other developed countries	16 098	15 915	3 456	49
Developing economies	**23 324**	**25 880**	**16 544**	**17 156**
Africa	503	1 167	809	1 774
East and South-East Asia	9 556	8 950	2 531	675
South Asia	566	598	826	64
West Asia	836	699	513	178
Latin America and the Caribbean	11 864	14 466	11 864	14 466
Transition economies	**2 018**	**370**	**10**	**-**

South America is the main driver of FDI growth to the region. FDI flows to Latin America and the Caribbean increased by 16 per cent to a record $217 billion in 2011, driven mainly by increasing inflows to South America (up 34 per cent). Inflows to Central America and the Caribbean, excluding offshore financial centres, increased by 4 per cent, while those to the offshore financial centres registered a 4 per cent decrease.

The high growth of FDI in South America was mainly due to its expanding consumer markets, high growth rates and natural-resource endowment. In 2011 Brazil remained by far the largest FDI target, with inflows increasing by 37 per cent to $67 billion – 55 per cent of the total in South America and 31 per cent of the total in the region. The size of Brazil's domestic market explains its attractiveness, as does its strategic position in South America, which brings within easy reach other emerging and fast-growing markets, such as Argentina, Chile, Colombia and Peru.

Another important driver for FDI growth to South America has been the relatively high rate of return on investments in the region. Since 2003, South American countries have witnessed significant growth of income on FDI: from an annual average of $11 billion during 1994–2002, equivalent to 0.84 per cent of the subregion's GDP, to an annual average of $60 billion during 2003–2011, equivalent to 2.44 per cent of GDP. In 2011, FDI income increased another 17 per cent, reaching $95 billion.[12]

The rise in FDI income during the 2000s, in parallel with the increase in FDI stock (a nine-fold increase between 1994 and 2011) and share in GDP (from 11 to 28 per cent share in current GDP), was in part driven by increased investment in extractive industries, which have enjoyed high profitability and have attracted a significant part of FDI inflows since the commodity price boom. For example, in Chile this industry accounted for 43 per cent of accumulated FDI inflows during 2006–2010. Its share in Brazil's FDI stock grew from 3 per cent at the end of 2005 to 15 per cent at the end of 2010. In Peru its share grew from 14 per cent at the end of 2003 to 26 per cent at the end of 2010, while in Colombia its share jumped from 17 per cent in 1994–2002 to 54 per cent in 2003–2011, attracting about two thirds of FDI inflows in 2009–2011.[13] The rates of return on inward FDI[14] in the

extractive industry in Argentina and Chile were 30 per cent and 20 per cent, respectively, in 2010, while those on total inward FDI were 11 per cent and 14 per cent, respectively.[15] The importance of FDI income is evident in the high share of reinvested earnings, which represented 45 per cent of FDI flows to South American countries other than Brazil[16] in 2003–2011, compared with 11 per cent in 1994–2002. Although high and rapidly growing FDI profits boost investment in productive capacity in host countries, they also entail risks, in that cash flows are available for repatriation or for short-term investment in local markets.

Offshore financial centres have surged as significant destinations for FDI since the beginning of the global financial crisis in 2007. After reaching a record $77 billion in 2008, FDI flows declined in 2009 by 9 per cent, after the OECD undertook initiatives to tackle banking secrecy and tax evasion through offshore financial centres. In 2011, flows decreased by 4 per cent to $67 billion, equivalent to 31 per cent for the region's total. However, they remained much higher than their pre-crisis level ($21 billion annual average in 2004–2006).

In 2011, inflows to the subregions of Central America and the Caribbean, excluding offshore financial centres, increased by 4 per cent to $29 billion – 13 per cent of total flows to Latin America and the Caribbean. A relatively more positive outlook for the United States, with which these countries have deep economic ties, offset the impact of the weakening global economy on FDI. Inflows to Mexico, which accounted for 69 per cent of total inflows to these countries, decreased by 6 per cent because of an 85 per cent drop in cross-border M&A sales, from $8 billion in 2010 to $1.2 billion in 2011. Nevertheless, FDI in Mexico's automotive and auto-component industry – an industry that is almost entirely foreign owned – was thriving. International auto companies continued to make new investments, especially in small and fuel-efficient vehicles and components. Investment by original equipment manufacturers has brought with it small and medium-sized firms in the auto parts industry. Investments for new automobile projects in Mexico from 2006 to 2012 are estimated to total $15 billion. Nissan, Ford and Honda have announced plans to invest $2 billion, $1.5 billion and $800 million.[17]

A reconfiguration of investments is taking place in the region. Although traditional investors from Europe and North America increased their investment in greenfield FDI projects in Latin America and the Caribbean in 2011 (up 17 per cent) and remained by far the main actors in such projects (72 per cent of the total in 2011), they have also divested more assets than they have purchased in the region's cross-border M&A market in the past three years. This changing pattern of FDI by traditional investors is occurring at the same time as the advance of TNCs from developing economies and Japan (table C). TNCs from Colombia, Mexico, China and India have been the most active investors from developing countries.

A retreat from the region by some major European financial institutions has been accelerating in 2012, as pressure to bolster their balance sheets grows – potentially leaving a gap to be filled by local or regional institutions looking to become international. For example, Banco Santander SA (Spain) announced in December 2011 an agreement to sell its Colombian unit to CorpBanca (Chile) for $1.2 billion, along with a 7.8 per cent stake in its Chilean unit.[18] Earlier in the year Santander announced sales of stakes in other Latin American businesses, including its bank in Brazil and 51 per cent of its Latin American insurance arm. These moves, driven by the need to boost capital at home in order to meet more stringent requirements from European regulators, constitute a major reversal of this bank's strategy of the 1990s, when its growing presence in the continent was seen as central to its global expansion plans. In a similar move driven by the same motives, ING (Netherlands) announced that it would sell its insurance and pensions businesses across much of Latin America to the Grupo de Inversiones Suramericana (Colombia), which will pay $3.85 billion for pension and investment units in a handful of countries, including Colombia.[19]

FDI outflows have become volatile. Outward FDI flows from Latin America and the Caribbean have become volatile since the global financial crisis. They decreased by 17 per cent in 2011, after a 121 per cent increase in 2010, which had followed a 44 per cent decline in 2009. This volatility is due to the growing importance of flows that are not necessarily related to investment in productive activity abroad, as reflected by the high share of offshore financial centres in total FDI flows from the region, and the increasing repatriation of intracompany loans by Brazilian outward investors, which reached a record $21 billion in 2011.

The global financial crisis has accelerated the shift towards industrial policy in Argentina and Brazil. This shift began in the early 2000s, during the recession that hit the region in 1998–2002. The recession was perceived as a failure of the economic model of the 1990s to deliver economic growth and reduce poverty. As a consequence, a number of Latin American countries entered a new phase, marked by a review of the role of the State in the economy and rehabilitation of industrial policy, which is slowly returning after practical exclusion from the previous economic model.[20] Some countries – Argentina in 2001, Mexico in 2002 and Brazil in 2003[21] – began announcing plans to promote specific industries and activities (Peres, 2011).[22]

More recently, the global economic crisis accelerated this shift towards industrial policy in Argentina and Brazil. Both countries implemented policies to support industries not only by fostering investment, innovation and foreign trade, but also by protecting the domestic market and local manufacturing – already weakened by the appreciation of local currencies[23] – from the flood of cheap manufactured goods seeking to counter weak demand in the United States and Europe. Both countries want their local industries to capitalize on their domestic consumption boom and aim to establish a homegrown high-technology industry that will help them diversify their economies and move up the value chain.

Since the global economic crisis began, a number of measures adopted by Argentina and Brazil have reversed some of the unilateral trade liberalization measures implemented in the 1990s, in efforts to make local manufacturing more cost-effective and persuade producers to set up locally. These measures include higher tariff barriers, more stringent criteria for licenses and increased preference margins for domestic production in public procurement in the case of Brazil.[24] In addition, Brazil increased the tax on manufactured products (Imposto sobre Produtos

Industrializados) levied on certain national and imported vehicles by 30 percentage points, while granting a rate reduction equivalent to 30 percentage points to vehicles that have at least 65 per cent regional content (defined as that of Brazil, the Mercado Común del Sur (MERCOSUR) or Mexico) and that meet other requirements.[25] Moreover, Brazil unveiled a new policy in August 2011. It included the replacement of the corporate payroll contribution to social security (20 per cent) by a 1.5 per cent tax on gross revenues for firms in labour-intensive sectors starting in December 2012, and the expansion of Banco Nacional do Desenvolvimento loan programmes. At the MERCOSUR level, members agreed in December 2011 to impose a 35 per cent tariff, the maximum allowed under WTO rules, on 100 additional goods, subject to MERCOSUR's common tariff on imports from outside the bloc. The new tariffs will be imposed until December 2014. Capital goods, textiles and chemical imports are the likely targets.[26]

These policies may induce "barrier hopping" FDI into the region. Indeed, they seem to have had an impact on the strategy of TNCs in these countries. In Brazil, TNC automakers announced a flurry of investments into the auto sector at the end of 2011. For instance, among the new investments planned for Brazil or already under way, Chery (China) has begun construction of a $400 million plant that will produce 150,000 vehicles a year; Volkswagen has announced plans to invest $4.5 billion in the country until 2016; and the Renault-Nissan alliance will invest $1.5 billion to build a new Nissan plant in Rio de Janeiro state, where production is due to begin in 2014, and $200 million in its existing Curitiba site. Another Chinese group, JAC Motors, is planning to invest RMB 900 million for a plant with a capacity of 100,000 units, while BMW is also reportedly looking to establish its first factory in Latin America in Brazil.[27] In addition, after being granted tax incentives, Foxconn (Taiwan Province of China) plans to build five additional factories in Brazil to help cater to demand for Apple iPads and other tablets, which together are expected to require an annual run rate of nearly 400 million units within five years.[28] In Argentina, in a context of a boom in agriculture exports and the domestic auto market (with growth of about 30 per cent per year), the Government began in 2011 negotiating with

automakers and agriculture-machinery producers to source and produce locally. In addition, a number of TNCs announced new investments in the country.[29]

More recently, after declaring the achievement of self-sufficiency in hydrocarbons and their exploitation, industrialization, transportation and marketing to be of national public interest, the Government renationalized 51 per cent of Argentina's largest oil company, YPF (see box III.4). The Government was prompted to retake control of the industry by Argentina's first fuels deficit in 17 years.[30] YPF has announced it will look for both local and international partners to finance exploration in the Vaca Muerta shale, which could hold the world's third largest reserves of unconventional gas and oil.

Argentina and Brazil are revising their development strategies as they pursue more active policies for promoting industrialization and broader development goals. This revival of industrial policies is likely to have an impact on both FDI policy and FDI strategy. FDI policy is likely to depend increasingly on the industry in question and the role the Governments want to assign to FDI, which in turn will affect FDI strategy. While the era of across-the-board liberalization policies for FDI seems to be over, this change does not seem to be deterring FDI flows, which have boomed in Brazil in recent years and steadily increased in Argentina since the region resumed growth in 2003–2004.

Short-term prospects of FDI to Latin America and the Caribbean are muted. The region is likely to remain attractive to foreign direct investors given its natural resources and its relatively higher growth prospects at a time of overall global uncertainty. In addition, the shift towards a greater use of industrial policy may induce "barrier-hopping" FDI into the region, and appears to have already had an effect on firms' investment plans. However, the uncertainty created at the global level by the European debt crisis is affecting the region's short-term prospects and impacting on FDI, which is likely to register, at the best, a slight growth in 2012.

6. Transition economies

Table A. Distribution of FDI flows among economies, by range,[a] 2011

Range	Inflows	Outflows
Above $5.0 billion	Russian Federation, Kazakhstan, Ukraine	Russian Federation
$1.0 to $4.9 billion	Belarus, Turkmenistan, Serbia, Croatia, Azerbaijan, Uzbekistan, Albania, Georgia	Kazakhstan
$0.5 to $0.9 billion	Kyrgyzstan, Montenegro, Armenia	Azerbaijan
Below $0.5 billion	Bosnia and Herzegovina, the former Yugoslav Republic of Macedonia, Republic of Moldova, Tajikistan	Ukraine, Serbia, Georgia, Armenia, Belarus, Croatia, Albania, Republic of Moldova, Bosnia and Herzegovina, Montenegro, the former Yugoslav Republic of Macedonia, Kyrgyzstan

[a] Economies are listed according to the magnitude of their FDI flows.

Figure A. FDI flows, top 5 host and home economies, 2010–2011
(Billions of dollars)

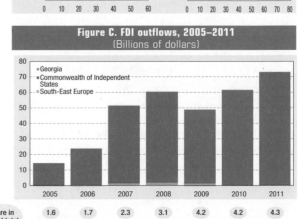

Figure B. FDI inflows, 2005–2011
(Billions of dollars)

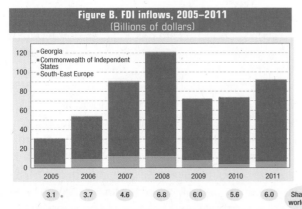

	2005	2006	2007	2008	2009	2010	2011	
Share in world total	3.1	3.7	4.6	6.8	6.0	5.6	6.0	

Figure C. FDI outflows, 2005–2011
(Billions of dollars)

	2005	2006	2007	2008	2009	2010	2011
	1.6	1.7	2.3	3.1	4.2	4.2	4.3

Table B. Cross-border M&As by industry, 2010–2011
(Millions of dollars)

Sector/industry	Sales		Purchases	
	2010	2011	2010	2011
Total	**4 499**	**32 970**	**5 693**	**13 510**
Primary	**20**	**18 271**	**2 268**	**12 143**
Mining, quarrying and petroleum	- 85	18 226	2 268	12 094
Manufacturing	**1 857**	**6 386**	**270**	**- 1 354**
Food, beverages and tobacco	1 366	5 243	325	111
Wood and wood products	51	68	126	-
Chemicals and chemical products	- 7	984	- 7	- 106
Metals and metal products	12	-	- 174	- 1 368
Services	**2 621**	**8 312**	**3 155**	**2 720**
Trade	391	2 464	13	-
Transport, storage and communications	1 065	5 761	- 442	- 3
Finance	503	198	2 459	2 222
Business services	191	- 361	7	65

Table C. Cross-border M&As by region/country, 2010–2011
(Millions of dollars)

Region/country	Sales		Purchases	
	2010	2011	2010	2011
World	**4 499**	**32 970**	**5 693**	**13 510**
Developed economies	**2 364**	**22 937**	**4 672**	**1 464**
European Union	7 537	10 516	3 094	2 062
United States	119	7 032	205	- 894
Japan	-	-	-	-
Other developed countries	- 5 291	5 389	1 373	296
Developing economies	**276**	**1 580**	**69**	**3 525**
Africa	388	-	51	- 130
East and South-East Asia	20	379	-	1 531
South Asia	24	- 245	-	-
West Asia	-	117	21	5
Latin America and the Caribbean	- 156	1 329	- 3	2 119
Transition economies	**952**	**8 520**	**952**	**8 520**

Table D. Greenfield FDI projects by industry, 2010–2011
(Millions of dollars)

Sector/industry	Transition economies as destination		Transition economies as investors	
	2010	2011	2010	2011
Total	**55 934**	**59 461**	**21 575**	**17 967**
Primary	**3 508**	**4 844**	**3 995**	**1 658**
Mining, quarrying and petroleum	3 508	4 844	3 995	1 658
Manufacturing	**30 867**	**35 602**	**12 386**	**12 030**
Coke, petroleum and nuclear fuel	3 332	10 164	3 218	7 861
Chemicals and chemical products	4 208	2 712	872	68
Non-metallic mineral products	1 455	3 219	88	6
Motor vehicles and other transport equipment	12 085	7 872	5 536	1 358
Services	**21 559**	**19 015**	**5 195**	**4 278**
Electricity, gas and water	2 656	4 915	847	681
Construction	7 400	2 591	343	-
Transport, storage and communications	4 063	4 162	1 437	720
Finance	2 444	2 871	1 686	1 982

Table E. Greenfield FDI projects by region/country, 2010–2011
(Millions of dollars)

Partner region/economy	Transition economies as destination		Transition economies as investors	
	2010	2011	2010	2011
World	**55 934**	**59 461**	**21 575**	**17 967**
Developed economies	**38 268**	**40 904**	**2 751**	**4 518**
European Union	32 539	31 444	2 164	2 238
United States	2 787	3 586	425	2 014
Japan	1 442	1 740	17	108
Other developed countries	1 501	4 134	145	159
Developing economies	**11 448**	**8 522**	**12 607**	**3 414**
Africa	8	-	2 612	727
East and South-East Asia	5 253	6 563	5 648	1 232
South Asia	1 069	824	576	389
West Asia	5 108	1 135	1 753	695
Latin America and the Caribbean	10	-	2 018	370
Transition economies	**6 218**	**10 035**	**6 218**	**10 035**

Recovery of FDI flows. FDI to economies in transition in South-East Europe, the CIS and Georgia[31] recovered strongly in 2011, prompted by the dynamism of cross-border M&A deals, although greenfield investments are still the dominant form of entry. Inflows rose by 25 per cent, to $92 billion (figure B). In South-East Europe, manufacturing FDI increased, buoyed by competitive production costs and open access to EU markets, while in the CIS, resource-based economies benefited from continued natural-resource-seeking FDI. Compared with foreign portfolio flows, FDI flows were remarkably stable, underscoring their importance for development. Large countries continued to account for the lion's share of inward FDI. Inflows remained concentrated in a few economies, with the top five destinations accounting for 87 per cent of the flows (figure A).

The Russian Federation saw FDI flows grow by 22 per cent, reaching $53 billion, the third highest level ever recorded. Foreign investors were motivated by the continued strong growth of the domestic market and affordable labour costs, coupled with productivity gains. They also continued to be attracted by high returns in energy and other natural-resource-related projects, as shown by the partnership deal between Exxon Mobil (United States) and the State-owned oil company Rosneft (Russian Federation) to develop the rich, untapped reserves of the Arctic zone.

Cross-border M&As were particularly dynamic. The FDI rebound was due mainly to a surge in the value of cross-border M&As, from $4.5 billion in 2010 to $33 billion in 2011 (tables B and C), driven by a number of large transactions. The takeover of Polyus Gold (Russian Federation) for $6.3 billion by the KazakhGold Group (Kazakhstan) was the largest. Although deals in energy, mining, oil and gas tend to attract the most media attention, the consumer market was also a target for cross-border M&As in 2011.[32]

TNCs from around the world invested in the region; "round-tripping" FDI was still high. Developed countries, mainly EU members, continued to account for the largest share of FDI projects (both cross-border M&As and greenfield investments), though projects from developing and transition economies gained importance. Overall, FDI flows

between transition countries remained relatively low, accounting for an average of 10 per cent of the region's total FDI projects, although they increased 20 per cent since 2010, mainly due to intraregional M&As. A large part of FDI flows to the transition economies continued to come from offshore centres, as "round-tripping" or transhipment transactions. As a result, Cyprus and the British Virgin Islands were the largest two investors in the region in 2011, representing almost one third of total inflows.

FDI in services remained sluggish but new impetus may come from the WTO accession of the Russian Federation. In 2011, FDI projects in transition economies rose in all three sectors of production (tables B and D). Compared with the pre-crisis level (2005–2007), the value of FDI in the primary sector increased almost four-fold; FDI in manufacturing rose by 28 per cent while FDI in services remained lower. Over the long run, however, FDI in services is expected to rise because of the accession of the Russian Federation to the WTO (box II.3). Through that accession the country has further committed to integrate itself into the global economic system, which will boost foreign investors' confidence and improve the overall investment environment. The services sector may well replace the manufacturing sector as the engine of FDI growth, while in the manufacturing sector, domestic and foreign investors will most likely consolidate as the landscape becomes more competitive. In the primary sector, the impact on FDI will vary by industry.

Record-high FDI outflows, and not only by natural-resource-based TNCs. FDI outflows from the transition economies, mainly from the Russian Federation, reached an all-time record level in 2011 (figure C). Natural-resource-based TNCs in transition economies, supported by high commodity prices and higher stock market valuations, continued their expansion into emerging markets rich in natural resources. For example, TNK-BP (Russian Federation) entered the Brazilian oil industry with a $1 billion acquisition of a 45 per cent stake in 21 oil blocks located in the Solimoes Basin. At the same time, the company base of outward FDI continued widening as other firms from various industries also invested. For example, Sberbank – the largest Russian bank and the third largest European one

Box II.3. The Russian Federation's accession to the WTO: implications for inward FDI flows

On 16 December 2011, at its Ministerial meeting in Geneva, the WTO formally approved the terms of the Russian Federation's entry to the WTO.[a] Fulfilling the WTO obligations will involve substantial trade and investment liberalization measures. These measures will have implications for FDI flows to the Russian Federation in all three sectors, which will be felt even more strongly after the transition to full compliance with WTO standards.

- The services sector. This sector accounts for more than 40 per cent of GDP in the Russian Federation. Liberalization will gradually open the country's services market to foreign investors. The Russian Federation has undertaken special obligations in 11 services industries and 116 sub-industries. For example:
  - In banking, foreign banks may now establish majority-owned affiliates, and the threshold of foreign participation has been raised to 50 per cent (with the exception of foreign investment in privatized banks, in which greater ownership is possible).[b] However, even though the country has allowed the establishment of branches of international banks, they must be registered as Russian entities, have their own capital and be subject to supervision by the Russian central bank.
  - In insurance, the share of foreign ownership has been expanded to 100 per cent in non-life insurance companies and to 50 per cent in the life insurance market (up from 15 per cent in both).
  - In trade, 100 per cent foreign firms are allowed to participate in both the wholesale and the retail segments.
  - In business services, the country has committed to market access and national treatment for a wide variety of professions. Foreign companies have been permitted to operate as 100 per cent foreign-owned entities.
  - In telecommunications, restrictions of foreign participation to 49 per cent will be eliminated within four years after the WTO accession.
  - In distribution services, 100 per cent foreign-owned companies have been allowed to engage in wholesale, retail and franchise activities, as well as express delivery services, including the distribution of pharmaceuticals.

- The manufacturing sector. Most manufacturing industries had been largely open to foreign investors and had already attracted a significant amount of FDI, so accession to the WTO may not immediately have substantial FDI-generating effects. Indeed, the reduction of import restrictions and the elimination of trade-related investment measures in industries such as automobiles and food industries may reduce incentives to FDI by eroding the possibility of "barrier-hopping". Nevertheless, over time, freer access to imported inputs could help improve the cost-quality conditions of manufacturing and increase the attractiveness of the economy as a site for efficiency-oriented manufacturing FDI. Some industries that are not competitive, such as mechanical engineering, may lose FDI potential as they undergo downsizing in the aftermath of WTO accession and the end of their current protection. Industries such as ferrous and non-ferrous metallurgy and chemical products may benefit from WTO accession and better access to foreign markets, but only in the long run. Metallurgy and chemicals are already competitive in world markets and operate without major subsidies.

- The primary sector. WTO accession may benefit FDI in the mining sector but hinder FDI in agriculture. Foreign investors may also be attracted to export-oriented oil and gas production (within the limits of the strategic sectors law) because these activities will benefit from the liberalization of markets and elimination of export quotas. Business opportunities are expected to be more scarce in agriculture, in which output may even contract. The Institute of Economic Forecasting of the Russian Academy of Sciences estimates that the country will lose $4 billion a year in agricultural production. This estimate is based on the assumption that local production will not be able to improve productivity and competitiveness. If local producers react by modernizing successfully, the losses may be more moderate. Competitive foreign producers would still find niche markets in food and beverages.

Upon accession, pursuant to the WTO Agreement on Trade-Related Investment Measures, the Russian Federation will be prohibited from imposing certain conditions on enterprises operating in the country, including those with foreign investments.

Source: UNCTAD, based on Kostyunina (2012).
[a] The Russian Federation will have until mid-July 2013 to ratify the accession agreement and will become a member 30 days after it notifies the WTO of its ratification.
[b] In addition, foreign affiliates in banking will be allowed to provide a variety of services, including asset management services, credit cards and other types of payments; to own and trade all kinds of securities available in the country, including government securities; and to participate in the privatization of State-owned enterprises.

in terms of market capitalization – was pursuing major acquisitions abroad (e.g. in 2011 the bank completed the acquisition of Volksbank (Austria) affiliates in four transition economies[33] and four new EU member countries[34]). As corporate customers of Russian banks venture abroad, they demand that their banks have a local presence in host countries to help finance their activities there. Russian technology-based firms also acquired large assets, especially in developed markets (e.g. Sky Technology acquired 10 per cent of Twitter (United States)).

The new privatization agenda in the aftermath of the crisis is expected to contribute to FDI growth. After two decades of transition, privatization is well advanced in large parts of South-East Europe and the CIS. Nevertheless, some countries retain assets that could be privatized. Privatization will be revived after the lull of 2008–2010. During the crisis, Governments' reluctance to bring politically sensitive companies to the market and international investors' lack of confidence left little room for privatization projects. However, with signs of an economic upturn and pressure on State budgets, the process is expected to gain new momentum.

For instance, the Government of the Russian Federation approved partial privatization of 10 major State-owned companies before 2013, which could bring an extra Rub 1 trillion ($33 billion) to the State budget. The effort includes minority shares in the major oil company Rosneft, the hydropower generator RusHydro, the Federal Grid Company of Unified Energy Systems, the country's largest shipping company (Sovcomflot), Sberbank, VTB Bank, the United Grain Company, the Rosagroleasing agricultural leasing company, the oil pipeline company Transneft and the national rail monopoly (Russian Railways). In Serbia, two large publicly owned enterprises are expected to be privatized in 2012: Telekom Srbija and the catering service of the national airline, JAT. In Bosnia and Herzegovina, the Government is hoping to raise about $5 billion in 2012–2013, mainly by privatizing assets in 25 large companies included in previous privatization plans. In Croatia, the State holds a minority stake in over 600 companies and more than 50 per cent of assets in over 60 companies. Seeking to leverage increased investor attention on

the back of its accession to the EU in 2013, Croatia is set to reinvigorate its privatization drive.

Both inflows and outflows are expected to rise further. FDI flows to transition economies are expected to continue to grow in the medium term, reflecting a more investor-friendly environment, WTO accession by the Russian Federation and new privatization programmes. FDI from developing countries is also expected to rise further, aided by joint initiatives to support direct investments in some transition economies. For example, CIC, China's main sovereign wealth fund, and the Russian Direct Investment Fund (RDIF) agreed to contribute $1 billion each to an RDIF-managed fund. The fund will make 70 per cent of its investments in the Russian Federation, Kazakhstan and Belarus. In 2012, CIC bought a small stake in VTB Bank (Russian Federation) as part of a deal to privatize 10 per cent of the bank. However, FDI inflows in the first quarter of 2012 are slightly lower compared with the same period in 2011.

Outward FDI, too, is set to thrive in 2012 and beyond, thanks to high commodity prices and economic recovery in home countries that have extensive natural resources. The increasing number of new outward investors is another factor driving the volume of outward FDI.

7. Developed countries

Table A. Distribution of FDI flows among economies, by range,ᵃ 2011

Range	Inflows	Outflows
Above $100 billion	United States	United States, Japan, United Kingdom
$50 to $99 billion	Belgium, United Kingdom	France, Belgium, Switzerland, Germany, Canada
$10 to $49 billion	Australia, France, Canada, Germany, Spain, Italy, Luxembourg, Netherlands, Poland, Denmark, Austria, Ireland, Sweden, Israel, Portugal	Italy, Spain, Netherlands, Austria, Sweden, Denmark, Norway, Australia, Portugal, Luxembourg
$1 to $9 billion	Czech Republic, Hungary, Norway, New Zealand, Romania, Slovakia, Bulgaria, Greece, Latvia, Lithuania, Iceland, Slovenia	Poland, Finland, Hungary, Israel, New Zealand, Cyprus, Greece, Czech Republic
Below $1 billion	Malta, Bermuda, Cyprus, Estonia, Gibraltar, Finland, Switzerland, Japan	Slovakia, Bulgaria, Lithuania, Slovenia, Latvia, Romania, Malta, Iceland, Bermuda, Estonia, Ireland

ᵃ Economies are listed according to the magnitude of their FDI flows.

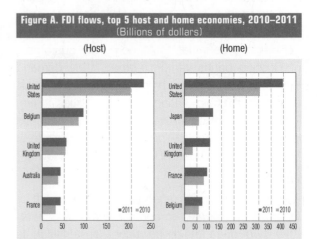

Figure A. FDI flows, top 5 host and home economies, 2010–2011
(Billions of dollars)
(Host)   (Home)

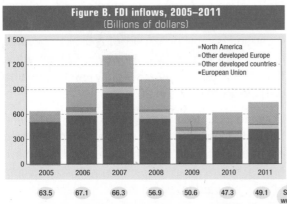

Figure B. FDI inflows, 2005–2011
(Billions of dollars)

Share in world total: 63.5 | 67.1 | 66.3 | 56.9 | 50.6 | 47.3 | 49.1

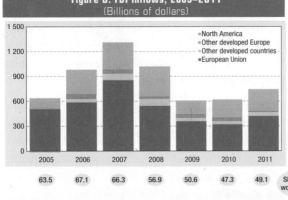

Figure C. FDI outflows, 2005–2011
(Billions of dollars)

Share in world total: 83.5 | 81.4 | 83.2 | 80.3 | 73.0 | 68.2 | 73.0

Table B. Cross-border M&As by industry, 2010–2011
(Millions of dollars)

Sector/industry	Sales 2010	Sales 2011	Purchases 2010	Purchases 2011
Total	**257 152**	**409 691**	**223 726**	**400 929**
Primary	52 783	81 186	31 837	32 085
Mining, quarrying and petroleum	47 971	80 306	31 330	31 904
Manufacturing	102 486	176 213	106 146	184 659
Food, beverages and tobacco	27 951	26 509	26 504	23 880
Chemicals and chemical products	26 987	78 517	41 085	76 684
Metals and metal products	569	5 729	5 812	19 394
Electrical and electronic equipment	10 585	23 043	6 383	17 145
Services	101 882	152 293	85 744	184 186
Trade	12 201	14 231	5 812	6 495
Transport, storage and communications	7 765	23 920	11 785	41 725
Finance	26 331	23 609	65 408	92 744
Business services	34 755	38 374	25 368	32 999

Table C. Cross-border M&As by region/country, 2010–2011
(Millions of dollars)

Region/country	Sales 2010	Sales 2011	Purchases 2010	Purchases 2011
World	**257 152**	**409 691**	**223 726**	**400 929**
Developed economies	185 916	334 673	185 916	334 673
European Union	13 958	89 785	85 102	144 085
United States	79 769	123 184	70 191	115 523
Japan	18 134	43 314	3 249	3 752
Other developed countries	74 056	78 391	27 374	71 313
Developing economies	53 668	67 049	35 446	43 319
Africa	1 371	4 265	6 722	4 308
East and South-East Asia	34 985	45 773	7 439	15 007
South Asia	7 836	5 239	7 439	14 870
West Asia	-2 555	2 599	2 257	8 222
Latin America and the Caribbean	12 036	9 173	2 744	908
Transition economies	**4 672**	**1 464**	**2 364**	**22 937**

Table D. Greenfield FDI projects by industry, 2010–2011
(Millions of dollars)

Sector/industry	Developed countries as destination 2010	Developed countries as destination 2011	Developed countries as investors 2010	Developed countries as investors 2011
Total	**300 648**	**276 430**	**643 504**	**643 490**
Primary	13 151	18 497	43 149	57 580
Mining, quarrying and petroleum	13 151	18 415	43 149	57 464
Manufacturing	149 458	116 105	334 910	312 495
Chemicals and chemical products	11 664	11 745	37 548	51 484
Metals and metal products	10 668	6 629	43 493	32 232
Electrical and electronic equipment	22 086	17 554	41 497	36 371
Motor vehicles and other transport equipment	27 356	25 318	78 501	70 814
Services	138 038	141 829	265 445	273 414
Electricity, gas and water	37 654	51 257	69 153	74 904
Transport, storage & communications	22 390	17 881	45 660	57 712
Finance	15 944	17 354	30 616	32 739
Business services	28 799	24 812	50 884	58 776

Table E. Greenfield FDI projects by region/country, 2010–2011
(Millions of dollars)

Partner region/economy	Developed countries as destination 2010	Developed countries as destination 2011	Developed countries as investors 2010	Developed countries as investors 2011
World	**300 648**	**276 430**	**643 504**	**643 490**
Developed economies	248 810	237 251	248 810	237 251
European Union	156 393	130 499	146 232	146 425
United States	52 863	52 733	53 161	43 643
Japan	13 616	21 107	5 967	5 371
Other developed countries	25 938	32 911	43 450	41 812
Developing economies	49 087	34 661	356 427	365 335
Africa	1 192	487	48 554	38 939
East and South-East Asia	32 559	16 470	136 798	133 339
South Asia	6 368	4 503	38 423	41 532
West Asia	3 769	9 687	36 532	38 990
Latin America and the Caribbean	5 200	3 499	94 771	112 431
Transition economies	**2 751**	**4 518**	**38 268**	**40 904**

Both inward and outward FDI up in 2011. Inflows to developed countries, which bottomed out in 2009, accelerated their recovery in 2011 to reach $748 billion, up 21 per cent from the previous year. The recovery has nonetheless made up only one fifth of the ground lost during the financial crisis. Inflows remained at 77 per cent of the average over the three years before the crisis began. Inflows to Europe, which were still in decline in 2010, showed a strong turnaround while robust recovery in the United States continued. Australia and New Zealand attracted significant volumes, and Japan saw a net divestment for the second successive year (annex table I.1).

Recovery of outward FDI from developed countries gathered pace in 2011 (up 25 per cent from 2010). Outflows reached $1.24 trillion, a level comparable with the pre-crisis average of 2005–2007. The growth came on the strength of outward FDI from the United States and Japan (figure A). Outward FDI from the United States reached $397 billion, exceeding the peak of 2007 ($394 billion). Japanese outward FDI doubled to $114 billion (annex table I.1). The trend in Europe is more mixed. While outward FDI from the United Kingdom almost tripled (up 171 per cent) to $107 billion, flows from Germany dropped by half ($54.4 billion) and from the Netherlands by nearly as much ($31.9 billion). Outflows from Denmark and Portugal were at a record high.

Re-emergence of Japan as the second largest investor. Outward FDI flows from Japan doubled in 2011 to $114 billion, approximating the peak in 2008 of $128 billion and showing a strong revival after the decline in 2009–2010. The underlying "push" factors for Japanese TNCs remained the same. In addition to manufacturing FDI seeking low-cost locations, the strength of the yen and the weak growth prospects of the home economy are prompting Japanese TNCs to seek growth opportunities and strategic assets in overseas markets.

One of the most notable examples in recent years is the acquisition of Nycomed (Switzerland) by the pharmaceutical company Takeda for $13.7 billion. This deal was the second largest cross-border purchase by a Japanese TNC ever. Access to markets in Europe and North America, as well as

emerging countries, was thought to be the rationale behind this acquisition. Similarly, the purchase of CaridianBCT (United States) for $2.6 billion gave Terumo, Japan's largest medical device maker, access to North American customers in the blood transfusion equipment market. Market-seeking motives were also behind the purchase by the Japanese beverage group Kirin of a 50.45 per cent stake in Schincariol (Brazil) for $2.5 billion and of a 14.7 per cent stake in Fraser and Neave (Singapore) for $970 million.

In addition to markets, the search for assets in the form of natural resources and technology has become prominent in recent acquisitions by Japanese TNCs. Examples include the acquisition of a 24.5 per cent stake in Anglo America Sur (Chile) by Mitsubishi Corp., which subsequently announced a plan to double its global copper production. Mitsubishi Corp. and other Japanese sogo shosha have re-emerged as important direct investors in commodity and natural resources.

Support measures by the Japanese Government may have played a role in promoting strategic-asset-seeking FDI. In August 2011, the Government established a $100 billion programme to encourage private sector firms to exchange yen funds for foreign currencies, as part of efforts to ease the negative effects of the strong yen. Such funds can be used to finance the acquisition of foreign firms and natural resources by Japanese TNCs.[35] Toshiba accessed this facility for its $2.3 billion acquisition of Landis+Gyr (Switzerland), a manufacturer of electricity meters that has expertise in smart grids. Sony used it to take full control of the joint venture Sony Ericsson.

Continuing boom in mining. The demand for commodities remains strong despite the slowdown in the global economy. Cross-border M&As nearly doubled in this sector in 2011 (table B). Greenfield data also show a 40 per cent increase from 2010 to 2011 (table D). The development of shale gas extraction in the United States was a major factor driving FDI. For example, BHP Billiton (Australia) purchased gas producer Petrohawk Energy (United States) for $12.1 billion. Other developed countries rich in natural resources, notably Australia and Canada, also continued to attract FDI in the mining industry for minerals such as coal, copper, gold and iron ore. Major deals in the industry included the purchase of Equinox Minerals (Australia) by the world's largest gold producer, Barrick Gold (Canada), for $7.35 billion as well as those of Consolidated Thompson Iron Mines (Canada) by Cliffs Natural Resources (United States) for $4.35 billion and Western Coal (Canada) by Walter Energy (United States) for $2.91 billion.

Behind the optimistic outlook for the extractive industry is the growing demand in emerging markets. Not surprisingly, therefore, TNCs from developing countries were also increasingly active in acquiring natural-resource assets overseas, including in developed countries. Sinopec (China) acquired the oil and gas explorer Daylight Energy (Canada) for $2.07 billion. GVK Power (India) acquired Hancock Coal (Australia) for $1.26 billion. Brazilian oil company HRT Participações acquired UNX Energy (Canada) for $711 million.

Restructuring in the financial industry continues. Financial institutions continued offloading overseas assets to repay the State aid they received during the financial crisis and also to strengthen their capital base so as to meet the requirements of Basel III and even tougher targets set by the European Banking Authority. In 2011, American International Group paid back an additional $2.15 billion to the Government of the United States following the sale of its life insurance unit, Nan Shan, in Taiwan Province of China. In another example cited earlier, Santander (Spain) sold its Colombian business, including Banco Santander Colombia, to CorpBanca (Chile) for $2.16 billion.

Divestments in the financial industry are not just about retrenchment but are also motivated by the desire to concentrate on fewer business areas and geographies to achieve scale. For instance, the French insurer AXA SA held a 54 per cent stake in AXA Asia Pacific, which ran life insurance and wealth management businesses in the Asia-Pacific region. In a deal worth $13.1 billion, AXA SA took full control of AXA Asia Pacific to pursue its focus on growing in Asia, while divesting AXA Asia Pacific's operations in Australia and New Zealand to AMP, which, for its part, sought scale and became the largest firm in the Australian wealth management sector with this acquisition. In a separate development, AXA sold its Canadian division to Intact Financial (Canada),

which was seeking to diversify its businesses, for $2.78 billion.

The eurozone crisis and FDI in Greece, Italy, Portugal and Spain. Despite the intensified eurozone crisis, total FDI flows into and out of the four most affected countries appeared to show little impact. FDI inflows were up in Portugal, Italy and Greece, and close to the average of the previous two years for Spain (table II.2). However, underlying variables showed signs of distress. Given the depth of recession, especially in Greece, reinvested earnings – one of three components of FDI – were down in all four countries (as they depend on the earnings of existing foreign affiliates in the host country). Intracompany loans ("other capital" in table II.2) were also down in Italy and Spain, indicating that TNCs withdrew debt capital from their foreign affiliates in these countries. The fact that intracompany loans were negative for Greece between 2007 and 2010 is indicative of the protracted nature of the crisis and of the level of adaptation on the part of TNCs.

M&A data do not show systematic patterns of divestment from the four countries by foreign TNCs, although sales of locally owned assets to foreign investors have increased. In Italy, the value of net M&A sales (acquisition of domestic firms by foreign TNCs) doubled from $6 billion in 2010 to $13 billion in 2011. A single large divestment worth $22 billion distorts the picture on divestment of assets. M&A sales in Spain and particularly in Portugal saw some acquisitions by Latin American TNCs. Consistent with M&A data, the equity components of FDI were at a relatively high level in all four countries, as their economic situation and asset valuations may have created acquisition targets.

Data on FDI outflows from the same countries show that outflows declined until 2009 or 2010 and then began to recover much as they did in other European countries – although the scale of outward FDI from Greece and Portugal has traditionally been low. Data on the components of outward FDI suggest that TNCs may have transferred some assets to foreign affiliates (or left assets there in the form of reinvested earnings). In Italy and Spain, for instance, total outward FDI flows in 2011 were, respectively, only 49 per cent and 27 per cent of the peaks of 2007 (table II.3). In contrast, outflows of "other capital" – mainly intracompany loans –

Table II.2. FDI inflows to Greece, Italy, Portugal and Spain, by component, 2007–2011 (Billions of dollars)						
Country	FDI components	2007	2008	2009	2010	2011
Greece	Total	2.1	4.5	2.4	0.4	1.8
	Equity	2.4	5	3.4	2.9	4.1
	Reinvested earnings	1.2	0.4	-0.5	-2.2	-2.3
	Other capital	-1.4	-0.9	-0.5	-0.3	-
Italy	Total	43.8	-10.8	20.1	9.2	29.1
	Equity	18.5	-3.7	7.5	-4.6	22.2
	Reinvested earnings	6.6	5	7.2	6.7	6.3
	Other capital	18.8	-12.1	5.3	7	0.6
Portugal	Total	3.1	4.7	2.7	2.6	10.3
	Equity	2.2	3	0.9	1	7.6
	Reinvested earnings	1.1	1.3	1.6	3.6	1.8
	Other capital	-0.3	0.3	0.3	-1.9	1
Spain	Total	64.3	77	10.4	40.8	29.5
	Equity	37.4	44.9	7.7	31	28.3
	Reinvested earnings	10.3	2.2	3.3	6.2	5.8
	Other capital	16.6	29.9	-0.6	3.6	-4.6

Source: UNCTAD, based on data from the central bank in respective country.

Table II.3. FDI outflows from Greece, Italy, Portugal and Spain, by component, 2007–2011 (Billions of dollars)						
Country	FDI components	2007	2008	2009	2010	2011
Greece	Total	5.2	2.4	2.1	1	1.8
	Equity	4.7	2.5	1.9	0.9	1.5
	Reinvested earnings	0.5	0.4	0.6	0.2	0.2
	Other capital	0.1	-0.4	-0.4	-0.1	-
Italy	Total	96.2	67	21.3	32.7	47.2
	Equity	99.7	26.8	12.1	11.6	20.7
	Reinvested earnings	-16.1	15.2	14.7	9.4	5.8
	Other capital	12.7	25	-5.5	11.6	20.7
Portugal	Total	5.5	2.7	0.8	-7.5	12.6
	Equity	1.9	2.3	-0.8	-11.1	3.9
	Reinvested earnings	0.5	1	0.9	2.7	1.4
	Other capital	3.2	-0.5	0.7	0.9	7.4
Spain	Total	137.1	74.7	13.1	38.3	37.3
	Equity	111.9	63.8	6.5	24	22.7
	Reinvested earnings	18.7	4.5	6.6	8.1	7.9
	Other capital	6.5	6.4	0	6.3	6.7

Source: UNCTAD, based on data from the central bank in respective country.

in 2011 were 163 per cent and 103 per cent of the 2007 level in Italy and Spain respectively. In the case of Portugal, "other capital outflows" were more than twice the level of 2007, taking total outward FDI to a record high at $12.6 billion.

Prospects for 2012 and beyond. The recovery of FDI will be tested severely in 2012. Data from the first five months show a fall of 60 per cent in cross-border M&A sales and 76 per cent in cross-border M&A purchases.

On the positive side, the factors driving FDI highlighted above – accumulated profits, the outward strategy of Japanese TNCs and the mining boom – are likely to remain active for some years to come. The restructuring of the financial industry is also likely to continue, although its net impact on FDI flows may be negative. In addition, the launch of privatization programmes by European countries that have gone through sovereign debt crises could encourage FDI. Greece plans to raise $50 billion by 2015 through the sale of State-owned companies and real estate. Italy is set to sell properties and utilities owned by the central Government and local authorities. The privatization programme in Spain envisages the sale of airports and the national lottery. Given the weakness of their domestic economies,

cross-border investment is likely to play a major role in these countries' privatization programmes.

However, a number of factors could dampen the recovery of FDI. The eurozone crisis and the apparent weakness of most major economies will weigh heavily on investors' sentiment. The difficulties in the banking industry mean that despite the significant cash balances of large TNCs, they may have difficulty raising capital for any leverage component of investments. Further restructuring among TNCs, especially in the financial industry, may well involve divestment of overseas assets, reducing outward FDI from developed countries.

B. TRENDS IN STRUCTURALLY WEAK, VULNERABLE AND SMALL ECONOMIES

1. Least developed countries

Table A. Distribution of FDI flows among economies, by range,[a] 2011

Range	Inflows	Outflows
Above $1.0 billion	Mozambique, Zambia, Sudan, Chad, Democratic Republic of the Congo, Guinea, Bangladesh, United Republic of Tanzania, Niger	Angola, Zambia
$0.5 to $0.9 billion	Madagascar, Cambodia, Myanmar, Uganda, Equatorial Guinea, Liberia	..
$0.1 to $0.4 billion	Lao People's Democratic Republic, Senegal, Ethiopia, Haiti, Mali, Solomon Islands, Benin, Central African Republic, Rwanda, Somalia	Liberia
Below $0.1 billion	Nepal, Afghanistan, Djibouti, Malawi, Vanuatu, Togo, Lesotho, Sierra Leone, Mauritania, Gambia, Timor-Leste, Guinea-Bissau, Eritrea, São Tomé and Principe, Bhutan, Samoa, Burkina Faso, Comoros, Kiribati, Tuvalu, Burundi, Yemen, Angola	Democratic Republic of the Congo, Sudan, Yemen, Senegal, Niger, Cambodia, Togo, Bangladesh, Lao People's Democratic Republic, Guinea, Mauritania, Burkina Faso, Solomon Islands, Benin, Mali, Guinea-Bissau, Vanuatu, Kiribati, São Tomé and Principe, Samoa, Mozambique

[a] Economies are listed according to the magnitude of their FDI flows.

Figure A. FDI flows, top 5 host and home economies, 2010–2011
(Billions of dollars)

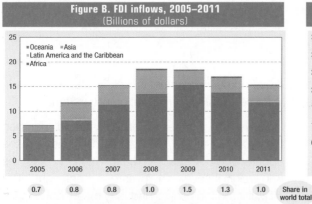

Figure B. FDI inflows, 2005–2011
(Billions of dollars)

Figure C. FDI outflows, 2005–2011
(Billions of dollars)

	2005	2006	2007	2008	2009	2010	2011	
Inflows	0.7	0.8	0.8	1.0	1.5	1.3	1.0	Share in world total
Outflows	0.1	0.0	0.1	0.2	0.1	0.2	0.2	

Table B. Cross-border M&As by industry, 2010–2011
(Millions of dollars)

Sector/industry	Sales		Purchases	
	2010	2011	2010	2011
Total	2 201	504	277	353
Primary	1 094	- 191	20	-
Mining, quarrying and petroleum	1 094	- 191	20	-
Manufacturing	94	624	1	-
Food, beverages and tobacco	65	632	-	-
Textiles, clothing and leather	10	-	-	-
Chemicals and chemical products	20	4	-	-
Metals and metal products	-	5	1	-
Services	1 013	70	257	353
Electricity, gas and water	110	-	-	-
Trade	-	6	-	-
Transport, storage and communications	903	50	-	-
Finance	-	14	257	353

Table C. Cross-border M&As by region/country, 2010–2011
(Millions of dollars)

Region/country	Sales		Purchases	
	2010	2011	2010	2011
World	2 201	504	277	353
Developed economies	1 655	436	20	-
European Union	786	180	1	-
United States	1 313	- 10	-	-
Japan	-	450	-	-
Other developed countries	- 445	- 183	20	-
Developing economies	511	68	257	353
Africa	252	- 14	257	353
East and South-East Asia	183	75	-	-
South Asia	356	4	-	-
West Asia	- 280	-	-	-
Latin America and the Caribbean		3	-	-
Transition economies	35	-	-	-

Table D. Greenfield FDI projects by industry, 2010–2011
(Millions of dollars)

Sector/industry	LDCs as destination		LDCs as investors	
	2010	2011	2010	2011
Total	39 714	33 304	732	923
Primary	11 871	11 796	-	-
Mining, quarrying and petroleum	11 871	11 796	-	-
Manufacturing	17 838	11 848	501	424
Food, beverages and tobacco	606	1 125	30	31
Coke, petroleum and nuclear fuel	10 525	5 197	466	393
Non-metallic mineral products	876	1 505	-	-
Metals and metal products	1 079	1 205	-	-
Services	10 006	9 660	231	499
Electricity, gas and water	3 430	4 499	-	-
Transport, storage and communications	1 549	1 908	11	-
Finance	1 824	1 478	207	426
Business services	1 297	929	7	26

Table E. Greenfield FDI projects by region/country, 2010–2011
(Millions of dollars)

Partner region/economy	LDCs as destination		LDCs as investors	
	2010	2011	2010	2011
World	39 714	33 304	732	923
Developed economies	20 910	16 729	98	122
European Union	14 615	9 367	98	33
United States	906	3 597	-	89
Japan	243	896	-	-
Other developed countries	5 146	2 869	-	-
Developing economies	16 305	15 859	635	802
Africa	7 059	3 703	141	572
East and South-East Asia	3 543	5 691	4	151
South Asia	2 729	4 219	9	70
West Asia	2 174	558	15	8
Latin America and the Caribbean	800	1 637	466	-
Transition economies	2 500	716	-	-

Further marginalization of LDCs[36] as a group. FDI inflows to LDCs remained small (figure B). With the continuous fall of FDI to Angola – by far the largest recipient country among 48 LDCs for a decade – 2011 inflows slid further, by 11 per cent, to $15 billion, the lowest level in five years (figure B). Even measured among the overall inflows to developing and transition economies, the share of inflows to LDCs has kept falling from 3.1 per cent in 2009, to 2.4 per cent in 2010 and to 1.9 per cent in 2011. These disappointing results reflected a 16 per cent decline in greenfield investments and a 77 per cent fall in cross-border M&A sales (tables B–E).

Although FDI inflows declined, the number of greenfield projects held steady. The bulk of investment in LDCs is in greenfield projects. Although the value of such projects dropped by 16 per cent, from $39.7 billion to $33.3 billion, the number of projects rose from 310 in 2010 to 338 in 2011. The total value of investments in LDCs depends largely on a few large-scale projects (table II.4). (These values exceed FDI flow data because they include total project values and different accounting methods.)

Greenfield investments in mining, quarrying and petroleum accounted for 35 per cent (table D). The overall share of manufacturing fell from 45 per cent to 36 per cent. In contrast, the increasing share of the services sector (from 25 per cent to 29 per cent) was supported by a 31 per cent rise in electric, gas and water and a 23 percent increase in transport, storage and communication.

Two large-scale greenfield projects in fossil fuel and electric power went to Mozambique and the United Republic of Tanzania. The largest project announced in 2011 (table II.4), a power plant to be built by Jindal, is the largest greenfield electricity investment for Mozambique since 2003.[37] If it materializes, this will be that company's second large-scale investment in the country, following the $1.6 billion project in manufacturing coal, oil and gas announced in 2008, for which Jindal received a 25-year mining concession. Two other TNCs – Vale (Brazil), which invested $1.2 billion in coal extraction in 2007 and $0.7 billion in electricity in 2009, and Riversdale (Australia), which invested $0.5 billion in coal extraction in 2008 – are also developing plans for coal-fired plants in the country.

The United Republic of Tanzania attracted a $0.8 billion investment in fossil fuel and electric power (table II.4), which accounted for more than 20 per cent of its total value of greenfield projects in 2011. This is the second electricity investment in the country, after the $0.7 billion investment by Globeleg (United States), recorded in 2004 (UNCTAD, 2011b: 215).

Alternative/renewable energy projects in the Lao People's Democratic Republic and Rwanda. Thai Biogas Energy in the Lao People's Democratic

Table II.4. The 10 largest greenfield projects in LDCs, 2011					
Host economy	Industry	Investing company	Home economy	Estimated investment ($ million)	Estimated jobs created
Mozambique	Fossil fuel electric power	Jindal Steel & Power	India	3 000	368
Uganda	Oil and gas extraction	Tullow Oil	United Kingdom	2 000	783
Mozambique	Natural, liquefied and compressed gas	Eni SpA	Italy	1 819	161
Mozambique	Natural, liquefied and compressed gas	Sasol Petroleum International	South Africa	1 819	161
Equatorial Guinea	Oil and gas extraction	Noble Energy	United States	1 600	626
Democratic Republic of the Congo	Copper, nickel, lead and zinc mining	Freeport McMoRan	United States	850	1 459
United Republic of Tanzania	Fossil fuel electric power	Castletown Enterprises	United Kingdom	799	118
Zambia	Copper, nickel, lead and zinc mining	Non-Ferrous China Africa (NFCA)	China	700	1 201
Democratic Republic of the Congo	Iron ore mining	Sundance Resources	Australia	620	1 063
Lao People's Democratic Republic	Biomass power	Thai Biogas Energy	Thailand	558	700

Source: UNCTAD, based on information from the Financial Times Ltd, fDi Markets (www.fDimarkets.com).

Republic was the 10th largest investment in 2011 among this group of countries (table II.4). The company, which is owned by Private Energy Market Fund (Finland) and Al Tayyar Energy (United Arab Emirates), creates biogas projects for heat and electricity generation, using wastewater discharged from agricultural industries. This project is supported by the Finnish Fund for Industrial Cooperation and the Energy and Environment Partnership Program, and is expected to generate employment for 700 factory workers and support 5,000 families in farming.[38] Before this investment, the Lao People's Democratic Republic had already reported six projects in alternative/renewable energy totalling $1.7 billion, of which $0.8 billion (for two electricity projects) came from Malaysia in 2007 and 2008 (UNCTAD, 2011b: 135).

On a smaller scale, Rwanda attracted $142 million in an alternative/renewable energy project from ContourGlobal (United States), which represented 18 per cent of Rwanda's total green-field investments in 2011. Part of this investment is financed by the Emerging Africa Infrastructure Fund, the Netherlands Development Finance Company, the African Development Bank and the Belgian Investment Company for Developing Countries.[39]

Developing and transition economies accounted for half of greenfield investments. About half of greenfield investments in LDCs came from developing (48 per cent) and transition economies (2 per cent) (table E). Although such sources are increasingly important, neither the share nor the value ($16.6 billion) of their 2011 investments quite recovered to the levels recorded in 2008–2009.

Among developing economies, India remained the largest investor in LDCs, contributing $4.2 billion in 39 projects, followed by China ($2.8 billion in 20 projects) and South Africa ($2.3 billion in 27 projects). Although the numbers of projects reported by these three countries are the highest since data collection started in 2003, in value terms more than 70 per cent of investment from India and more than 80 per cent from South Africa were directed to the two projects in Mozambique (table II.4).

2. Landlocked developing countries

Table A. Distribution of FDI flows among economies, by range,ª 2011

Range	Inflows	Outflows
Above $1 billion	Kazakhstan, Mongolia, Turkmenistan, Zambia, Chad, Azerbaijan, Uzbekistan, Niger	Kazakhstan, Zambia
$500 to $999 million	Plurinational State of Bolivia, Uganda, Kyrgyzstan, Botswana, Armenia	Azerbaijan
$100 to $499 million	Lao People's Democratic Republic, the former Yugoslav Republic of Macedonia, Zimbabwe, Paraguay, Republic of Moldova, Ethiopia, Mali, Central African Republic, Rwanda	..
$10 to $99 million	Nepal, Swaziland, Afghanistan, Malawi, Lesotho, Bhutan, Tajikistan	Mongolia, Armenia, Niger, Republic of Moldova, Zimbabwe
Below $10 million	Burkina Faso, Burundi	Lao People's Democratic Republic, Swaziland, Burkina Faso, Botswana, Mali, the former Yugoslav Republic of Macedonia, Kyrgyzstan

ª Economies are listed according to the magnitude of their FDI flows.

Figure A. FDI flows, top 5 host and home economies, 2010–2011
(Billions of dollars)

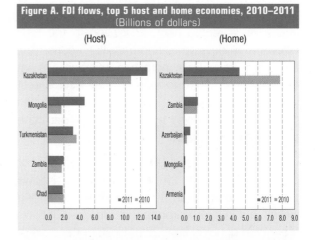

Figure B. FDI inflows, 2005–2011
(Billions of dollars)

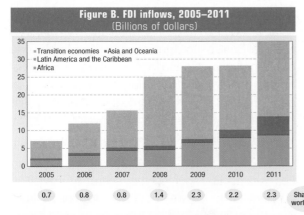

| 0.7 | 0.8 | 0.8 | 1.4 | 2.3 | 2.2 | 2.3 | Share in world total |

Figure C. FDI outflows, 2005–2011
(Billions of dollars)

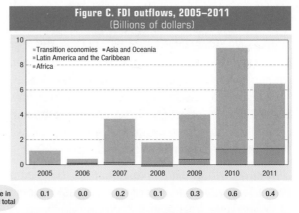

| 0.1 | 0.0 | 0.2 | 0.1 | 0.3 | 0.6 | 0.4 | |

Table B. Cross-border M&As by industry, 2010–2011
(Millions of dollars)

Sector/industry	Sales		Purchases	
	2010	2011	2010	2011
Total	621	716	1 727	8 083
Primary	45	357	123	7 921
Mining, quarrying and petroleum	45	312	123	7 921
Manufacturing	44	189	-	-
Food, beverages and tobacco	-	163	-	-
Textiles, clothing and leather	-	-	-	-
Chemicals and chemical products	42	10	-	-
Metals and metal products	-	33	-	-
Services	532	170	1 603	162
Trade	-	1	-	-
Transport, storage and communications	371	77	-	-
Finance	69	66	1 604	162
Health and social services	-	27	-	-

Table C. Cross-border M&As by region/country, 2010–2011
(Millions of dollars)

Region/country	Sales		Purchases	
	2010	2011	2010	2011
World	621	716	1 727	8 083
Developed economies	69	- 111	1 471	159
European Union	71	268	1 469	159
United States	- 17	- 4	-	-
Japan	- 3	-	-	-
Other developed countries	19	- 375	2	-
Developing economies	550	895	257	5
Africa	303	3	257	-
East and South-East Asia	166	783	-	-
South Asia	80	32	-	-
West Asia	-	77	-	5
Latin America and the Caribbean	-	-	-	-
Transition economies	-	- 69	- 1	7 919

Table D. Greenfield FDI projects by industry, 2010–2011
(Millions of dollars)

Sector/industry	LLDCs as destination		LLDCs as investors	
	2010	2011	2010	2011
Total	29 217	39 360	1 394	1 137
Primary	3 126	13 062	-	-
Mining, quarrying and petroleum	3 126	13 062	-	-
Manufacturing	18 575	18 692	551	192
Coke, petroleum and nuclear fuel	9 906	9 786	358	30
Rubber and plastic products	34	1 479	-	-
Non-metallic mineral products	293	1 661	-	-
Motor vehicles and other transport equipment	736	2 010	-	3
Services	7 517	7 606	842	945
Electricity, gas and water	1 311	1 315	-	100
Transport, storage and communications	1 893	2 248	198	5
Finance	1 208	1 424	329	366
Business services	1 358	2 004	-	39

Table E. Greenfield FDI projects by region/country, 2010–2011
(Millions of dollars)

Partner region/economy	LLDCs as destination		LLDCs as investors	
	2010	2011	2010	2011
World	29 217	39 360	1 394	1 137
Developed economies	15 387	15 745	366	231
European Union	11 836	11 873	359	221
United States	1 146	1 116	7	10
Japan	184	97	-	-
Other developed countries	2 221	2 661	-	-
Developing economies	11 962	16 136	227	205
Africa	5 664	2 638	198	143
East and South-East Asia	2 066	7 022	2	-
South Asia	1 301	5 367	4	31
West Asia	2 287	711	23	31
Latin America and the Caribbean	644	398	-	-
Transition economies	1 868	7 479	801	701

Inflows to landlocked developing countries (LLDCs) reached a record high. In 2011, FDI inflows to 31 LLDCs[40] grew by 24 per cent to $35 billion (figure B), a record high. In relation to the total inflows to all developing and transition economies, the share of LLDCs increased marginally (from 4.1 per cent in 2010 to 4.5 per cent). The largest recipient of inflows was again Kazakhstan (37 per cent), followed by Mongolia (14 per cent) and Turkmenistan (9 per cent) (figure A).

Inflows to 15 African LLDCs represented 21 per cent, compared with 25 per cent in 2010. Inflows to Kazakhstan rose by 20 per cent, led by strong investment in hydrocarbons.[41] In Mongolia, inflows more than doubled from 2010 to 2011 because of large-scale projects in extractive industries (section A.2), allowing this county to surpass Turkmenistan in FDI. Nevertheless, 12 of 31 LLDCs (39 per cent) recorded declines, of which 5 – Armenia, Bhutan, Burkina Faso, Mali and Turkmenistan – experienced falls for the second year in a row. For example, although Turkmenistan attracted $3.2 billion of FDI inflows (figure A), these inflows have followed a downward trajectory since 2009.

Strong growth in extractive industries, but some diversification in manufacturing. The vast majority of inward investments in this group continued to be in the form of greenfield investments, which increased by 35 per cent to $39 billion (table D). The value of greenfield investments in the primary sector grew four-fold over 2010, reaching the highest level in eight years. In the manufacturing sector, growth was strong in three industries: rubber and plastic products (from $34 million in 3 projects in 2010 to $1.5 billion in 6 projects), non-metallic mineral products (from $0.3 billion in 7 projects to $1.7 billion in 11 projects), and motor vehicles and other transport equipment (from $0.7 billion in 8 projects to $2.0 billion in 22 projects).

The recipients of the largest investments were Kazakhstan ($8.0 billion, compared with $2.5 billion in 2010), and Uzbekistan ($7.6 billion, compared with $2.4 billion in 2010), reflecting the destinations of large-scale projects (table II.5). The receipts of these two countries represent 40 per cent of all greenfield investments in LLDCs, greater than the share of combined greenfield investments in the 15 African LLDCs (38 per cent).

Investments in the extractive industry accounted for almost 80 per cent of greenfield investments in Uzbekistan. Following the previous $1.3 billion investment from the United Arab Emirates in chemicals (*WIR11*: 81), in 2011 the country attracted another large-scale investment in the manufacturing sector (table II.3). Indorama (Singapore), a petrochemicals group, announced a joint-venture project with the Uzbek national gas company, Uzbekneftegaz, and the Uzbekistan Fund for Reconstruction and Development to build a polyethylene production plant under a government programme to enhance and develop polymers production.[42]

Indorama also has a stake in Uzbekistan's textile industry. The Kokand Textile joint venture, established in 2010 by Indorama and the country's National Bank of Foreign Economic Activity,[43] is one of 100 projects intended to triple the export potential of the textile industry; Indorama announced an additional $54 million investment in 2011. A similar investment in textiles ($60 million) was reported by Textile Technologies Group (Republic of Korea).

More investments from Asia and the Russian Federation. By source, the share of transition economies in inflows to LLDCs increased from 6 per cent in 2010 to 19 per cent in 2011 (table E). This was due to the $7.2 billion in investments (27 projects) from the Russian Federation, in which the $5 billion investment in Uzbekistan (table II.5) accounted for 70 per cent.

Greenfield investments from developing economies reached the highest level in three years, but their share in the total greenfield investments in LLDCs remained the same as in 2010 (41 per cent). Investments from South, East and South-East Asia jumped substantially, from $3.4 billion in 2010 to $12.4 billion in 2011. India was the largest investor among developing economies ($4.9 billion in 27 projects – record highs in both value and number – compared with $1.2 billion in 21 projects in 2010), followed by China ($2.9 billion in 14 projects), Singapore ($1.3 billion in 3 projects) and the Republic of Korea ($1.3 billion in 8 projects).

The high level of investments from India, however, was mostly attributed to the single project in Zimbabwe (table II.5), which accounted for more

Table II.5. The 10 largest greenfield projects in LLDCs, 2011					
Host economy	Industry	Investing company	Home economy	Estimated investment ($ million)	Estimated jobs created
Uzbekistan	Natural, liquefied and compressed gas	LUKOIL	Russian Federation	5 000	3 000
Zimbabwe	Iron ore mining	Essar Group	India	4 000	3 000
Kazakhstan	Iron ore mining	Eurasian Natural Resources Corporation (ENRC)	United Kingdom	2 100	3 000
Uganda	Oil and gas extraction	Tullow Oil	United Kingdom	2 000	783
Uzbekistan	Urethane, foam products and other compounds	Indorama	Singapore	1 190	3 000
Kazakhstan	Basic chemicals	Nitol Group	United Kingdom	1 000	1 200
Turkmenistan	Natural, liquefied and compressed gas	Thermo Design Engineering	Canada	923	356
Kazakhstan	Other petroleum and coal products	Tethys Petroleum	United Kingdom	923	356
Turkmenistan	Natural, liquefied and compressed gas	China National Petroleum Corp (CNPC)	China	923	356
Zambia	Copper, nickel, lead and zinc mining	Non-Ferrous China Africa (NFCA)	China	700	1 201

Source: UNCTAD, based on information from the Financial Times Ltd, fDi Markets (www.fDimarkets.com).

than 80 per cent of the $4.9 billion. Similarly, the two projects from China in table II.5 represented 56 per cent of its greenfield investments in LLDCs, and the Indorama project in Uzbekistan (table II.5) accounted for 89 per cent of Singapore's greenfield investments in LLDCs.

In Africa, Zimbabwe attracted the largest greenfield investment. The $4 billion investment from the Essar Group (India) (table II.5) contributed the bulk of the rise in Zimbabwe's greenfield investments from $0.8 billion in 2010 to $5.8 billion in 2011, making this country the largest recipient among African LLDCs. The Essar Group expected to implement this investment for the construction of a steel plant to process domestic iron ore through two newly established joint ventures with the Government.[44] Their establishment concluded the transaction process that began in August 2010 for the revival of the operational assets of the Zimbabwe Iron and Steel Company.[45] Although the amount thus far committed by Essar Africa Holdings was reported at $750 million, the country counts on additional investments in related infrastructure to ensure sustainable operations at one of the joint ventures.

3. Small island developing States

Table A. Distribution of FDI flows among economies, by range,[a] 2011

Range	Inflows	Outflows
Above $1 billion	Bahamas	..
$500 to $999 million	Trinidad and Tobago	Bahamas
$100 to $499 million	Barbados, Maldives, Mauritius, Jamaica, Fiji, Solomon Islands, Seychelles, Saint Kitts and Nevis, Saint Vincent and the Grenadines	..
$50 to $99 million	Cape Verde, Saint Lucia, Antigua and Barbuda, Vanuatu	Mauritius, Jamaica
$1 to $49 million	Grenada, Dominica, Timor-Leste, São Tomé and Principe, Samoa, Tonga, Federated States of Micronesia, Marshall Islands, Comoros, Kiribati, Palau, Tuvalu	Seychelles, Solomon Islands
Below $1 million	Nauru, Papua New Guinea	Vanuatu, Papua New Guinea, Tonga, Kiribati, São Tomé and Principe, Cape Verde, Samoa, Fiji, Barbados

[a] Economies are listed according to the magnitude of their FDI flows.

Figure A. FDI flows, top 5 host and home economies, 2010–2011
(Billions of dollars)

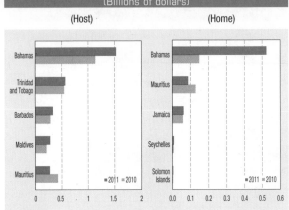

Figure B. FDI inflows, 2005–2011
(Billions of dollars)

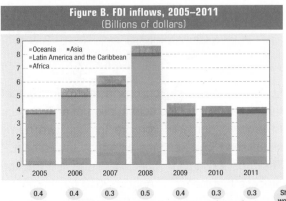

Table B. Cross-border M&As by industry, 2010–2011
(Millions of dollars)

Sector/industry	Sales		Purchases	
	2010	2011	2010	2011
Total	**9 650**	**1 223**	**60**	**- 210**
Primary	**9 037**	**938**	**- 11**	**- 17**
Mining, quarrying and petroleum	9 037	929	- 11	- 17
Manufacturing	**-**	**19**	**-**	**525**
Food, beverages and tobacco	-	19	-	-
Non-metallic mineral products	-	-	-	- 78
Metals and metal products	-	-	-	603
Services	**614**	**266**	**70**	**- 718**
Electricity, gas and water	82	-	-	-
Trade	-	-	-	-
Transport, storage and communications	-	210	- 3	-
Business services	1	56	3	-

Table C. Cross-border M&As by region/country, 2010–2011
(Millions of dollars)

Region/country	Sales		Purchases	
	2010	2011	2010	2011
World	**9 650**	**1 223**	**60**	**- 210**
Developed economies	**8 953**	**- 992**	**113**	**193**
European Union	28	216	18	-
United States	- 175	- 1 048	100	193
Japan	-	- 288	1	-
Other developed countries	9 100	128	- 5	-
Developing economies	**698**	**2 215**	**- 53**	**158**
Africa	-	-	- 88	62
East and South-East Asia	440	2 215	5	- 78
South Asia	163	-	35	209
West Asia	-	-	-	-
Latin America and the Caribbean	94	-	- 5	- 35
Transition economies	**-**	**-**	**-**	**- 561**

Table D. Greenfield FDI projects by industry, 2010–2011
(Millions of dollars)

Sector/industry	SIDS as destination		SIDS as investors	
	2010	2011	2010	2011
Total	**5 957**	**7 429**	**2 698**	**3 591**
Primary	**1 260**	**3 000**	**-**	**-**
Mining, quarrying and petroleum	1 260	3 000	-	-
Manufacturing	**1 982**	**160**	**1 612**	**78**
Food, beverages and tobacco	21	138	3	15
Textiles, clothing and leather	14	22	-	-
Coke, petroleum and nuclear fuel	1 904	-	1 550	-
Metals and metal products	20	-	35	-
Services	**2 716**	**4 270**	**1 086**	**3 514**
Construction	1 254	1 966	-	-
Transport, storage and communications	2	1 057	13	-
Finance	180	277	79	180
Business services	23	618	188	1 891

Table E. Greenfield FDI projects by region/country, 2010–2011
(Millions of dollars)

Partner region/economy	SIDS as destination		SIDS as investors	
	2010	2011	2010	2011
World	**5 957**	**7 429**	**2 698**	**3 591**
Developed economies	**3 002**	**1 884**	**16**	**42**
European Union	1 054	1 156	-	15
United States	401	564	-	20
Japan	-	-	-	-
Other developed countries	1 547	164	16	7
Developing economies	**2 955**	**5 545**	**2 682**	**3 549**
Africa	52	4 223	2 592	3 287
East and South-East Asia	1 872	214	63	18
South Asia	553	810	-	-
West Asia	453	74	-	-
Latin America and the Caribbean	18	92	19	110
Transition economies	**-**	**-**	**-**	**-**

Inflows fell for the third year in a row and dipped to their lowest level in six years. Compared with 2010, FDI inflows to SIDS[46] fell by 2 per cent in 2011. Although FDI has been a major contributor to capital formation in SIDS (23 per cent in 2011), this group's position in global FDI remained miniscule (figure B). The marginal share of its inflows in relation to those to developing and transition economies also dropped, from 0.6 per cent in 2010 to 0.5 per cent in 2011. The distribution of FDI remains highly skewed, with two economies (the Bahamas and Trinidad and Tobago) (figure A) receiving 51 per cent of the total.

Greenfield investments to SIDS more important than M&As. Unlike in LDCs and LLDCs, the dominance of greenfield investments over cross-border M&As in value has not always been evident in SIDS. Depending on small numbers of larger investments, the relative importance of M&As and greenfield investments shifts from one year to another. In 2011, in the absence of megadeals in mining, quarrying and petroleum, the total values of cross-border M&A sales in SIDS dropped significantly (tables B and C). The total net sales value of $1.2 billion is much smaller than the gross sum of the transaction values recorded by the six largest deals in table II.6 (i.e. $4.4 billion).[47]

In contrast, total greenfield investments in SIDS increased by 25 per cent and reached a record high of $7.4 billion (tables D and E). The largest project recorded for the year in Papua New Guinea (table II.7) represented 40 per cent of all greenfield

investments in SIDS, and three construction projects in Mauritius and the Maldives, amounting to almost $2 billion, accounted for 30 per cent of such investments. Furthermore, transport, storage and communications attracted record high greenfield investments ($1.1 billion in 8 projects) (table D), which accounted for 14 per cent of such investments.

China was the most active in M&A sales, while South Africa was the largest source of greenfield investments in SIDS. Unlike in many regions and other groups of economies, the increasing importance of investments from the South had not been a clear trend in SIDS until 2011. Total sales to developed economies were negative, while developing economies accounted for inflows of $2.2 billion (table C), of which more than $1.9 billion was generated by M&A sales to China in three deals. In addition to the two deals presented in table II.6, China spent $9 million to purchase sugarcane plantations in Jamaica.

In greenfield investments in SIDS, the share of developing economies advanced from 50 per cent in 2010 to 75 per cent in 2011 (table E). Investments from South Africa jumped from less than $0.1 billion in 2010 to $4.2 billion. The $3 billion investment from Harmony Gold Mining (South Africa) (table II.7) contributed to a 57 per cent growth in greenfield investments in Papua New Guinea. Among other investors from developing economies, India continued to hold the key position by investing $0.8 billion in five projects in Jamaica and Maldives.

Table II.6. Selected largest M&A sales in SIDS, 2011

Target country	Industry of target company	Acquiring company	Home economy	Value ($ million)	Shares acquired (%)	Ultimate target country
Bahamas	Special warehousing and storage	Buckeye Partners LP	United States	1 641	80	United States
Barbados	Deep sea transportation of freight	Investor Group	China	1 048	100	United States
Trinidad and Tobago	Natural gas liquids	China Investment Corp	China	850	10	Trinidad and Tobago
Bahamas	Special warehousing and storage	Buckeye Partners LP	United States	340	20	United States
Jamaica	Electric services	Korea East-West Power Co Ltd	Korea, Republic of	288	40	Japan
Bahamas	Radiotelephone communications	Cable & Wireless Communications Plc	United Kingdom	210	51	Bahamas

Source: UNCTAD, cross-border M&A database.

Table II.7. The 10 largest greenfield projects in SIDS, 2011					
Host economy	Industry	Investing company	Home economy	Estimated investment ($ million)	Estimated jobs created
Papua New Guinea	Gold ore and silver ore mining	Harmony Gold Mining Co Ltd	South Africa	3 000	3 000
Mauritius	Commercial and institutional building construction	Atterbury Property Developments	South Africa	1 223	1 102
Mauritius	Computer facilities management services	Cybernet Software Systems	United States	500	3 000
Maldives	Residential building construction	Tata Housing	India	372	2 297
Maldives	Residential building construction	Tata Housing	India	372	2 297
Jamaica	Wireless telecommunication carriers	LIME	United Kingdom	282	97
Bahamas	Wireless telecommunication carriers	Bahamas Telecommunications Company	United Kingdom	282	97
Barbados	Wireless telecommunication carriers	LIME	United Kingdom	282	97
Maldives	Accommodation	Six Senses	Thailand	206	232
Jamaica	Water transportation	CMA CGM	France	100	1 000

Source: UNCTAD, based on information from the Financial Times Ltd, fDi Markets (www.fDimarkets.com).
Note: According to the data source, Tata Housing had two identical projects in Maldives.

A series of large-scale investments announced in Papua New Guinea. Thanks to the recent investment boom in metals and LNG, during 2008–2011 Papua New Guinea attracted 11 greenfield projects, including related education and training, and business services, with reported investment values exceeding $9 billion. Among them, the Exxon-led LNG project has been reported as the largest public-private partnership in the country.[48] Despite this activity, FDI inflows to Papua New Guinea fell from the peak of $0.4 billion in 2009 to $29 million in 2010 and, owing to the equity purchase by the Government from a Canadian mining TNC, became -$0.3 billion in 2011.

For many SIDS, attracting more or larger-scale investments does not guarantee more positive development outcomes. In Papua New Guinea, for example, efforts are under way to ensure that revenue flows expected from the recent investment boom will materialize and be used effectively to achieve development goals. In addition to the LNG projects, the prospects of large-scale investments in metals remain high, because of newfound gold, silver and other mineral deposits. These investments lead to increasing concerns about the environmental impacts of mining and to domestic pressures, calling for legislative reforms to increase

State control over mining projects and tax revenues from foreign investments.[49] A Government initiative, reported in the first quarter of 2012, to set up a sovereign wealth fund to ensure that LNG project revenues will be used for infrastructure development and education, is an important step towards making better use of FDI for development.[50]

Notes

1. In the United Nations' terminology, sub-Saharan Africa refers to the countries of East, West, Southern and Central Africa plus the Sudan and South Sudan in North Africa.

2. For instance, Oclaro (United States) announced in March 2012 that it would relocate its production and testing businesses in Shenzhen, China, to Malaysia within the next three years.

3. JETRO, based on Ben Bland, "Japanese companies make big move into Vietnam", *Financial Times*, 9 February 2012.

4. For instance, Master Lock and Whirlpool (both United States) have relocated part of their production from Asia to the United States, though the scale of the relocation is small.

5. For instance, Ford (United States) is to build five new assembly plants in China, with a total investment of $5 billion.

6. During the visit of Vice President Xi Jinping to the United States in February 2012, China announced the opening of the automotive insurance market to investors from the United States.

7. For instance, Citigroup (United States) expects to double the number of its branches in China to 100 by 2014 or 2015. The bank has bought stakes in a number of Chinese financial institutions, such as Shanghai Pudong Development Bank. In early 2012, Citigroup was granted a licence for credit card business, the first time a foreign bank has obtained such a licence in China.

8 See "Outlook hazy for MENA project financing", *Middle East Economic Survey*, LIV(52), 26 December 2011.

9 Citigroup, MENA Construction Projects Tracker, November 2011, cited in press articles. See, for example, *Construction Week Online*, "$133bn worth of KSA projects on hold", 2 April 2012, www.constructionweekonline.com/article-16262-133bn-worth-of-ksa-projects-on-hold--report. Examples in Dubai include up to 500 property projects that were to be cancelled and about 90,000 units under review, according to the Real Estate Regulatory Agency. There has also been a slowdown in Abu Dhabi's construction market, as companies cut jobs and postpone projects. Delays have occurred on beachfront apartments, the first office building that will make more energy than it uses and branches of the Louvre and Guggenheim museums.

10 BBVA (Spain) acquired 24.89 per cent of Turkiye Garanti Bankasi for $5.9 billion, and Vallares (United Kingdom) acquired Genel Enerji for $2.1 billion.

11 "Turkey's policies to draw foreign investments to the country are shifting towards a more sector-specific approach", 13 January 2012. www.balkans.com.

12 UNCTAD FDI/TNC database.

13 UNCTAD estimations based on central banks' data.

14 The rate of return is the ratio of income from FDI to the average inward FDI stock (average of the inward FDI stock at the ends of the year and the previous year).

15 Based on data from the respective central banks in Argentina and Chile. See: www.bcra.gov.ar/pdfs/estadistica/Anexo%20 Estadístico%20IED%2020101231.xls, and www.bcentral.cl/ estadisticas-economicas/series-indicadores/xls/IED_sector_ pais.xls.

16 The Central Bank of Brazil does not collect data on reinvested earnings.

17 See Economist Intelligence Unit, "Mexico components; second thought", 13 March 2012, and *Investment Properties Mexico*, "Mexico's automotive industry receives billions in foreign investment dollars", 18 April 2012.

18 Santander, Press Release, "Santander vende su negocio en Colombia al grupo chileno CorpBanca por 1.225 millones de dólares", 6 December 2011; and *El País*, "El Santander vende el 7,8 per cent de su filial chilena por 710 millones de euros", 8 December 2011.

19 See Economist Intelligence Unit, "Latin America finance: Banco Santander retreats", 7 December 2011.

20 Although some governments maintained certain sectoral policies, in particular for the automotive industry.

21 In 2003 Brazil announced its Guidelines for an Industrial, Technology and Foreign Trade Policy, then in 2008 launched its Productive Development Policy: Innovate and Invest to Sustain Growth. In 2001, Argentina selected nine sectors to support. In 2002, Mexico launched its Economic Policy for Competitiveness, which defined 12 branches to be promoted through sectoral programmes.

22 Other countries focused on the extractive industry, taking a more regulatory approach in order to benefit from soaring global commodity prices and to foster State control over natural resources (see chapter III). Among the latter, some choose to exclusively increase – to different degrees – taxes and royalties in extractive industries (such as Chile, Colombia, Guatemala, Honduras and Peru), others have chosen the paths of contract renegotiations (such as Ecuador and the Bolivarian Republic of Venezuela) and nationalization (such as the Plurinational State of Bolivia, Ecuador and the Bolivarian Republic of Venezuela), extending nationalization in some cases to other sectors of the economy (Bolivarian Republic of Venezuela).

23 In Brazil, the appreciation was taking place in both nominal and real terms, whereas in Argentina, there has been a depreciation

in nominal terms but an appreciation in real terms, owing to a higher level of inflation.

24 In Argentina, the law increasing this margin (law 25.551) has been adopted by the Senate but not yet approved by the Parliament.

25 In other requirements, the automotive manufacturing company must invest at least 0.5 per cent of its gross revenues in innovation and research and development activities within Brazil and must carry out at least 6 of 11 activities in Brazil for at least 80 per cent of its production. This new tax regime is valid for one year, up to December 2012.

26 See *Other News*, "South American Trade Group Raises Import Tariffs", 21 December 2011, www.other-news.info.

27 *Financial Times*, "Peugeot Citroën plans drive on Brazil", 27 October 2011; Economist Intelligence Unit, "China has become Brazil's biggest economic partner – and its most difficult one", 16 January 2012, and "Brazil industry: Cars at any cost", 26 October 2011, www.eiu.com.

28 Brazil's Interministerial Ordinance No. 34 provides benefits for a reduction in, or elimination of, taxes relating to production of touch-screen devices that do not have a physical keyboard and weigh less than 750 grams. See *AppleInsider*, "Foxconn to build 5 new Brazilian factories to help make Apple products", 31 January 2012, www.appleinsider.com.

29 Volkswagen announced investments of $138 million to boost production of gearboxes for export, while Renault and PSA Peugeot Citroën agreed to boost exports and use more locally made auto parts to reduce their imports. Agriculture machinery makers also announced investment plans: Deere & Co. (United States) said it will start making tractors, combines and parts in Argentina; Fiat (Italy) said it will invest $100 million in a factory to make combines and tractors; and AGCO (United States) has agreed to invest $140 million in a new factory that will produce tractors and motors. (See *Farm Equipment*, "AGCO to Invest $140 Million in New Argentina Factory", 21 October 2011, www. farm-equipment.com; Bloomberg, "Porsche Sells Malbec to Keep Autos Coming into Argentina: Cars", 3 November 2011, www.bloomberg.com).

30 Ministry of Economy and Public Finance, Argentina.

31 Georgia ceased to be member of the CIS in 2009.

32 Examples of large transactions include the €835 million acquisition of a 43 per cent stake in the Russian retail hypermarket chain OOO Lenta by the buyout group TPG Capital (United States), and the €604 million that Unilever (United Kingdom) spent on the Russian cosmetics manufacturer Concern Kalina.

33 Bosnia and Herzegovina, Croatia, Serbia and Ukraine.

34 The Czech Republic, Hungary, Slovakia and Slovenia.

35 The primary objective of this measure was to contain the rapid appreciation of the yen.

36 Afghanistan, Angola, Bangladesh, Benin, Bhutan, Burkina Faso, Burundi, Cambodia, the Central African Republic, Chad, the Comoros, the Democratic Republic of the Congo, Djibouti, Equatorial Guinea, Eritrea, Ethiopia, the Gambia, Guinea, Guinea-Bissau, Haiti, Kiribati, the Lao People's Democratic Republic, Lesotho, Liberia, Madagascar, Malawi, Maldives, Mali, Mauritania, Mozambique, Myanmar, Nepal, the Niger, Rwanda, Samoa, São Tomé and Principe, Senegal, Sierra Leone, the Solomon Islands, Somalia, the Sudan, Timor-Leste, Togo, Tuvalu, Uganda, the United Republic of Tanzania, Vanuatu, Yemen and Zambia.

37 See the table on p. 162 in UNCTAD (2011b).

38 Thai Biogas, Press Release, "DPS-TBEC Contract Signing Ceremony on May 26, 2011, Lao PDR". Available at: www.tbec. co.th/e_news15.htm (accessed 16 May 2012).

39 "Rwanda: Contourglobal Wins Award for Kivuwatt Project", 17 February 2012. Available at: www.allAfrica.com.

[40] The countries in this group are Afghanistan, Armenia, Azerbaijan, Bhutan, the Plurinational State of Bolivia, Botswana, Burkina Faso, Burundi, the Central African Republic, Chad, Ethiopia, Kazakhstan, Kyrgyzstan, the Lao People's Democratic Republic, Lesotho, the former Yugoslav Republic of Macedonia, Malawi, Mali, the Republic of Moldova, Mongolia, Nepal, the Niger, Paraguay, Rwanda, Swaziland, Tajikistan, Turkmenistan, Uganda, Uzbekistan, Zambia and Zimbabwe. Sixteen LLDCs are LDCs, and nine are economies in transition.

[41] "Country Report: Kazakhstan", April 2012. Available at: www.eiu.com.

[42] "US$1.2 bln upgrade of a PE gas-chemical complex in Uzbekistan", 2 February 2011. Available at: www.plastemart.com; "Singapore's Indorama signs Uzbek polyethylene deal", 10 February 2011. Available at: www.PRW.com.

[43] "Indorama launches $30 million textile mill in Kokand", 27 November 2011. Available at: www.timesca.com.

[44] "Govt of Zimbabwe confirms agreement with Essar for revival of Zisco", 16 December 2011. Available at: www.essar.com.

[45] "Government of Zimbabwe and Essar Africa Holdings announce new steel and mining entity", 3 August 2011. Available at: www.essar.com.

[46] Twenty-nine countries (of which eight are LDCs) are included in this group: Antigua and Barbuda, the Bahamas, Barbados, Cape Verde, the Comoros, Dominica, Fiji, Grenada, Jamaica, Kiribati, Maldives, the Marshall Islands, Mauritius, the Federated States of Micronesia, Nauru, Palau, Papua New Guinea, Saint Kitts and Nevis, Saint Lucia, Saint Vincent and the Grenadines, Samoa, São Tomé and Principe, Seychelles, the Solomon Islands, Timor-Leste, Tonga, Trinidad and Tobago, Tuvalu and Vanuatu.

[47] The ownership of targeted companies in SIDS often rests outside SIDS, as explained in chapter I (see box I.1). Consequently, reported M&A deals in SIDS often reflect a change in ownership of existing foreign assets in SIDS from one foreign investor to another. Among the six deals in table II.6, four worth $3.3 billion are linked to the United States and Japan as the home economies of targeted companies. The two deals by the United States in the Bahamas involved the same targeted company, Vopak Terminal Bahamas, and the same acquiring company, Buckeye Partners LP. The ultimate ownership of the 100 per cent interest of Vopak Terminal Bahamas belonged to First Reserve Corp. (United States). The second largest deal, by China, was the acquisition of the assets of a Barbados affiliate of GE (United States). Thus, the inflow to Barbados in relation to this transaction was most likely not recorded at all. A similar explanation applies to the fifth deal, by the Republic of Korea, in which KEPCO acquired a 40 per cent interest in Jamaica Public Service Co. Ltd. from Marubeni Corp. (Japan).

[48] A joint-venture project between ExxonMobil, including Esso Highlands as operator (33.2 per cent), Oil Search Limited (29 per cent), the Government of Papua New Guinea (16.6 per cent), Santos Limited (13.5 per cent), JX Nippon Oil Exploration (4.7 per cent), Papua New Guinea landowners (2.8 per cent) and Petromin PNG Holdings Limited (0.2 per cent) (www.pnglng.com).

[49] Based on personal communication with the Lead Media and Communications Adviser of Esso Highlands, 31 May 2012, in reference to ExxonMobil's "Financial and Operating Review 2011", p. 41, www.exxonmobil.com.

[50] "Papua New Guinea. Brighter metals prospects", 8 May 2012. Available at: www.oxfordbusinessgroup.com/economic_updates; Economist Intelligence Unit, "Country Report: Papua New Guinea", April 2012. Available at: www.eiu.com.

RECENT POLICY DEVELOPMENTS

CHAPTER III

Many countries continued to liberalize and promote foreign investment in various industries to stimulate growth in 2011. At the same time, new regulatory and restrictive measures continued to be introduced, partly for industrial policy reasons. They became manifest primarily in the adjustment of entry policies for foreign investors (e.g. in agriculture and pharmaceuticals), in extractive industries (e.g. through nationalization and divestment requirements) and in a more critical approach towards outward FDI.

International investment policymaking is in flux. The annual number of new bilateral investment treaties (BITs) continues to decline, while regional investment policymaking is intensifying. Sustainable development is gaining prominence in international investment policymaking. Numerous ideas for reform of the investor–State dispute settlement (ISDS) system have emerged, but few have been put into action.

Suppliers need support for CSR compliance. Corporate social responsibility (CSR) codes of transnational corporations (TNCs) often pose challenges for suppliers in developing countries (particularly small and medium-sized enterprises (SMEs)). They have to comply with and report under multiple, fragmented standards. Policymakers can alleviate these challenges and create new opportunities for suppliers by incorporating CSR into enterprise development and capacity-building programmes. TNCs can also harmonize standards and reporting requirements at the industry level.

A. NATIONAL POLICY DEVELOPMENTS

Key features of investment policies included continuous liberalization and promotion, the adjustment of entry policies with regard to FDI, more state influence in extractive industries and a more critical approach towards outward FDI.

In 2011, at least 44 countries and economies adopted 67 policy measures affecting foreign investment (table III.1). Of these measures, 52 related to investment liberalization, promotion and facilitation, while 15 introduced new restrictions or regulations for foreign investors.

The percentage of more restrictive policy measures decreased significantly, from approximately 32 per cent in 2010 to 22 per cent in 2011. However, it would be premature to interpret this decrease as an indication of a reversal of the trend towards a more stringent policy environment for investment observed in previous years (figure III.1). The share of measures introducing new restrictions or regulations was roughly equal for both developing and transition economies, on the one hand, and for developed countries, on the other hand. To extract these figures, UNCTAD applied a revised methodology (see box III.1).

Of the 67 measures adopted, almost half (29) were directed specifically at foreign investment. These measures offered special incentives to foreign investors, reduced existing discrimination or introduced new restrictions on foreign investors. In total, 21 more favourable measures for foreign investors and 8 less favourable ones were reported. Of the more favourable policy measures, just over half (11) related to FDI liberalization, another 6 to promotion and facilitation activities, and 4 to the operational conditions of FDI. The less favourable

policy changes related in particular to new restrictions on the entry and establishment of foreign investment (6 measures). Finally, four measures were directed at outward investment, with two aiming at promoting investment and two having a restrictive or discouraging nature.

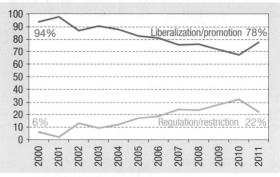

Figure III.1. National regulatory changes, 2000–2011
(Per cent)

Source: UNCTAD, Investment Policy Monitor database.

The overall policy trend towards continuous liberalization and promotion of investment often targeted specific industries (table III.2). Extractive industries were again the main exception, inasmuch as most policy measures related to them were less favourable, although the effect was less pronounced than in previous years (see section A.2). Agriculture and financial industries also had relatively high shares of less favourable measures. In agriculture, new entry restrictions were introduced. For financial industries, these measures included two restrictions affecting ownership and control of foreign investors, one in banking and one in insurance, and a measure restricting access to local finance for foreign-funded investment firms.

Table III.1. National regulatory changes, 2000–2011
(Number of measures)

Item	2000	2001	2002	2003	2004	2005	2006	2007	2008	2009	2010	2011
Number of countries that introduced changes	45	51	43	59	80	77	74	49	41	45	57	44
Number of regulatory changes	81	97	94	126	166	145	132	80	69	89	112	67
Liberalization/promotion	75	85	79	114	144	119	107	59	51	61	75	52
Regulation/restriction	5	2	12	12	20	25	25	19	16	24	36	15
Neutral/indeterminate	1	10	3	0	2	1	0	2	2	4	1	0

Source: UNCTAD, Investment Policy Monitor database.

Box III.1. Investment Policy Monitor database: revised methodology

UNCTAD has been collecting information on changes in national FDI policies on an annual basis since 1992. This collection has provided input to the analysis of global and regional investment policy trends in this *Report*, the quarterly *Investment Policy Monitor* (since 2009) and the *UNCTAD-OECD Reports on G-20 Investment Measures*.

Policy measures are collected in the Investment Policy Monitor (IPM) database. The measures are identified through a systematic review of government and business intelligence sources and verified, to the fullest extent possible, by referencing government sources.

In 2011, to further improve the quality of reporting, UNCTAD revised the methodology to monitor investment policy measures. The new approach allows a more detailed and focused analysis of policy changes by introducing three distinct categories of measures:

1. FDI-specific measures: measures which apply only to foreign investors, such as entry conditions or ownership restrictions for foreign investors, FDI screening procedures and investment incentives reserved to foreign investors.

2. General investment measures: measures which apply to both domestic and foreign investors, such as private ownership restrictions, licensing procedures for new businesses, privatization schemes and general investment incentives.

3. General business climate measures: measures which indirectly affect investors in general, such as corporate taxation changes, labour and environmental regulations, competition policies and intellectual property laws.

FDI-specific and general investment measures are divided into three types, on the basis of the policy area they address: entry and establishment, treatment and operation, and promotion and facilitation.

The count of national investment policy measures is limited to FDI-specific measures and general investment measures; in the past, relevant measures related to the general business climate were also included.[a] However, UNCTAD's analysis will continue to present main changes in the business climate when they provide relevant insights into investment-related policy developments.

Furthermore, the database registers whether the expected impact of a measure is likely to be more favourable or less favourable to investors. More favourable measures are measures that are directly or indirectly geared towards creating a more attractive environment for foreign investment, for instance, through liberalization or the provision of incentives. Less favourable measures are measures that have the opposite effect. They include, for instance, the introduction of new entry restrictions, discriminatory treatment and limitations on the repatriation of profits.

Source: UNCTAD.

[a] As a result of the exclusion of policy measures related to the general business climate, the number of annual investment policy measures reported in 2011 is significantly reduced from the number reported in previous *WIRs*. To maintain the tradition of presenting investment policy developments over an extended period of time and to allow comparisons between developments in different years, UNCTAD has recalculated the number of policy measures adopted over the last 10 years (table III.1).

Table III.2. National regulatory changes in 2011, by industry

Industry	Total number of measures	More favourable (%)	Less favourable (%)
Total	**71**	**78**	**22**
No specific industry	36	89	11
Agribusiness	2	50	50
Extractive industries	7	43	57
Manufacturing	7	71	29
Electricity, gas and water	2	100	0
Transport, storage and communications	7	86	14
Financial services	6	50	50
Other services	4	100	0

Source: UNCTAD, Investment Policy Monitor database.
Note: Overall total differs from that in table III.1 because some changes relate to more than one industry.

1. Investment liberalization and promotion remained high on the policy agenda

In 2011, at least eight countries undertook measures to open industries for FDI. Targeted industries included agriculture, media services and finance. By far the highest concentration of measures liberalizing entry and establishment conditions for foreign investors occurred in Asia (see box III.2). Several countries pursued privatization policies, particularly in airport and telecommunications services.

Countries worldwide continued to liberalize and promote foreign investment in various industries to foster economic growth and development.

Box III.2. Examples of investment liberalization measures in 2011–2012

Brazil adopted a law lifting the 49 per cent cap on foreign ownership of cable operators. The law also entitles telecom operators to offer combined packages including voice, broadband and television services.[a]

Canada increased the threshold for review for investors from WTO member countries from $312 million in 2011 to $330 million for 2012.[b]

India allowed full foreign ownership in parts of the agriculture sector, namely in the development and production of seeds and planting material, animal husbandry, pisciculture, aquaculture under controlled conditions and services related to agribusiness and related sectors.[c] In addition, the country expanded the degree of foreign investment allowed in single-brand retail trading to 100 per cent from the previous limit of 51 per cent.[d]

The Russian Federation relaxed the approval requirement for foreign acquisitions in companies that extract subsoil resources, from 10 per cent of shares to 25 per cent.[e]

Thailand allowed foreign banks operating branches in the country to convert such branches into subsidiaries.[f]

Source: UNCTAD, Investment Policy Monitor database. Additional examples of FDI-specific policy measures can be found in UNCTAD's *IPMs* published in 2011 and 2012.
[a] Law No. 12485, *Official Gazette*, 13 September 2011.
[b] Investment Canada Act: Amount for 2012, *Official Gazette* of the Government, 25 February 2012.
[c] Ministry of Commerce and Industry, Consolidated FDI Policy Circular 1 (2011), 31 March 2011.
[d] Ministry of Commerce and Industry, Press Note No. 1 (2012 Series), 10 January 2012.
[e] Federal Law No. 322-FZ, 17 November 2011.
[f] Bank of Thailand, Policy Guideline Permitting Foreign Banks to Establish a Subsidiary in Thailand, 15 December 2011.

Box III.3. Examples of investment promotion and facilitation measures in 2011–2012

Angola introduced a new investment regime applicable to national and foreign investors that invest in developing areas, special economic zones or free trade zones. Provided certain conditions are fulfilled, it offers investors several incentives in a wide range of industries, including agriculture, manufacturing, rail, road, port and airport infrastructure, telecommunications, energy, health, education and tourism.[a]

China published new guidelines encouraging FDI in strategic emerging industries involved in energy efficiency, environmental protection and high-tech, as well as some other industries in the manufacturing and services sectors.[b]

The *Russian Federation* issued a decree appointing investment ombudsmen, one for each of the country's eight federal districts. The decree states that ombudsmen are meant to assist businesses in realizing investment projects and to facilitate their interaction with authorities at the federal, regional and local levels.[c]

The *United States* established the "SelectUSA" initiative, the first coordinated federal initiative to attract foreign investment and to encourage United States investors abroad to relocate their business operations back home. The initiative aims to (i) market the country's strengths in a better way; (ii) provide clear, complete, and consistent information on the investment climate in the United States; and (iii) remove unnecessary obstacles to investment. It also aims to support private-sector job creation and retain industries needed for economic growth.[d]

Uzbekistan adopted a new decree that offers additional incentives and guarantees to foreign investors, including a "grandfathering" clause, assistance with the construction of infrastructure, and tax benefits.[e]

Source: UNCTAD, Investment Policy Monitor database. Additional examples of FDI-specific policy measures can be found in UNCTAD's *IPMs* published in 2011 and 2012.
[a] New Private Investment Law, *Republic Gazette*, 20 May 2011.
[b] National Development and Reform Commission, Catalogue for the Guidance of Foreign Investment Industries (amended in 2011), 29 December 2011.
[c] Presidential Decree No. 535-rp, 3 August 2011.
[d] United States Department of Commerce, Press Release, 15 June 2011.
[e] President of Uzbekistan, Decree No. UP-4434: "On additional measures for attraction of foreign direct investment", 10 April 2011.

A large share (32 per cent) of the policy measures undertaken in 2011 related to investment promotion and facilitation. Among them were administrative and procedural changes to facilitate foreign investments. Others provided new incentives for investors in industries such as extractive industries, electricity generation, information communications and technology, and education and health care. Some countries also took steps to set up new or expand existing special economic zones (see box III.3).

2. State regulation with regard to inward FDI continued

Regulatory measures affecting FDI included the adjustment of entry policies in some key sectors and more state control of extractive industries. The past year saw a continuation of regulatory policies on FDI. The manifold motivations for these policies included considerations of national security, food security and industrial policy, as well as the wish to control strategic industries and infrastructure (box III.4). Restrictions appeared not only in the regulatory framework itself, but also in more stringent administrative practices, for instance, in screening procedures for incoming investment and in a broader interpretation of national security concerns.

State regulation became manifest in particular in two policy areas: (i) an adjustment of entry policies with regard to inward FDI, and (ii) more regulatory policies in extractive industries. In both areas, changes were partly driven by industrial policy considerations (see also chapter II).

a. Adjusting entry policies with regard to inward FDI

Some countries modified their policy approach with regard to FDI in 2011–2012 by introducing new entry barriers or by reinforcing screening procedures. Particularly in Latin America and Africa, concerns are growing about an excessive purchase of land by large-scale foreign firms and government-controlled entities (e.g. sovereign wealth funds), the environmental consequences of overexploitation; and their implications for the promotion of rural economic development among domestic rural producers.[1] At least two countries

(*Argentina* and the *Democratic Republic of Congo*) adopted restrictive measures on agriculture. These changes reflect the fact that agriculture is a strategic sector for food security and an important source for economic growth.

Despite similar concerns about FDI in agriculture, the two countries chose different forms and degrees of restriction on access to land by foreigners. The *Democratic Republic of Congo* opted for a strict nationality requirement, under which only Congolese citizens or companies that are majority-owned by Congolese nationals are allowed to hold land.[2] By contrast, *Argentina* opted for a solution that sets quantitative quota for foreign ownership of agricultural land (see box III.4).

Other means deployed in 2011 to enhance government control over inward FDI – without going so far as to formally restrict FDI entry – were admission and screening procedures. For example, *India* decided that FDI proposals for mergers and acquisitions in the pharmaceutical sector would have to pass through the Government approval route.[3] This decision was allegedly made to ensure a balance between public health concerns and attracting FDI in the pharmaceutical industry.

b. More State influence in extractive industries

In 2011–2012, a number of countries rich in natural resources took a more regulatory approach to extractive industries. The several reasons for this development include Governments' desire to benefit from soaring global commodity prices and their wish to foster State control over natural resources, as well as their dissatisfaction with the performance of private operators.

To obtain more control over extractive industries, governments have chosen different paths. These paths have led to *nationalization*, *expropriation* or *divestment requirements* (see box III.4). Some countries preferred to *increase – to different degrees – taxes and royalties in extractive industries*; they include *Colombia*,[4] *Ghana*,[5] *Guatemala*,[6] *Honduras*,[7] *Peru*,[8] the *Bolivarian Republic of Venezuela*,[9] *Zambia*[10] and *Zimbabwe*.[11] A major difference between countries that introduced new taxes relates to the participation of the private sector in the reform process. In some countries,

Box III.4. Examples of FDI restrictions and regulations in 2011–2012

Argentina adopted a law that declares to be in the public interest and subject to expropriation 51 per cent of the share capital of YPF S.A., owned by Repsol YPF S.A. (Spain), and 51 per cent of the share capital of Repsol YPF Gas S.A., owned by Repsol Butano S.A. (Spain).[a]

The country also adopted legislation on land, limiting ownership by foreigners (both individuals and companies) to 15 per cent of productive rural land, a restriction that is compounded by a limit of 30 per cent for foreigners of the same nationality. In addition, no single foreign person or firm may own more than 1,000 hectares of land in certain core productive districts.[b]

In the *Plurinational State of Bolivia*, the President ordered the take-over of the subsidiary of the power company REE (Spain), which owns and runs about three quarters of the country's power grid.[c]

The *Democratic Republic of the Congo* adopted a law allowing land to be held only by Congolese citizens or by companies that are majority-owned by Congolese nationals.[d]

India decided that FDI proposals for mergers and acquisitions in the pharmaceutical sector will be permitted only under the Government approval route – no longer under the "automatic" route.[e]

In *Indonesia*, new legislation requires foreign firms operating in coal, minerals and metals to progressively divest their holdings to Indonesians, including the central Government, regional authorities, State-owned enterprises and private domestic investors. Foreign holders of mining business permits are required to divest their shares gradually, starting five years after production, so that by the tenth year at least 51 per cent of the shares are owned by Indonesian entities.[f]

The *Russian Federation* amended the federal law "On mass media". Foreign legal entities, as well as Russian legal entities that have a foreign share exceeding 50 per cent, are prohibited from establishing radio stations that broadcast in an area covering more than half of the Russian regions or in an area where more than 50 per cent of the country's population lives.[g]

Sri Lanka passed a law that provides for the appointment of a competent authority to control, administer and manage 37 domestic and foreign enterprises. The legislation aims to revive underperforming companies and underutilized assets in places where the land belongs to the Government.[h]

Source: UNCTAD, Investment Policy Monitor database. Additional examples of investment-related policy measures can be found in UNCTAD's *IPM*s published in 2011 and 2012.

[a] Law No. 26.741, *Official Gazette*, 7 May 2012.
[b] Law No. 26.737, *Official Gazette*, 28 December 2011.
[c] Decreto Supremo 1214, 1 May 2012.
[d] Loi No. 11/022 du 24 Décembre 2011 Portant Principes Fondamentaux Relatifs à L'agriculture. Available at: www.digitalcongo.net/UserFiles/file/PDF_files/2012/loi_principes_fondam.pdf (accessed 18 April 2012). The Law was due to come into effect in June 2012.
[e] Ministry of Commerce and Industry, Press Note No. 3 (2011 series), 8 November 2011.
[f] Presidential Decree No. 24/2012, 21 February 2012.
[g] Federal Law of 14 June 2011, No. 142-FZ, "On amending selected legislative acts of the Russian Federation in order to improve legal regulation of mass media".
[h] Central Bank of Sri Lanka, Press Release, 17 November 2011.

the new laws that raised royalties and taxes were passed following negotiations with the mining business associations.

Yet another policy approach was the *renegotiation of investment contracts*. In 2010, *Ecuador* had passed a law compelling private oil companies to renegotiate their service contracts in order to replace the taxation arrangement in production-sharing agreements with a flat rate per barrel of oil.[12] Several foreign companies renegotiated their contracts with the Government; however, in the case of Petrobras, the Government took over its operations after the contract renegotiation failed.[13]

3. More critical approach towards outward FDI

Several countries took a more critical approach towards outward FDI, including restrictions on FDI and incentives to repatriate FDI.

In 2011–2012, some countries adopted more critical policies on outward FDI. In light of high domestic unemployment, concerns are rising that outward FDI contributes to job exports and a weakening of the domestic industrial base. Other policy concerns include the stability of the foreign exchange market and improvements in the balance of payments. To address these concerns, countries took different policy approaches, including (i) restrictions on outward FDI and (ii) incentives to bring investments home.

With regard to measures falling into the first category, Argentina required its insurance companies to repatriate all their investments abroad before the end of 2011.[14] Through this measure, the Government sought to stem capital flight.

The second category includes incentives and other facilitation measures to repatriate investments abroad. For example, in June 2011, *India* allowed Indian-controlled companies abroad to disinvest – under certain conditions – without prior approval from the Reserve Bank of India, where the amount repatriated on disinvestment was less than the amount of the original investment.[15] In a similar vein, the "SelectUSA" initiative (see box III.3) encourages United States investors abroad to relocate their business operations to the United States.[16]

4. Policy measures affecting the general business climate remain important

Policy measures affecting the general business climate for FDI mainly related to changes in corporate tax rates.

In 2011, numerous policy measures related to the general business climate, affecting the treatment and operation of foreign investment. Many measures included increases in corporate taxation rates, mainly in the extractive industries in Africa and in Latin America and the Caribbean (see section A.3). Other policy measures affecting the general business climate included changes in the competition regime, labour regulation, immigration rules and company laws (see box III.5).

> **Box III.5. Selected policy measures affecting the general business climate in 2011–2012**
>
> *Brazil* allowed the establishment of one-person limited liability companies ("EIRELI").[a]
>
> *Ecuador* issued a law on restrictive business practices.[b]
>
> *South Africa* took additional steps towards the implementation of a new Companies Act, bringing a host of changes, such as a restructuring of corporate categories.[c]
>
> *Source*: UNCTAD, Investment Policy Monitor database. Additional examples of policy measures related to the general business climate can be found in UNCTAD's *IPM*s published in 2011 and 2012.
> [a] Law 12.441, *Official Gazette*, 12 July 2011. The legislation entered into force on 9 January 2012.
> [b] Secretary of National Planning and Development, "Organic Law on the Regulation of Restrictive Business Practices", 29 September 2011.
> [c] Act 34243, *Official Gazette*, 20 April 2011.

5. Conclusion: Common challenges in designing FDI policies

The policy examples given above show the considerable challenges that countries face in finding the "right" approach to foreign investment. These

Governments need to pursue a consistent approach when adjusting their FDI policies, and investment protectionism has to be avoided.

challenges may arise in making decisions in several areas: how much to liberalize or restrict FDI; what operational conditions to impose on FDI; and how to deal with outward FDI. This section discusses eight such challenges.

First, when it comes to choosing whether to liberalize or restrict FDI, the decision often requires a more nuanced answer than a simple "yes" or "no". Countries need to consider a menu of options, including the various alternatives of foreign ownership ceilings versus quantitative quota, formal restrictions versus more flexible screening procedures, and mandatory requirements versus voluntary measures. Even within an industry, different choices can be made about the extent to which it should be open for FDI.

Second, countries need to carefully consider the pros and cons of different policy options to find the "right" degree of State regulation. For instance, although it is the sovereign right of each country to expropriate private property in the public interest – subject to conditions stipulated by the domestic law of the host State and its obligations under international law – such actions also carry numerous risks, such as potential damage to the investment climate, the likelihood of exposure to investment disputes, the danger of economic retaliation, and the risk of economic inefficiency owing to a lack of sufficient capacity and technical expertise. Compared with nationalization and expropriation, increases in taxes and royalties or renegotiations of investment contracts are likely to have less negative consequences and may therefore be less disruptive to the relationship between the host–country government and TNCs.

Third, deciding only on the degree of openness to FDI may not be sufficient to address the specific policy issue at stake. Attracting FDI requires a stable, predictable and enabling investment climate. To encourage FDI, countries also need to offer "hard" support through a qualified workforce and good infrastructure. Industry-specific challenges also exist. For instance, in agriculture, opening or restricting the degree of access to land by foreigners may be inadequate if authorities do not first create modern, harmonized registration and cadastre systems that can actually measure the extent to which foreign acquisitions take place. In addition, depending on the country, the definition of rural and urban land can vary by region, and productivity ratios may differ regionally or by crops grown. These variations open doors for loopholes in legislation that can be abused on both sides.

Fourth, the issue of openness to FDI also entails a range of sensitive and important issues in connection to trade. They include the potential effects of trade-related investment measures or investment-related trade measures on FDI, and the implications of re-introducing local content requirements or research and development requirements for existing obligations under the WTO or BITs. As recent examples in Latin America show (see chapter II), a raise in import tariffs can induce "barrier-hopping" FDI or trigger new patterns of FDI in the region, such as industrial re-clustering or the breaking down of global supply chains into multi-domestic industries.

Fifth, countries need to ensure that their FDI-related policies address the roots of the problem rather than curing only the symptoms. For instance, the most promising way to motivate domestic companies to keep their production and operations at home is to foster favourable conditions which encourage them to invest domestically rather than to create distortions by preventing or discouraging them from investing abroad. Policies to actively discourage outward FDI can hurt recipient countries, in particular developing countries that depend on the inflow of foreign capital, technology and know-how. They can also result in the disruption of international supply chains into which domestic companies are integrated.

Sixth, countries need to decide on their institutional set-up for designing and adjusting FDI policies. Many countries follow an approach of making policy changes ad hoc, as need arises. Others, such as *China* and *India*, have established specific guidelines and policies under which their approach to FDI is constantly reviewed and adapted if necessary. In *China*, new policies are reflected in specific lists that identify the industries where FDI is encouraged, restricted or prohibited. *India* regularly reviews its FDI policy measures and publishes changes in a "Consolidated FDI Policy" document, which contains general conditions of FDI as well as industry-specific conditions (e.g. industries in which FDI is prohibited or permitted).

Seventh, inconsistent policy changes and adjustment can create considerable uncertainty about the direction of FDI policies, potentially producing negative effects on the investment climate. These risks call for governments to have a long-term perspective on FDI policies and to focus on stable investment conditions. Prior consultations with affected stakeholders at the national and international levels, as well as full transparency in the process of regulatory and administrative changes, help to reduce uncertainty and at the same time promote good governance. Complementary institutional reforms can enhance government capacities to implement laws effectively.

Eighth, in times of economic crisis, there is a considerable risk of countries resorting to protectionist investment measures when addressing FDI. Attention is also warranted to ensure that regulations related to sustainable development do not become a pretext for "green" protectionism (see box III.6). International organizations, such as UNCTAD and the Organization for Economic Cooperation and Development (OECD), continue to monitor national investment policies. In 2011 and 2012, the two organizations issued two joint reports on the investment measures of G-20 countries.[17] More international cooperation is needed to avoid creating unnecessary costs to the global economy or provoking instances of retaliation.

Box III.6. FDI and "green" protectionism

Recently, a debate has started about whether policies aimed at "green" growth could have the side-effect of investment protectionism.[a] This is primarily a concern for developing countries.

The promotion of a "green economy" offers significant opportunities and benefits for countries, including the opening of new business fields, the improvement of production processes and improvements in energy efficiency, as well as positive effects on the local natural environment. In contrast, raising the level of environmental protection might both directly and indirectly discourage FDI.

As regards the *direct* effects, stricter requirements on emission standards and other energy-efficiency measures may significantly increase the costs of investment and production and therefore potentially discourage companies from investing. The issue also becomes relevant with regard to public investment projects, such as infrastructure development, for which the state seeks the participation of private investors. In particular companies from developing countries may not have the capital and know-how to comply with these requirements. In addition, government incentives in developed countries for investing in a green economy may have the side-effect of discouraging companies from investing in developing countries where they could not expect comparable government support.

Environmental considerations may also *indirectly* discourage FDI. For example, a country's *trade policies* may impose import restrictions on goods ("investment-related trade measures") that are produced by an investment in another country in a manner that the importing country considers not environmentally friendly. Companies may hesitate to make an investment in country A if they have to fear that subsequently they cannot export the produced goods to country B. Similar problems may arise in connection with *public procurement policies.*

There is no internationally accepted definition of "investment protectionism". Broadly speaking, the term targets country measures that directly or indirectly hinder foreign investment without a public policy justification (see also chapter IV, section B.1). Countries may have different perceptions of whether any of the above-mentioned policies constitute a disguised investment restriction.

More international coordination could help avoid policy conflicts arising from the impact of environmental regulations on FDI. In particular, it could contribute to prevent a "race to the top" as regards incentives for FDI for a green economy, or a "race to the bottom" with regard to lowering environmental standards. UNCTAD, together with the OECD, already monitor investment protectionism at the general level, following a request from G-20 countries.

Source: UNCTAD.

[a] The issue has been discussed, for instance, in the context of the United Nations Sustainable Development Conference (Rio+20) and the OECD Freedom of Investment Roundtable. See "Countries agree to extend negotiations on Rio+20 outcome document", UN news center, 5 May 2012. www.un.org; OECD, "Harnessing Freedom of Investment for Green Growth", 5 May 2011. www.oecd.org.

B. INTERNATIONAL INVESTMENT POLICIES

1. Regional treaty making is gradually moving to centre stage

Negotiations on BITs are losing momentum as regional investment policymaking is intensifying. With 47 international investment agreements (IIAs) signed in 2011 (33 BITs and 14 "other IIAs"), traditional investment treaty making continues to lose momentum. This trend is expected to persist through 2012, which saw only 10 BITs and 2 "other IIAs" concluded during the first five months of the year.[18]

"Other IIAs", which include agreements such as free trade agreements or economic partnership agreements, continue to fall into one of three categories: IIAs including obligations commonly found in BITs (9); agreements with limited investment-related provisions (2); and IIAs focusing on investment cooperation and/or providing for a future negotiating mandate on investment (3).[19] Like chapter IV, this chapter takes a focused approach to IIAs and no longer covers double taxation treaties.[20]

The overall trend of reduced treaty making may have several causes, including (i) a gradual shift towards regional treaty making, where a single regional treaty takes the place of a multitude of bilateral pacts and where regional blocs (instead of their individual members) negotiate with third States, and (ii) the fact that IIAs are becoming increasingly controversial and politically sensitive, primarily owing to the spread of IIA-based investor–State arbitrations.

By the end of 2011, the overall IIA universe consisted of 3,164 agreements, which included 2,833 BITs and 331 "other IIAs". In quantitative terms, bilateral agreements still dominate international investment policymaking; however, in terms of economic significance, there has been a gradual shift towards regionalism. Several developments in Asia, Europe and North America illustrate this trend.

Discussions on the *Trans-Pacific Partnership Agreement* continue, with the 12th negotiation round concluded in May 2012. Currently, nine countries participate (Australia, Brunei Darussalam, Chile, Malaysia, New Zealand, Peru, Singapore, the United States and Viet Nam); Canada and Mexico have been formally invited to join the negotiations and Japan has also expressed an interest. The agreement is expected to establish a free trade area and to include a fully fledged investment chapter with high standards for investment liberalization and protection – an issue that has sparked some

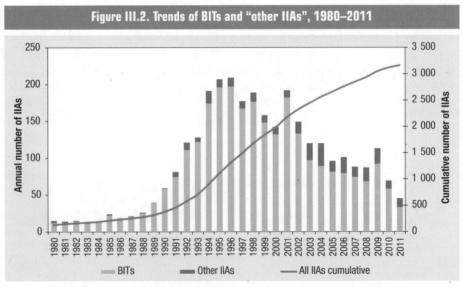

Figure III.2. Trends of BITs and "other IIAs", 1980–2011

Source: UNCTAD.

Figure III.3. BITs and "other IIAs", 2006–2011
(Numbers and country coverage)

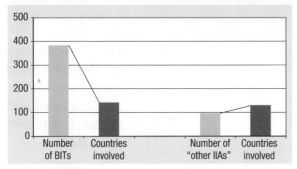

Source: UNCTAD.

controversy among investment stakeholders.[21] If all 12 countries sign the deal, their combined economic weight would amount to 35 per cent of global gross domestic product (GDP), and the treaty could potentially replace 47 IIAs (18 BITs and 29 other IIAs) currently existing between these countries.

The *2012 trilateral investment agreement between China, Japan and the Republic of Korea* has an economic weight that is not far from that of the North American Free Trade Agreement. Together, the three signatories, who have also agreed to start negotiating a free trade pact, account for one fifth of both world population and global GDP. Substantively, the investment agreement is a carefully crafted instrument that (i) offers detailed regulation of key concepts (e.g. definition of investment, fair and equitable treatment, indirect expropriation and most-favoured-nation treatment); (ii) does not apply to certain domestic investment policies (e.g. governments retain control over the establishment of investments, they can maintain existing discriminatory measures and they have not undertaken extensive commitments on performance requirements); and (iii) grants regulatory space for the pursuit of certain policy objectives (e.g. through detailed exceptions with respect to taxation, essential security interests and prudential measures as well as temporary derogation from the free-transfer obligation). The treaty also includes some new disciplines, most importantly regarding the enforcement of domestic intellectual property rights.[22] The agreement does not terminate BITs previously signed between the

parties and provides that nothing in the agreement shall be construed to prevent investors from relying on existing BITs that may be more favourable to them.[23] By including such a clause, the parties ensure that the new agreement does not lower the standards that otherwise exist under other treaties.[24]

At the *European Union* (EU) level, the European Commission now negotiates not only regarding the liberalization of trade and investment, but also on conditions related to protection of investment on behalf of all member States (see *WIR10*, *WIR11*). Given that the EU countries together account for a quarter of global GDP and almost half of global FDI outflows,[25] any agreement concluded by the EU will have significant economic weight. In September 2011, the EU Council issued the first three negotiating directives to the EU Commission to conduct negotiations on investment protection for free trade agreements (FTAs) with Canada, India and Singapore. As addressed in the Communication of the European Commission, "Towards a comprehensive European international investment policy"[26] and the Conclusions by the European Council,[27] the objective for future agreements containing provisions on investment protection is to preserve the high level of investment protection contained in existing member State BITs (e.g. the inclusion of intellectual property rights as protected investment; provisions for the fair and equitable, most-favoured-nation and national treatment of investors; and ISDS). In December 2011, the EU Council adopted negotiating directives for deep and comprehensive FTAs with Egypt, Jordan, Morocco and Tunisia, which will also include provisions on investment protection.

Taken together, EU member States account for about half of the world's BITs. Since *new EU-wide investment treaties* will replace BITs between the EU's respective treaty partner and individual EU member States, they will entail important changes to the global investment policy landscape. For example, once concluded, the EU–India FTA is expected to replace 21 BITs signed by India with individual EU members. At the same time, individual EU member States have continued to conclude BITs with third States: since the EU Lisbon Treaty's entry into force (1 December 2009), 45 such agreements have been signed, including 10 in 2011.[28] The BITs signed by member States will remain in force until replaced by EU agreements, but they will have to be amended if they are not in line with EU legislation.

Another example of a regional organization negotiating as a group with outside countries is the *Association of Southeast Asian Nations* (ASEAN).[29] For example, ASEAN has concluded agreements with Australia and New Zealand (2008) and China (2010) and is negotiating one with India. The conclusion of new ASEAN+ agreements has not led to the termination of existing BITs and FTAs between individual ASEAN members and third countries. This might be the case because the contracting parties may wish to ensure the most favourable treatment to foreign investors arising from the different treaties in force. The ASEAN–China Investment Agreement co-exists with nine BITs between individual ASEAN countries and China.[30]

The past year also saw the conclusion of negotiations on the *Mexico–Central America FTA* (Costa Rica, El Salvador, Guatemala, Honduras, Mexico and Nicaragua). Together, the six countries account for almost a quarter of Latin America's GDP. This treaty establishing a free trade area, with its fully fledged investment chapter, will replace three earlier FTAs which Mexico had in place with the participating countries.[31]

On the whole, the balance is gradually shifting from bilateral to regional treaty making, thereby increasing the impact of regions in IIA rulemaking. In most cases, regional treaties are at the same time FTAs. By comprehensively addressing the trade and investment elements of international economic activities, such broader agreements can better respond to the needs of today's economic realities, where international trade and investment are increasingly interconnected (see *WIR11*). It is also notable that investment chapters in new regional agreements typically contain more refined and precise provisions than in earlier treaties.

This shift can bring about the consolidation and harmonization of investment rules and represent a step towards multilateralism. However, where new treaties do not entail the phase-out of old ones, the result can be the opposite: instead of simplification and growing consistency, regionalization may lead to a multiplication of treaty layers, making the IIA network even more complex and prone to overlaps and inconsistencies.

2. Growing discontent with ISDS

In 2011, the number of known ISDS cases filed under IIAs grew by at least 46 (figure III.4). This constitutes the highest number of known treaty-based disputes ever filed in one year.

While investors continue to use the ISDS mechanism, some States have expressed their discontent with current dispute settlement proceedings.

Venezuela faced 10 new cases, followed by Egypt (4) and Ecuador (4), Peru (3) and Poland (2), Philippines (2) and Turkmenistan (2).[32] By the end of 2011, the total number of known treaty-based cases had reached 450.[33]

The rapid increase of ISDS cases in the last decade can be explained by a number of factors, including the growing number of IIAs, the increasing awareness about ISDS among investors and their legal counsel, and the significant rise of FDI flows. The growing number of ISDS cases may also – at least in part – reflect investors' responses to *governments' reassertion of their role in regulating and steering the economy*, as implemented through a number of national regulatory changes. Increased nationalizations, especially in Latin America, triggered multiple disputes and explain Venezuela's position as the "top respondent" in 2011. More recently, following Argentina's expropriation of Repsol's controlling stake in YPF, the country's largest oil company,[34] Repsol threatened the commencement of arbitration through the International Centre for Settlement of Investment Disputes (ICSID) (see box III.4).

In other recent cases, *investors challenged core public policies* that had negatively affected their business prospects. Having filed a similar action against Uruguay in February 2010, Philip Morris initiated arbitral proceedings against Australia, claiming that the country's new packaging and labelling requirements for cigarettes violate BIT provisions.[35] Vattenfall, a Swedish energy company, filed an ICSID case against Germany over that country's decision to phase out nuclear energy facilities.[36] Following cases against Argentina, notably the joint claim under the Argentina–Italy BIT (1990) by over 60,000 Italian bondholders arising

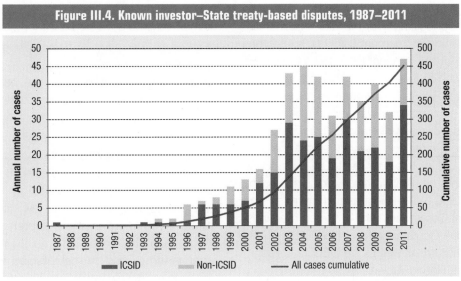

Figure III.4. Known investor–State treaty-based disputes, 1987–2011

Source: UNCTAD.

from Argentina's debt default and restructuring,[37] the restructuring of Greece's sovereign debt has led to considerations of how aggrieved bondholders can use IIAs to recover their losses.

Some *States have expressed their concerns* with today's ISDS system. In April 2011, the Australian Government issued a trade policy statement announcing that it would stop including ISDS clauses in its future IIAs. Explaining this decision, the Government stated that ISDS would give foreign businesses greater legal rights than domestic businesses and would constrain the Government's public policymaking ability (e.g. the adoption and implementation of social, environmental and economic law), explicitly referring to the country's tobacco packaging and labelling legislation.[38] In January 2012, Venezuela notified its intention to withdraw from the ICSID Convention, becoming the third State to do so (after the Plurinational State of Bolivia and Ecuador).[39] In June 2011, the Plurinational State of Bolivia denounced its BIT with the United States, thereby terminating the ISDS mechanisms (after the "sunset" period elapses).[40]

The *enforcement of awards* is not straightforward. Following Argentina's failure to pay two long-standing ICSID arbitral awards of more than $300 million to United States companies and its insistence that the claimants must resort to Argentine courts for execution of ICSID awards in the country,

in March 2012 the United States suspended Argentina's right to benefit from the United States Generalized System of Preferences (GSP). The GSP entitles exporters from developing countries to pay lower customs duties on their exports to the United States.[41] This is the first time a country has been suspended from a GSP programme for failing to pay an arbitration award, raising concerns about "re-politicization" of investment disputes.

Another notable development is Ecuador's initiation, in June 2011, of *State–State proceedings* against the United States. By doing so, Ecuador effectively seeks to overturn the interpretation of a particular clause in the Ecuador–United States BIT, adopted earlier by an investor–State tribunal in the *Chevron v. Ecuador* case.[42] In the absence of a proper mechanism for an appellate review, this represents one way to pursue correction of perceived mistakes by an arbitral tribunal.

Increasing numbers of *requests for disqualification of arbitrators*, filed by both investors and States, are another sign of dissatisfaction with ISDS procedures.[43] This is particularly so where an arbitrator is perceived as biased owing to multiple appointments in different proceedings by the same party or by the same law firm, or where the arbitrator has taken a position on a certain issue in a previous award or in academic writings. So far, all such requests have been dismissed.

Over time, the *public discourse* about the usefulness and legitimacy of the ISDS mechanism has been gaining momentum (*WIR11*), sometimes taking place at the national level and focusing on a country's choice to embrace ISDS in a particular IIA (e.g. India, Republic of Korea) and sometimes having an international dimension, involving stakeholders from a wide range of countries (as with the open letter from lawyers about the TPP Agreement). All of this has led to an intensifying debate in international forums, including in the context of UNCTAD's Investment, Enterprise and Development Commission and its expert meetings, the annual IIA Conference, and UNCTAD's World Investment Forum, as well as the OECD's Freedom of Investment Round Tables.

3. ISDS: unfinished reform agenda

Ideas for reforming ISDS abound, but few have been translated into actions. The shortcomings of the ISDS system have been well documented. Concerns include (i) an expansive use of IIAs that reaches beyond what was originally intended; (ii) contradictory interpretations of key IIA provisions by ad hoc tribunals, leading to uncertainty about their meaning; (iii) the inadequacy of ICSID's annulment or national judicial review mechanisms to correct substantive mistakes of first-level tribunals; (iv) the emergence of a "club" of individuals who serve as counsel in some cases and arbitrators in others, often obtaining repeated appointments, thereby raising concerns about potential conflicts of interest; (v) the practice of nominating arbitrators who are likely to support the position of the party appointing him/her; (vi) the secrecy of many proceedings; (vii) the high costs and considerable length of arbitration proceedings; and (viii) overall concerns about the legitimacy and equity of the system.

The growing engagement of policymakers, academics, businesses and civil society with ISDS issues has produced a variety of suggestions for reform:

- *Reining in the growing number of ISDS cases* by (i) promoting the use of mediation and conciliation instead of arbitration; (ii) implementing national dispute prevention policies (e.g. ombudsman offices); (iii) setting a time limit for bringing investor

claims (e.g., three years) or (iv) more carefully circumscribing possible bases for claims.

- *Fostering legitimacy and increasing the transparency of ISDS proceedings* by allowing public access to relevant documents, holding public hearings, and accepting *amicus curiae* briefs.

- *Dealing with inconsistent readings of key provisions in IIAs and poor treaty interpretation* by (i) improving the applicable IIA provisions, thus leaving less room for interpretation; (ii) requiring tribunals to interpret treaties in accordance with customary international law; (iii) increasing State involvement in the interpretative process (e.g. through renvoi and joint interpretation mechanisms); and (iv) establishing an appellate body to review awards.

- *Improving the impartiality and quality of arbitrators* by establishing a neutral, transparent appointment procedure with permanent or quasi-permanent arbitrators and abolishing the system of unilateral party appointments.

- *Reducing the length and costs of proceedings* by introducing mechanisms for prompt disposal of "frivolous" claims and for the consolidation of connected claims, as well as caps on arbitrator fees.

- *Assisting developing countries in handling ISDS cases* by establishing an advisory facility or legal assistance centre on international investment law and increasing capacity-building and technical assistance.

- *Addressing overall concerns about the functioning of the system*, including the lack of coherence between awards, by establishing a fully fledged international investment court with permanent judges to replace ad hoc arbitrations under multiple rules, or by requiring the exhaustion of local remedies.

Some of these *changes have already made their way into recent IIAs*, e.g. those concerning time limits for bringing claims, enhanced roles for States in treaty interpretation, prompt disposal of "frivolous" claims, consolidation of related proceedings and transparency. Some States have preferred a more radical solution of "exiting" the system (e.g. denouncing the ICSID Convention, terminating BITs or avoiding ISDS in future IIAs). Still others have not changed anything in their IIA practice. What is lacking is a systematic assessment of individual reform options – their feasibility, potential effectiveness and implementation methods (e.g., through IIAs, arbitral rules or institutions) – as well as an evaluation of the steps taken to date. A multilateral policy dialogue on ISDS could help in developing a consensus about the preferred course for the reform and ways to put it into action.

4. Enhancing the sustainable development dimension of international investment policies

a. IIA-related developments

Sustainability considerations are gaining prominence in the negotiation of IIAs as well as in other investment policymaking processes. A number of recent developments indicate that sustainable development elements are starting to play a more prominent role in international investment policies. Although some IIAs concluded in 2011 follow the traditional BIT model that focuses solely on investment protection, *others include innovations*. Several of these features are meant to ensure that the treaty does not interfere with, but instead contributes to, countries' sustainable development strategies that focus on inclusive economic growth, policies for industrial development, and the environmental and social impacts of investment (see examples in table III.3).

In the IIA context, paying due regard to sustainable development implies that a treaty should (i) promote and protect those investments that are conducive to host-country development; (ii) provide treatment and protection guarantees to investors without hindering the government's power to regulate in the public interest (e.g. for environmental, public health or safety purposes); (iii) not overexpose a country to costly litigation and the risk of exorbitant financial liabilities; and (iv) stimulate responsible business practices by investors. (For a full appraisal of the sustainable development implications of IIA provision, see UNCTAD's Investment Policy Framework for Sustainable Development (IPFSD) in chapter IV.)

In addition, a number of other recent developments in investment policymaking indicate increased attention to sustainable development considerations.

The *2012 revision of the United States Model BIT* turns the best-endeavour commitment not to relax domestic environmental and labour laws into a binding obligation. It also explicitly recognizes the importance of environmental laws and policies, and multilateral environmental agreements and reaffirms commitments under the International Labour Organization Declaration on Fundamental Principles and Rights at Work.[44]

The *2012 Joint Statement by the European Union and the United States*, issued under the auspices of the Transatlantic Economic Council, sets out a number of principles for investment policymaking. They include broad market access for foreign investors, non-discrimination, a high level of legal certainty and protection against unfair or harmful treatment of investors and investments, and effective and transparent dispute settlement procedures. The Joint Statement also refers to the need to promote responsible business conduct, preserve government authority to regulate in the public interest and avoid attracting foreign investment by weakening or failing to apply regulatory measures.[45]

This year saw the continuation of the work by *the Southern African Development Community (SADC) on its model BIT template*. Expected to be finalized later this year, the template is meant to embody harmonized approaches that will assist the 15 SADC member States in their individual and collective IIA negotiations with third countries. The draft template represents a distinct effort to enhance the sustainable development dimension of future IIAs, by including provisions on environmental and social impact assessments; measures against corruption; standards for human rights, environment and labour; corporate governance; and the right of States to regulate and pursue their development goals.

The *Secretariat of the Commonwealth*, a voluntary association of 54 countries, is preparing a handbook entitled *"Integrating Sustainable Development into International Investment Agreements: A Guide for Developing Countries"*. Scheduled for release in the summer of 2012, the guide is designed to help developing countries to negotiate IIAs that better promote sustainable development. It does so by identifying best practices in existing IIAs, proposing new and innovative sample provisions, and discussing pros and cons of various policy options.

Table III.3. Examples of sustainable-development-friendly aspects of selected IIAs signed in 2011

Columns (sustainable-development-friendly aspects of IIA provisions, in order of frequency):

- C1: Detailed exceptions from the free-transfer-of-funds obligation, including balance-of-payments difficulties and/or enforcement of national laws
- C2: Omission of the so-called "umbrella" clause
- C3: Clarification of what does and does not constitute an indirect expropriation
- C4: Fair and equitable treatment standard equated to the minimum standard of treatment of aliens under customary international law
- C5: References to the protection of health and safety, labour rights, environment or sustainable development in the treaty preamble
- C6: Explicit recognition that parties should not relax health, safety or environmental standards to attract investment
- C7: A carve-out for prudential measures in the financial services sector
- C8: General exceptions, e.g. for the protection of human, animal or plant life or health; or the conservation of exhaustible natural resources
- C9: Exclusion of sovereign debt obligations from the range of assets protected by the treaty
- C10: Exclusion of portfolio investment (shares representing less than 10 per cent of a company's capital) from the range of assets protected by the treaty
- C11: No provision for investor–State arbitration

Treaty / Policy Objective	C1	C2	C3	C4	C5	C6	C7	C8	C9	C10	C11
United Republic of Tanzania–Turkey BIT	×	×	×	×			×		×		
Nigeria–Turkey BIT	×	×	×	×		×			×		×
Mexico–Peru FTA	×	×	×	×	×	×		×			
Republic of Korea–Peru FTA	×	×	×	×	×	×	×	×			
Panama–Peru FTA	×	×	×	×	×	×	×	×			
Japan–Papua New Guinea BIT	×	×			×	×	×				
India–Slovenia BIT	×	×	×	×							
India–Nepal BIT		×	×	×							
India–Malaysia FTA	×	×	×	×			×	×			
India–Lithuania BIT		×	×	×							
India–Japan EPA	×		×	×	×	×	×	×			
Guatemala–Peru FTA	×	×	×	×				×			
Czech Republic–Sri Lanka BIT	×	×									
Costa Rica–Peru FTA	×	×	×	×	×	×	×	×			
Colombia–Japan BIT	×	×	×	×	×	×	×	×			
China–Japan–Republic of Korea TIA	×	×	×	×	×	×	×				
Central America–Mexico FTA	×	×	×	×	×	×	×	×			
Bosnia and Herzegovina–San Marino BIT		×									
Azerbaijan–Czech Republic BIT	×	×		×							
Australia–New Zealand Investment Protocol	×	×	×	×	×		×				×
Policy Objectives: Stimulate responsible business practices					×	×					
Avoid overexposure to ISDS claims	×	×	×	×			×	×	×		×
Preserve the right to regulate in the public interest	×		×	×			×	×			×
Focus on investments conducive to development					×	×			×		

Source: UNCTAD.
Note: Based on treaties signed in 2011 for which the full text is available.

b. Other developments

Sustainable development considerations also figure prominently in a number of other policy developments related to foreign investment.

The *2011 UN Guiding Principles on Business and Human Rights*,[46] a set of non-binding recommendations for governments and businesses, recommend that IIAs preserve States' ability to protect human rights (principle 9)[47] and that businesses assess their human rights impact, prevent and mitigate adverse effects (principles 17–20), and provide information on their human rights impact to relevant stakeholders (principle 21). Because the Guiding Principles concern a broad range of human rights including civil, political, economic, cultural, social and labour rights, they contribute to a comprehensive effort to ensure that business is conducted sustainably and ethically.

The *2011 Revision of the OECD Guidelines for Multinational Enterprises* (1976)[48] primarily focuses on public policy concerns such as human rights,[49] employment and the environment, while strengthening the principles relating to bribery and taxation. The Guidelines remain voluntary, but the new proactive and detailed implementation agenda can help to ensure stricter adherence by individual enterprises, thereby fostering more responsible and sustainable investment.

The *2012 revision of the International Chamber of Commerce's Guidelines for International Investment* (1972)[50] calls for responsible investment that would benefit sustainable economic development in host States. In addition to the general obligation of investors to comply with host-State laws, the Guidelines call on investors to respect national and international labour laws even where they are not effectively enforced. They encourage investors to conduct environmental impact assessments before starting a new activity or project and before decommissioning a facility or leaving a site. The Guidelines also call on home States to promote outward FDI that would contribute to the economic development of the host country. The revision includes a new chapter on CSR.

The Doha Mandate,[51] *adopted at the UNCTAD XIII Ministerial Conference 2012*, highlights sustainable development and inclusive growth as the two guiding principles for UNCTAD's work on investment and enterprise, placing it in the context of productive capacity-building, industrialization and economic diversification, and job creation. Building on the 2008 Accra Accord, the Doha Mandate will guide the work of UNCTAD's Investment and Enterprise Division for the next four years, accentuating four linkages – namely, between FDI and trade, official development assistance, domestic investment and regional integration – and highlighting the importance of non-equity modes, global supply chains, quantifiable indicators, operational methodologies and policy guidelines, barriers to investment and investment in agriculture. With respect to IIAs, the Doha Mandate recognizes the need to balance the interests of different investment stakeholders.

The *June 2012 G-20 Los Cabos Summit*[52] reiterated the G-20's support for the *Principles for Responsible Agricultural Investment* (PRAI), developed jointly by UNCTAD, the Food and Agriculture Organization, the International Fund for Agricultural Development and the World Bank (*WIR11*).[53] In addition, the Summit commended the progress achieved and supported by the G-20 Development Working Group, which includes, in the private investment and job creation pillar, work by an Inter-agency Working Group under coordination from UNCTAD to develop key indicators for measuring and maximizing the economic and employment impact of private sector investment (*WIR11*).[54] Within the same pillar, work on the report, "Promoting Standards for Responsible Investment in Value Chains", was also concluded.[55]

At the *2012 Rio+20 Conference*, world leaders adopted the Outcome Document, "The Future We Want",[56] which urges governments to create enabling environments that facilitate public and private sector investment in relevant and needed cleaner-energy technologies; encourages the promotion of investment in sustainable tourism, including eco-tourism and cultural tourism; notes the role of foreign direct investment in the transfer of environmentally sound technologies; and calls upon countries to promote investment in science, innovation and technology for sustainable development including through international cooperation. Governments also took note of the PRAI. They also acknowledged the importance of corporate sustainability reporting.

The Conference, which government representatives attended along with thousands of participants from the private sector, NGOs and other groups, focused on two themes: (i) a green economy in the context of sustainable development and poverty eradication; and (ii) the institutional framework for sustainable development,[57] with the overall objective of shaping future steps to reduce poverty, advance social equity and ensure environmental protection.

The run-up to the Conference also saw a new commitment by stock exchanges to promote long-term, sustainable investment in their markets through the Sustainable Stock Exchanges Initiative, which had been co-convened by UNCTAD, the UN Global Compact, the UN-backed Principles for Responsible Investment, and the United Nations Environment Programme in 2009.[58]

C. CORPORATE SOCIAL RESPONSIBILITY IN GLOBAL SUPPLY CHAINS

1. Supplier codes of conduct and implementation challenges[59]

The complexity of CSR codes among TNCs in global supply chains poses compliance challenges for suppliers, particularly SMEs. Policymakers and TNCs can alleviate these challenges and create new opportunities for suppliers through various capacity development initiatives.

An ongoing investment policy issue is the corporate social responsibility (CSR) of TNCs. As noted in WIR11, the past decade has seen the rise of an increasingly complex mix of CSR codes and standards. CSR codes in global supply chains hold out the promises of promoting sustainable, inclusive development in host countries and transferring knowledge on how to address critical social and environmental issues. Compliance with such codes presents challenges for many suppliers in developing countries, especially SMEs. Policymakers can support SME suppliers by, inter alia, mainstreaming CSR into domestic enterprise development programmes and working with TNCs to harmonize standards and simplify compliance procedures.

a. Proliferation of CSR codes

Across a broad range of industries, it is now common for TNCs to set supplier codes of conduct that detail social and environmental performance standards for their global supply chains. Since the early 2000s, there has been a significant proliferation of CSR codes in global supply chains, both individual TNC codes and industry-level codes. Thousands of individual company codes exist. They are especially common in large TNCs: more than 90 per cent have policies on social and environmental issues.[60] Together with company codes, the many dozens of industry association codes and multi-stakeholder initiative codes create a broad, interconnected web of CSR codes.[61]

Furthermore, CSR codes and standards themselves are becoming more complex and their applications more complicated. TNCs .send suppliers CSR auditing questionnaires that can be more than 20 pages, covering up to 400 items. Supplier that have more than one factory have to fill in a questionnaire for each facility. Furthermore, many questions are formulated using non-specific terms. Questions such as "Are all workers free to leave your employment upon giving reasonable notice?" are very common. If the customer does not define in specific terms what is meant by "reasonable", the answer will be, at best, difficult to produce, and at worst, meaningless. Because processes in each company differ, it might not be possible to answer a question with a simple "yes" or "no", yet the questionnaires rarely provide suppliers the option for further explanation.[62]

Most leading companies not only adopt a supplier code of conduct and communicate this code to their suppliers, but also have an implementation programme to try to ensure suppliers comply with the code. Such implementation programmes consist of multi-step assessment and monitoring procedures. Although the use of self-evaluation and capacity-building initiatives varies among companies and industries, the majority of companies focus their code implementation programmes on on-site audits, improvements and re-audits.

b. Challenges for suppliers (particularly SMEs) in developing countries

The proliferation and application of CSR codes poses a series of serious challenges for suppliers, particularly SMEs in developing countries. Challenges include, inter alia:

- the use of international standards that exceed current regulations and common market practices in the host country;

- the existence of diverging and sometimes conflicting requirements from different TNCs;

- the capacity constraints of suppliers in understanding and applying international standards in their day-to-day operations;

- an overload of multiple on-site inspections and complex reporting procedures;

- consumer and civil society concerns about technical or quality standards for products and for marketing, in addition to suppliers' existing challenges in meeting them; and

• competitiveness concerns for firms that bear the cost of fully complying with CSR standards relative to other SMEs that do not attempt to fully comply.

Suppliers that operate in countries that are categorized by TNCs as "high-risk sourcing zones" are subject to particularly strong scrutiny from their customers. These suppliers are more frequently subject to CSR assessments, such as self-evaluation questionnaires and monitoring or auditing processes. Because most suppliers serve multiple customers, they often need to undergo multiple social audits throughout the year. This is especially challenging, because each auditor or purchasing company has its own factory evaluation checklist, differing in specificity, length, requirements and topics addressed.

An additional structural challenge results from the fact that the purchasing practices and the CSR practices of many TNC buyers remain independent of one another. As a consequence, suppliers receive messages that are sometimes at odds (i.e. CSR demands vs. price, quality and delivery-time demands). In the absence of greater coordination among companies to harmonize CSR codes and simplify evaluation processes, and within companies to align CSR with other more conventional business demands, SMEs face the burden of a large number of audits and the challenge of meeting sometimes contradictory policies on CSR and purchasing.

Almost all companies expect their suppliers to implement "corrective action plans" to address deficiencies identified during audits, yet these plans are often inadequate for creating long-lasting change in a supplier's operation. Some companies have begun to create supplier development programmes with a CSR focus. However, most only offer such programmes to their key suppliers, which are often large companies in their own right, leaving SMEs without direct support.

To fill the gap left by the private sector, various civil society and governmental stakeholders have engaged in supplier development programmes for SMEs. However, such programmes are still limited in number and scope. Where they exist,

they are mostly initiated, funded and implemented by development agencies, intergovernmental organizations or civil society, with very limited involvement of local governments. The main challenges with externally funded programmes are scalability (i.e. how to apply them to a broader group of companies) and sustainability (i.e. how to ensure the programmes can continue over the long term). To address these challenges, some stakeholders are calling for government action in CSR capacity-building. Most national governments, however, have not yet mainstreamed CSR into their SME and supplier development programmes.

2. Policy options for effective promotion of CSR standards in global supply chains

To ensure continued growth and international competitiveness, SME suppliers in developing countries need support to cope with the challenges presented by CSR codes. Ways and means of providing such support include the following four:

• *National governments and international organizations should mainstream CSR issues into national enterprise development programmes.* CSR has become a commonplace demand in most industries, yet SMEs in developing countries are rarely provided the tools they need to address this challenge. Policymakers should therefore consider promoting training on environmental management, human resource management, and occupational safety and health.

• *National governments and international organizations should do more to assist enterprises with operational guidance for international standards.* Because most private codes of conduct refer to international standards, it is necessary to provide more practical guidance on how to implement these standards on the factory floor.

• *TNCs should be encouraged to harmonize their CSR codes at the industry level and to streamline application procedures.* Suppliers today can be subject to multiple audits or factory inspections per year. Most of these inspections are largely redundant, with different buyers asking the same questions. Initiatives such as the Supplier Ethical Data Exchange[63] can help rationalize supplier inspections, promote sharing of information among buyers, harmonize reporting practices and generally reduce unnecessary burdens on suppliers. Policymakers should encourage and support such initiatives.

• *TNCs should be encouraged to integrate CSR policies into purchasing policies, with the aim of ensuring that suppliers are effectively motivated and supported to meet all the demands being placed on them.* There is a need for greater policy coherence within TNCs. For example, purchasing policies on price and delivery time, on the one hand, and CSR policies on pay and excessive overtime hours, on the other, need to have some degree of alignment to avoid mutual exclusivity. Private CSR policies that are not fully aligned with private purchasing policies send mixed signals and can create situations in which compliance becomes impossible.

Consumer and civil society concerns are driving CSR, raising the bar for market entry for developing-country suppliers. Meeting these demands will require an upgrade of management skills. Governments can assist through capacity development programmes and by strengthening national institutions that promote compliance with labour and environmental laws. Countries that equip their SMEs with the capacity to meet CSR codes will create new opportunities for their enterprises in global supply chains.

* * *

All in all, investment policies – at both the national and the international level – are developing in a constantly changing economic environment with evolving political goals. Whereas in the past the focus was very much on investment liberalization and quantitative growth, policy concerns are nowadays more about how to make FDI instrumental for qualitative and inclusive growth, how to find the "right" balance between investment liberalization and regulation for the public good, and how to harness CSR in this context. This raises considerable challenges in terms of how best to calibrate FDI, how to promote responsible investment and how to improve the international investment regime. Chapter IV is devoted to these issues.

Notes

[1] See FAO (2011) *Land Grabbing: Case studies in 17 countries of Latin American and the Caribbean*, p. 27. Available at: www.rlc.fao.org/es/prensa/noticias/estudio-de-la-fao-halla-intensos-procesos-de-concentracion-y-extranjerizacion-de-tierras-en-america-latina-y-el-caribe (accessed 11 April 2012).

[2] See Loi No. 11/022 du 24 Décembre 2011 Portant Principes Fondamentaux Relatifs a L'agriculture. Available at: www.digitalcongo.net/UserFiles/file/PDF_files/2012/loi_principes_fondam.pdf (accessed 18 April 2012).

[3] Previously, foreign investment in the pharmaceutical sector of up to 100 per cent was permitted under the automatic route of the FDI Scheme.

[4] Ministerio de Minas y Energía, Resolución 18.0241, "Por la cual se declaran y delimitan unas áreas estratégicas mineras y se adoptan otras determinaciones", 24 February 2012.

[5] Ministry of Finance and Economic Planning, "Ghana Budget 2012 – corporate tax rate of mining companies". 16 November 2011. Available at: www.ghana.gov.gh/documents/2012budgethi.pdf.

[6] "Gobierno y mineras suscriben acuerdo voluntario de regalías", *Diario de Centroamérica*, 27 January 2012.

[7] Decree 105, *Official Gazette* No. 32561, 8 July 2011.

[8] See laws No. 29788, 29789 and 29790, *Official Gazette*, 28 September 2011.

[9] Decree 8163, *Official Gazette* No. 6022, 18 April 2011.

[10] "Zambia Budget Highlights 2012". Available at: www.zra.org.zm/BudgetHighlights_2012.pdf.

[11] Commissioner General, 2012 Budget Overview of Tax Changes, 11 November 2011. Available at: www.zra.org.zm/BudgtHighlights_2012.pdf.

[12] Ley Reformatoria a la Ley de Hidrocarburos y a la Ley de Régimen Tributario Interno, 24 June 2010.

[13] See *WIR11*, p. 98.

[14] See *Official Gazette*, "Government orders repatriation of assets owned by insurance companies abroad", 27 October 2011. Only under exceptional circumstances could certain types of investments be authorized to remain abroad, and in any case they could not exceed 50 per cent of the assets of any individual firm.

[15] Address delivered by Shri. Harun R. Khan, Deputy Governor, Reserve Bank of India at the Bombay Chamber of Commerce & Industry, Mumbai, 2 March 2012.

[16] President of the United States, Executive Order 13577 of 15 June 2011 "On the Establishment of the SelectUSA Initiative". Available at: www.gpo.gov/fdsys/pkg/FR-2011-06-20/pdf/2011-15443.pdf.

[17] See *OECD-UNCTAD Report on G-20 Trade and Investment Measures* (6th Report, October 2011, and 7th Report, May 2012). Available at: http://unctad.org/en/Pages/DIAE/G-20/UNCTAD-OECD-reports.aspx (accessed 13 June 2012).

[18] For regular reporting on IIA developments, see UNCTAD's *IPMs* at www.unctad.org/ipm.

[19] See also chapters III in *WIR10* and *WIR11*.

[20] It is notable, though, that 2011 saw the conclusion of 57 double taxation treaties (on income or income and capital), bringing the total number to 3,091.

[21] For example, over 100 lawyers from future signatories to the TPP Agreement voiced their concern with the prospect of including investor–State arbitration in the agreement and signed an open letter that calls for "rejecting the Investor–State dispute mechanism and reasserting the integrity of our domestic legal processes". See http://tpplegal.wordpress.com/open-letter.

[22] More specifically, it includes a novel provision which may be interpreted as giving investors a direct right of action for damages against host States that fail to enforce their Intellectual property rights laws.

[23] Article 25 of the trilateral investment agreement between China, Japan and the Republic of Korea.

[24] China–Japan BIT (1988); China–Republic of Korea BIT (1992) replaced by a new agreement in 2007; and Japan–Republic of Korea BIT (2002).

[25] In 2005–2010, the EU countries on average accounted for approximately 47 per cent of the annual global FDI outflows. See also *WIR11*, p. 187.

[26] See COM(2010)343, 7 July 2010.

[27] Conclusions on a comprehensive European international investment policy (3041st Foreign Affairs Council meeting, 25 October 2010).

[28] The Czech Republic has signed the highest number of agreements (10), followed by Romania (5) and Portugal (4). Estonia, Germany, Malta and the Slovakia have signed 3 BITs each. The most frequent treaty partner for post-Lisbon BITs has been India (4 treaties), which is surprising given that the EU is negotiating an FTA with India that will have an investment chapter. Twenty out of the 45 signed BITs are the renegotiated ones.

[29] Member States of ASEAN are Brunei Darussalam, Cambodia, Indonesia, the Lao People's Democratic Republic, Malaysia, Myanmar, the Philippines, Singapore, Thailand and Viet Nam. ASEAN member States also continue concluding BITs and other IIAs individually. For example, in 2011–2012, Viet Nam concluded a BIT with Oman, and Malaysia concluded FTAs with India and with Australia.

[30] Each ASEAN country, except for Brunei Darussalam, has a BIT with China.

[31] Mexico–Costa Rica FTA (1994), Mexico–Nicaragua FTA (1997) and Mexico–El Salvador–Guatemala–Honduras FTA (2000).

[32] Over the past years, at least 89 governments have responded to one or more investment treaty arbitrations. The largest number of claims were filed against Argentina (51 cases), Venezuela (25), Ecuador (23), Mexico (19), and the Czech Republic (18). The number of concluded cases had reached 220 by the end of 2011. Of these, approximately 40 per cent were decided in favour of the State and approximately 30 per cent in favour of the investor. Approximately 30 per cent were settled.

[33] For more statistical data and substantive analysis of the 2011 developments in ISDS, see UNCTAD (2012a), "Latest Developments in Investor–State Dispute Settlement", *IIA Issues Note*, No. 1.

[34] See box III.4 for details.

[35] *Philip Morris Asia Limited v. Australia*, UNCITRAL, Notice of Claim, 22 June 2011.

[36] *Vattenfall AB and others v. Federal Republic of Germany* (ICSID Case No. ARB/12/12).

[37] See also UNCTAD (2011f). "Sovereign Debt Restructuring and International Investment Agreements", *IIA Issues Note*, No. 2.

[38] See Australian Government, Gillard Government Trade Policy Statement: "Trading our way to more jobs and prosperity", April 2011. Available at: http://www.dfat.gov.au/publications/trade/trading-our-way-to-more-jobs-and-prosperity.pdf.

[39] Venezuela's announcement of 24 January 2012 is available at: www.mre.gov.ve/index.php?option=com_content&view=article&id=18939:mppre&catid=3:comunicados&Itemid=108. See also UNCTAD (2010) "Denunciation of the ICSID Convention and BITs: Impact on Investor–State Claims", *IIA Issues Note*, No. 2.

[40] The termination of the treaty took effect on 10 June 2012; pursuant to the treaty terms, it will continue to apply for another 10 years to investments established by the time of termination. United States, *Federal Register*, "Notice of Termination of United States–Bolivia Bilateral Investment Treaty", 23 May 2012.

[41] United States, Presidential Proclamation, "To Modify Duty-free Treatment Under the Generalized System of Preferences and for Other Purposes", *Federal Register*, 26 March 2012.

[42] The provision in question, enshrined in Article II(7) of the BIT, prescribes that Governments provide foreign investors with "effective means" for asserting claims and enforcing rights. Arbitrators in *Chevron v. Ecuador* held that Article II(7) prohibited "undue" delay in local court systems and that the threshold for finding a violation of this obligation was lower than for denial of justice under international law. See *Chevron Corporation (USA) and Texaco Petroleum Company (USA) v. The Republic of Ecuador*, UNCITRAL, PCA Case No. 34877, Partial Award on the Merits, 30 March 2010.

[43] In 2011, at least seven arbitrators were challenged by one of the disputing parties.

[44] www.state.gov/documents/organization/188371.pdf.

[45] http://trade.ec.europa.eu/doclib/docs/2012/april/tradoc_149331.pdf.

[46] The principles, adopted by the UN Human Rights Council in 2011, are aimed at the implementation of the "Protect, Respect and Remedy" Framework presented by UN Special Representative John Ruggie in 2008. The UN Guiding Principles (UN Doc A/HRC/17/31) and the "Protect, Respect and Remedy" Framework (UN Doc A/HRC/8/5) are available at: www.ohchr.org/EN/Issues/Business/Pages/Reports.aspx. See also UN Human Rights Council resolution (UN Doc A/HRC/RES/17/4). Available at: http:ap.ohchr.org/documents/dpage_e.aspx?si=A/HRC/RES/17/4.

[47] Principle 9 recommends that, when concluding investment treaties, "States should maintain adequate domestic policy space to meet their human rights obligations".

[48] The Guidelines establish a comprehensive code of responsible business conduct adhered to by 42 Governments and apply to companies operating in or from the relevant countries. Available at: www.oecd.org/dataoecd/43/29/48004323.pdf.

[49] This is set out in a new chapter in line with the UN Guiding Principles on Business and Human Rights.

[50] Available at: www.iccwbo.org/Advocacy-Codes-and-Rules/Document-centre/2012/2012-ICC-Guidelines-for-International-Investment.

[51] The "Doha Mandate" (TD/L.427) was adopted at the UNCTAD XIII Conference, held in Doha, Qatar. Accompanying the Mandate, UNCTAD member States also adopted the "Doha Manar", a political declaration in which member States commend UNCTAD as the focal point of the United Nations system for the integrated treatment of trade and development and interrelated issues in finance, technology, investment and sustainable development and reiterate their commitment to the organization.

[52] G-20 Leaders Declaration, G2012 Los Cabos, www.g20.org/images/stories/docs/g20/conclu/G20_Leaders_Declaration_2012.pdf.

[53] For more information, see UNCTAD website and UNCTAD (2011e).

[54] See UNCTAD website and UNCTAD (2011d).

[55] Ibid.

[56] Available at: www.uncsd2012.org/content/documents/727The%20Future%20We%20Want%2019%20June%201230pm.pdf.

[57] See Rio+20 Conference website, available at: www.uncsd2012.org/rio20/about.html (accessed 30 June 2012).

[58] Stock exchange leaders committed to the following pledge: "We voluntarily commit, through dialogue with investors, companies and regulators, to promoting long-term sustainable investment and improved environmental, social and corporate governance disclosure, and performance among companies listed on our exchange." See also www.unctad.org/diae and www.SSEinitiative.org.

[59] For a deeper analysis of this subject, see UNCTAD (2012) "Corporate Social Responsibility in Global Value Chains: evaluation and monitoring challenges for small and medium-sized suppliers in developing countries".

[60] UNCTAD (2011g).

[61] UNCTAD (2011c)

[62] UNCTAD (2012b).

[63] SEDEX is a not-for-profit organization whose membership comprises private companies that use SEDEX's information sharing platform. See www.sedexglobal.com (accessed 10 June 2012).

INVESTMENT POLICY FRAMEWORK FOR SUSTAINABLE DEVELOPMENT

CHAPTER IV

Mobilizing investment and ensuring that it contributes to sustainable development is a priority for all countries. A new generation of investment policies is emerging, as governments pursue a broader and more intricate development policy agenda, while building or maintaining a generally favourable investment climate.

"New generation" investment policies place inclusive growth and sustainable development at the heart of efforts to attract and benefit from investment. This leads to specific investment policy challenges at the national and international levels. At the national level, these include integrating investment policy into development strategy, incorporating sustainable development objectives in investment policy and ensuring investment policy relevance and effectiveness. At the international level, there is a need to strengthen the development dimension of international investment agreements (IIAs), balance the rights and obligations of States and investors, and manage the systemic complexity of the IIA regime.

To address these challenges, UNCTAD has formulated a comprehensive Investment Policy Framework for Sustainable Development (IPFSD), consisting of (i) Core Principles for investment policymaking, (ii) guidelines for national investment policies, and (iii) options for the design and use of IIAs.

UNCTAD's IPFSD can serve as a point of reference for policymakers in formulating national investment policies and in negotiating or reviewing IIAs. It provides a common language for discussion and cooperation on national and international investment policies. It has been designed as a "living document" and incorporates an online version that aims to establish an interactive, open-source platform, inviting the investment community to exchange views, suggestions and experiences related to the IPFSD for the inclusive and participative development of future investment policies.

A. INTRODUCTION

A dynamic phase in the investment policy environment provides a window of opportunity to strengthen the sustainable development dimension of national and international investment policies.

The policy environment for cross-border investment is subject to constant change. At the national level, governments continue to adopt investment policy measures (at a rate of about 150 annually over the past decade according to UNCTAD's monitoring of such measures, see chapter III), not to speak of countless measures taken every year that influence the overall business environment for investors. At the international level, new investment agreements have been concluded at a rate of more than one per week for the past few years. At the level of "soft law", the universe of codes and standards that govern the behaviour of corporate investors also continues to expand.

Over the last two decades, as more and more governments have come to realize the crucial role of private investment, including foreign direct investment (FDI), in fuelling economic growth and development, great strides have been made to improve both national and international investment policies. Very significant efforts have been made by governments in developing countries in particular, often aided by the international development community through policy frameworks, model treaties and technical assistance (such as UNCTAD's Investment Policy Reviews). A lot of experience has been gained and documented that now helps policymakers identify what measures work well, or less well, under what circumstances and in what context.

Despite the progress made, and despite the lessons learned, important questions remain unanswered for policymakers. Some perceived or acknowledged shortcomings in investment policy regimes are addressed only partially, or not at all, by existing models and frameworks intended to support policymakers.

This year's *WIR* takes a fresh look at investment policymaking – *focusing on direct private investment in productive assets* (i.e. excluding other capital flows which should be addressed by the financial system and policies) – by taking a systemic approach that examines the universe of national and international policies through the lens of today's key investment policy challenges. It also aims explicitly to strengthen the development dimension of investment policies, and presents a comprehensive *Investment Policy Framework for Sustainable Development* (IPFSD).

Encouragement to pick up this gauntlet comes from discussions with senior policymakers in numerous forums, including at UNCTAD's biennial World Investment Forum; at its Commission on Investment, Enterprise and Development; and at its regular intergovernmental expert group meetings on investment and enterprise. It also stems from discussions with academics and business advisors in UNCTAD's round tables on investment policy, and from UNCTAD's technical assistance work with developing countries. Further encouragement has emerged from other important policy platforms, most notably the G-20, which in its Seoul Declaration in 2010 and the accompanying Multi-Year Action Plan for Development specifically refer to the need to strengthen the sustainable development dimension of national and international investment policies.

The IPFSD also comes at a time when many other investment stakeholders are putting forward suggestions for the future of investment policymaking. At UNCTAD's 2012 World Investment Forum, the International Chamber of Commerce (ICC) launched its contribution in the form of (revised) Guidelines for International Investment. The OECD has announced its intention to start work on an update of its policy framework for investment. The recently adopted European Union-United States Statement on Shared Principles for International Investment and the release of the new United States' model BIT are also testimony of policy dynamism. These developments appear to signal a window of opportunity to strengthen the sustainable development dimension of investment policies.

The remainder of this chapter first details the drivers of change in the investment policy environment – introducing a "new generation" of investment policies

– and the challenges that need to be addressed in a comprehensive IPFSD (section B). It then proposes a set of Core Principles for investment policymaking, which serve as "design criteria" for national and international investment policies (section C). Section D presents a framework for national investment policy. Section E focuses on IIAs and translates the

Core Principles into options for the formulation and negotiation of such instruments, with a particular focus on development-friendly options. The final section looks at the way forward, suggesting how policymakers and the international development community could make use of the IPFSD, and how it could be further improved.

B. A "NEW GENERATION" OF INVESTMENT POLICIES

1. The changing investment policy environment

Changes in the global investor landscape, a stronger role for governments in the economy, and a greater need for global coordination are giving rise to a new generation of investment policies.

Investment policy is not made in a vacuum. It is made in a political and economic context that, at the global and regional levels, has been buffeted in recent years by a series of crises in the areas of finance, food security and the environment, and that faces persistent global imbalances and social challenges, especially with regard to poverty alleviation. These crises and challenges are having profound effects on the way policy is shaped at the global level. First, the economic and financial crisis has accentuated a longer-term shift in economic weight from developed countries to emerging markets. Global challenges such as food security and climate change, where developing country engagement is an indispensable prerequisite for any viable solution, have further added to a greater role for those countries in global policymaking. Second, the financial crisis in particular has boosted the role of governments in the economy, in both the developed and the developing world. Third, the nature of the challenges, which no country can address in isolation, makes better international coordination imperative. And fourth, the global political and economic context and the challenges that need to be addressed – with social and environmental concerns taking center stage – are leading policymakers to reflect on an emerging new development paradigm that places inclusive and sustainable development goals on the same footing as economic growth and development goals.

Trends in investment policy naturally mirror these developments.

There have been fundamental changes in the investment and investor landscape.

Developing countries and economies in transition are now primary FDI destinations, and their importance as FDI recipients continues to increase. In 2010, for the first time, developing countries received more than half of global FDI flows – in part as a result of the fall in investment in developed countries. This increases the opportunities, but also multiplies the stakes, for strategic investment targeting, promotion and protection policies in developing countries.

Emerging economies have not only become important recipients of FDI, they are increasingly large investors themselves, with their share in world outflows approaching 30 per cent. Although these countries might previously have been more concerned with the pressure they faced to provide protection for investments made by others, they now also consider the security and treatment of their own investors' interests abroad.

There are also new types of investors on the scene. State-owned enterprises (SOEs) are becoming important FDI players; UNCTAD counted some 650 multinational SOEs in 2010, operating about 8,500 foreign affiliates (*WIR11*). Although SOEs account for only 1 per cent of the total number of multinational enterprises, their overseas investments amount to roughly 11 per cent of global FDI flows. Sovereign wealth funds (SWFs), similarly, are gaining importance as FDI players. Their total FDI stock amounted to some $110 billion in 2011, and their overseas investments make up less than 1 per cent of global FDI flows. But with total assets under management of $4-5 trillion, the scope for further direct investment in productive assets is significant.

Clearly the patterns and types of investment of these new players (in terms of home and host countries and in terms of investors) are different, and so are their policy priorities. Furthermore, it is necessary to be vigilant concerning waning support for open investment climates in developed market economies in the face of competition from increasingly active developing-country investors.

Governments are playing a greater role in the economy and are giving more direction to investment policy.

Governments have become decidedly less reticent in *regulating* and *steering* the economy. More and more governments are moving away from the hands-off approach to economic growth and development that prevailed previously.[1] Industrial policies and industrial development strategies are proliferating in developing and developed countries alike (*WIR11*). These strategies often contain elements of targeted investment promotion or restriction, increasing the importance of integrated and coherent development and investment policies.

Governments are also becoming more active in their efforts to integrate domestic companies into global value chains (GVCs). They promote such integration through local capacity-building, technological upgrading and investment promotion activities, such as matchmaking or the establishment of special economic zones. Expectations of governments' promotion efforts have become higher as they increasingly focus on the *quality* – and not only on the *quantity* – of investment.

Fears and, to some extent, evidence of a job-less (or job-poor) recovery in many regions are also adding pressure on governments to look for *"the right types"* of investment, and to adopt measures to maximize the job-creation impact of investment. In developed countries, such fears have at times sparked debate on whether and how to discourage domestic companies from investing abroad or to promote the repatriation of foreign investment back home. In developing countries, the same fears are fuelling the debate on whether investment is bringing enough jobs for the poor and is sufficiently inclusive.

A stronger role of the State also manifests itself with regard to other sustainability issues. New social and environmental regulations are being introduced or existing rules reinforced – all of which has implications for investment. In addition to regulatory activities, governments are increasing efforts to promote actively the move towards sustainable development, for example through the encouragement of low-carbon FDI. They are also placing more emphasis on corporate responsibility by promoting the adoption of private codes of corporate conduct.

The trend for policymakers to intervene more in the economy and, to an extent, to steer investment activity, is visible in the constantly increasing share of regulatory and restrictive policies in total investment policy measures over the last five years. This trend reflects, in part, a renewed realism about the economic and social costs of unregulated market forces but it also gives rise to concerns that an accumulation of regulatory activities may gradually increase the risk of over-regulation or investment protectionism that hinders inward and outward FDI (see box IV.1).

There is a greater need for global coordination on investment policy.

The need to address common sustainable development challenges and to respond effectively to global economic and financial turmoil to avoid future crises has instigated calls for new models of global economic governance. In the area of investment, there are compelling reasons for such improved international coordination. It could help keep protectionist tendencies and discriminatory treatment of foreign investors in check. Further, in a world in which governments increasingly "compete" for their preferred types of investment it could help avoid a "race to the bottom" in regulatory standards or a "race to the top" in incentives.

A number of specific investment issues accentuate the need for better global coordination on investment policy as, by their nature, they can be addressed effectively only in a cooperative manner. For one, better international coordination would help overcome coherence problems posed by the highly atomized system of IIAs, which consists of more than 3,100 core treaties (i.e. bilateral investment treaties (BITs) and other agreements with investment

Box IV.1. Defining investment protectionism

Despite the fact that international policy forums at the highest level (e.g. the G-20[2]) frequently make reference to "investment protectionism", there is no universally agreed definition of the term. Different schools of thought take different approaches.

Broadly, protectionist measures related to investment would include: (1) measures directed at foreign investors that explicitly or "de facto" discriminate against them (i.e. treating them differently from domestic investors) and that are designed to prevent or discourage them from investing in, or staying in, the country. And (2) measures directed at domestic companies that require them to repatriate assets or operations to the home country or that discourage new investments abroad.[3] In this context, "measures" refer to national regulatory measures, but also include the application of *administrative procedures* or, even less tangible, *political pressure*.

The above reasoning ignores any possible *justification* of investment protectionism – i.e. measures may be motivated by legitimate policy concerns such as the protection of national security, public health or environmental objectives, or a desire to increase the contribution of FDI to economic development. It also does not refer to any assessment of *proportionality* of measures relative to such legitimate policy concerns. Nor does it attempt to assess the *legality* of relevant measures under any applicable international normative framework (whether investment-specific, i.e. international investment agreements; trade-related, e.g. WTO rules; or otherwise). Disregarding these considerations is analogous to the situation in trade, where a tariff may be applied to imports for legitimate policy reasons and may be legal under WTO rules, but is often still considered a protectionist measure.

From a development perspective this approach is clearly unsatisfactory: measures taken for legitimate public policy objectives, relevant and proportional to those objectives and taken in compliance with relevant international instruments, should not be considered protectionist. The challenge lies in defining the boundaries of legitimacy, relevance and proportionality, in order to distinguish between measures taken in good faith for the public good and measures with underlying discriminatory objectives.

For many policymakers the term "protectionism" has a negative connotation. The lack of a common language among policymakers and the investment community – one country's protectionism is another country's industrial policy – is not helpful to efforts to maintain an international investment policy environment that aims to balance openness and pursuit of the public good while minimizing potentially harmful distortionary effects on investment flows.

Source: UNCTAD.

provisions). Another issue on which policymakers are increasingly engaged in international dialogue is international tax cooperation. Unsustainable levels of public deficits and sovereign debt have made governments far more sensitive to tax avoidance, manipulative transfer pricing, tax havens and similar options available to multinational firms to unduly reduce their tax obligations in host and home countries.

Other, non-financial, global challenges also require better coordination on investment, as witnessed by efforts to promote green investment in support of environmentally friendly growth, and international collaboration on investment in agriculture to help improve food security (*WIR09, WIR10*).

A new generation of investment policies is emerging.

As a result of the developments described above, a new generation of investment policies is emerging,

with governments pursuing a broader and more intricate development policy agenda within a framework that seeks to maintain a generally favourable investment climate. This new generation of investment policies has been in the making for some time, and is reflected in the dichotomy in policy directions over the last few years – with simultaneous moves to further liberalize investment regimes and promote foreign investment, on the one hand, and to regulate investment in pursuit of public policy objectives on the other. It reflects the recognition that liberalization, if it is to generate sustainable development outcomes, has to be accompanied – if not preceded – by the establishment of proper regulatory and institutional frameworks. The key policy challenge is to strike the right balance between regulation and openness (Epilogue *WIR10*).

"New generation" investment policies place inclusive growth and sustainable development at the heart of efforts to attract and benefit from investment. Sustainable development issues – including environmental, social and poverty alleviation concerns – as well as investor responsibility in these areas, are not "new" in and by themselves. However, to date, the myriad of solutions and options developed over the years to address sustainable development concerns have not been part and parcel of mainstream investment policymaking, and the international consensus on sustainable development is not reflected in it. "New generation" investment policies aim to *systematically integrate* sustainable development and *operationalize* it in concrete measures and mechanisms at the national and international levels, and at the level of policymaking and implementation.

Broadly, "new generation" investment policies are characterized by (i) a recognition of the role of investment as a primary driver of economic growth and development and the consequent realization that investment policies are a *central part of development strategies*; and (ii) a desire to pursue sustainable development through *responsible investment*, placing social and environmental goals on the same footing as economic growth and development objectives. Furthermore, (iii) a shared recognition of the need to promote responsible investment as a cornerstone of economic growth and job creation is giving renewed impetus to

efforts to resolve, in a comprehensive manner, long-standing issues and shortcomings of investment policy that may hamper *policy effectiveness* and risk causing uncertainty for investors. These three broad aspects of "new generation" investment policies translate into specific investment policy challenges at the national and international levels.

2. Key investment policy challenges

At the national level, key investment policy challenges are (table IV.1):

- To *connect the investment policy framework to an overall development strategy* or industrial development policy that works in the context of national economies, and to *ensure coherence with other policy areas*, including overall private sector or enterprise development, and policies in support of technological advancement, international trade and job creation. "New generation" investment policies increasingly incorporate targeted objectives to channel investment to areas key for economic or industrial development and for the build-up, maintenance and improvement of productive capacity and international competitiveness.

> **New generation investment policies aim to integrate sustainable development and CSR into mainstream investment policymaking at the national and international levels, and in design and implementation. This poses new challenges for policymakers.**

Table IV.1. National investment policy challenges	
Integrating investment policy in development strategy	• Channeling investment to areas key for the build-up of productive capacity and international competitiveness • Ensuring coherence with the host of policy areas geared towards overall development objectives
Incorporating sustainable development objectives in investment policy	• Maximizing positive and minimizing negative impacts of investment • Fostering responsible investor behaviour
Ensuring investment policy relevance and effectiveness	• Building stronger institutions to implement investment policy • Measuring the sustainable development impact of investment

- To *ensure that investment supports sustainable development and inclusiveness* objectives. Investment policymaking will focus increasingly on *qualitative* aspects of investment. Because the behaviour of firms, including international investors, with respect to social and environmental issues is driven in part by corporate responsibility standards developed outside the traditional regulatory realm, one aspect of this challenge is finding the right balance between regulatory and private sector initiatives. A focus on sustainable development objectives also implies that investment policy puts increasing emphasis on the promotion of specific *types* of investment, e.g. "green investments" and "low-carbon investment" (*WIR10*).

- To *ensure continued investment policy relevance and effectiveness*, by building stronger institutions to implement investment policy and to manage investment policy dynamically, especially by measuring the sustainable development impact of policies and responding to changes in the policy environment. With the greater role that governments are assuming in steering investment to support sustainable development objectives, and with the selective departure from an open and liberal approach to investment, comes greater responsibility on the part of policymakers to ensure the effectiveness of their measures, especially where such measures imply restrictions on the freedom of economic actors or outlays of public funds (e.g. in the case of incentives or the establishment of special economic zones).

Similarly, *at the international level*, the changing investment policy environment is giving rise to three broad challenges (table IV.2):

- To *strengthen the development dimension* of the international investment policy regime. In the policy debate this development dimension principally encompasses two aspects:

  - Policymakers in some countries, especially those seeking to implement industrial development strategies and targeted investment measures, have found that IIAs can unduly constrain national economic development policymaking.

  - Many policymakers have observed that IIAs are focused almost exclusively on protecting investors and do not do enough to promote investment for development.

- To *adjust the balance between the rights and obligations of States and investors*, making it more even. IIAs currently do not set out any obligations on the part of investors in return for the protection rights they are granted. Negotiators could consider including obligations for investors to comply with

Table IV.2. International investment policy challenges	
Strengthening the development dimension of IIAs	• Safeguarding policy space for sustainable development needs • Making investment promotion provisions more concrete and consistent with sustainable development objectives
Balancing rights and obligations of States and investors	• Reflecting investor responsibilities in IIAs • Learning from and building on corporate social responsibility (CSR) principles
Managing the systemic complexity of the IIA regime	• Dealing with gaps, overlaps and inconsistencies in IIA coverage and content and resolving institutional and dispute settlement issues • Ensuring effective interaction and coherence with other public policies (e.g. climate change, labour) and systems (e.g. trading, financial)

national laws of the host country. In addition, and parallel to the debate at the level of national policies, corporate responsibility initiatives, standards and guidelines for the behaviour of international investors increasingly shape the investment policy landscape. Such standards could serve as an indirect way to add the sustainable development dimension to the international investment policy landscape, although there are concerns among developing countries that they may also act as barriers to investment and trade.

- To *resolve issues stemming from the increasing complexity of the international investment policy regime*. The current regime is a system of thousands of treaties (mostly bilateral investment treaties, free trade agreements with investment provisions, and regional agreements), many ongoing negotiations and multiple dispute-settlement mechanisms, which nevertheless offers protection to only two-thirds of global FDI stock, and which covers only one-fifth of bilateral investment relationships (*WIR11*). Most governments continue to participate in the process of adding ever more agreements to the system, despite the fact that many are not fully satisfied with its overall design. It has a number of systemic problems, including gaps, overlaps and inconsistencies in coverage and content;

ambiguities in treaty interpretation by arbitral tribunals; onerous arbitration procedures and unpredictability of arbitration awards. Also, the "interconnect" between international investment policies and other policy areas such as trade, finance, competition or environmental (e.g. climate change) policies, is absent.

3. Addressing the challenges: UNCTAD's Investment Policy Framework for Sustainable Development

To address the challenges discussed in the previous section, UNCTAD proposes a comprehensive *Investment Policy Framework for Sustainable Development* (IPFSD), consisting of a set of Core Principles for investment policymaking, guidelines for national investment policies, and guidance for policymakers on how to engage in the international investment policy regime, in the form of options for the design and use of IIAs (figure IV.1 and box IV.2). These build on the experience and lessons learned of UNCTAD and other organizations in designing investment policies for development. By consolidating good practices, the IPFSD also attempts to establish a benchmark for assessing the quality of a country's

UNCTAD's Investment Policy Framework for Sustainable Development addresses the challenges posed by the new investment policy agenda.

Figure IV.1. Structure and components of the IPFSD

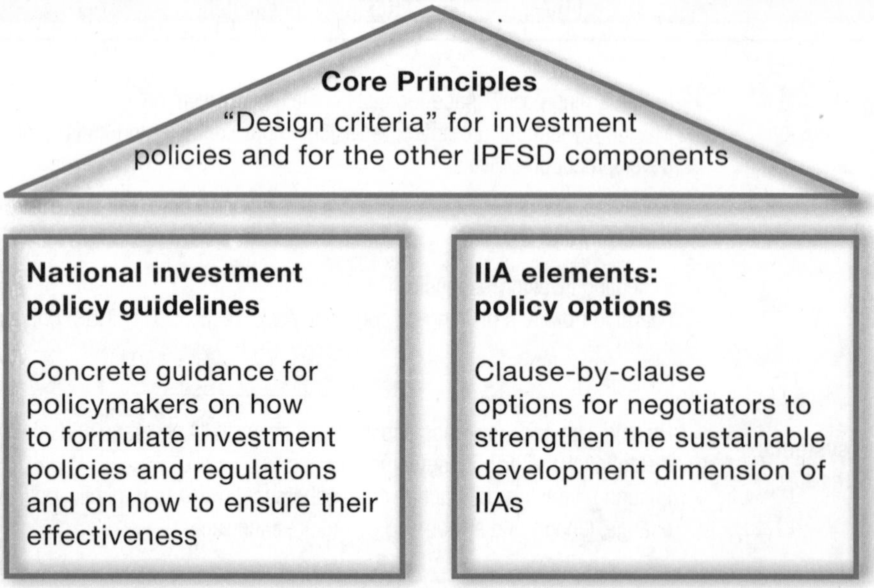

Core Principles
"Design criteria" for investment policies and for the other IPFSD components

National investment policy guidelines	IIA elements: policy options
Concrete guidance for policymakers on how to formulate investment policies and regulations and on how to ensure their effectiveness	Clause-by-clause options for negotiators to strengthen the sustainable development dimension of IIAs

Box IV.2. Scope of the IPFSD

This box addresses a number of key questions relating to the scope, coverage and target audience of the IPFSD:

What policies are covered by the IPFSD?
The IPFSD is meant to provide guidance on investment policies, with a particular focus on FDI. This includes policies with regard to the establishment, treatment and promotion of investment. In addition, a comprehensive framework needs to look beyond investment policies per se and include investment-related aspects of other policy areas.

Does the IPFSD deal with national and international investment policies?
Investment policies and related policy areas covered by the IPFSD comprise national and international policies, as coherence between the two is fundamental.

Does the IPFSD cover domestic and foreign investment?
The IPFSD's focus on FDI is evident in sections on, for example, the entry and establishment of investment, the promotion of outward investment and the section on international investment policies. However, many of the guidelines in the section on national investment policies have relevance for domestic investment as well.

Does the IPFSD consider portfolio investment?
The IPFSD focuses on direct investment in productive assets. Portfolio investment is considered only where explicitly stated in the context of IIAs, which in many cases extend coverage beyond direct investment.

Is the IPFSD concerned with inward and outward investment?
The IPFSD primarily offers policy advice for countries where the investment – domestic or foreign – is made, as this is typically the principal concern of investment policies. However, the IPFSD does not ignore the fact that policies with regard to *outward* investment may also be part of a country's development strategy.

Is the IPFSD addressed to policymakers from developing and developed countries?
The addressees of the IPFSD are, in principle, both developing and developed countries. It has been designed with the particular objective to assist the former in the design of investment policies in support of sustainable development objectives, but is equally relevant for developed countries.

Does the IPFSD focus on the attraction of investment or on its impact?
The policy guidelines of the IPFSD serve a dual purpose. On the one hand, they intend to assist governments in improving the attractiveness of their countries as investment locations. To this end, they contain specific recommendations concerning the institutional set-up, the general business climate and the treatment of investors. On the other hand, they also provide guidance on how countries can maximize the sustainable development benefits from investment, in particular foreign investment.

Source: UNCTAD.

policy environment for foreign investment – taking into account that one single policy framework cannot address the specific investment policy challenges of individual countries (see boxes IV.4, IV.6 and IV.7 on the need for custom-designed investment policy advice).

Although there are a number of existing international instruments that provide guidance to investment policymakers,[4] UNCTAD's IPFSD distinguishes itself in several ways. First, it is meant as a comprehensive instrument dealing with all aspects of national and international investment policymaking. Second, it puts a particular emphasis on the relationship between foreign investment and sustainable development, advocating a balanced approach between the pursuit of purely economic growth objectives by means of investment liberalization and promotion, on the one hand, and the need to protect people and the environment, on the other hand. Third, it underscores the interests of developing countries in investment policymaking. Fourth, it is neither a legally binding text nor a voluntary undertaking between States, but expert guidance by an international organization, leaving national policymakers free to "adapt and adopt" as appropriate.

C. CORE PRINCIPLES FOR INVESTMENT POLICYMAKING

1. Scope and objectives of the Core Principles

The Core Principles for investment policymaking are the "design criteria" for national and international investment policies.

The Core Principles for investment policymaking aim to guide the development of national and international investment policies. To this end, they translate the challenges of investment policymaking into a set of "design criteria" for investment policies. Taking the challenges discussed in the previous section as the starting point, they call for integrating investment policy in overall development strategies, enhancing sustainable development as part of investment policies, balancing rights and obligations of States and investors in the context of investment protection and promotion, including CSR in investment policymaking, and encouraging international cooperation on investment-related challenges.

The Core Principles are not a set of rules per se. They are an integral part of the IPFSD, as set out in this chapter, which attempts to convert them, collectively and individually, into a concrete set of policy guidelines for national investment policymakers and for negotiators of IIAs (sections D and E). As such, they do not always follow the traditional "policy areas" of a national investment policy framework, nor the usual articles of IIAs.

The Core Principles are grouped as follows:

- Principle 1 states the overarching objective of investment policymaking.
- Principles 2, 3 and 4 relate to the general process of policy development and the policymaking environment as relevant for investment policies.
- Principles 5 through 10 address the specifics of investment policymaking.
- Principle 11 refers to cooperation in investment-related matters at the international level.

The design of the Core Principles has been inspired by various sources of international law and politics. Some of these instruments have importance for the entire set of the Core Principles as they relate – to various degrees – to sustainable development. Several other international instruments relate to individual Core Principles (see box IV.3).

Box IV.3. The origins of the Core Principles in international law

The Core Principles can be traced back to a wide range of existing bodies of international law, treaties and declarations.

The UN Charter (Article 55) promotes, inter alia, the goal of economic and social progress and development. The UN Millennium Development Goals call for a Global Partnership for Development. In particular, Goal 8 (Target 12) encourages the further development of an open, rule-based, predictable, non-discriminatory trading and financial system, which includes a commitment to good governance, development, and poverty reduction, both nationally and internationally – concepts that apply equally to the investment system. The "Monterrey Consensus" of the UN Conference on Financing for Development of 2002 acknowledges that countries need to continue their efforts to achieve a transparent, stable and predictable investment climate, with proper contract enforcement and respect for property rights, embedded in sound macroeconomic policies and institutions that allow businesses, both domestic and international, to operate efficiently and profitably and with maximum development impact. The UN Johannesburg Plan of Implementation of September 2002, following up on the "Rio Declaration", calls for the formulation and elaboration of national strategies for sustainable development, which integrate economic, social and environmental aspects. The 4th UN Conference on LDCs in May 2011 adopted the Istanbul Programme of Action for the LDCs 2011-2020 with a strong focus on productive capacity-building and structural transformation as core elements to achieve more robust, balanced, equitable, and inclusive growth and sustainable development. Finally, the 2012 UNCTAD XIII Conference – as well as previous UNCTAD Conferences – recognized the role of FDI in the development process and called on countries to design policies aimed at enhancing the impact of foreign investment on sustainable development and inclusive growth, while underlining the importance of stable, predictable and enabling investment climates.

/...

Box IV.3. The origins of the Core Principles in international law (concluded)

Several other international instruments relate to individual Core Principles. They comprise, in particular, the Universal Declaration of Human Rights and the UN Guiding Principles on Business and Human Rights, the Convention on the Establishment of the Multilateral Investment Guarantee Agency, the World Bank Guidelines on the Treatment of Foreign Direct Investment, the UN Global Compact, the OECD Guidelines for Multinational Enterprises and the ILO Tripartite Declaration of Principles concerning Multinational Enterprises and Social Policy, and several WTO-related agreements, including the GATS, the TRIMs Agreement and the Agreement on Government Procurement.

Source: UNCTAD.

2. Core Principles for investment policymaking for sustainable development

Area	Core Principles
1 **Investment for sustainable development**	• The overarching objective of investment policymaking is to promote investment for inclusive growth and sustainable development.
2 **Policy coherence**	• Investment policies should be grounded in a country's overall development strategy. All policies that impact on investment should be coherent and synergetic at both the national and international levels.
3 **Public governance and institutions**	• Investment policies should be developed involving all stakeholders, and embedded in an institutional framework based on the rule of law that adheres to high standards of public governance and ensures predictable, efficient and transparent procedures for investors.
4 **Dynamic policymaking**	• Investment policies should be regularly reviewed for effectiveness and relevance and adapted to changing development dynamics.
5 **Balanced rights and obligations**	• Investment policies should be balanced in setting out rights and obligations of States and investors in the interest of development for all.
6 **Right to regulate**	• Each country has the sovereign right to establish entry and operational conditions for foreign investment, subject to international commitments, in the interest of the public good and to minimize potential negative effects.
7 **Openness to investment**	• In line with each country's development strategy, investment policy should establish open, stable and predictable entry conditions for investment.
8 **Investment protection and treatment**	• Investment policies should provide adequate protection to established investors. The treatment of established investors should be non-discriminatory.
9 **Investment promotion and facilitation**	• Policies for investment promotion and facilitation should be aligned with sustainable development goals and designed to minimize the risk of harmful competition for investment.
10 **Corporate governance and responsibility**	• Investment policies should promote and facilitate the adoption of and compliance with best international practices of corporate social responsibility and good corporate governance.
11 **International cooperation**	• The international community should cooperate to address shared investment-for-development policy challenges, particularly in least developed countries. Collective efforts should also be made to avoid investment protectionism.

3. Annotations to the Core Principles

Principle 1: Investment for sustainable development

This overarching principle defines the overall objective of the Investment Policy Framework for Sustainable Development. It recognizes the need to promote investment not only for economic growth as such, but for growth that benefits all, including the poorest. It also calls for the mainstreaming of sustainable development issues – i.e. development that meets the needs of the present without compromising the ability of future generations to meet theirs – in investment policymaking, at both the national and international levels.

Principle 2: Policy coherence

This principle recognizes that investment is a means to an end, and that investment policy should thus be integrated in an overarching development strategy. It also acknowledges that success in attracting and benefiting from investment depends not only on investment policy "stricto sensu" (i.e. entry and establishment rules, treatment and protection) but on a host of investment-related policy areas ranging from tax to trade to environmental and labour market policies. It recognizes that these policy areas interact with each other and that there is consequently a need for a coherent overall approach to make them conducive to sustainable development and to achieve synergies. The same considerations apply with respect to the interaction between national investment policies and international investment rulemaking. Successful experiences with investment for development often involved the establishment of special agencies with a specific mandate to coordinate the work of different ministries, government units and policy areas, including the negotiation of IIAs.

Principle 3: Public governance and institutions

The concept of good public governance refers to the efficiency and effectiveness of government services, including such aspects as accountability, predictability, clarity, transparency, fairness, rule of law, and the absence of corruption. This principle recognizes the importance of good public governance as a key factor in creating an environment conducive to attracting investment. It also stresses the significance of a participatory approach to policy development as a basic ingredient of investment policies aimed at inclusive growth and fairness for all. The element of transparency is especially important, as in and by itself it tends to facilitate dialogue between public and private sector stakeholders, including companies, organized labour and non-governmental organizations (NGOs).

Principle 4: Dynamic policymaking

This principle recognizes that national and international investment policies need flexibility to adapt to changing circumstances, while recognizing that a favourable investment climate requires stability and predictability. For one, different policies are needed at different development stages. New factors may emerge on the domestic policy scene, including government changes, social pressures or environmental degradation. International dynamics can have an impact on national investment policies as well, including through regional integration or through international competition for the attraction of specific types of foreign investment. The increasing role of emerging economies as outward investors and their corresponding desire better to protect their companies abroad drives change in investment policies as well.

The dynamics of investment policies also imply a need for countries continuously to assess the effectiveness of existing instruments. If these do not achieve the desired results in terms of economic and social development, or do so at too high a cost, they may need to be revised.

Principle 5: Balanced rights and obligations

Investment policies need to serve two potentially conflicting purposes. On the one hand, they have to create attractive conditions for foreign investors. To this end, investment policies include features of investment liberalization, protection, promotion and facilitation. On the other hand, the overall regulatory framework of the host country has to ensure that any negative social or environmental effects are minimized. More regulation may also be warranted to find appropriate responses to crises (e.g. financial crisis, food crisis, climate change).

Against this background, this core principle suggests that the investment climate and policies of a country should be "balanced" as regards the overall treatment of foreign investors. Where and how to strike this balance is basically an issue for the domestic law of host countries and therefore requires adequate local capacities. International policies vis-à-vis foreign investors likewise play a role and – if not carefully designed – might tilt the balance in favour of those investors. The principle does not mean that each individual investment-related regulation of a host country would have to be balanced.

Principle 6: Right to regulate

The right to regulate is an expression of a country's sovereignty. Regulation includes both the general legal and administrative framework of host countries as well as sector- or industry-specific rules. It also entails effective implementation of rules, including the enforcement of rights. Regulation is not only a State right, but also a necessity. Without an adequate regulatory framework, a country will not be attractive for foreign investors, because such investors seek clarity, stability and predictability of investment conditions in the host country.

The authority to regulate can, under certain circumstances, be ceded to an international body to make rules for groups of states. It can be subject to international obligations that countries undertake; with regard to the treatment of foreign investors this often takes place at the bilateral or regional level. International commitments thus reduce "policy space". This principle advocates that countries maintain sufficient policy space to regulate for the public good.

Principle 7: Openness to investment

This principle considers a welcoming investment climate, with transparent and predictable entry conditions and procedures, a precondition for attracting foreign investment conducive for sustainable development. The term "openness" is not limited to formal openness as expressed in a country's investment framework and, possibly, in entry rights granted in IIAs. Equally important is the absence of informal investment barriers, such as burdensome, unclear and non-transparent administrative procedures. At the same time, the principle recognizes that countries have legitimate reasons to limit openness to foreign investment, for instance in the context of their national development strategies or for national security reasons.

In addition, the issue of "openness" reaches beyond the establishment of an investment. Trade openness can be of crucial importance, too; in particular, when the investment significantly depends on imports or exports.

Principle 8: Investment protection

This principle acknowledges that investment protection, although only one among many determinants of foreign investment, can be an important policy tool for the attraction of investment. It therefore closely interacts with the principle on investment promotion and facilitation (Principle 9). It has a national and an international component. Core elements of protection at the national level include, inter alia, the rule of law, freedom of contract and access to courts. Key components of investment protection frequently found in IIAs comprise the principles of non-discrimination (national treatment and most-favoured-nation treatment), fair and equitable treatment, protection in case of expropriation, provisions on movement of capital and effective dispute settlement.

Principle 9: Investment promotion and facilitation

Most countries have set up promotion schemes to attract and facilitate foreign investment. Promotion and facilitation measures often include the granting of fiscal or financial incentives, and the establishment of special economic zones or "one-stop shops". Many countries have also set up special investment promotion agencies (IPAs) to target foreign investors, offer matchmaking services and provide aftercare.

The principle contains two key components. First, it stipulates that in their efforts to improve the investment climate, countries should not compromise sustainable development goals, for instance by lowering regulatory standards on social or environmental issues, or by offering incentives that annul a large part of the economic benefit of the investment for the host country. Second, the principle acknowledges that, as more and more countries seek to boost investment and target specific types of investment, the risk of harmful competition for investment increases; i.e. a race to the regulatory bottom or a race to the top of incentives (with negative social and environmental consequences or escalating commitments of public funds). Investment policies should be designed to minimize this risk. This underlines the importance of international coordination (see Principle 11 below).

Principle 10: Corporate governance and responsibility

This principle recognizes that corporate governance and CSR standards are increasingly shaping investment policy at the national and international levels. This development is reflected in the proliferation of standards, including several intergovernmental organization standards of the United Nations, the ILO, the IFC and the OECD, providing guidance on fundamental CSR issues;[5] dozens of multi-stakeholder initiatives; hundreds of industry association codes; and thousands of individual company codes (*WIR11*). Most recently, the UN Human Rights Council adopted a resolution endorsing the Report of the Special Representative of the Secretary-General on the issue of human rights and transnational corporations and other business enterprises.

CSR standards are voluntary in nature and so exist as a unique dimension of "soft law". The principle calls on governments to actively promote CSR standards and to monitor compliance with them. Promotion also includes the option to adopt existing CSR standards as part of regulatory initiatives, turning voluntary standards into mandatory requirements.

Principle 11: International cooperation

This principle considers that investment policies touch upon a number of issues that would benefit from more international cooperation. The principle also advocates that particular efforts should be made to encourage foreign investment in LDCs.

Home countries can support outward investment conducive to sustainable development. For a long time, developed countries have provided investment guarantees against certain political risks in host countries or offered loans to companies investing abroad. The Multilateral Investment Guarantee Agency (MIGA) provides investment insurance at the international level. The principle builds upon examples of countries that have started to condition the granting of investment guarantees on an assessment of social and environmental impacts.

The importance of international cooperation also grows as more and more countries make use of targeted investment promotion policies. Better international coordination is called for to avoid a global race to the bottom in regulatory standards, or a race to the top in incentives, and to avoid a return of protectionist tendencies.

More international coordination, in particular at the regional level, can also help to create synergies so as to realize investment projects that would be too complex and expensive for one country alone. Another policy area that would benefit from more international cooperation is investment in sensitive sectors. For example, recent concerns about possible land grabs and the crowding out of local farmers by foreign investors have resulted in the development by the FAO, UNCTAD, the World Bank and IFAD of Principles for Responsible Investment in Agriculture (PRAI).

* * *

Some Core Principles relate to a specific investment policy area (e.g. openness to investment, investment protection and promotion, corporate governance and social responsibility) and can therefore relatively easily be traced to specific guidelines and options in the national and international parts of the framework. Other Core Principles (e.g. on public governance and institutions, balanced rights and obligations, the right to regulate) are important for investment policymaking as a whole. As a consequence, they are reflected in guidelines dispersed across the entire range of relevant policy issues covered by the framework.

The Core Principles interact with each other. The individual principles and corresponding guidelines therefore must not be applied and interpreted in isolation. In particular, Principle 1 – as the overarching rule within the policy framework – has relevance for all subsequent principles. Integrating investment policies into sustainable development strategies requires a coherent policy framework. Good public governance is needed in its design and implementation. Sustainable development is an ongoing challenge, which underlines the importance of policymaking dynamics. And an IPFSD needs to comprise elements of investment regulation and corporate governance, on the one hand, and openness, protection and promotion, on the other hand, thereby contributing to an investment climate with balanced rights and obligations for investors.

D. NATIONAL INVESTMENT POLICY GUIDELINES

This section translates the Core Principles for investment policymaking into concrete guidelines at the national level, with a view to addressing the policy challenges discussed in section B. To address these policy challenges – ensuring that investment policy is coherent with other policy areas supporting a country's overall development strategy; enhancing the sustainable development impact of investment and promoting responsible investment; and improving policy effectiveness, while maintaining an attractive investment climate – this section, including the detailed policy guidelines it contains, argues for policy action at three levels:

1. At the *strategic* level, policymakers should ground investment policy in a broad road map for economic growth and sustainable development – such as those set out in formal economic or industrial development strategies in many countries.

2. At the *normative* level, through the setting of rules and regulations, on investment and in a range of other policy areas, policymakers can promote and regulate investment that is geared towards sustainable development goals.

3. At the *administrative* level, through appropriate implementation and institutional mechanisms, policymakers can ensure continued relevance and effectiveness of investment policies.

The following sections will look at each of these levels in turn.

1. Grounding investment policy in development strategy

Development strategy should define a clear role for private and foreign investment in building productive capacity and ensure coherence across all policy areas geared towards overall development objectives.

Many countries have elaborated explicit development strategies that set out an action plan to achieve economic and social objectives and to strengthen international competitiveness. These strategies will vary by country, depending on their stage of development, their domestic endowments and individual preferences, and depending on the degree to which the political and economic system allows or requires the participation of the State in economic planning. Because investment is a key driver of economic growth, a prerequisite for the build-up of productive capacity and an enabler of industrial development and upgrading, investment policy must be an integrated part of such development strategies (see box IV.4).

Defining the role of public, private, domestic and foreign direct investment

Mobilizing investment for sustainable development remains a major challenge for developing countries, particularly for LDCs. Given the often huge development financing gaps in these countries, foreign investment can provide a necessary complement to domestic investment, and it can be particularly beneficial when it interacts in a synergetic way with domestic public and private investment. Agriculture, infrastructure and climate change-related investments, among others, hold significant potential for mutually beneficial interaction between foreign and domestic, and public and private investment. For example, public-private partnerships (PPPs) have become important avenues for infrastructure development in developing countries, although experience has shown that high-quality regulatory and institutional settings are critical to ensure the development benefits of such infrastructure PPPs (*WIR08*).

Given the specific development contributions that can be expected from investment – private and public, domestic and foreign – policymakers should consider carefully what role each type can play in the context of their development strategies. In particular the opportunities and needs for *foreign* investment – intended as direct investment in productive assets (i.e. excluding portfolio investment) – differ from country to country, as does the willingness to open sectors and industries to foreign investors. Examples include the improvement of infrastructure, investment in skills and education, investments to secure food supply, or investments in other specific

Box IV.4. Integrating investment policy in development Strategy: UNCTAD's Investment Policy Reviews

UNCTAD's Investment Policy Review (IPR) program was launched in 1999 in response to growing demand from member States for advice on FDI policy. The IPRs aim to provide an independent and objective evaluation of the policy, regulatory and institutional environment for FDI and to propose customized recommendations to governments to attract and benefit from increased flows of FDI. To date IPRs have been undertaken for 34 countries, including 17 developing countries, 4 transition economies and 13 LDCs, of which 5 in post-conflict situations (box table IV.4.1).

Box table IV.4.1. Beneficiaries of the UNCTAD IPR program, 1999–2011

Categories	Countries
Developing countries	Algeria, Botswana, Colombia, Dominican Republic, Ecuador, Egypt, El Salvador, Ghana, Guatemala, Kenya, Mauritius, Morocco, Mongolia, Nigeria, Peru, Sri Lanka, Viet Nam
Transition economies	Belarus, the former Yugoslav Republic of Macedonia, Republic of Moldova, Uzbekistan
Least developed countries	Benin, Burkina Faso, Burundi, Ethiopia, Lesotho, Mauritania, Mozambique, Nepal, Rwanda, Sierra Leone, United Republic of Tanzania, Uganda, Zambia

UNCTAD coordinates its IPR activities with the work of other development partners (including other UN agencies such as the UNDP and UNIDO, the OECD, the World Bank, national and regional development banks, local development institutions and NGOs) in order to create synergies.

IPRs are carried out through a structured process, starting with (i) a formal request from the national government to UNCTAD expressing commitment to policy reforms; (ii) preparation of the IPR advisory report and its presentation at a national workshop where government and national stakeholders review findings; (iii) intergovernmental peer review and sharing of best practices in investment policy in Geneva; (iv) implementation and follow-up technical assistance and capacity-building; and (v) preparation of an implementation assessment and additional follow-up actions.

Substantively, key areas of recommendations common to nearly all IPRs conducted to date include (i) Defining the strategic role of investment (and in particular FDI) in countries' development strategies; (ii) Reforming investment laws and regulations; (iii) Designing policies and measures for attracting and benefitting from FDI; and (iv) Addressing institutional issues related to FDI promotion and facilitation.

A number of case-specific areas for recommendations or themes have included privatizations, the promotion of investment in target industries, promotion and facilitation of infrastructure investment, private sector development initiatives and business linkages, skill building and technology transfer, and regional cooperation initiatives.

Recently, the IPR approach has been strengthened further with the inclusion of sections on specific priority industries, containing a quantitative assessment of the potential for investment in those industries and the potential development impact of investment through such indicators as value added, employment generation, and export generation, with a view to helping governments attract and negotiate higher value added types of investment.

Source: UNCTAD; www.unctad.org/diae/ipr.

industries that are of crucial importance for a country.

Even looking at the role of foreign investment per se, policymakers should be aware of different types, each with distinct development impacts. Greenfield investment has different impacts than investment driven by mergers and acquisitions (M&As). The former will generally imply a greater immediate contribution to productive capacity and job creation; the latter may bring benefits such as technology upgrading or access to international

markets (or survival in case of troubled acquisition targets), but may also have negative effects (e.g. on employment in case of restructurings). Similarly, efficiency-seeking investments will have different development impacts than market-seeking investments, both with potential positive and negative contributions. And foreign investment also comes in different financial guises: FDI does not always imply an influx of physical capital (e.g. reinvested earnings), nor does it always translate into actual capital expenditures for the build-up of productive assets (e.g. retained earnings) and can sometimes behave in a manner not dissimilar to portfolio investment.

Furthermore, the role of foreign investors and multinational firms in an economy is not limited to FDI. They can also contribute to economic development through non-equity modes of international production (NEMs), such as contract manufacturing, services outsourcing, licensing, franchising or contract farming. Because this form of involvement is based on a contractual relation between the foreign company and domestic business partners, it requires that the host country has sufficiently qualified local entrepreneurs, which calls for coordinated policies on investment, enterprise development and human resource development (*WIR11*).

A key aspect in defining the role of investment in economic growth and development strategies is the need for calibrated policies to stimulate job creation and to maximize the job content of investment, both quantitatively and qualitatively. This has become especially urgent in light of the cumulative employment losses during the global financial crisis, and the relatively low job content of economic growth since, leading to a global employment deficit estimated at over 200 million workers.[6]

Harnessing investment for productive capacity-building and enhancing international competitiveness

The potential contribution of foreign investment to building or reinforcing local productive capacities should guide investment policy and targeting efforts. This is particularly important where investment is intended to play a central role in industrial upgrading and structural transformation in developing economies. The most crucial aspects of productive capacity-building include human resources and skills development, technology and know-how, infrastructure development, and enterprise development.

Human resources and skills. Human resources development is a crucial determinant of a country's long-term economic prospects. In addition, the availability of skilled, trainable and productive labour at competitive costs is a major magnet for efficiency-

seeking foreign investors. As such, education and human resource development policy should be considered a key complement to investment policy. Particular care should be given to matching skills needs and skills development, including in terms of vocational and technical training. Vocational training that prepares trainees for jobs involving manual or practical activities related to a specific trade or occupation is a key policy tool, for instance, to enhance the capacity of local suppliers.

As economies develop, skills needs and job opportunities evolve, making constant adaptation and upgrading of education and human development policies a necessity. The latter are essential not just to provide the necessary skills to investors, but more crucially to ensure that the population can gain access to decent work opportunities.

FDI – as well as NEMs – is particularly sensitive to the availability of local skills, which can frequently be a "make or break" factor in investment location decisions. Where local skills are partially lacking, foreign and national investors may wish to rely on expatriate workers to fill the gaps. Although particular care should be paid to promoting employment by nationals and to protecting national security, countries have a lot to gain from enabling investors to tap foreign skills readily and easily where needed. Well-crafted immigration and labour policies have had demonstrated benefits in countries that have allowed foreign skills to complement and fertilize those created locally. Knowledge spillovers also occur through international employees. An adequate degree of openness in granting work permits to skilled foreign workers is therefore important not only to facilitate investments that may otherwise not materialize for lack of skills, but also to support and complement the national human resource development policy through education.

Technology and know-how. An important policy task is to encourage the dissemination of technology. For example, governments can promote technology clusters that promote R&D in a particular industry and that can help upgrade industrial activities by bringing together technology firms, suppliers and research institutes. Disseminating and facilitating the acquisition of technology can also improve the involvement of domestic producers in GVCs (e.g.

call centers, business processing operations or contract farming).

Appropriate protection of intellectual property rights is an important policy tool because it is often a precondition for international investors to disclose technology to licensees in developing countries, especially in areas involving easily imitable technologies (e.g. software, pharmaceuticals), and hence can affect chances of attracting equity investments (e.g. joint ventures) or non-equity modes of involvement (e.g. licensing). At the same time the level of protection should be commensurate with the level of a country's development and conducive to the development of its technological capacities. It can be a means of encouraging independent research activities by local companies, because businesses are more likely to invest resources in R&D and technological upgrading if their innovations are protected.

Infrastructure. The development of domestic infrastructure may necessitate investments of such magnitude that it is impossible for domestic companies to undertake them alone. Infrastructure development may also require certain technological skills and know-how, which domestic firms do not have (e.g. telecommunication, energy, exploration of natural resources in remote areas). Likewise, the move to a low-carbon economy will often necessitate bringing in the technological capacities of foreign investors.

Most developing countries, especially LDCs, continue to suffer from vast deficiencies in infrastructure, in particular electricity, water and transport, and to a lesser extent telecommunications. Following technological progress and changes in regulatory attitudes, many countries have succeeded in introducing private (foreign) investment and competition in what used to be public sector monopolies, e.g. mobile telecommunications or power generation.

Given the potential contribution of FDI to building high-quality infrastructure, countries should consider the extent to which certain sectors or sub-sectors could be opened to (foreign) private investment, and under what conditions – balancing considerations of public service provision, affordability and accessibility. National security-related concerns with regard to the liberalization of critical infrastructure can be taken care of by screening procedures. A clear vision of what is doable and desirable socially, technically and from a business perspective is essential given the dependence of economic growth on infrastructure development.

All too many developing countries have attempted to privatize infrastructure or public services only to fail or achieve less than optimal outcomes.[7] Governments need to develop not only a clear assessment of what can be achieved and at what costs, but also a comprehensive understanding of the complex technicalities involved in infrastructure investments and their long-term implications in terms of cost, quality, availability and affordability of services. A sound legal framework to guide concessions, management contracts and all forms of public-private partnerships is a key piece in the infrastructure development and investment strategies (*WIR08*).

Enterprise development. Domestic enterprise development is a key transfer mechanism for the development benefits of investment to materialize. At the same time, especially for foreign investors, the presence of viable local enterprise is a crucial determinant for further investment and for partnerships in NEMs. A comprehensive discussion of policy options to foster domestic entrepreneurial development – including in areas such as the regulatory environment, access to finance, education and training, and technological development – can be found in UNCTAD's Entrepreneurship Policy Framework (box IV.5).

Enterprise development policies aimed at enhancing the benefits from investment focus on building capacity to absorb and adapt technology and know-how, to cooperate with multinational firms, and to compete internationally.

Another important policy task is the promotion of linkages and spillover effects between foreign investment and domestic enterprises (*WIR01*). Policy coordination is needed to ensure that investment promotion is targeted to those industries that could have the biggest impact in terms of creating backward and forward linkages and contribute not just to direct, but also to

Box IV.5. UNCTAD's Entrepreneurship Policy Framework

Entrepreneurship is vital for economic growth and development. The creation of new business entities generates value added, fiscal revenues, employment and innovation, and is an essential ingredient for the development of a vibrant small and medium-sized business sector. It has the potential to contribute to specific sustainable development objectives, such as the employment of women, young people or disadvantaged groups. Entrepreneurship development can also contribute to structural transformation and building new industries, including the development of eco-friendly economic activities.

UNCTAD's Entrepreneurship Policy Framework (EPF) aims to support developing-country policymakers in the design of initiatives, measures and institutions to promote entrepreneurship. It sets out a structured framework of relevant policy areas, embedded in an overall entrepreneurship strategy, which helps guide policymakers through the process of creating an environment that facilitates the emergence of start-ups, as well as the growth and expansion of new enterprises.

The EPF recognizes that in designing entrepreneurship policy "one size does not fit all". Although the national economic and social context and the specific development challenges faced by a country will largely determine the overall approach to entrepreneurship development, UNCTAD has identified six priority areas that have a direct impact on entrepreneurial activity (box figure IV.5.1). In each area the EPF suggests policy options and recommended actions.

Box figure IV.5.1. Key components of UNCTAD's Entrepreneurship Policy Framework

The EPF further proposes checklists and numerous references in the form of good practices and case studies. The case studies are intended to equip policymakers with implementable options to create the most conducive and supportive environment for entrepreneurs. The EPF includes a user guide, a step-by-step approach to developing entrepreneurship policy, and contains a set of indicators that can measure progress. An on-line inventory of good practices in entrepreneurship development, available on UNCTAD's web-site, completes the EPF. This online inventory will provide an opportunity for all stakeholders to contribute cases, examples, comments and suggestions, as a basis for the inclusive development of future entrepreneurship policies.

Source: UNCTAD; www.unctad.org/diae/epf.

indirect employment creation. At the same time, policymakers in developing countries need to address the risk of foreign investment impeding domestic enterprise development by crowding out local firms, especially SMEs. Industrial policies may play a role in protecting infant industries or other sensitive industries with respect to which host countries see a need to limit foreign access.

In the long run, enterprise development is essential if host countries are to improve international

competitiveness. Promotion efforts should therefore not be limited to low value added activities within international value chains, but gradually seek to move to higher value added segments. This is crucial for remaining competitive once developing countries lose their low labour cost advantage. However, switching from labour-intensive low-value activities to more capital-intensive, higher-value production methods may raise unemployment in the transition phase and thus calls for vigilant labour market and social policies. This confirms the important dynamic dimension of investment and enterprise development strategies, calling for regular reviews and adaptation of policy instruments.

Ensuring coherence between investment policies and other policy areas geared towards overall development objectives

The interaction between investment policy and other elements of a country's overall economic development and growth strategy – including human resource development, infrastructure, technology, enterprise development, and others – is complex. It is critical that government authorities work coherently towards the common national objective of sustainable development and inclusive growth, and seek to create synergies. This requires coordination at the earliest stages of policy design, as well as the involvement of relevant stakeholders, including the investor community and civil society.

2. Designing policies for responsible investment and sustainable development

Maximizing positive and minimizing negative impacts of investment requires balancing investment promotion and regulation. CSR standards can complement the regulatory framework. From a development perspective, FDI is more than a flow of capital that can stimulate economic growth. It comprises a package of assets that includes long-term capital, technology, market access, skills and know-how (*WIR99*). As such, it can contribute to sustainable development by providing financial resources where such resources are often scarce; generating employment (*WIR94*); strengthening export capacities (*WIR02*); transferring skills and disseminating technology; adding to GDP through investment and value added, both directly and indirectly; and generating fiscal revenues. In addition, FDI can support industrial diversification and upgrading, or the upgrading of agricultural productivity (*WIR09*) and the build up of productive capacity, including infrastructure (*WIR08*). Importantly, it can contribute to local enterprise development through linkages with suppliers (*WIR01*) and by providing access to GVCs (*WIR11*). The growing importance of GVCs

can have an important pro-poor dynamic to the extent that marginalized communities and small suppliers can integrate into global or regional value chains as producers, suppliers or providers of goods and services.

These positive development impacts of FDI do not always materialize automatically. And the effect of FDI can also be negative in each of the impact areas listed above. For example, it can lead to outflows of financial resources in the form of repatriated earnings or fees; it can, under certain circumstances, crowd out domestic investment and domestic enterprise (*WIR97*); it can at times reduce employment by introducing more efficient work practices or through restructurings (*WIR94*, *WIR00*), or jobs created may be unstable due to the footloose nature of some investment types; it can increase imports more than exports (or yield limited net export gains), e.g. in case of investment operations requiring intermediate inputs or for market-seeking investments (*WIR02*, *WIR11*); technology dissemination might not take place, or only at high cost (e.g. through licensing fees) (*WIR11*), and local technological development may be slowed down; skills transfers may be limited by the nature of jobs created; fiscal gains may be limited by tax avoidance schemes available to international investors, including transfer pricing; and so forth.

The balance of potential positive and negative development contributions of FDI is proof that investment policy matters in order to maximize the positive and minimize the negative impacts. Reaping the development benefits from investment requires not only an enabling policy framework that combines elements of investment promotion and regulation and that provides clear, unequivocal and transparent rules for the entry and operation of foreign investors (see box IV.6), it also requires adequate regulation to minimize any risks associated with investment.

The host of different impact types listed above indicates that such regulations need to cover a broad range of policy areas beyond investment policies per se, such as trade, taxation, intellectual property, competition, labour market regulation, environmental policies and access to land. The coverage of such a multitude of different policy areas confirms the need for consistency and coherence in policymaking across government.

Fostering sustainable development and inclusive growth through investment requires a balance of promotion and regulation. On the promotion side, attracting low-carbon investment, for example, may imply the need to set up new policy frameworks

for a nascent renewable energy sector, which may also require government assistance in the start-up phase, be it through tax incentives or measures aimed at creating a market (*WIR10*). Encouraging investment in sectors that are crucial for the poor may imply building sound regulatory frameworks and facilitating responsible investment in agriculture (including contract farming), as agriculture

---

Box IV.6. Designing sound investment rules and procedures: UNCTAD's Investment Facilitation Compact

UNCTAD's Investment Facilitation Compact combines a number of programmes aimed at assisting developing countries in strengthening their policy and institutional framework for attracting and retaining foreign investment, and in developing a regulatory climate in which investors can thrive.

The *UNCTAD-ICC Investment Guides* aim to provide accurate and up-to-date information on regulatory conditions in participating countries (as well as on the investment climate and emerging investment opportunities). They are prepared in collaboration with governments, national chambers of commerce and investors and are distributed by investment promotion agencies, foreign missions and other government departments, as well as by the International Chamber of Commerce.

The guides aim to provide a reliable source of third-party information for investors looking to invest in countries that are rarely covered by commercial publishers. They highlight often under-reported economic and investment policy reform efforts, including fiscal incentives, regional integration, easier access to land, establishment of alternative dispute settlement mechanisms, simplified border procedures, facilitation of permits and licenses and laws enabling private investment in power generation and infrastructure. Because the guides are produced through a collaborative process they also build capacities of governments to promote investment opportunities and understand investors' needs.

UNCTAD's *Business Facilitation* program aims to help developing countries build a regulatory and institutional environment that facilitates investment and business start-ups. It works through a methodology that first provides full transparency on existing rules and procedures for investors; it does so by offering online detailed, practical and up-to-date descriptions of the steps investors have to follow for procedures such as business or investment registration, license and permit issuance, payment of taxes, or obtaining work permits. Once full transparency has been created, the program helps governments simplify procedures by identifying unnecessary steps or developing alternatives.

The programme promotes good governance by increasing the awareness of administrative rules and procedures, establishing the conditions for a balanced dialogue between the users of the public services, including investors, and civil servants. It also sets a basis for regional or international harmonization of rules by facilitating the exchange of good practices among countries.

Individual programmes within the Investment Facilitation Compact have to date been undertaken in more than 35 countries and regions, with a strong focus on LDCs (box table IV.6.1).

Box table IV.6.1. Beneficiaries of selected programs of UNCTAD's Investment Facilitation Compact

Categories	Countries/regions
Investment Guides	Bangladesh, Benin, Bhutan, Burkina Faso, Cambodia, Comoros, East African Community, Ethiopia, Kenya, Lao People's Democratic Republic, Mali, Morocco, Oriental Region of Morocco, Mauritania, Mozambique, Nepal, Rwanda, United Republic of Tanzania, Silk Road Region, Uganda, Uzbekistan, Zambia
Business Facilitation	Benin, Burkina Faso, Cape Verde, Cameroon, Colombia, Comoros, Costa Rica, El Salvador, Guatemala, Mali, Nicaragua, Togo, Russian Federation (City of Moscow), Rwanda, Viet Nam

Source: UNCTAD; www.unctad.org; www.theiguides.org; www.eregulations.org.

continues to be the main source of income in many developing countries (*WIR09*).

At the same time, on the regulatory side, sustainability considerations should be a key consideration when deciding on the granting of investment incentives. The short-term advantages of an investment need to be weighed against the potential long-term environmental effects. And the sensitive issue of access to land requires careful balancing of the rights and obligation of agricultural investors. For many developing countries, it is a key challenge to strengthen such environmental and social protection while maintaining an attractive investment climate.

Sustainability issues should also be a main consideration in investment contracts between the host country and individual investors. Such contracts can be a means to commit investors to environmental or social standards beyond the level established by the host country's general legislation, taking into account international standards and best practices.

While laws and regulations are the basis of investor responsibility, voluntary CSR initiatives and standards have proliferated in recent years, and they are increasingly influencing corporate practices, behaviour and investment decisions. Governments can build on them to complement the regulatory framework and maximize the development benefits of investment (*WIR11*).

Because CSR initiatives and voluntary standards are a relatively new area that is developing quickly and in many directions, the management of their policy implications is a challenge for many developing countries. In particular, the potential interactions between soft law and hard law can be complex, and the value of standards difficult to extract for lack of monitoring capacity and limited comparability. A number of areas can benefit from the encouragement of CSR initiatives and the voluntary dissemination of standards; for example, they can be used to promote responsible investment and business behaviour (including the avoidance of corrupt business practices), and they can play an important role in promoting low-carbon and environmentally sound investment. Care needs to be taken to avoid these standards becoming undue barriers to trade and investment flows.

3. Implementation and institutional mechanisms for policy effectiveness

Investment policy and regulations must be adequately enforced by impartial, competent and efficient public institutions, which is as important for policy effectiveness as policy design itself. Policies to address implementation issues should be an integral part of the investment strategy and should strive to achieve both integrity across government and regulatory institutions and a service orientation where warranted. As a widely accepted best practice, regulatory agencies should be free of political pressure and have significant independence, subject to clear reporting guidelines and accountability to elected officials or representatives. These principles are particularly relevant for investors in institutions including courts and judiciary systems; sectoral regulators (e.g. electricity, transport, telecommunications, banking); customs; tax administration or revenue authorities; investment promotion agencies; and licensing bodies.

Ensuring policy effectiveness implies building institutional capability, monitoring implementation, and measuring results against objectives.

As stated in the fourth Core Principle, managing investment policy dynamically is of fundamental importance to ensure the continued relevance and effectiveness of policy measures. Revisions in investment policy may be driven by changes in strategy – itself caused by adaptations in the overall development strategy – or by external factors and changing circumstances. Countries require different investment policies at different stages of development, policies may need to take into account those in neighbouring countries, and be cognizant of trade patterns or evolving relative shares of sectors and industry in the economy. Policy design and implementation is a continuous process of fine-tuning and adaptation to changing needs and circumstances.

Beyond such adaptations, investment policy may also need adjustment where individual measures, entire policy areas, or the overall investment policy regime is deemed not to achieve the intended objectives, or to do so at a cost higher than intended. Understanding when this is the case, understanding it in time for corrective action to be taken, and understanding the reasons for the failure of measures to have the desired effect, is the essence of measuring policy effectiveness.

A significant body of academic literature exists on methodologies for evaluating policy effectiveness. Specifically in the area of investment policy, there are three objective difficulties associated with the measurement of policy effectiveness:

- It is often difficult to assess the effectiveness of discrete investment policy measures, such as the provision of incentives, let alone the effectiveness of the overall investment policy framework. Many *exogenous factors* and investment determinants beyond policy drive the investment attraction performance of a country – e.g. market size and growth, the presence of natural resources, the quality of basic infrastructure, labour productivity, and many others (see UNCTAD's Investment Potential Index).

- Investment policy effectiveness measures should also provide an indication of the extent to which policies help realize the benefits from investment and maximize its development impact. However, it is often difficult to find solid evidence for the discrete impact on various dimensions of *investment*, let alone for the impact of the *policies* that led to that investment or that guide the behaviour of investors.

- Much of the impact of investment policies and thus their effectiveness depends on the way such policies are applied, and on the capabilities of institutions charged with *the implementation and enforcement of policies and measures*, rules and regulations.

Given these objective difficulties in measuring the effectiveness of investment policies, and to ensure that potentially important policy changes are not delayed by complex analyses of the impact of individual measures, policymakers may be guided by a few simplifying rules in evaluating the effectiveness of their policies:

- Investment policy should be based on a set of explicitly formulated policy objectives with clear priorities, a time frame for achieving them, and the principal measures intended to support

the objectives. These objectives should be the principal yardstick for measuring policy effectiveness.

- The detailed quantitative (and therefore complex) measurement of the effectiveness of individual policy measures should focus principally on those measures that are most costly to implement, such as investment incentives.

- Assessment of progress in policy implementation and verification of the application of rules and regulations at all administrative levels is at least as important as the measurement of policy effectiveness. A review process should be put in place to ensure that policies are correctly implemented as a part of the assessment of policy effectiveness.

Goals and objectives for investment policy, as set out in a formal investment strategy in many countries, should be SMART:[8]

- *Specific:* they should break down objectives for investment attraction and impact for priority industries or activities as identified in the development strategy.

- *Measurable:* investment goals and objectives should identify a focused set of quantifiable indicators.

- *Attainable:* as part of investment policy development, policymakers should compare investment attraction and investment impact with peer countries to inform realistic target setting.

- *Relevant:* objectives (and relevant indicators) should relate to impacts that can be ascribed to investment (and by implication investment policy), to the greatest extent possible filtered for "general development strategy" impacts.

- *Time-bound:* objectives should fall within a variety of time frames. Even though broad development and investment-related objectives are of a long-term nature (e.g. 10-20 years), intermediate and specific objectives should refer to managerially and politically relevant time frames, e.g. 3-4 years. In addition, short-term benchmarks should be set within shorter time periods (a few quarters or a year) to ensure effective progress and implementation.

Objectives of investment policy should ideally include a number of quantifiable goals for both the *attraction of investment* and the *impact of investment*. To measure policy effectiveness for the attraction of investment, UNCTAD's Investment Potential and Attraction Matrix can be a useful tool. This matrix compares countries with their peers, plotting investment inflows against potential based on a standardized set of economic determinants, thereby providing a proxy for the effect of policy determinants. Similarly, for the measurement of policy effectiveness in terms of impact, UNCTAD's Investment Contribution Index may be a starting point.

Also important is the choice of impact indicators. Policymakers should use a focused set of key indicators that are the most direct expression of the core development contributions of private investments, including direct contributions to GDP growth through additional value added, capital formation and export generation; entrepreneurial development and development of the formal sector and tax base; and job creation. The indicators could also address labour, social, environmental and development sustainability aspects.

The impact indicator methodology developed for the G-20 Development Working Group by UNCTAD, in collaboration with other agencies, may provide guidance to policymakers on the choice of indicators of investment impact and, by extension, of investment policy effectiveness (see table IV.3). The indicator framework, which has been tested in a number of developing countries, is meant to serve as a tool that countries can adapt and adopt in accordance with their national economic development priorities and strategies. At early stages of development, pure GDP contribution and job creation impacts may be more relevant; at

more advanced stages, quality of employment and technology contributions may gain relevance.

4. The IPFSD's national policy guidelines

The national investment policy guidelines are organized in four sections, starting from the strategic level, which aims to ensure integration of investment policy in overall development strategy, moving to investment policy "stricto sensu", to investment-related policy areas such as trade, taxation, labour and environmental regulations, and intellectual property policies, to conclude with a section on investment policy effectiveness (table IV.4).

The national investment policy guidelines help policymakers integrate investment and development strategy, design investment-specific policies, ensure coherence with other policy areas, and improve policy effectiveness.

While the national guidelines in the IPFSD are meant to establish a generally applicable setting for investment-related policymaking, they cannot provide a "one-size-fits-all" solution for all economies. Countries have different development strategies and any policy guide must acknowledge these divergences. Governments may have different perceptions about which industries to promote and in what manner, and what role foreign investors should play in this context. Social, cultural, geographical and historical differences play a role as well. Furthermore, the investment climate of each country has its individual strengths and weaknesses; therefore, policies aimed at building upon existing strengths and reducing perceived deficiencies will differ. Thus investment policies need to be fine-tuned on the basis of specific economic contexts, sectoral investment priorities and development issues faced by individual countries. The IPFSD's national investment policy guidelines establish a basic framework. Other tools are available to complement the basic framework with customized best practice advice (box IV.7).

Table IV.3. Possible indicators for the definition of investment impact objectives and the measurement of policy effectiveness

Areas	Indicators	Details and examples
Economic value added	1. Total value added	• Gross output (GDP contribution) of the new/additional economic activity resulting from the investment (direct and induced)
	2. Value of capital formation	• Contribution to gross fixed capital formation
	3. Total and net export generation	• Total export generation; to some extent, net export generation (net of imports) is also captured by the local value added indicator
	4. Number of formal business entities	• Number of businesses in the value chain supported by the investment; this is a proxy for entrepreneurial development and expansion of the formal (tax-paying) economy
	5. Total fiscal revenues	• Total fiscal take from the economic activity resulting from the investment, through all forms of taxation
Job creation	6. Employment (number)	• Total number of jobs generated by the investment, both direct and induced (value chain view), dependent and self-employed
	7. Wages	• Total household income generated, direct and induced
	8. Typologies of employee skill levels	• Number of jobs generated, by ILO job type, as a proxy for job quality and technology levels (including technology dissemination)
Sustainable development	9. Labour impact indicators	• Employment of women (and comparable pay) and of disadvantaged groups • Skills upgrading, training provided • Health and safety effects, occupational injuries
	10. Social impact indicators	• Number of families lifted out of poverty, wages above subsistence level • Expansion of goods and services offered, access to and affordability of basic goods and services
	11. Environmental impact indicators	• Greenhouse gas emissions, carbon offset/credits, carbon credit revenues • Energy and water consumption/efficiency hazardous materials • Enterprise development in eco-sectors
	12. Development impact indicators	• Development of local resources • Technology dissemination

Source: "Indicators for measuring and maximizing economic value added and job creation arising from private sector investment in value chains", Report to the G-20 Cannes Summit, November 2011; produced by an inter-agency working group coordinated by UNCTAD. UNCTAD has included this methodology in its technical assistance work on investment policy, see box IV.4.

Table IV.4. Structure of the National Investment Policy Guidelines

Investment and sustainable development strategy	• Integrating investment policy in sustainable development strategy • Maximizing the contribution of investment to productive capacity-building and international competitiveness

Investment regulation and promotion	• Designing investment-specific policies regarding:
	  – Establishment and operations
	  – Treatment and protection of investments
	  – Investor responsibilities
	  – Investment promotion and facilitation

Investment-related policy areas	• Ensuring coherence with other policy areas, including trade, taxation, intellectual property, competition, labour market regulation, access to land, corporate responsibility and governance, environmental protection, and infrastructure and public-private partnerships
Investment policy effectiveness	• Building effective public institutions to implement investment policy • Measuring investment policy effectiveness and feeding back lessons learned into new rounds of policymaking

Box IV.7. Investment policy advice to "adapt and adopt": UNCTAD's Series on Best Practices in Investment for Development

As with UNCTAD's IPR approach (see box IV.4), in which each IPR is custom-designed for relevance in the specific context of individual countries, the UNCTAD work program on Best Practices in Investment for Development acknowledges that *one size does not fit all*.

The program consists of a series of studies on investment policies tailored to:
  – specific sectors of the economy (e.g. infrastructure, natural resources);
  – specific development situations (e.g. small economies, post-conflict economies);
  – specific development issues (e.g. capacity-building, linkages).

The program aims to build an inventory of best policy practices in order to provide a reference framework for policymakers in developing countries through concrete examples that can be adapted to their national context. Each study therefore looks at one or two specific country case studies from which lessons can be drawn on good investment policy practices related to the theme of the study. The following studies are currently available:
  – How to Utilize FDI to Improve Transport Infrastructure: Roads – Lessons from Australia and Peru;
  – How to Utilize FDI to Improve Transport Infrastructure: Ports – Lessons from Nigeria;
  – How to Utilize FDI to Improve Infrastructure: Electricity – Lessons from Chile and New Zealand;
  – How to Attract and Benefit from FDI in Mining – Lessons from Canada and Chile;
  – How to Attract and Benefit from FDI in Small Countries – Lessons from Estonia and Jamaica;
  – How Post-Conflict Countries Can Attract and Benefit from FDI – Lessons from Croatia and Mozambique;
  – How to Integrate FDI and Skill Development – Lessons from Canada and Singapore;
  – How to Create and Benefit from FDI-SME Linkages – Lessons from Malaysia and Singapore;
  – How to Prevent and Manage Investor-State Disputes – Lessons from Peru.

Source: UNCTAD; www.unctad.org.

UNCTAD Investment Policy Framework for Sustainable Development
National investment policy guidelines

Sections	Sub-sections		Policy Guidelines
1 Investment and sustainable development strategy	**1.1 Strategic investment policy priorities**	1.1.1	Investment policy should be geared towards the realization of national sustainable development goals and grounded in a country's overall development strategy. It should set out strategic priorities, including: - Investment in specific economic activities, e.g. as an integral part of an industrial development strategy. - Areas for mutual reinforcement of public and private investment (including a framework for public-private partnerships). - Investment that makes a significant development contribution by creating decent work opportunities, enhancing sustainability, and/or by expanding and qualitatively improving productive capacity (see 1.2) and international competitiveness. Investment policy priorities should be based on a thorough analysis of the country's comparative advantages and development challenges and opportunities, and should address key bottlenecks for attracting FDI.
		1.1.2	Strategic investment policy priorities may be effectively formalized in a published document (e.g. investment strategy), making explicit the intended role of private and foreign investment in the country's sustainable development strategy and development priorities, and providing a clear signal to both investors and stakeholders involved in investment policymaking.
	1.2 Investment policy coherence for productive capacity-building		
	Human resource development	1.2.1	The potential for job creation and skills transfer should be one of the criteria for determining investment priorities. Taking into account the mutually reinforcing link between human resource development (HRD) and investment, investment policy should inform HRD policy to prioritize skill building in areas crucial for development priorities, whether technical, vocational, managerial or entrepreneurial skills.
	Technology and know-how	1.2.2	The potential for the transfer of appropriate technologies and the dissemination of know-how should be one of the criteria for determining investment priorities, and should be promoted through adequate investment-related policies, including taxation and intellectual property.
	Infrastructure	1.2.3	The potential for infrastructure development through FDI, in particular under PPPs, should be an integral part of investment policy. Infrastructure development policies should give due consideration to basic infrastructure areas crucial for the building of productive capacities, including utilities, roads, sea- and airports or industrial parks, in line with investment priorities.
		1.2.4	A specific regulatory framework for PPPs should be in place to ensure that investor-State partnerships serve the public interest (see also section 3.9 below).
	Enterprise development	1.2.5	The potential for FDI to generate business linkages and to stimulate local enterprise development should be a key criterion in defining investment policy and priorities for FDI attraction. Enterprise development and business facilitation policies (including access to finance) should promote entrepreneurial activity where such activity yields particularly significant benefits through linkages and acts as a crucial locational determinant for targeted foreign investments.
2 Investment regulation and promotion	**2.1 Entry, establishment and operations of foreign investors**		
	Policy statement on FDI and degree of openness	2.1.1	Investment policy benefits from a clear message towards the international business community on FDI (e.g. in a country's investment strategy or law on foreign investment, where these exist). Attracting high levels of diverse and beneficial FDI calls for a general policy of openness and avoidance of investment protectionism, subject to qualifications and selective restrictions to address country-specific development needs and policy concerns, such as regarding the provision of public goods or the control over strategic industries and critical infrastructure.

Sections	Sub-sections		Policy Guidelines
Investment regulation and promotion (continued)	Screening and entry restrictions	2.1.2	Ownership restrictions or limitations on the entry of foreign investment, in full accordance with countries' right to regulate, should be justified by legitimate national policy objectives and should not be influenced by special interests. They are best limited to a few explicitly stated aims, including: - protecting the national interest, national security, control over natural resources, critical infrastructure, public health, the environment; or - promoting national development objectives in accordance with a published development strategy or investment strategy. Such restrictions need to be in conformity with international commitments.
		2.1.3	Restrictions on foreign ownership in specific industries or economic activities should be clearly specified; a list of specific industries where restrictions (e.g. prohibitions, limitations) apply has the advantage of achieving such clarity while preserving a policy of general openness to FDI.
		2.1.4	A periodic review should take place of any ownership restrictions and of the level of ownership caps to evaluate whether they remain the most appropriate and cost-effective method to ensure achievement of these objectives.
		2.1.5	Screening procedures for investment entry and establishment, where applicable, should be conducted following pre-established objective criteria.
	Property registration	2.1.6	Investors should be able to register ownership of or titles to land and other forms of property securely, effectively and timely, including in order to facilitate access to debt finance, bearing in mind specific development challenges in this regard (see also 3.6 below).
	Freedom of operations	2.1.7	Governments should avoid direct or indirect intrusions in business management and respect the freedom of operations of private companies, subject to compliance with domestic laws. This includes the freedom of investors to decide whether they want to invest at home or abroad.
	Performance requirements	2.1.8	Performance requirements and related operational constraints should be used sparingly and only to the extent that they are necessary to achieve legitimate public policy purposes. They need to be in compliance with international obligations and would typically be imposed principally as conditions for special privileges, including fiscal or financial incentives.
2.2 Treatment and protection of investors	Treatment under the rule of law	2.2.1	Established investors and investments, foreign or domestic, should be granted treatment that is based on the rule of law.
	Core standards of treatment	2.2.2	As a general principle, foreign investors and investments should not be discriminated against vis-à-vis national investors in the post-establishment phase and in the conduct of their business operations. Where development objectives require policies that distinguish between foreign and domestic investment, these should be limited, transparent and periodically reviewed for efficacy against those objectives. They need to be in line with international commitments, including REIOs.
		2.2.3	While recognizing that countries have not only the *right* to regulate, regulatory changes should take into account the need to ensure stability and predictability of the investment climate.
	Transfer of funds	2.2.4	Where the level of development or macro-economic considerations warrant restrictions on the transfer of capital, countries should seek to treat FDI-related transactions differently from other (particularly short-term) capital account transactions. Countries should guarantee the freedom to transfer and repatriate capital related to investments in productive assets, subject to reporting requirements (including to fight money laundering) and prior compliance with tax obligations, and subject to potential temporary restrictions due to balance of payment crises and in compliance with international law. Controls should be periodically reviewed for efficacy.

Sections	Sub-sections		Policy Guidelines
Investment regulation and promotion (continued)		2.2.5	Countries should guarantee the free convertibility of their currency for current account transactions, including FDI-related earnings and dividends, interests, royalties and others. Any restriction to convertibility for current account transactions should be in accordance with existing international obligations and flexibilities, in particular the IMF Articles of Agreement.
	Contract enforcement and dispute settlement	2.2.6	All investors should be entitled to equal treatment in the enforcement of contracts. Mechanisms and proceedings for the enforcement of contracts should be timely, efficient and effective, and available to all investors so as to duly operate under the rule of law.
	Investment contracts	2.2.7	States should honour their obligations deriving from investment contracts with investors, unless they can invoke a fundamental change of circumstances or other legitimate reasons in accordance with national and international law.
	Expropriation	2.2.8	When warranted for legitimate public policy purposes, expropriations or nationalization should be undertaken in a non-discriminatory manner and conform to the principle of due process of law, and compensation should be provided. Decisions should be open to recourse and reviews to avoid arbitrariness.
	International commitments	2.2.9	Governments should assign explicit responsibility and accountability for the implementation and periodic review of measures to ensure effective compliance with commitments under IIAs. Strong alternative dispute resolution (ADR) mechanisms can be effective means to avoid international arbitration of disputes.
	2.3 Investor obligations		
	Responsible investment	2.3.1	Investors' first and foremost obligation is to comply with a host country's laws and regulations. This obligation should apply and be enforced indiscriminately to national and foreign investors, as should sanctions for non-compliance.
	Standards	2.3.2	Governments should encourage adherence to international standards of responsible investment and codes of conduct by foreign investors. Standards which may serve as reference include the ILO Tri-partite Declaration, the OECD Guidelines for Multinational Enterprises, the UNCTAD, FAO IFAD and World Bank Principles for Responsible Agricultural Investment, the UN Guiding Principles on Business and Human Rights and others. In addition, countries may wish to translate soft rules into national legislation.
	2.4 Promotion and facilitation of investment		
	Investment authority and investment promotion agency	2.4.1	Explicit responsibility and accountability should be assigned to an investment promotion agency (IPA) to encourage investment and to assist investors in complying with administrative and procedural requirements with a view towards facilitating their establishment, operation and development.
		2.4.2	The mission, objectives and structure of the IPA should be grounded in national investment policy objectives and regularly reviewed. The core functions of IPAs should include image building, targeting, facilitation, aftercare and advocacy.
		2.4.3	As the prime interface between Government and investors, IPAs should support efforts to improve the general business climate and eliminate red tape.
		2.4.4	Where screening or preliminary approval is imposed on foreign investors, responsibility and accountability for such procedures should be clearly separate from investment promotion and facilitation functions in order to avoid potential conflicts of interest.
		2.4.5	IPAs should be in a position to resolve cross-ministerial issues through its formal and informal channels of communication, and by reporting at a sufficiently high level of Government. Its governance should be ensured through an operational board that includes members from relevant ministries and from the private sector.
		2.4.6	The effectiveness of the IPA in attracting investment should be periodically reviewed against investment policy objectives. The efficiency of the IPA and its working methods should also be reviewed in light of international best practice.

Sections	Sub-sections		Policy Guidelines
Investment regulation and promotion (continued)	Investment incentives and guarantees	2.4.7	The work of national and sub-national IPAs, as well as that of authorities promoting investment in special economic zones, should be closely coordinated to ensure maximum efficiency and effectiveness.
		2.4.8	Being at the core of Government efforts to promote and facilitate investment, the IPA should establish close working relationships (including through secondment of staff) with regulatory agencies dealing directly with investors. It should seek to promote a client-oriented attitude in public administration. It may enlist the diplomatic service to strengthen overseas promotion efforts.
		2.4.9	Investment incentives, in whatever form (fiscal, financial or other), should be carefully assessed in terms of long-term costs and benefits prior to implementation, giving due consideration to potential distortion effects. The costs and benefits of incentives should be periodically reviewed and their effectiveness in achieving the desired objectives thoroughly evaluated.
		2.4.10	Where investment incentives are granted to support nascent industries, self-sustained viability (i.e. without the need for incentives) should be the ultimate goal so as to avoid subsidizing non-viable industries at the expense of the economy as a whole. A phase-out period built in the incentive structure is good practice, without precluding permanent tax measures to address positive or negative externalities.
		2.4.11	The rationale and justification for investment incentives should be directly and explicitly derived from the country's development strategy. Their effectiveness for achieving the objectives should be fully assessed before adoption, including through international comparability.
		2.4.12	The granting and administration of incentives should be the responsibility of an independent entity or ministry that does not have conflicting objectives or performance targets for investment attraction.
		2.4.13	Environmental, labour and other regulatory standards should not be lowered as a means to attract investment, or to compete for investment in a "regulatory race to the bottom".
		2.4.14	Investment incentives should be granted on the basis of a set of pre-determined, objective, clear and transparent criteria. They should be offered on a non-discriminatory basis to projects fulfilling these criteria. Compliance with the criteria (performance requirements) should be monitored on a regular basis as a condition to benefit from the incentives.
		2.4.15	Investment incentives over and above pre-defined incentives must be shown to make an exceptional contribution to development objectives, and additional requirements should be attached, including with a view to avoiding a "race to the top of incentives".
		2.4.16	Investment incentives offered by sub-national entities which have the discretion to grant incentives over and above the pre-defined limits, should be coordinated by a central investment authority to avoid investors "shopping around".
	Promotion of business linkages and spillovers	2.4.17	As business linkages between foreign investors and national companies do not always develop naturally, Governments and IPAs should actively nurture and facilitate them. Undue intrusion in business partnerships should be avoided as mutually beneficial and sustainable linkages cannot be mandated.
		2.4.18	Measures that Governments should consider to promote linkages include: (1) direct intermediation between national and foreign investors to close information gaps; (2) support (financial and other) to national companies for process or technology upgrading; (3) selective FDI targeting; (4) establishment of national norms and standards, along the lines of international ones (e.g ISO standards); and (5) incentives for foreign investors to assist in upgrading of local SMEs and promotion of entrepreneurship.
		2.4.19	Mandatory practices to promote linkages, such as joint-venture requirements, should be used sparingly and carefully considered to avoid unintended adverse effects.
		2.4.20	Explicit responsibility and accountability should be assigned to the investment authority or IPA to nurture and promote business linkages established by foreign investors as part of its aftercare mandate.
		2.4.21	Specific policies should encourage businesses to offer training to employees in skill areas deemed crucial in the country's policy on human resource development, including through performance requirements linked to investment incentives.

Sections	Sub-sections		Policy Guidelines
3 Investment-related policies	**3.1 Trade policy**		
	International trade agreements	3.1.1	Access to global markets is essential for resource- and efficiency-seeking foreign investors, and the size of local/regional markets is equally important for market-seeking investors. Active participation in international trade agreements (in particular the WTO) and enhanced integration at the regional level should be considered an integral part of development strategy and a key factor in promoting investment.
	Trade restriction and promotion	3.1.2	Trade policies, including tariffs and non-tariff barriers, and trade promotion/facilitation measures (e.g. export finance, import insurance schemes, support to obtain compliance with international standards and norms) can selectively promote or discourage investment in specific industries. They should be defined in line with (industrial) development objectives and investment policy.
	Customs and border procedures	3.1.3	Compliance costs and efficiency of border procedures should be periodically benchmarked against international best practice and should avoid as much as possible forming an obstacle to the attraction of export-oriented investment or investment that relies on imports of intermediate goods.
	3.2 Tax policy		
	Corporate taxation	3.2.1	A periodic review, including international benchmarking, of corporate taxation (and fiscal incentives) for effectiveness, costs and benefits should be an integral part of investment policy. Reviews should consider costs linked to the structure of the tax regime, including (1) administrative and compliance costs for investors, (2) administrative and monitoring costs for the tax authorities, and (3) forgone revenue linked to tax evasion and/or tax engineering.
		3.2.2	Undue complexity of income tax law and regulations should be avoided and they should be accompanied by clear guidelines, as transparency, predictability and impartiality of the tax regime are essential for all investors, foreign and national alike.
		3.2.3	The tax system should tend to neutrality in its treatment of domestic and foreign investors.
	Fiscal incentives	3.2.4	In line with a country's development strategy, incentives can be used for the encouragement of investment in specific industries or in order to achieve specific objectives (e.g. regional development, job creation, skills upgrading, technology dissemination). Fiscal incentives for investors should not by nature seek to compensate for an unattractive or inappropriate general tax regime.
		3.2.5	The general corporate income tax regime should be the norm and not the exception and proliferation of tax incentives should be avoided as they quickly lead to distortions, generate unintended tax avoidance opportunities, become difficult to monitor, create administrative costs and may end up protecting special interests at the expense of the general public.
	Transfer pricing and international cooperation	3.2.6	Well-established and clearly defined transfer pricing rules are essential to minimize tax engineering and tax evasion. Developing countries can build on international best practices. International cooperation between tax authorities is key to fight manipulative transfer pricing practices.
	Double taxation treaties	3.2.7	Double taxation treaties are an effective tool to promote inward and outward FDI. Developing countries should carefully negotiate such treaties to ensure that the principle of "taxation at the source" prevails.
		3.2.8	A country's international tax treaty network should focus on major countries of origin for the types of investment prioritized in its investment policy.
	3.3 Intellectual property		
		3.3.1	Laws and regulations for the protection of intellectual property rights and mechanisms for their enforcement should meet the need of prospective investors (especially where investment policy aims to attract investment in IP-sensitive industries) and encourage innovation and investment by domestic and foreign firms, while providing for sanctions against the abuse by IPR holders of IP rights (e.g. the exercise of IP rights in a manner that prevents the emergence of legitimate competing designs or technologies) and allowing for the pursuit of the public good. As national investors are frequently less aware of their IP rights they should be educated on the issue.

Sections	Sub-sections		Policy Guidelines
Investment-related policies (continued)		3.3.2	Developing countries are encouraged to integrate the flexibilities in IP protection granted under international treaties, including the WTO's TRIPS agreement, into national legislation and consider the extent to which these flexibilities can create opportunities for investment attraction (e.g. in the production of pharmaceuticals).
	3.4 Competition policy		
	Competition laws and regulations	3.4.1	Competition laws and regulations, covering practices in restraint of competition, abuse of market power and economic concentration together with effective monitoring and enforcement mechanisms, are essential to reap the benefits from investment and should provide fair rules and a level playing field for all investors, foreign and domestic.
	Coordination of investment and competition authorities	3.4.2	Investment policymakers should cooperate closely with competition authorities, with a view to addressing any anti-competitive practices by incumbent enterprises that may inhibit investment. Particular attention should be paid to priority industries and investment types.
		3.4.3	Where investment policy pursues objectives for sectors that may be considered to fall under a public services obligation or for regulated sectors (e.g. public transport, utilities, telecommunications), competition authorities should be actively involved in shaping relevant policies and measures, coordinating closely with sectoral regulators.
	M&As and privatizations	3.4.4	Competition laws and decisions related to M&As, as well as the policy framework for privatizations, should support development strategy and investment policy objectives, and should ensure continued attractiveness of the relevant sector for further investment by avoiding market exclusivity and preventing abuse of dominant market power.
		3.4.5	Close coordination between competition authorities in neighbouring countries should be pursued in case of cross-border M&As, particularly in small economies.
	3.5 Labour market regulation		
	Balancing labour market flexibility and protection of employees	3.5.1	Labour market regulations should support job creation objectives in investment policy, including through an appropriate degree of labour market flexibility. At the same time, employees should be protected from abusive labour practices.
	Core labour standards	3.5.2	Countries need to guarantee internationally recognized core labour standards, in particular regarding child labour, the right for collective representation and other core protections as guaranteed by the ILO conventions the country is a party to. Effective mechanisms to promote core labour standards should be put in place and applied equally to foreign and domestic firms.
	Adjustment costs of investment policy	3.5.3	Adjustment costs or friction caused by shifting productive capacity and employment to priority investment areas, industries or activities in accordance with investment policy should be addressed both in labour market policies (e.g. re-training, social support) and in investment policy (e.g. encouraging investors to help ease transition costs).
	Hiring of international staff	3.5.4	Expatriate staff can at times be critical to the success of individual investment projects. Labour policy and/or immigration policy should avoid unduly restricting or delaying the employment of foreign personnel, including in skilled trades/artisan jobs, by investors in order not to hinder the build-up of productive capacity. At the same time, employment opportunities for nationals in jobs they can adequately fill should be promoted.
		3.5.5	Transfer of skills from expatriate staff to nationals should be actively encouraged, including through technical and vocational training requirements at the company level whenever expatriates are employed. The use of foreign employees in skilled trades/artisan jobs may be time-bound in order to encourage foreign invested firms to establish local linkages.

Sections	Sub-sections		Policy Guidelines
Investment-related policies (continued)	**3.6 Access to land**		
	Titles	3.6.1	More than the nature of land titles (full ownership, long-term lease, land-use rights or other), predictability and security are paramount for investors. Governments should aim to ease access to land titles, adequately register and protect them, and guarantee stability. Developing and properly administering a national cadastre system can be an effective tool to encourage investment.
		3.6.2	Full ownership of land or tradable land titles can help companies secure financing for investment, as land can be used as collateral. Transferable titles should be encouraged where specific country circumstances do not prevent this option.
	Agricultural land	3.6.3	Foreign ownership or user titles over agricultural land is particularly sensitive in most countries, in particular those with large rural populations and where food security is an issue. Governments should pay particular care in putting in place and enforcing regulations to protect the long-term national interest and not compromise it for short-term gains by special interest groups. Adherence to the UNCTAD, FAO, IFAD, and World Bank Principles for Responsible Agricultural Investment should be encouraged.
	Industrial land and industrial parks	3.6.4	The development of industrial, technology or services parks as public-private partnerships has worked well in a number of countries and can be an effective tool to facilitate access to fully-serviced land by (foreign) investors.
	3.7 Corporate responsibility and governance		
	CSR standards	3.7.1	Governments should encourage compliance with high standards of responsible investment and corporate behaviour, including through: (1) capacity-building and technical assistance to local industry to improve their ability to access markets or work with investors that prefer or require certified products; (2) public procurement criteria; (3) incorporating existing standards into regulatory initiatives, and/or turning voluntary standards (soft law) into regulation (hard law).
	Corporate governance	3.7.2	Countries should aim to adopt international standards of corporate governance for large formal businesses under their company law or commercial code, in particular: (1) protection of minority shareholders; (2) transparency and disclosure on a timely, reliable and relevant basis; (3) external auditing of accounts; and (4) adoption of high standards and codes of good practices on corruption, health, environment, and safety issues. The OECD Principles of Corporate Governance and the UNCTAD Guidance on Good Practices in Corporate Governance Disclosure may serve as guidance.
	Reporting standards	3.7.3	Corporate reporting standards should provide for disclosure by foreign-controlled firms on local ownership and control structures, finances and operations, and health, safety, social and environmental impacts, following international best practice. Recommendations by the UNCTAD Intergovernmental Working Group of Experts on International Standards of Accounting and Reporting (ISAR) may serve as guidance.
	3.8 Environmental policy		
	Environmental impact of investment	3.8.1	Environmental impact assessments (EIA) should be part of investment policies; it is useful to classify projects based on a number of pre-defined criteria, including sector, nature, size and location to place more stringent or less stringent requirements on preliminary environmental impact assessments (or absence thereof).
		3.8.2	Environmental norms, including EIA requirements, should be transparent, non-discriminatory vis-à-vis foreign investors, predictable and stable; Governments should ensure that environmental licensing procedures are conducted without undue delay and in full technical objectivity.
	Environmental dumping	3.8.3	Foreign investors should be encouraged to adhere to international standards of environmental protection and committed not to engage in environmental dumping; in specific cases (e.g. mining or oil extraction), Governments may wish to legally require international best practices (including the use of technologies) to be strictly adhered to.

Sections	Sub-sections	Policy Guidelines	
Investment-related policies (continued)	**3.9 Infrastructure, concessioning and PPP policies**		
	Opening infrastructure sectors to investors	3.9.1	Given the potential contribution of private investment to building high-quality infrastructure, countries should consider the extent to which basic infrastructure sectors can be opened to domestic and foreign private investment, and under what conditions.
		3.9.2	In sectors opened to private investment, careful efforts should go into identifying specific projects to be taken up by private investors. Shortlists of projects for concessioning are a useful tool, and Governments should initially focus on projects of moderate complexity, where commercial gains are easier to realize for investors, and where the socio-economic gains are clearly measurable.
	Concessioning rules and regulations	3.9.3	Following strategic decisions on which sectors to open to private investment, Governments should put in place a carefully crafted legal framework for concession contracts and public-private partnerships. Given the long-term nature of concession agreements in infrastructure, the legal framework should provide significant assurances to investors, including regarding contractual terms and their enforcement, and property rights.
		3.9.4	The legal framework for concession contracts needs to adequately protect the long-term national interest and consumers, ensuring adequate sharing of risks between the private and public partners.
	Competitive outcomes	3.9.5	Wherever possible, concessioning to private investors should aim to introduce competition so as not to replace a public monopoly with a private one. Placing natural monopolies under private concession should be limited to cases where it increases efficiency and the delivery of services. Putting in place appropriate competition and sectoral regulations should be considered a pre-requisite for the successful concessioning of infrastructure services.
	Institutional framework for concessioning and PPPs	3.9.6	Given the complexity of contractual terms involved in large infrastructure concessions, strong institutions need to be put in place first in order to achieve desirable outcomes; in addition to strengthening sectoral regulators, countries should consider the establishment of a dedicated PPP unit.
4 Investment policy effectiveness	**4.1 Public governance and institutions**		
	From framework to implementation	4.1.1	In the implementation of investment policies Governments should strive to achieve: (1) integrity and impartiality across Government and independence of regulatory institutions, subject to clear reporting lines and accountability to elected officials; (2) transparency and predictability for investors; (3) a service-orientation towards investors, where warranted.
	Inter-agency cooperation	4.1.2	Close cooperation and formal communication channels should be in place between institutions and agencies dealing with investors. The IPA should play a coordinating role given its comprehensive perspective on issues confronting investors.
	Anti-corruption efforts	4.1.3	Governments should adopt effective anti-corruption legislation and fight corruption with appropriate administrative, institutional and judicial means, for which international best practices should serve as guidance. Investors should be held to good corporate governance principles, which include refraining from paying bribes and denouncing corrupt practices.

Sections	Sub-sections		Policy Guidelines
Investment policy effectiveness (continued)	4.2 Dynamic policy development	4.2.1	Policy design and implementation is a continuous process of fine-tuning and adaptation to changing needs and circumstances. Periodic review (every 3-4 years) of performance against objectives should take place, with a view to: - verifying continued coherence of investment policy with overall development strategy - assessing investment policy effectiveness against objectives through a focused set of indicators - identifying and addressing underlying causes of underperformance - evaluating return on investment of the more costly investment policy measures (e.g. incentives).
	4.3 Measuring investment policy effectiveness	4.3.1	Objectives for investment policy should be the yard-stick for measurement of policy effectiveness. (Where countries have a formal investment strategy it should set out such objectives, see 1.1 above.) They should break down objectives for investment attraction and development impact, and set clear priorities. Performance (especially in terms of investment attraction) should be benchmarked against peers.
		4.3.2	Indicators for objectives related to the *attraction of investment* may include: - investment inflows (e.g. total, by industry, activity) - investment flows as a share of gross output and capital formation (e.g. total, by industry, activity) - greenfield investment as a share of total investment - positioning on UNCTAD's *"Investment Potential and Attraction Matrix"*.
		4.3.3	Indicators for objectives related to the *impact of investment* may include: - value added of investment activity - value of capital formation - export generation - contribution to the creation of formal business entities - fiscal revenues - employment generation and wage contribution - technology and skills contribution (e.g. as measured through the skill-types of jobs created) - social and environmental measures - positioning on UNCTAD's *"Investment Contribution Matrix"*.

E. ELEMENTS OF INTERNATIONAL INVESTMENT AGREEMENTS: POLICY OPTIONS

Countries can address international investment policy challenges in their strategic approach to IIAs, in the negotiation of IIAs and the design of specific clauses, and through multilateral consensus building. The guidance on international investment policies set out in this section aims to translate the Core Principles into concrete options for policymakers, with a view to addressing today's investment policy challenges. While national investment policymakers address these challenges through rules, regulations, institutions and initiatives, at the international level policy is translated through a complex web of treaties (including, principally, bilateral investment treaties, free trade agreements with investment provisions, economic partnership agreements and regional agreements).[9] As discussed in section B, the complexity of that web, which leads to gaps, overlaps and inconsistencies in the system of IIAs, is itself one of the challenges to be addressed. The other is the need to strengthen the development dimension of IIAs, balancing the rights and obligations of States and investors, ensuring sufficient policy space for sustainable development policies and making investment promotion provisions more concrete and aligned with sustainable development objectives.

International investment policy challenges must be addressed at three levels:

1. When formulating their *strategic approach to international engagement on investment*, policymakers need to embed international investment policymaking into their countries' development strategies. This involves managing the interaction between IIAs and national policies (e.g. ensuring that IIAs support industrial policies (*WIR11*)) and that between IIAs and other international policies or agreements (e.g. ensuring that IIAs do not contradict international environmental agreements *(WIR10)* or human rights obligations). The overall objective is to ensure coherence between IIAs and sustainable development needs.

2. *In the detailed design of provisions in investment agreements* between countries, policymakers need to incorporate sustainable development considerations, addressing concerns related to policy space (e.g., through reservations and exceptions), balanced rights and obligations of States and investors (e.g., through encouraging compliance with CSR standards), and effective investment promotion (e.g., through home-country measures).

3. *Multilateral consensus building on investment policy*, in turn, can help address some of the systemic challenges stemming from the multi-layered and multi-faceted nature of the IIA regime, including the gaps, overlaps and inconsistencies in the system, its multiple dispute resolution mechanisms, and its piecemeal and erratic expansion.

This section, therefore, first discusses how policymakers can strategically engage in the international investment regime at different levels and in different ways in the interest of sustainable development. It then provides a set of options for the detailed design of IIAs. The final section of this chapter suggests an avenue for further consensus building and international cooperation on investment policy.

UNCTAD's proposed options for addressing the challenges described above come at a time when a multitude of investment stakeholders are putting forward suggestions for the future of IIA policymaking. With the recently adopted European Union–United States Statement on Shared Principles for International Investment, the revision of the International Chamber of Commerce (ICC) Guidelines for International Investment, and the release of the new United States model BIT, IIA policymaking is in one of its more dynamic evolutionary stages, providing a window of opportunity to strengthen the sustainable development dimension of IIAs.

1. Defining the role of IIAs in countries' development strategy and investment policy

When engaging in IIAs, policymakers should be aware of what IIAs can and cannot do for their national development, and set clear priorities. International investment instruments are an integral part of investment policymaking that supports investment promotion objectives but that can also constrain investment and development policymaking. As a promotion tool, IIAs complement national rules and regulations by offering additional assurances to foreign investors concerning the protection of their investments and the stability, transparency and predictability of the national policy framework. As to the constraints, these could take many forms: they could limit options for developing countries in the formulation of development strategies that might call for differential treatment of investors, e.g. industrial policies (see *WIR11*); or they could hinder policymaking in general, including for sustainable development objectives, if investors perceive new measures as unfavourable to their interests and resort to IIA-defined dispute settlement procedures outside the normal domestic legal process.

Given such potential constraints on policymaking, it is important to ensure the coherence of IIAs with other economic policies (e.g. trade, industrial, technology, infrastructure or enterprise policies that aim at building productive capacity and strengthening countries' competitiveness) as well as with non-economic policies (e.g. environmental, social, health or cultural policies).[10] Policymakers should carefully set out an agenda for international engagement and negotiation on investment (including the revision and renegotiation of existing agreements).

When considering the pros and cons of engaging in IIAs, policymakers should have a clear understanding of what IIAs can and cannot achieve.

- IIAs *can*, by adding an international dimension to investment protection and by fostering stability, predictability and transparency, reinforce investor confidence and thus promote investment. From an investor's perspective, IIAs essentially act as an insurance policy, especially important for investments in countries with unfavourable country-risk ratings.

- IIAs *can* promote investment in other ways beyond granting investor protection. Some IIAs include commitments on the part of home countries to promote outward investment or to engage in collaborative initiatives for this purpose (although this is currently a small minority of treaties).[11]

- IIAs *can* help to build and advertise a more attractive investment climate. By establishing international commitments, they can foster good governance and facilitate or support domestic reforms.

- By contrast, IIAs alone *cannot* turn a bad domestic investment climate into a good one and they cannot guarantee the inflow of foreign investment. There is no mono-causal link between the conclusion of an IIA and FDI inflows; IIAs play a complementary role among many determinants that drive firms' investment decisions.[12] Most importantly, IIAs cannot be a substitute for domestic policies and a sound national regulatory framework for investment.

Host countries' engagement in the current IIA system may not be driven solely by a clear and explicit design that grounds their treaties in a solid development purpose, but rather influenced by the negotiation goals of their treaty partners or other non-economic considerations.[13] As such, there is a risk that IIAs, in number and substance, may become largely a vehicle for the protection of interests of investors and home countries without giving due consideration to the development concerns of developing countries. Not surprisingly, a detailed analysis of the substance of model treaties of major outward investing countries shows that, on average, treaty provisions are heavily skewed towards providing a high level of protection, with limited concessions to development aspects that can be a trade-off against investor protection (i.e. leaving countries more policy space generally implies granting less protection to investors). This trade-off suggests that there may be an inherent development challenge in IIAs: developing countries with the most unfavourable risk ratings are most in need of the protecting qualities of IIAs to attract investment, but they are generally also the countries most in need of flexibility (or policy space) for specific development policies.

Moreover, not only low-income developing countries may experience IIAs as a straightjacket, but also higher income countries, and even developed market economies, are sometimes faced with unexpected consequences of their own treaties. As more and more countries with sound and credible domestic legal systems and stable investment climates continue to conclude IIAs granting high levels of investor protection, they risk being confronted themselves with investor-State dispute settlement (ISDS) rules originally intended to shield their investors abroad. This risk is exacerbated by the changing investor landscape, in which more and more developing countries, against whose policies the IIA protective shield was originally directed, are becoming important outward investors in their own right, turning the tables on the original developed country IIA *demandeurs*. Spelling out the underlying drivers and objectives of a country's approach to IIAs thus becomes important not only for developing countries, but also for developed ones.

In addition to taking into account the development purpose of IIAs, in defining their agenda for international engagement and negotiation on investment, IIA policymakers should:

- *Consider the type of agreements to prioritize*, and whether to pursue dedicated agreements on investment or investment provisions integrated in broader agreements, e.g. covering also trade, competition and/ or other policy areas. The latter option provides for comprehensive treatment of inter-related issues in different policy areas. It also recognizes the strong interaction between trade and investment and the blurring boundaries between the two (due to the phenomenon of non-equity modes of international production; see *WIR11*), as well as the FDI and trade inducing effect of enlarged markets.

- *Consider whether to pursue international engagement* on investment policy in the context of regional economic cooperation or integration or through bilateral agreements. For smaller developing countries, with

limited potential to attract market-seeking investment in their own right, opportunities for regional integration and collaboration on investment policy, particularly when combined with potentially FDI-inducing regional *trade* integration (UNCTAD 2009), may well take priority over other types of investment agreements. The benefits of this approach may be largest when combined with technical assistance and efforts towards regulatory cooperation and institution building.

- *Set priorities – where countries pursue bilateral collaboration on investment – in terms of treaty partners* (i.e. prioritize the most important home countries of international investors in sectors that are key to the country's development strategy and where foreign involvement is desired).

Furthermore, international engagement on investment policy should recognize that international agreements interact with each other and with other bodies of international law. Policymakers should be aware, for example, that commitments made to some treaty partners may easily filter through to others through most-favoured-nation (MFN) clauses, with possibly unintended consequences. Commitments may clash, or hard-won concessions in a negotiation (e.g. on policy space for performance requirements) may be undone through prior or subsequent treaties.

Finally, a particularly sensitive policy issue is whether to include liberalization commitments in IIAs by granting pre-establishment rights to foreign investors. Most IIAs grant protection to investments from the moment they are established in the host State; the host country thus retains discretion with respect to the admission of foreign investors to its market. However, in recent years an increasing number of IIAs include provisions that apply in the pre-establishment phase of investment, contributing to a more open environment for investment, at the cost of a lower degree of discretion in regulating entry matters domestically. When granting pre-establishment rights, managing the interaction between international and national policies is particularly crucial: policymakers can use IIAs to bind – at the international level – the degree of openness granted in domestic laws; or they can use IIA negotiations as a driving force for change, fostering greater openness at the national level (*WIR04*).[14] Granting pre-establishment rights also adds new complexities to the interaction between agreements. For example, a question may arise whether an unqualified MFN clause of a pre-establishment IIA could allow investors to enforce host countries' obligations under the WTO GATS agreement through ISDS.[15]

The following section, which discusses how today's investment policy challenges can be addressed in the content and detailed provisions of IIAs, covers both pre- and post-establishment issues. Policymakers have so far mostly opted for agreements limited to the post-establishment phase of investment; where they opt for pre-establishment coverage, numerous tools are available to calibrate obligations in line with their countries' specific needs.

2. Negotiating sustainable-development-friendly IIAs

Sustainable-development-friendly IIAs incorporate stronger provisions to promote responsible investment, to balance State and investor obligations, and to safeguard regulatory space.

Addressing sustainable development challenges through the detailed design of provisions in investment agreements principally implies four areas of evolution in treaty-making practice. Such change can be promoted either by including new elements and clauses in IIAs, or by taking a fresh approach to existing, traditional elements.

1. *Incorporating concrete commitments to promote and facilitate investment for sustainable development*: Currently, IIAs mostly promote foreign investment only indirectly through the granting of investment protection – i.e. obligations on the part of host countries – and do not contain commitments by home countries to promote responsible investment. Most treaties include hortatory language on encouraging investment in preambles or non-binding provisions on investment promotion. Options to improve the investment promotion aspect of treaties include concrete facilitation mechanisms (information sharing, investment promotion forums), outward investment promotion schemes (insurance and guarantees), technical assistance and capacity-building initiatives targeted at sustainable investment, supported by appropriate institutional arrangements for long-term cooperation.

2. *Balancing State commitments with investor obligations and promoting responsible investment*: Most IIAs currently provide for State obligations but do not specify investor obligations or responsibilities. Legally binding obligations on companies and individuals are stipulated by national law but are absent in international treaties, which traditionally do not apply to private parties directly.[16] However, there are examples of IIAs that impose obligations on investors (e.g. COMESA Investment Agreement of 2007[17]) or of international conventions that establish criminal responsibility of individuals (e.g. the Rome Statute of the International Criminal Court). These examples, together with the changes in the understanding of the nature and functions of international law, would suggest that international treaties can, in principle, impose obligations on private parties.[18] While stopping short of framing IIAs so as to impose outright obligations on investors, a few options may merit consideration.

For example, IIAs could include a requirement for investors to comply with investment-related national laws of the host State when making and operating an investment, and even at the post-operations stage (e.g. environmental clean-up), provided that such laws conform to the host country's international obligations, including those in the IIA.[19] Such an investor obligation could be the basis for further stipulating in the IIA the consequences of an investor's failure to comply with domestic laws, such as the right of host States to make a counterclaim in ISDS proceedings with the investor.

In addition, IIAs could refer to commonly recognized international standards (e.g. the United Nations Guidelines on Business and Human Rights). This would not only help balance State commitments with investor obligations but also support the spread of CSR standards – which are becoming an ever more important feature of the investment policy landscape (WIR11). Options for treaty language in this regard could range from commitments to promote best international CSR standards to ensuring that tribunals consider an investor's compliance with CSR standards when deciding an ISDS case.

3. *Ensuring an appropriate balance between protection commitments and regulatory space for development*: IIAs protect foreign investment by committing host country governments to grant certain standards of treatment and protection to foreign investors; it is the very nature of an IIA's standards of protection, and the attendant stabilizing effect, to place limits on government regulatory freedom. For example, where host governments aim to differentiate between domestic and foreign investors, or require specific corporate behaviour, they would be constrained by IIA provisions on non-discrimination or on performance requirements. In addition, to the extent that foreign investors perceive domestic policy changes to negatively affect their expectations, they may challenge them under IIAs by starting arbitration proceedings against host States. Countries can safeguard some policy space by carefully crafting the structure of IIAs, and by clarifying the scope and meaning of particularly vague treaty provisions such as the fair and equitable treatment standard and expropriation as well as by using specific flexibility mechanisms such as general or national security exceptions and reservations. More recent IIA models, such as the one adopted by the United States in 2004, offer examples in this regard. The right balance between protecting foreign investment and maintaining policy space for domestic regulation should flow from each country's development strategy, ensuring that flexibility mechanisms do not erode a principal objective of IIAs – their potential investment-enhancing effect.

4. *Shielding host countries from unjustified liabilities and high procedural costs*: Most IIAs reinforce their investment protection provisions by allowing investors directly to pursue relief through investor-State dispute settlement (ISDS). The strength of IIAs in granting protection to foreign investors has become increasingly evident through the number of ISDS cases brought over the last decade, most of which have been directed at developing countries. Host countries have faced claims of up to $114 billion[20] and awards of up to $867 million.[21] Added to these financial liabilities are the costs of procedures, all together putting a significant burden on defending countries and exacerbating the concerns related to policy space. Host countries – both developed and developing – have experienced that the possibility of bringing ISDS claims can be used by foreign investors in unanticipated ways. A number of recent cases have challenged measures adopted in the public interest (e.g. measures to promote social equity, foster environmental protection or protect public health), and show that the borderline between protection from political risk and undue interference with legitimate domestic polices is becoming increasingly blurred. Shielding countries from unjustified liabilities and excessive procedural costs through treaty design thus involves looking at options both in ISDS provisions themselves and in the scope and application of substantive clauses (see below).

These areas of evolution are also relevant for "pre-establishment IIAs", i.e. agreements that – in addition to protecting established investors – contain binding rules regarding the establishment of new investments. While a growing number of countries opt for the pre-establishment approach, it is crucial to ensure that any market opening through IIAs is in line with host countries' development strategies. Relevant provisions opt for selective liberalization, containing numerous exceptions and reservations designed to protect a country from over-committing and/or ensuring flexibilities in the relevant treaty obligations (see box IV.8).

Box IV.8. Pre-establishment commitments in IIAs

Pre-establishment IIAs signal that a country is generally committed to an open investment environment, although the fact that a country only concludes post-establishment IIAs does not necessarily mean that it follows a restrictive FDI policy. Also, pre-establishment commitments in IIAs do not necessarily have to mirror the actual degree of openness of an economy. Establishment rights in IIAs can remain below this level or go beyond it, i.e. IIAs can be used to open hitherto closed industries to foreign investors.

Pre-establishment IIAs typically operate by extending national treatment and MFN treatment to the "establishment, acquisition and expansion" of investments. This prevents each contracting party from treating investors from the other contracting party less favourably than it treats its own investors and/or investors from other countries in these matters.

Properly defining the scope of pre-establishment commitments is key. The two main mechanisms are the positive and negative listing of sectors/industries. Under the latter, investors benefit from pre-establishment commitments in all industries except in those that are explicitly excluded. The negative-list approach is more demanding in terms of resources: it requires a thorough audit of existing domestic policies. In addition, under a negative-list approach and in the absence of specific reservations, a country commits to openness also in those sectors/activities, which, at the time the IIA is signed, may not yet exist in the country, or where regulatory frameworks are still evolving. In contrast, a positive-list approach offers selective liberalization by way of drawing up a list of industries in which investors will enjoy pre-establishment rights. Another, more limited method is to include a positive list of "committed" industries and complement it with a list of reservations preserving certain measures or aspects in those industries ("hybrid", or GATS-type approach).

Pre-establishment treaties display a range of options – typically through country-specific reservations – for preserving policy flexibility even in "committed" industries (see the IPFSD IIA-elements table, Part B, on pre-establishment options).

Source: UNCTAD.

These four types of evolution in current treaty practice filter through to specific clauses in different ways. The following are examples of how this would work, focusing on some of the key provisions of current treaty practice – scope and definition, national treatment, most-favoured nation treatment, fair and equitable treatment, expropriation and ISDS. In addition to shaping specific clauses, sustainable development concerns can also be addressed individually, e.g. through special and differential treatment (SDT), a key aspect of the multilateral trading system but largely unknown in IIA practice (see box IV.9).

- *Scope and Definition*: An IIA's coverage determines the investments/investors that benefit from the protection offered by the IIA. Past disputes have demonstrated the potential for broad interpretation of IIAs, so as to apply to types of transactions that were originally not envisaged to benefit from the IIA (such as government debt securities).[22] When negotiating an IIA with a stronger sustainable development dimension, it may thus be

appropriate to safeguard policy space and exclude some types of financial transactions (e.g. portfolio investment or short-term, speculative financial flows) from a treaty's scope and to focus application of the treaty on those types of investment that the contracting parties wish to attract (e.g. direct investment in productive assets).

Whether IIAs should exclude portfolio investment is a policy choice that has been subject to intense debate. Portfolio investment can make a contribution to development by providing financial capital. However, the sometimes volatile nature of portfolio investment flows can be damaging. At the practical level, portfolio and direct investment are often difficult to differentiate, both in terms of identifying relevant financial flows of either type, and in terms of targeted policy instruments.

It may also be appropriate to exclude from a treaty's scope specific areas of public policy or specific (sensitive) economic sectors. Or,

Box IV.9. Special and differential treatment (SDT) and IIAs

A large number of IIAs are concluded between developed and developing countries. SDT gives legal expression to the special needs and concerns of developing countries and/or least developed countries in international (economic) agreements. It is based on the notion that treaty parties at different stages of development should not necessarily be bound by the same obligations.

Expression of the principle can be found in a multilateral context in over 145 provisions of WTO agreements[23] essentially i) granting less onerous obligations to developing countries – either permanently or temporarily; and/or ii) imposing special obligations on developed countries vis-à-vis developing countries.[24] Over time, SDT has found its way into other aspects of international relations, most prominently international environmental law, including the climate change framework.

Thus far, SDT has largely been absent from IIAs. Despite incorporating the general concepts of policy space and flexibility for development, IIAs – being mostly of a bilateral nature – are based on legal symmetry and reciprocity, meaning that the rights and obligations of the parties are generally the same. Moreover, IIAs typically do not deal with pre-establishment/market access issues, for which SDT considerations are particularly relevant.

Exceptionally, however, the COMESA Investment Agreement contains an SDT clarification with respect to the fair and equitable treatment standard: *"For greater certainty, Member States understand that different Member States have different forms of administrative, legislative and judicial systems and that Member States at different levels of development may not achieve the same standards at the same time."*[25]

Reinvigorating SDT with a view to making IIAs work better for sustainable development could take a number of forms. For example, lower levels of obligations for developing countries could be achieved through i) development-focused exceptions from obligations/commitments; ii) best endeavour commitments for developing countries; iii) asymmetrically phased implementation timetables with longer time frames for developing countries; or iv) a development-oriented interpretation of treaty obligations by arbitral tribunals. Best endeavour commitments by more advanced countries could, for example, relate to: i) technical assistance and training (e.g. assisting in the handling of ISDS cases or when putting in place appropriate domestic regulatory systems to ensure compliance with obligations); ii) promotion of the transfer/dissemination of technology; iii) support and advice for companies from developing countries (e.g. to become outward investors or adopt CSR standards); iv) investment promotion (e.g. provide outward investment incentives such as investment guarantees, tax breaks).

While SDT remains largely absent from IIAs, negotiators could consider adding SDT elements, offering a further promising tool for making IIAs more sustainable-development-friendly, particularly for least-developed and low-income countries.

Source: UNCTAD.

in order to limit liability and to avoid "treaty shopping" and "roundtrip investment", it may be appropriate to confine application to genuine investors from the contracting parties, excluding investments that are only channelled through legal entities based in the contracting parties.

- *National Treatment (NT):* National treatment protects foreign investors against discrimination vis-à-vis comparable domestic investors, with a view to ensuring a "level playing field". Non-discriminatory treatment is generally considered conducive to good governance and is, in principle, enshrined in many countries' domestic regulatory frameworks. Nevertheless, even if national treatment is provided under domestic legislation, countries may be reluctant to "lock in" all aspects of their domestic regulatory framework at the international level (e.g. private sector development initiatives, including regulatory, financial or fiscal incentives) and, depending on their development strategy, States may wish to afford preferential treatment to national investors/investments as part of industrial development policies or for other reasons. In such cases, negotiators could circumscribe the scope of national treatment clauses and/or allow for derogations (e.g. through the lodging of reservations excluding sectors, policy areas or specific measures from its application (see *WIR11*)).

- *Most-Favoured-Nation (MFN) Treatment:* MFN clauses aim to prevent discrimination between comparable investors of different foreign nationality. The meaning of such treatment has been subject to diverging and unanticipated interpretations by tribunals. Several arbitral decisions have interpreted MFN as allowing investors to invoke more investor-friendly language from treaties between the respondent State and a third country, thereby effectively sidelining the "base" treaty (i.e. the treaty between the investor's home and host country on the basis of which the case was brought). This practice can be seen in a positive light as "upward harmonization" of IIA standards or in a negative one as "cherry picking" best clauses from different treaties, endangering individual treaty bargains. MFN treatment needs to be carefully considered, particularly in light of countries' growing networks of IIAs with different obligations and agreements including pre-establishment issues. To avoid misinterpretation, IIAs have started explicitly excluding dispute settlement issues as well as obligations undertaken in treaties with third States from the scope of the MFN obligation. Other options include limiting the clause's reach through country-specific reservations.

- *Fair and Equitable Treatment (FET):* The obligation to accord fair and equitable treatment to foreign investments appears in the great majority of IIAs. Investors (claimants) have frequently – and with considerable success – invoked it in ISDS. There is a great deal of uncertainty concerning the precise meaning of the concept, because the notions of "fairness" and "equity" do not connote a clear set of legal prescriptions in international investment law and allow for a significant degree of subjective judgment. Some tribunals have read an extensive list of disciplines into the FET clause, which are taxing on any State, but especially on developing and least-developed countries; lack of clarity persists regarding the appropriate threshold of liability. The use of FET to protect investors' legitimate expectations can indirectly restrict countries' ability to change investment-related policies or to introduce new policies – including those for the public good – that may have a negative impact on individual foreign investors. Options to reduce uncertainty regarding States' liabilities and to preserve policy space include qualifying or clarifying the FET clause, including by way of an exhaustive list of State obligations under FET, or even considering omitting it.

- *Expropriation:* An expropriation provision protects foreign investors/investments against dispossession or confiscation of their property by the host country without compensation. As most IIAs also prohibit indirect expropriation (i.e. apply to regulatory takings), and as some arbitral tribunals have tended to interpret this broadly (i.e. including legitimate regulatory measures in the pursuit of the public interest), the expropriation clause has the potential to impose undue constraints on a State's regulatory capacity. To avoid this, policymakers could clarify the notion of indirect expropriation and introduce criteria to distinguish between indirect expropriation and legitimate regulation that does not require compensation.

- *Investor–State Dispute Settlement (ISDS):* Originally, the system of international investor-State arbitration was conceived as an effective tool to enforce foreign investors' rights. It offered direct access to international arbitration for investors to avoid national courts of host countries and to solve disputes in a neutral forum that was expected to be cheap, fast, and flexible. It was meant to provide finality and enforceability, and to depoliticize disputes. While some of these advantages remain valid, the ISDS system has more recently displayed serious shortcomings (e.g. inconsistent and unintended interpretations of clauses, unanticipated uses of the system by investors, challenges against policy measures taken in the public interest, costly and lengthy procedures, limited or no transparency), undermining its legitimacy. While some ISDS concerns can be addressed effectively only through a broader approach requiring international collaboration, negotiators can go some way to improving the institutional and procedural aspects of ISDS and to limiting liability and the risk of becoming embroiled in costly procedures. They can do so by qualifying the scope of consent given to ISDS, promoting the use of alternative dispute resolution (ADR) methods, increasing transparency of procedures, encouraging arbitral tribunals to take into account standards of investor behaviour when settling investor-State disputes, limiting resort to ISDS and increasing the role of domestic judicial systems, providing for the possibility of counterclaims by States, or even refraining from offering ISDS.[26]

3. IIA elements: policy options

Options to craft more sustainable-development-friendly IIAs include adjusting existing provisions in IIAs, adding new ones, or introducing the concept of Special and Differential Treatment.

The IPFSD table on IIA-elements (see pages 143–159) contains a comprehensive compilation of policy options available to IIA negotiators, including options to operationalize sustainable development objectives (also see table IV.5). The options include both mainstream IIA provisions as well as more idiosyncratic treaty language used by fewer countries. In some instances, the IPFSD IIA-elements table contains new suggestions by UNCTAD.[27]

As a comprehensive set of policy options, the IPFSD IIA-elements table aims to represent two different approaches on the design of IIAs. At one end of the spectrum is the school of thought that prefers IIAs with straightforward provisions focusing on investment protection and limiting clarifications and qualifications to the minimum. At the other end, a comprehensive approach to investment policymaking adds a host of considerations – including on sustainable development – in the wording of IIA clauses.

The objective of the IPFSD IIA -elements table is to provide policymakers with an overview of options for designing an IIA. It offers a broad menu from which IIA negotiators can pick and choose. This table is not meant to identify preferred options for IIA negotiators or to go so far as to suggest a model IIA. However, the table briefly comments on

the various drafting possibilities with regard to each IIA provision and highlights – where appropriate – their implications for sustainable development. It is hoped that these explanations will help IIA negotiators identify those drafting options that best suit their countries' needs, preferences and objectives.

The IPFSD IIA-elements table includes various options that could be particularly supportive of sustainable development. Examples are:

- Including a carefully crafted scope and definitions clause that excludes portfolio, short-term or speculative investments from treaty coverage.

- Formulating an FET clause as an exhaustive list of State obligations (e.g. not to (i) deny justice in judicial or administrative procedures, (ii) treat investors in a manifestly arbitrary manner, (iii) flagrantly violate due process, etc.).

- Clarifying – to the extent possible – the distinction between legitimate regulatory activity and regulatory takings (indirect expropriations) giving rise to compensation.

- Limiting the Full Protection and Security (FPS) provision to "physical" security and protection only and specifying that protection shall be commensurate with the country's level of development.

- Limiting the scope of a transfer of funds clause by providing an exhaustive list of covered payments/transfers; including exceptions in case of serious balance-of-payments difficulties; and conditioning the transfer right on the investor's compliance with its fiscal and other transfer-related obligations in the host country.

- Including carefully crafted exceptions to protect human rights, health, core labour standards and the environment, with well-functioning checks and balances, so as to guarantee policy space while avoiding abuse.

- Considering, in light of the quality of the host country's administrative and judicial system, the option of "no ISDS" or of designing the dispute settlement clause to make ISDS

Table IV.5. Policy options to operationalize sustainable development objectives in IIAs

Options	Mechanisms	Examples
Adjusting existing/common provisions to make them more sustainable-development-friendly through clauses that: • safeguard policy space • limit State liability	Hortatory language	- *Preamble*: stating that attracting responsible foreign investment that fosters sustainable development is one of the key objectives of the treaty.
	Clarifications	- *Expropriation*: specifying that non-discriminatory good faith regulations pursuing public policy objectives do not constitute indirect expropriation. - *FET*: including an exhaustive list of State obligations.
	Qualifications/ limitations	- *Scope and definition*: requiring covered investments to fulfill specific characteristics, e.g., positive development impact on the host country.
	Reservations/ carve-outs	- *Country-specific reservations* to NT, MFN or pre-establishment obligations, carving out policy measures (e.g. subsidies), policy areas (e.g. policies on minorities, indigenous communities) or sectors (e.g. social services).
	Exclusions from coverage/ exceptions	- *Scope and definition*: excluding portfolio, short-term or speculative investments from treaty coverage. - *General exception* for domestic regulatory measures that aim to pursue legitimate public policy objectives.
	Omissions	- Omit FET, umbrella clause.
Adding new provisions or new, stronger paragraphs within provisions for sustainable development purposes to: • balance investor rights and responsibilities • promote responsible investment • strengthen home-country support	Investor obligations and responsibilities	- Requirement that investors comply with host State laws at both the entry and the post-entry stage of an investment. - Encouragement to investors to comply with universal principles or to observe applicable CSR standards.
	Institutional set-up for sustainable development impact	- Institutional set-up under which State parties cooperate to e.g. review the functioning of the IIA or issue interpretations of IIA clauses. - Call for cooperation between the Parties to promote observance of applicable CSR standards.
	Home-country measures to promote responsible investment	- Encouragement to offer incentives for sustainable-development-friendly outward investment; investor compliance with applicable CSR standards may be an additional condition. - Technical assistance provisions to facilitate the implementation of the IIA and to maximize its sustainable development impact, including through capacity-building on investment promotion and facilitation.
Introducing Special and Differential Treatment for the less developed Party – with effect on both existing and new provisions – to: • calibrate the level of obligations to the country's level of development	Lower levels of obligations	- Pre-establishment commitments that cover fewer economic activities.
	Development-focused exceptions from obligations/ commitments	- Reservations, carving out sensitive development related areas, issues or measures.
	Best endeavour commitments	- FET, NT commitments that are not legally binding.
	Asymmetric implementation timetables	- Phase-in of obligations, including pre-establishment, NT, MFN, performance requirements, transfer of funds and transparency.

Source: UNCTAD.

the last resort (e.g. after exhaustion of local remedies and ADR).

- Establishing an institutional set-up that makes the IIA adaptable to changing development contexts and major unanticipated developments (e.g. ad hoc committees to assess the effectiveness of the agreement and to further improve its implementation through amendments or interpretations).

The IPFSD IIA-elements table recognizes that specific policy objectives can be pursued by different treaty elements, thereby inviting treaty drafters to choose their "best-fit" combination. For example, a country that wishes to preserve regulatory space for policies aimed at ensuring access to essential services can opt for (i) excluding investments in essential services from the scope of the treaty; (ii) excluding essential services policies from the scope of specific provisions (e.g. national treatment); (iii) scheduling reservations (for national treatment or the prohibition of performance requirements) for specific (existing and/or future) essential services policies; (iv) including access to essential services as a legitimate policy objective in the IIA's general exceptions; or (v) referring to the importance of ensuring access to essential services in the preamble of the agreement.

The IPFSD IIA-elements table likewise reflects that negotiators can determine the normative intensity of IIA provisions: they can ensure the legally binding and enforceable nature of some obligations while at the same time resorting to hortatory, best endeavour language for others. These choices can help negotiators design a level of protection best suited to the specific circumstances of negotiating partners and in line with the need for proper balancing between investment protection and policy space for sustainable development.

The ultimate shape of an IIA is the result of a specific combination of options that exist in respect of each IIA provision. It is this blend that determines where on a spectrum between utmost investor protection and maximum policy flexibility a particular IIA is located. The same holds true for the IIA's impact on sustainable development. Combinations of and interactions between IIA provisions can take a number of forms:

- *Interaction between a treaty's scope/definitions and the obligations it establishes for the contracting parties*: An agreement's "protective strength" stems not only from the substantive and procedural standards of protection it offers to investors, but also from the breadth and variety of categories of investors and investments it covers (i.e. that benefit from the standards of protection offered by the IIA). Hence, when designing a particular IIA and calibrating the degree of protection it grants, negotiators can use different combinations of the two. For example, (i) a broad open-ended definition of investment could be combined with few substantive obligations, or with obligations formulated in a manner reducing their "bite"; or (ii) a narrow definition of investment (e.g. covering direct investments in a few priority sectors only) could be combined with more expansive protections such as an unqualified FET standard or the prohibition of numerous performance requirements.

- *Interaction between protection-oriented clauses*: Some IIAs combine narrowly drafted clauses in some areas with broad provisions in others. An example is the combination between a carefully circumscribed expropriation clause and an unqualified FET provision. Another option is to limit the impact of ISDS by either formulating substantive standards of protection as best endeavour (i.e. hortatory) clauses, or by precluding the use of ISDS for particularly vague treaty articles, such as the FET standard.[28] Under such scenarios, protective standards may still have a good-governance-enhancing effect on host countries' regulatory framework, while reducing the risk of being drawn into ISDS. Consideration also has to be given to the interaction with the MFN provision: with the inclusion of a "broad" MFN clause, investors may be tempted to circumvent "weak" protection clauses by relying on more protective (i.e. "stronger") clauses in treaties with third parties.

- *Interaction between protection and exceptions*: Strong protection clauses and effective

UNCTAD's Investment Policy Framework for Sustainable Development

Elements of International Investment Agreements: Policy Options
Summary of contents

Sections	Description
Part A. Post-establishment	
1 Preamble	… sets out objectives of the treaty and the intentions of the Contracting Parties
2 Treaty scope	… defines the investment and investors protected under the treaty and its temporal application
3 Admission	… governs entry of investments into the host State
4 Standards of treatment and protection	… prescribe the treatment, protection and rights which host States are required to accord foreign investors/investments
5 Public policy exceptions	… permit public policy measures, otherwise inconsistent with the treaty, to be taken under specified, exceptional circumstances
6 Dispute settlement	… governs settlement of disputes between the Contracting Parties and those between foreign investors and host States
7 Investor obligations and responsibilities	… promote compliance by investors with domestic and/or international norms at the entry and operation stage
8 Relationship to other agreements	… establishes a hierarchy in case of competing international norms
9 Not lowering of standards clause	… discourages Contracting Parties from attracting investment through the relaxation of labour or environmental standards
10 Investment promotion	… aims to encourage foreign investment through additional means beyond investment protection provisions in IIAs
11 Institutional set-up	… establishes an institutional platform for collaboration between the Contracting Parties
12 Final provisions	… define the duration of the treaty, including its possible prolongation
Part B. Pre-establishment	
1 Pre-establishment obligations	… govern establishment of foreign investments in the host State
Part C. Special and Differential Treatment (SDT)	
1 Asymmetrical obligations	… enable imposition of less onerous obligations on a less developed Contracting Party
2 Additional tools	… encourage positive contributions by a more developed Contracting Party

UNCTAD's Investment Policy Framework for Sustainable Development

Policy options for IIAs
Part A. Post-establishment

The different sections of the table, starting with the preamble and closing with the final provisions, follow the order of articles as commonly found in IIAs. Where possible, the policy options are organized along a scale ranging from i) the most investor-friendly or most protective to ii) the options providing more flexibility to the State, balance and/or legal precision. In some sections, two or more policy options can be combined.

Sections	Policy options for IIAs	Sustainable development (SD) implications
1 Preamble ... sets out objectives of the treaty and the intentions of the Contracting Parties	1.1.0 Refer to the objective of creating and maintaining favourable conditions for investment and intensifying economic cooperation between the Parties.	The treaty preamble does not set out binding obligations but plays a significant role in interpreting substantive IIA provisions.
	1.1.1 Clarify that the Parties conclude this IIA with a view to - attracting and fostering responsible inward and outward foreign investment that contributes to SD - promoting good governance .	When a preamble refers to the creation of "a stable framework for investments" or "favourable conditions for investments" as the sole aim of the treaty (i.e. if the IIA only refers to those objectives), tribunals will tend to resolve interpretive uncertainties in favour of investors. In contrast, where a
	1.1.2 Clarify that the investor protection objectives shall not override States' right to regulate in the public interest as well as with respect to certain important policy goals, such as: - SD - protection of human rights - maintenance of health, labour and/or environmental standards - corporate social responsibility and good corporate governance.	preamble complements investment promotion and protection objectives with other objectives such as SD, the Millennium Development Goals (MDGs) or the Contracting Parties' right to regulate, this can lead to more balanced interpretations and foster coherence between different policy objectives/ bodies of law.
	1.1.3 Indicate that the promotion and protection of investments should be pursued in compliance with the Parties' obligations under international law including in particular their obligations with respect to human rights, labour rights and protection of the environment.	
2 Treaty scope		
2.1 Definition of investment ... sets out the types of investment covered by the treaty	2.1.0 Offer coverage of *any* tangible and intangible assets in the host State (through an illustrative/open-ended list), directly or indirectly owned/controlled by covered investors.	A traditional open-ended definition of "investment" grants protection to all types of assets. It may have the strongest attraction effect but can end up covering economic transactions not contemplated by the Parties or investments/assets with questionable SD contribution. It may also expose States to unexpected liabilities.
	2.1.1 Compile an exhaustive list of covered investments and/or exclude specific types of assets from coverage, e.g.: - portfolio investment - sovereign debt instruments - commercial contracts for the sale of goods or services - assets for non-business purposes - intellectual property rights not protected under domestic law.	States may want to tailor their definition of investment to target assets conducive to SD by granting protection only to investments that bring concrete benefits to the host country, e.g. long-term capital commitment, employment generation etc. To that effect, the Parties may wish to develop criteria for development-friendly investments.
	2.1.2 Require investments to fulfil specific characteristics, e.g. that the investment: - involves commitment of capital, expectation of profit and assumption of risk - involves assets acquired for the purpose of establishing lasting economic relations - must be made in "accordance with host country laws and regulations" - delivers a positive development impact on the host country (i.e. Parties could list specific criteria according to their needs and expectations).	A treaty may further specifically exclude certain types of assets from the definition of "investment" (e.g. portfolio investment – which can include short-term and speculative investments – intellectual property rights that are not protected under domestic legislation).

Sections	Policy options for IIAs	Sustainable development (SD) implications
2.2 Definition of investor ... sets out the types of investors protected under the treaty	**2.2.0** Offer coverage of any natural and legal persons originating from the other Contracting Party. With respect to legal entities, cover all those established in the other Contracting Party.	A broad definition of "investor" can result in unanticipated or unintended coverage of persons (natural or legal). For example, if a treaty determines the nationality of a legal entity solely on the basis of the place of incorporation, it creates opportunities for treaty shopping or free riding by investors not conceived to be beneficiaries (e.g. a third-country/host-country investor may channel its investment through a "mailbox" company established in the territory of a Party, in order to obtain treaty protection). A related set of issues arises with respect to dual nationals where one nationality is that of the host State.
	2.2.1 Exclude certain categories of natural or legal persons from treaty coverage, e.g.: - investors with double nationality (of which one is the host country nationality) - permanent residents of the host country - legal entities that do not have their seat or any real economic activity in the home country.	There are various options to narrow the range of covered persons. For example, to eliminate the risk of abuse and enhance legal predictability, a treaty may add a requirement that a company must have its seat in the home State and carry out real economic activities there. An alternative is to supplement the country-of-incorporation approach to determining nationality of a company with a denial-of-benefits clause.
	2.2.2 Include a denial-of-benefits clause that enables the host State to deny treaty protection to: - legal entities that are owned/controlled by third-country nationals or host State nationals and that do not have real economic activity in the of the home Party ("mailbox" companies) - legal entities owned/controlled by investors from countries with which the host country does not have diplomatic relations or those countries that are subject to an economic embargo.	
2.3 Exclusions from the scope ... carve out specific policy areas and/or industries from the scope of the treaty	**2.3.0** No exclusions.	The broader a treaty's scope, the wider its protective effect and its potential contribution to the attraction of foreign investment. However, a broad treaty also reduces a host State's policy space and flexibility and ultimately heightens its exposure to investors' claims. States can tailor the scope of the agreement to meet the country's SD agenda.
	2.3.1 Exclude specific policy areas from treaty coverage, e.g.: - subsidies and grants - public procurement - taxation.	
	2.3.2 Exclude specific sectors and industries from treaty coverage, e.g.: - essential social services (e.g. health, education) - specific sensitive industries (e.g. cultural industries, fisheries, nuclear energy, defence industry, natural resources).	By carving out specific policy areas and sectors/industries from treaty coverage, States preserve flexibility to implement national policies, such as industrial policies (e.g. to grant preferential treatment to domestic investors or to impose performance requirements), or to ensure access to essential/public services.
2.4 Temporal scope ... determines whether the treaty applies to investments and/or measures pre-dating the treaty	**2.4.0** Extend the treaty scope to investments established both before and after the treaty's entry into force.	The treaty's scope will be widest if its application is extended to all investments, regardless of the time of their establishment in the host State. Another approach is to exclude already "attracted" (i.e. pre-treaty) investments: it could be seen as preventing free-riding by "old" investors but at the same time would result in discrimination between "old" and "new" investments. Moreover, this can create uncertainty with respect to re-investments by "old" investors.
	2.4.1 Limit temporal scope to investments made after the conclusion/entry into force of the treaty.	
	2.4.2 Clarify that the treaty shall not allow IIA claims arising out of any State acts which ceased to exist prior to the IIA's entry into force, even though it may still have an ongoing effect on the investor.	Policymakers should consider the effect of the treaty on State acts, adopted prior to the treaty's entry into force, but with a lasting effect: «continuing» breaches (e.g. maintenance of an earlier legislative provision which comes into conflict with treaty obligations), individual acts whose effects continue over time (e.g. effect of a direct expropriation on the former owner of the asset) and "composite" acts, i.e. a series of actions or omissions which, taken together, are wrongful. It is useful to provide additional language to clarify whether the treaty would cover or exclude such lasting acts or effects.
	2.4.3 Clarify that the treaty shall not allow IIA claims based on measures adopted prior to conclusion of the treaty.	

Sections	Policy options for IIAs	Sustainable development (SD) implications
3 Admission ... govern entry investments into the host State (see also "Part B: Pre-establishment")	3.1.0 Provide that investments are admitted in accordance with domestic laws of the host State.	An express provision that precludes application of the treaty to acts that ceased to exist before the treaty's entry into force would enhance legal certainty, especially with regard to the period between the date of the treaty's signature and its entry into force. This approach would nevertheless keep open to challenge those prior laws and regulations that come into contradiction with the new treaty once it enters into force. An alternative is to apply the treaty only to those measures that are adopted after the treaty's entry into force: this would automatically preclude all of the State's earlier non-conforming measures from being challenged (e.g., preferential treatment to domestic investors in a particular industry in violation of the National Treatment obligation), eliminating the need to identify and schedule such measures individually. Most IIAs provide for admission of investments in accordance with the host State's national laws. Thus, unlike in the treaties that belong to the "pre-establishment" type, in this case States do not give any international guarantees of admission and can change relevant domestic laws as they deem appropriate. However, the promise to admit investments in accordance with domestic law still has a certain value as it affords protection to investors in case a host State refuses admission in contradiction or by disregarding its internal laws.
	3.1.1 No clause.	
4 Standards of treatment and protection		
4.1 National treatment (NT) ... protects foreign investors/investments against discrimination vis-à-vis domestic investors	4.1.0 Prohibit less favourable treatment of covered foreign investors/investments vis-à-vis comparable domestic investors/investments, without restrictions or qualifications.	NT guarantees foreign investors a level-playing field vis-à-vis comparable domestic investors and is generally considered conducive to good governance. Yet under some circumstances, and in accordance with their SD strategies, States may want to be able to accord preferential treatment to national investors/investments (e.g. through temporary grants or subsidies) without extending the same benefits to foreign-owned companies. In this case, NT provisions need to allow flexibility to regulate for SD goals. For example, countries with a nascent/emerging regulatory framework that are reluctant to rescind the right to discriminate in favour of domestic investors can make the NT obligation "subject to their domestic laws and regulations". This approach gives full flexibility to grant preferential (e.g. differentiated) treatment to domestic investors as long as this is in accordance with the country's legislation. However, such a significant limitation to the NT obligation may be perceived as a disincentive to foreign investors. Even more so, omitting the NT clause from the treaty may significantly undermine its protective value. There can be a middle ground between full policy freedom, on the one hand, and a rigid guarantee of non-discrimination, on the other. For example, States may exempt specific policy areas or measures as well as sensitive or vital economic sectors/industries from the scope of the obligation in order to meet both current and future regulatory or public-policy needs such as addressing market failures (this can be done either as an exception applicable to both Contracting Parties or as a country-specific reservation).
	4.1.1 Circumscribe the scope of the NT clause (for both/all Contracting Parties), noting that it, e.g.: - subordinates the right of NT to a host country's domestic laws - reserves the right of each Party to derogate from NT - does not apply to certain policy areas (e.g. subsidies, government procurement).	
	4.1.2 Include country-specific reservations to NT, e.g. carve-out: - certain policies/measures (e.g. subsidies and grants, government procurement, measures regarding government bonds) - specific sectors/industries where the host countries wish to preserve the right to favour domestic investors - certain policy areas (e.g. issues related to minorities, rural populations, marginalized or indigenous communities) - measures related to companies of a specific size (e.g. SMEs).	
	4.1.3 Omit NT clause.	

Sections	Policy options for IIAs		Sustainable development (SD) implications
4.2 Most-favoured nation (MFN) treatment … protects foreign investors/investments against discrimination vis-à-vis other foreign investors	4.2.0	Prohibit less favourable treatment of covered investors/investments vis-à-vis comparable investors/investments of any third country.	The MFN provision ensures a level-playing field between investors from the IIA home country and comparable investors from any third country. However, competing objectives and implications may come into play when designing an MFN clause. While an MFN clause may be used to ensure upward harmonization of IIA treaty standards, it can also result in the unanticipated incorporation of stronger investor rights from IIAs with third countries and complicate conscious treaty design. This is particularly the case if the MFN clause extends to pre-establishment issues or when the treaty includes carefully balanced provisions that could be rendered ineffective by an overly broad MFN clause.
	4.2.1	Limit the application of the MFN clause, noting that MFN does not apply to more favourable treatment granted to third-country investors under, e.g.: - Economic integration agreements - Double taxation treaties - IIAs concluded prior to (and/or after) the conclusion of the IIA in question (e.g. if the latter contains rules that are less favourable to investors, as compared to earlier IIAs) - ISDS clauses / procedural rights.	An example of the latter are recent arbitral decisions that have read the MFN obligation as allowing investors to invoke more investor-friendly provisions from third treaties, e.g. to incorporate standards not included in the base treaty, to benefit from higher protection standards compared to the ones found in the base treaty or to circumvent procedural (ISDS-related) requirements in the base treaty.
	4.2.2	Limit the application of the MFN clause to treatment accorded to foreign investors under domestic laws, regulations, administrative practices and de facto treatment.	Should a country wish to preclude the MFN clause from applying to any relevant international agreement, it can do so by excluding specific types of instruments from the scope of the MFN clause (see section 4.2.1) or, in a broader manner, by restricting the scope of the MFN clause to domestic treatment (see section 4.2.2). Carving out certain sectors/industries or policy measures through country-specific reservations, catering for both current and future regulatory needs, is an additional tool that allows managing the scope of the MFN clause in a manner targeted to the specific needs of individual IIA Parties.
	4.2.3	Include country-specific reservations to MFN, e.g. carve out: - certain policies/measures (e.g. subsidies, etc.) - specific sectors/industries - certain policy areas (e.g. issues related to minorities, rural populations, marginalized or indigenous communities)	
4.3 Fair and equitable treatment (FET) … protects foreign investors/investments against, e.g. denial of justice, arbitrary and abusive treatment	4.3.0	Give an unqualified commitment to treat foreign investors/investments "fairly and equitably".	FET is a critical standard of treatment: while it is considered to help attract foreign investors and foster good governance in the host State, almost all claims brought to date by investors against States have included an allegation of the breach of this all-encompassing standard of protection.
	4.3.1	Qualify the FET standard by reference to: - minimum standard of treatment of aliens under customary international law (MST/CIL) - international law or principles of international law.	Through an *unqualified* promise to treat investors "fairly and equitably", a country provides maximum protection for investors but also risks posing limits on its policy space, raising its exposure to foreign investors' claims and resulting financial liabilities. Some of these implications stem from the fact that there is a great deal of uncertainty concerning the precise meaning of the concept, because the notions of "fairness" and "equity" do not connote a clear set of legal prescriptions and are open to subjective interpretations. A particularly problematic issue concerns the use of the FET standard to protect investors "legitimate expectations", which may restrict the ability of countries to change policies or to introduce new policies that - while pursuing SD objectives - may have a negative impact on foreign investors.
	4.3.2	Include an exhaustive list of State obligations under FET, e.g. obligation not to - deny justice in judicial or administrative proceedings - treat investors in a manifestly arbitrary manner - flagrantly violate due process - engage in manifestly abusive treatment involving continuous, unjustified coercion or harassment - infringe investors' legitimate expectations based on investment-inducing representations or measures.	
	4.3.3	Clarify (with a view to giving interpretative guidance to arbitral tribunals) that: - the FET clause does not preclude States from adopting good faith regulatory or other measures that pursue legitimate policy objectives - the investor's conduct (including the observance of universally recognized standards, see section 7) is relevant in determining whether the FET standard has been breached - the country's level of development is relevant in determining whether the FET standard has been breached - a breach of another provision of the IIA or of another international agreement cannot establish a claim for breach of the clause.	Several options exist to address the deficiencies of *unqualified* FET standard, each with its pros and cons. The reference to customary international law may raise the threshold of State liability and help to preserve States' ability to adapt public policies in light of changing objectives (except when these measures constitute manifestly arbitrary conduct that amounts to egregious mistreatment of foreign investors), but the exact contours of MST/CIL remain elusive. An omission of the FET clause would reduce States' exposure to investor claims, but foreign investors may perceive the country as not offering a sound and reliable investment climate. Another solution would be to replace the general FET clause with an exhaustive list of more specific obligations. While agreeing on such a list may turn out to be a challenging endeavour, its exhaustive nature would help avoid unanticipated and far-reaching interpretations by tribunals.
	4.3.4	Omit FET clause.	

Sections	Policy options for IIAs	Sustainable development (SD) implications
4.4 Full protection and security (FPS) ...requires host States to exercise due diligence in protecting foreign investments	**4.4.0** Include a guarantee to provide investors/investments full protection and security.	Most IIAs include a guarantee of full protection and security (FPS), which is generally regarded as codifying customary international law obligations to grant a certain level of police protection and physical security. However, some tribunals may interpret the FPS obligation so as to cover more than just police protection: if FPS is understood to include economic, legal and other protection and security, it can constrain government regulatory prerogatives, including for SD objectives.
	4.4.1 Clarify the FPS clause by: - specifying that the standard refers to "physical" security and protection - linking it to customary international law (e.g. specifying that this obligation does not go beyond what is required by CIL) - providing that the expected level of police protection should be commensurate with the level of development of the country's police and security forces.	Policymakers may follow a recent trend to qualify the FPS standard by explicitly linking it to customary international law or including a definition of the standard clarifying that it is limited to "physical" security. This would provide predictability and prevent expansive interpretations that would constrain regulatory prerogatives.
	4.4.2 Omit FPS clause.	
4.5 Expropriation ...protects foreign investors in case of dispossession of their investments by the host country	**4.5.0** Provide that an expropriation must comply with/respect four conditions: public purpose, non-discrimination, due process and payment of compensation.	An expropriation provision is a fundamental element of an IIA. IIAs with expropriation clauses do not take away States' right to expropriate property, but protect investors against arbitrary or uncompensated expropriations, contributing to a stable and predictable legal framework, conducive to foreign investment.
	4.5.1 Limit protection in case of indirect expropriation (regulatory taking) by - establishing criteria that need to be met for indirect expropriation to be found - defining in general terms what measures do not constitute indirect expropriation (non-discriminatory good faith regulations relating to public health and safety, protection of the environment, etc.) - clarifying that certain specific measures do not constitute an indirect expropriation (e.g. compulsory licensing in compliance with WTO rules).	IIA provisions typically cover "indirect" expropriation, which refers to regulatory takings, creeping expropriation and acts "tantamount to" or "equivalent to" expropriation. Such provisions have been used to challenge general regulations with an alleged negative effect on the value of an investment. This raises the question of the proper borderline between expropriation and legitimate public policymaking (e.g. environmental, social or health regulations).
	4.5.2 Specify the compensation to be paid in case of lawful expropriation: - appropriate, just or equitable compensation - prompt, adequate and effective compensation, i.e. full market value of the investment ("Hull formula").	To avoid undue constraints on a State's prerogative to regulate in the public interest, an IIA may set out general criteria for State acts that may (or may not) be considered an indirect expropriation. While this does not exclude liability risks altogether, it allows for better balancing of investor and State interests.
	4.5.3 Clarify that only expropriations violating any of the three substantive conditions (public purpose, non-discrimination, due process), entail full reparation.	The standard of compensation for lawful expropriation is another important aspect. The use of terms such as "appropriate", "just" or "fair" in relation to compensation gives room for flexibility in the calculation of compensation. States may find it beneficial to provide further guidance to arbitrators on how to calculate compensation and clarify what factors should be taken into account.
4.6 Protection from strife ...protects investors in case of losses incurred as a result of armed conflict or civil strife	**4.6.0** Grant non-discriminatory (i.e. NT, MFN) treatment with respect to restitution/compensation in case of armed conflict or civil strife.	IIAs often contain a clause on compensation for losses incurred under specific circumstances, such as armed conflict or civil strife. Some countries have expanded the coverage of such a clause by including compensation in case of natural disasters or force majeure situations. Such a broad approach increases the risk for a State to face financial liabilities arising out of ISDS claims for events outside of the State's control.
	4.6.1 Guarantee – under certain circumstances – compensation in case of losses incurred as a result of armed conflict or civil strife as an absolute right (e.g. by requiring reasonable compensation).	Most IIAs only confer a relative right to compensation on foreign investors, meaning that a host country undertakes to compensate covered investors in a manner at least equivalent to comparable host State nationals or investors from third countries. Some IIAs provide an absolute right to compensation obliging a State to restitute or pay for certain types of losses (e.g. those caused by the requisitioning of their property by government forces or authorities). The latter approach is more burdensome for host States but provides a higher level of protection to investors.
	4.6.2 Define civil strife as not including "acts of God", natural disasters or force majeure.	
	4.6.3 Omit protection-from-strife clause.	

Sections	Policy options for IIAs	Sustainable development (SD) implications
4.7 Transfer of funds ... grants the right to free movement of investment-related financial flows into and out of the host country	4.7.0 Grant foreign investors the right to freely transfer any investment-related funds (e.g. open ended list) into and out of the host country.	IIAs virtually always contain a clause regarding investment-related transfers. The objective is to ensure that a foreign investor can make free use of invested capital, returns on investment and other payments related to the establishment, operation or disposal of an investment.
	4.7.1 Provide an exhaustive list of types of qualifying transfers.	
	4.7.2 Include exceptions (e.g. temporary derogations): - in the event of serious balance-of-payments and external financial difficulties or threat thereof - where movements of funds cause or threaten to cause serious difficulties in macro-economic management, in particular, related to monetary and exchange rate policies. Condition these exceptions to prevent their abuse (e.g. application in line with IMF rules and respecting conditions of temporality, equity, non-discrimination, good faith and proportionality).	However, an unqualified transfer-of-funds provision significantly reduces a host country's ability to deal with sudden and massive outflows or inflows of capital, balance-of-payments (BoP) difficulties and other macroeconomic problems. An exception increasingly found in recent IIAs allows States to impose restrictions on the free transfer of funds in specific circumstances, usually qualified by checks and balances (safeguards) to prevent misuse. Countries may also need to reserve their right to restrict transfers if this is required for the enforcement of the Party's laws (e.g. to prevent fraud on creditors etc.), again with checks and balances to prevent abuse.
	4.7.3 Reserve the right of host States to restrict an investor's transfer of funds in connection with the country's (equitable, non-discriminatory, and good faith application of its) laws, relating to, e.g.: - fiscal obligations of the investor/investment in the host country - reporting requirements in relation to currency transfers - bankruptcy, insolvency, or the protection of the rights of creditors - issuing, trading, or dealing in securities, futures, options, or derivatives - criminal or penal offences (e.g. imposing criminal penalties) - prevention of money laundering - compliance with orders or judgments in judicial or administrative proceedings.	
4.8 Transparency ... fosters access to information	4.8.0 Require Contracting Parties to promptly publish documents which may affect covered investments, including e.g. - laws and regulations - procedures/administrative rulings of general application - IIAs.	Some IIAs include a clause requiring countries to promptly publish laws and regulations. Providing investors (prospective and established ones) with access to such information improves a country's investment climate. This might, however, also pose administrative difficulties for some countries that do not have the human resources and technological infrastructure required. The treaty may incorporate commitments to provide technical assistance to developing countries to support implementation. The administrative burden imposed by transparency obligations could be lessened by using phrases such as "to the extent possible".
	4.8.1 Require countries to grant investment-related information upon request.	
	4.8.2 Require countries to publish in advance measures that they propose to adopt regarding matters covered by the IIA and to provide a reasonable opportunity for affected stakeholders (investors) to comment (prior-comment procedures).	The few IIAs that contain so-called "prior-comment procedures" require an even higher level of action by governments and may expose States to lobbying and pressure in the process of developing those laws.
	4.8.3 Explicitly reserve host States' rights and/or encourage State Parties - to implement policies placing transparency and disclosure requirements on investors - to seek information from a potential (or already established) investor or its home State - to make relevant information available to the public Qualify with an obligation upon the State to protect confidential information.	Transparency obligations are often excluded from the scope of ISDS (see 6.2.4). They can still be useful, given that any related problems can be discussed on a State-State level and addressed through technical assistance. Transparency provisions generally do not include any reference to transparency obligations applicable to investors. This contributes to the perception that IIAs lack i) corporate governance enhancing features; and ii) balance in the rights and obligations. IIAs could encourage States to strengthen domestic transparency requirements (e.g. including mechanisms for due diligence procedures).
	4.8.4 No clause.	

Sections	Policy options for IIAs	Sustainable development (SD) implications
4.9 Performance requirements ... regulate the extent to which host States can impose certain operational conditions on foreign investors/ investments	**4.9.0** Preclude Contracting Parties from placing trade-related performance requirements (e.g. local content requirements) on investments operating in the goods sector (in accordance with/incorporating the WTO TRIMs Agreement). **4.9.1** Preclude Contracting Parties from placing performance requirements on investments, beyond trade-related ones, e.g. requirements to transfer technology, to achieve a certain level of R&D operations or to employ a certain percentage of local personnel (TRIMs +). **4.9.2** Preclude Contracting Parties from imposing performance requirements unless they are linked to the granting of incentives (usually in combination with the above TRIMs + option). **4.9.3** Include country-specific reservations to the TRIMs+ obligation, e.g. carving out: - certain policies/measures (e.g. subsidies) - specific sectors/industries (e.g. banking, defence, fisheries, forestry, transport, infrastructure, social services) - certain policy areas (e.g. issues related to minorities, rural populations, marginalized or indigenous communities) - measures related to companies of a specific size (e.g. SMEs). **4.9.4** No clause prohibiting imposition of performance requirements	Performance requirements (PRs) refer to the imposition of conditions on businesses limiting their economic choices and managerial discretion (e.g. requirements to use locally produced inputs or to export a certain percentage of production). While PRs may be considered as creating economic inefficiencies, they can also be a potentially important tool for industrial or other economic development policies. From the transfer of technology to the employment of local workers, PRs can help materialize expected spill-over effects from foreign investment. Thus, to reap the full benefits of foreign investment and to align investment policy with SD objectives, policymakers need to carefully consider the need for policy flexibility when devising clauses on PRs. This is important, even if the IIA simply refers to the WTO TRIMs Agreement (because even though this does not add any new obligations on States who are also WTO members, the incorporation of TRIMs into an IIA gives investors the opportunity to directly challenge a TRIMs violation through ISDS). It is particularly important when considering the prohibition of an extensive list of PRs beyond TRIMs (e.g. requirements to transfer technology or employ local workers). The relevant exceptions and reservations should be considered from the point of view of both current and future regulatory needs. Finally, even if the IIA does not contain a clause explicitly ruling out PRs, the NT clause would prohibit the discriminatory imposition of PRs on foreign investors only.
4.10 "Umbrella" clause ... establishes a commitment on the part of the host State to respect its obligations regarding specific investments (including in investment contracts)	**4.10.0** Include a clause that requires each Party to observe any obligation (e.g. contractual) which it has assumed with respect to an investment of a covered investor. **4.10.1** Clarify that a breach of the "umbrella" clause may only result from an exercise of sovereign powers by a government (i.e. not an ordinary breach of contract by the State) and that disputes arising from such breaches shall be settled in the forum prescribed by the contract. **4.10.2** Introduce a "two-way" umbrella clause that requires both the State and the investor to observe their specific obligations related to the investment. **4.10.3** No "umbrella" clause.	An "umbrella" clause requires a host State to respect any obligation assumed by it with regard to a specific investment (for example, in an investment contract). The clause thus brings contractual and other individual obligations under the "umbrella" of the IIA, making them potentially enforceable through ISDS. By subjecting contractual violations to IIA arbitration an umbrella clause therefore makes it even more important for countries to have the technical capacity to carefully craft the respective contractual arrangements (e.g. when they enter into investment or concession contracts). The main difficulties with "umbrella" clauses are that they (1) effectively expand the scope of the IIA by incorporating non-treaty obligations of the host State into the treaty, which may increase the risk of being faced with costly legal proceedings, and (2) have given rise to conflicting interpretations by investor-State tribunals resulting in a high degree of unpredictability. One way of solving these problems – followed by many countries – would be to omit the "umbrella" clause from their IIAs. This means that an investor party to an investment contract would always have to show a breach of an IIA obligation, and not a breach of the contract. Alternatively, a country may clarify the scope of the umbrella clause and the competent dispute settlement forum to avoid conflicting interpretations. Finally, there is an option to make the umbrella clause work both ways, that is, to use it to incorporate into the IIA not only a State's obligations but also those of an investor, which would give States an opportunity to bring counterclaims against investors in the relevant ISDS proceedings.

Sections	Policy options for IIAs	Sustainable development (SD) implications
4.11 Personnel and staffing ... facilitates the entry, sojourn and employment of foreign personnel	4.11.0 Provide for the facilitation of entry, sojourn and issuing of work permits for nationals of one Party (or individuals regardless of nationality) into the territory of the other Party for purposes relating to an investment, subject to national immigration and other laws, covering: - all personnel, including families - only senior management and key personnel. 4.11.1 Ensure the right of investors to make appointments to senior management positions without regard to nationality. 4.11.2 Include country-specific reservations to the senior-management obligation (section 4.11.1), e.g. carve out: - certain policies/measures - specific sectors/industries - certain policy areas (minorities, indigenous communities) - measures related to companies of a specific size. 4.11.3 No clause.	Facilitating the entry and sojourn of foreign employees and the right to hire expatriate personnel (including senior management and members of the board of directors) can help to attract foreign investment. At the same time these provisions interact with host State's immigration laws - a particularly sensitive area of policymaking. It is important that host States retain control over their immigration policies or ensure coherence between relevant international and national regulations. Moreover, States may wish to encourage SD-related spill-overs such as employment for domestic or indigenous workers and trickle-down effects with respect to technological knowledge (e.g. by requiring foreign investments to employ indigenous personnel or by limiting the number of expatriate personnel working for the investor). Carefully choosing the right normative intensity (e.g. opting for a best-efforts approach), and other mechanisms for preserving flexibility (e.g. ensuring the priority of national laws) are key.
5 Public policy exceptions ... permit public policy measures, otherwise inconsistent with the treaty, to be taken under specified, exceptional circumstances	5.1.0 No public policy exceptions. 5.1.1 Include exceptions for national security measures and/or measures related to the maintenance of international peace and security: - formulate the exception as not self-judging (can be subject to arbitral review) - formulate the exception as self-judging. 5.1.2 Broaden the exception by clarifying that national security may encompass economic security. 5.1.3 Limit the exception by specifying: - that the exception only relates to certain types of measures, e.g. those relating to trafficking in arms or nuclear non-proliferation; or taken in pursuance of States' obligations under the UN Charter for the maintenance of international peace and security - that it only applies in times of war or armed conflict or an emergency in international relations. 5.1.4 Include exceptions for domestic regulatory measures that aim to pursue legitimate public policy objectives, e.g. to: - protect human rights - protect public health - preserve the environment (e.g. biodiversity, climate change) - protect public morals or maintain public order - preserve cultural and/or linguistic diversity - ensure compliance with laws and regulations that are not inconsistent with the treaty - allow for prudential measures (e.g. to preserve the integrity and stability of the financial system) - ensure the provision of essential social services (e.g. health, education, water supply) - allow for broader safeguards, including on developmental grounds (to address host countries' trade, financial and developmental needs) - prevent tax evasion - protect national treasures of artistic, historic or archaeological value (or "cultural heritage").	To date few IIAs include public policy exceptions. However, more recent treaties increasingly reaffirm States' right to regulate in the public interest by introducing general exceptions. Such provisions make IIAs and other public policy objectives, and reduce States' exposure to claims arising from any conflict that may occur between the interests of a foreign investor and the promotion and protection of legitimate public-interest objectives. Exceptions allow for measures, otherwise prohibited by the agreement, to be taken under specified circumstances. General exceptions identify the policy areas for which flexibility is to be preserved. A number of features determine how easy or difficult it is for a State to use an exception. To avoid review of the relevant measure by a court or a tribunal, the general exception can be made self-judging (i.e. the necessity/ appropriateness of the measure is judged only by the invoking State itself). This approach gives a wide margin of discretion to States, reduces legal certainty for investors and potentially opens possibilities for abuse. In contrast, exceptions designed as not self-judging imply that in case of a dispute, a court or tribunal will be able to determine whether the measure in question is allowed by the exception. In order to facilitate the use of exceptions by States, the provision may adjust the required link between the measure and the alleged policy objective pursued by this measure. For example, instead of providing that the measure must be "necessary" to achieve the policy objective, the IIA could require that the measure be "related" to the policy objective. Finally, in order to prevent abuse of exceptions, it is useful to clarify that "exceptional" measures must be applied in a non-arbitrary manner and not as disguised investment protectionism.

Sections		Policy options for IIAs	Sustainable development (SD) implications
	5.1.5	Prevent abuse of the exceptions by host States: - provide that «exceptional» measures shall not be applied in a manner that would constitute arbitrary or unjustifiable discrimination between investments or investors, or a disguised restriction on international trade or investment - choose the appropriate threshold which an "exceptional" measure must meet, e.g. the measure must be "necessary" (indispensable) to achieve the alleged policy objective, or be "related" (making a contribution) to this policy objective.	
6 Dispute settlement			
6.1 State-State … governs dispute settlement between the Contracting Parties	6.1.0	Establish that any unresolved IIA-related disputes can be submitted to State-State dispute settlement (arbitration).	To date, State-State arbitrations under IIAs have been very rare. This is a natural consequence of including ISDS into IIAs (and investors themselves taking host States to arbitration) to complement the system of diplomatic protection.
	6.1.1	Provide an option or require that the States engage in prior consultations and negotiations and/or resort to conciliation or mediation.	However, if a question about the meaning of a specific IIA obligation arises, and the Contracting Parties fail to resolve the uncertainty through consultations, a State-State arbitration can be a useful mechanism to clarify it. In this sense, State-State procedures retain their "supportive" function for ISDS.
6.2 Investor-State … provides foreign investors with access to international arbitration to resolve investment-related disputes with the host State	6.2.0	Grant investors the right to bring any investment-related dispute with the host country to international arbitration.	ISDS allows foreign investors to sue a host State if the latter violates its IIA obligations. Most IIAs allow investors to bypass domestic courts of host States and bring international arbitration proceedings (e.g. to constitute an *ad hoc* 3-person tribunal, most often at ICSID or under the UNCITRAL arbitration rules). The goal is to take the dispute out of the domestic sphere, to ensure independence and impartiality of the arbitrators, speed and effectiveness of the process and finality and enforceability of arbitral awards.
	6.2.1	Define the range of disputes that can be subject to ISDS: - any investment-related disputes (regardless of the legal basis for a claim, be it IIA, contract, domestic law or other) - disputes arising from specifically listed instruments (e.g. IIAs, contracts, investment authorisations/licenses) - disputes regarding IIA violations only - States' counterclaims.	As the number of ISDS cases increases, questions have arisen with regard to the effectiveness and the SD implications of ISDS. Many ISDS procedures are very expensive and often take several years to resolve. ISDS cases increasingly challenge domestic regulatory measures implemented for public policy objectives. Almost all ISDS cases lead to the break down of the relationship between the investor and the host State. Due to the lack of a single, unified mechanism, different tribunals have issued divergent interpretations of similarly worded treaty provisions, resulting in contradictory outcomes of cases involving identical/similar facts and/or treaty language. Many ISDS proceedings are conducted confidentially, which has raised concerns when tribunals address matters of public policy.
	6.2.2	Promote the use of alternative dispute resolution (ADR) methods - encourage resort to conciliation (e.g. ICSID or UNCITRAL conciliation rules) or mediation - agree to cooperate in developing dispute prevention mechanisms (including by creating investment ombudsmen or "ombuds" offices).	A number of policy options are available to deal with these problems. If the Contracting Parties consider each other's judicial systems to be effective and efficient, ISDS can be omitted from their IIA altogether. The Parties may also choose to subject only the most fundamental IIA protections to ISDS (e.g. the protection against uncompensated expropriation), reserve the right to give consent to arbitration on a case-by-case basis or minimize States' exposure to ISDS by other means (e.g. by removing certain areas from its purview, introducing limitation periods).
	6.2.3	Clarify that investors can only resort to international arbitration - after local remedies have been exhausted or a manifest ineffectiveness/bias of domestic courts has been demonstrated - if the investor agrees not to bring ("fork-in-the-road"), or undertakes to discontinue ("no U-turn"), the same case in another forum - within a limitation period, in order to prevent claims resulting from «old» measures (e.g. claim has to be brought within three years) - with respect to claims that arose after the treaty's entry into force (see section 2.4).	Parties may also consider promoting the use of alternative dispute resolution (ADR) methods, such as conciliation and mediation. If employed at the early stages of a dispute, ADR can help to prevent escalation of the conflict,
	6.2.4	Limit States' exposure to ISDS, e.g.: - clarify that certain treaty provisions and/or sensitive areas are excluded from ISDS, e.g. national security issues, including review of incoming investments; measures to protect the environment, health and human rights; prudential measures; measures relating to transfer of funds (or respective IIA provisions); tax measures that do not amount to expropriation; IIA provisions on transparency - specify only those issues/provisions to which ISDS should apply (e.g. only to the expropriation provision).	

Sections	Policy options for IIAs	Sustainable development (SD) implications
	6.2.5 Reserve State's consent to arbitration, so that it would be given separately for each specific dispute.	preserve the investment relationship, and find a workable common-sense solution in a faster, cheaper and more flexible manner. As part of the IIA rebalancing, a treaty may refer to the possibility of States bringing counterclaims for investors' non-compliance with the host State's national laws (section 7.1.1) or breach of investor's specific obligations undertaken in relation to its investment (section 4.10.3).
	6.2.6 Omit investor-State arbitration (i.e. do not consent to investor-State arbitration in the treaty) and nominate host State's domestic courts as the appropriate forum.	
6.3 ISDS institutions and procedures ... propose improvements of an institutional and procedural nature	6.3.0 Improve the institutional set-up of ISDS, e.g.: - consider a system with permanent or quasi-permanent arbitrators and/or an appellate mechanism - foster accessibility of documents (e.g. information about the case, party submissions, decisions and other relevant documents) - foster public participation (e.g. amicus curiae and public hearings) - specify that disputes concerning certain sensitive policy areas, such as tax and/or prudential measures, shall be submitted to the competent authorities of the Parties for a preliminary joint determination of whether they are in breach of the treaty - consider cooperation on training and assistance for adequate State representation in investor-State disputes, including through establishing an investment advisory centre.	The institutional set-up of the ISDS system is the cause of numerous concerns including perceived lack of legitimacy, inconsistent decisions, secrecy or participatory challenges for developing countries. IIA policymakers can improve the institutional set-up of ISDS in the treaty. An appellate mechanism could contribute to more coherent interpretation and foster trust in the system. Enhanced transparency of ISDS claims could enable broader and informed public debate as well as a more adequate representation of stakeholder interests, prevent non-transparent deals and stimulate balanced and well-reasoned arbitral decisions. Procedural improvements such as simplified disposals of «frivolous» claims, consolidation of claims and caps on arbitrator fees, could help streamline the arbitral process and make it less expensive and more effective. A reference to customary international law as controlling interpretation of the IIA, coupled with a possibility for the State Parties to issue joint interpretations, would ensure a common interpretative framework and the ability of the contracting States to influence this process, thereby limiting the discretion of arbitrators.
	6.3.1 Add features that would improve the arbitral process, e.g.: - mechanism for prompt/simplified disposal of "frivolous" claims - mechanism for consolidation of claims - requirement to interpret the IIA in accordance with customary international law (as codified in the Vienna Convention on the Law of Treaties) - mechanism for joint interpretation of the treaty by the Parties in case of ambiguities - caps on arbitrator fees.	
6.4 Remedies and compensation ... determines remedies available in case of treaty breach and gives guidance on compensation	6.4.0 No clause.	Most IIAs are silent on the issue of remedies and compensation. In theory this permits arbitral tribunals to apply any remedy they deem appropriate, including, for example, an order to the country to modify or annul its law or regulation. Remedies of the latter type could unduly intrude into the sovereign sphere of a State and impede its policymaking powers; thus, Parties to an IIA may consider limiting available remedies to monetary compensation and restitution of property (or compensation only).
	6.4.1 Limit available remedies to monetary compensation and restitution of property (or to compensation only).	
	6.4.2 Provide that the amount of compensation shall be equitable in light of circumstances of the case and set out specific rules on compensation for a treaty breach, e.g.: - exclude recoverability of punitive and/or moral damages - limit recoverability of lost profits (up to the date of award) - ensure that the amount is commensurate with the country's level of development.	As regards the amount of compensation for a treaty breach, international law requires compensation to be "full", which may include moral damages, loss of future profits and consequential damages. States may find it beneficial to provide guidance to arbitrators on applicable remedies and, similar to the case of expropriation above, on calculation of compensation. If the Contracting Parties believe that certain types of damages should not be recoverable by investors (e.g. punitive or moral damages), they can explicitly rule them out in their IIA. They can also restrict recoverability of future profits and provide that compensation should cover a claimant's direct losses and not exceed the capital invested plus interest. However, such rules may be seen as undermining the protective quality of the IIA.

Sections	Policy options for IIAs	Sustainable development (SD) implications
7 Investor obligations and res-ponsibilities ... promote compliance by investors with domestic and/ or international norms at the entry and operation stage	**7.1.0** No clause.	Most IIAs only set out obligations for States. To correct this asymmetry, an IIA could also set out investor obligations/responsibilities. Noting the evolving views on the capacity of international law to impose obligations on private parties, IIA policymakers could consider a number of options, each with its advantages and disadvantages.
	7.1.1 Require that investors comply with host State laws at both the entry and the post-entry stage of an investment. Establish sanctions for non-compliance: - deny treaty protection to investments *made in* violation of the host State law - deny treaty protection to investments *operating in* violation of those host State laws that reflect international legally binding obligations (e.g. core labour standards, anti-corruption, the environment conventions) and other laws as identified by the Contracting Parties - provide for States' right to bring counterclaims in ISDS arising from investors' violations of host State law.	These IPFSD options (i) condition treaty protection upon certain investor behaviour; (ii) raise the obligation to comply with domestic laws to the international level (increasing its relevance in arbitration); and (iii) take a best-endeavour approach to universally recognised standards or applicable CSR standards.
	7.1.2 Encourage investors to comply with universally recognized standards such as the ILO Tripartite MNE Declaration and the UN Guiding Principles on Business and Human Rights, and to carry out corporate due diligence relating to economic development, social and environmental risks. Provide that non-compliance may be considered by a tribunal when interpreting and applying treaty protections (e.g. FET) or determining the amount of compensation due to the investor.	A far-reaching option is to include an obligation for investors to comply with domestic laws and regulations of the host State at both, the entry and post-entry stage. While investors' observance of domestic laws can generally be enforced through national courts, including this obligation in an IIA could further improve means to ensure compliance (e.g. by way of denying treaty protection to non-complying investors or giving States a right to bring counterclaims in ISDS proceedings). Challenges may arise from the fact that domestic laws are usually directed at local enterprises as opposed to those who own or control them and from the need to ensure that minor/technical violations should not lead to complete denial of treaty benefits. Also, the elevation to a treaty level of the obligation to comply with domestic law should not affect the general principle that domestic laws must not be contrary to a country's international obligations - this can be made explicit in option 7.1.1 (e.g. by specifying that relevant domestic laws must not be inconsistent with the IIA and international law).
	7.1.3 Encourage investors to observe applicable CSR standards: - without specifying the relevant CSR standards - by giving a list of relevant CSR standards (e.g. in an annex) - by spelling out the content of relevant CSR standards (e.g. as best endeavour clauses). Provide that non-observance may be considered by a tribunal when interpreting and applying treaty protections (e.g. FET) or determining the amount of compensation due to the investor.	Another option is to promote responsible investment through IIA language that encourages investors to comply with relevant universal principles or with applicable CSR standards. Such a best-endeavour clause would be given additional weight if the treaty instructs tribunals to take into account investors' compliance with relevant principles and standards when deciding investors' ISDS claims. Given the multitude of existing CSR standards, it may be useful to refer to specific documents such as the UN Global Compact.
	7.1.4 Call for cooperation between the Parties to promote observance of applicable CSR standards, e.g. by - supporting the development of voluntary standards - building local industries' capacity for the uptake of voluntary standards - considering investors' adoption/compliance with voluntary standards when engaging in public procurement - conditioning the granting of incentives on the observance of CSR standards - promoting the uptake of CSR-related reporting (e.g. in the context of stock exchange listing rules).	
	7.1.5 Encourage home countries to condition the granting of outward investment promotion incentives on an investor's socially and environmentally sustainable behaviour (see also 10.1.1 on investment promotion).	
8 Relationship to other agreements ... establishes a hierarchy in case of competing international norms	**8.1.0** No clause.	IIAs usually provide that more favourable treatment of investors granted under another international treaty (e.g. a multilateral treaty to which both IIAs signatories are Parties) would take precedence. It is much less usual to address a relationship between an IIA and a treaty that governs a different policy area (e.g. protection of environment, human rights, etc.). Addressing this issue would help arbitral tribunals to take into account these other international commitments in order to ensure, as much as possible, harmonious interpretation of IIA provisions and see them as part of general international law.
	8.1.1 Stipulate that if another international treaty, to which the contracting States are parties, provides for more favourable treatment of investors/investments, that other treaty shall prevail in the relevant part.	
	8.2.0 Stipulate that in case of a conflict between the IIA and a host State's international commitments, such conflicts should be resolved in accordance with customary international law, including with reference to the Vienna Convention on the Law of Treaties.	
	8.2.1 Stipulate that in case of a conflict between the IIA and a host State's international commitments under a multilateral agreement in another policy area, such as environment and public health, the latter shall prevail.	

Sections	Policy options for IIAs	Sustainable development (SD) implications
9 Not lowering of standards clause …discourages Contracting Parties from attracting investment through the relaxation of labour or environmental standards	9.1.0 No clause. 9.1.1 Include environmental, human rights and labour clauses that - include a commitment to refrain from relaxing domestic environmental and labour legislation to encourage investment (expressed as a binding obligation or as a soft law clause) - reaffirm commitments under, e.g. international environmental agreements or with regard to international health standards, internationally recognized labour rights or human rights. 9.1.2 Encourage cooperation between treaty Parties to provide enhanced environmental, human rights and labour protection and hold expert consultations on such matters.	There is a concern that international competition for foreign investment may lead some countries to lower their environmental, human rights and labour standards and that this could lead to a "race to the bottom" in terms of regulatory standards. Some recent IIAs include language to address this concern. "Not lowering standards" provisions, for example, prohibit or discourage host States to compromise on environmental and labour protection for the purpose of attracting foreign investment. In doing so, the IIA goes beyond its traditional role of investment protection and pursues the goal of maintaining a regulatory framework that would be conducive to SD. While current IIAs often exclude "not lowering standards" clauses from ISDS or dispute settlement as such, it may be beneficial to foster consultations on this issue, including through institutional mechanisms, so as to ensure that the clause will effectively be implemented.
10 Investment promotion … aims to encourage foreign investment through additional means beyond investment protection provisions in IIAs	10.1.0 No clause. 10.1.1 Establish provisions encouraging investment flows, with a special emphasis on those which are most beneficial in light of a country's development strategy. Possible mechanisms include, e.g.:: - encourage home countries to provide outward investment incentives, e.g. investment guarantees, possibly conditioned on the SD enhancing effect of the investment and investors' compliance with universal principles and applicable CSR standards - organise joint investment promotion activities such as exhibitions, conferences, seminars and outreach programmes - exchange information on investment opportunities - ensure regular consultations between investment promotion agencies - provide technical assistance programmes to developing host countries to facilitate FDI flows - strengthen promotion activities through IIAs' institutional set up (see 11.1.1 below). 10.1.2 Include a subrogation clause.	While host States conclude IIAs to attract development-enhancing investment, the investment enhancing effect of IIAs is mostly indirect (through the protection offered to foreign investors). Only a few IIAs include special promotional provisions to encourage investment flows and increase investors' awareness of investment opportunities (e.g. by exchanging information or joint investment-promotion activities). Creating a joint committee responsible for investment promotion may help to operationalize the relevant provisions. Through these committees, the Parties can set up an agenda, organize and monitor the agreed activities and take corrective measures if necessary. The "promotional" provisions are "soft" (unenforceable), and their ultimate usefulness largely depends on the will and action of the Parties. The mechanism of subrogation supports investment promotion by ensuring the effective functioning of investment insurance schemes maintained by home States, or their respective agencies, to support their outward FDI. If the insurer covers the losses suffered by an investor in the host State, it acquires the investor's right to bring a claim and may exercise it to the same extent as, previously, the investor. Subrogation makes it possible for the insurer to be a direct beneficiary of any compensation by the host State to which the investor would have been entitled.

Sections	Policy options for IIAs	Sustainable development (SD) implications
11 Institutional set-up ...establishes an international platform collaboration between the Contracting Parties	11.1.0 No clause. 11.1.1 Set up an institutional framework under which the Parties (and, where relevant, other IIA stakeholders such as investors, local community representatives etc.) shall cooperate and hold meetings from time to time, to foster the implementation of the agreement with a view to maximising its contribution to SD. More specifically, this can include a commitment to: - issue interpretations of IIA clauses - review the functioning of the IIA - discuss and agree upon modification of commitments (in line with special procedures) and facilitate adaptation of IIAs to the evolving SD policies of State Parties, e.g. through renegotiation - organize and review investment promotion activities, including by involving investment promotion agencies, exchanging information on investment opportunities, organizing seminars on investment promotion - discuss the implementation of the agreement, including by addressing specific bottlenecks, informal barriers, red tape and resolution of investment disputes - regularly review Parties' compliance with the agreement's not-lowering standards clauses - provide technical assistance to developing Contracting Parties to enable them to engage in the institutionalized follow-up to the treaty - identify/update relevant CSR standards and organize activities to promote their observance.	While countries have concluded numerous IIAs, generally, there has been little follow-up to ensure that IIAs are properly implemented and kept up-to-date. Recent IIAs have started to include provisions for permanent institutional arrangements that perform a number of specific functions. For example, agreed interpretation can help ensure consistency in arbitral awards. Similarly, deliberations can ensure informed decision making on further investment liberalization, or prolonging or amending IIAs. All of this can help maximize the contribution of IIAs to SD, for example, by monitoring the development implications of IIAs and by engaging in dispute prevention activities and CSR promotion. A clear treaty mandate facilitates the implementation of the listed activities. Furthermore, it provides a forum to reach out to other relevant investment stakeholders including investors, local community representatives and academia.
12 Final provisions ...define the duration of the treaty and its possible prolongation	12.1.0 Specify the temporal application of the treaty (e.g. 10 or 20 years) with quasi-automatic renewal (the treaty is renewed unless one of the Parties notifies the other(s) of its intention to terminate). 12.1.1 State a specific duration of the treaty but stipulate that renewal is based on a written agreement of both Parties on the basis of a (joint) informed review of the IIA. 12.1.2 Include a "survival" clause which guarantees that in case of unilateral termination of the treaty, it will remain in effect for a number of years after the termination of the treaty (e.g. for another 5, 10 or 15 years) with respect to investments, made prior to the termination. 12.1.3 Do not specify minimum initial temporal duration but allow for termination of the treaty at any time upon the notification of either Party.	There is an emerging concern about aging treaty networks that may eventually be unsuitable for changing economic realities, novel or emerging forms of investment and new regulatory challenges. This partly results from the fact that IIAs often provide for a fixed period of duration and quasi-automatic renewal (in an attempt to provide a stable investment regime). An alternative would be to provide for renewal if both Parties explicitly agree to it in writing after a joint review of the treaty and an assessment of its impact on FDI flows and any attendant development implications. This exercise would help to assess whether the treaty is still needed and whether any amendments are required. Another issue concerns the protection of investors after the IIA's termination. An IIA may include a "survival" clause, which effectively locks in treaty standards for a number of years after the treaty is terminated. While it provides longer-term legal security for investors, which may be necessary for investors with long-term projects involving substantial commitment of capital (e.g. in the extractive industries), it may limit States' ability to regulate their economies in accordance with new realities (especially if the treaty's provisions do not grant sufficient policy flexibility). Negotiators may opt for a balanced solution by ensuring that the "survival" clause is not overly long.

UNCTAD's Investment Policy Framework for Sustainable Development

Policy options for IIAs

Part B. Pre-establishment

Policy options in Part B are supplementary to those in Part A and can be used by countries that wish to extend their IIA to pre-establishment matters. As in Part A, policy options are organized from most investor-friendly (i.e. highest level of liberalization) to those providing fewer establishment rights and more flexibility to the prospective host State.

Sections	Policy options for IIAs	Sustainable development (SD) implications
1 Pre-establishment obligations … govern establishment of foreign investments in the host State	**1.1.0** Grant the right of establishment, subject to restrictions on public policy grounds (EU Treaty approach).	Most IIAs grant protection to investors and their investments only after their establishment in the host State; the host country thus retains full regulatory freedom as regards the admission of foreign investors to its territory. For example, it can impose limits on foreign ownership of domestic companies or assets, apply screening procedures and block acquisitions for industrial or other policy reasons (e.g. national security).
	1.1.1 Undertake to refrain from imposing specific restrictions, including of a non-discriminatory nature, on the establishment in the host State's market (GATS approach), such as: - limitations on the participation of foreign capital in terms of maximum percentage limits on foreign shareholding - limitations on the number of establishments (quotas, monopolies, exclusive rights) - limitations on the total value of transactions or assets.	However, in recent years an increasing number of IIAs include provisions that apply at the pre-establishment phase of investment, with the aim of liberalizing access for investors from the other Party. This is usually achieved by (i) prohibiting countries to impose certain restrictions on market access (quotas, monopolies, exclusive rights and others), (ii) prohibiting countries to discriminate against covered investors at the stage of establishment and acquisition of investments, or (iii) using both approaches concurrently.
	1.1.2 Extend national treatment and/or MFN treatment to foreign investors with respect to "establishment, acquisition and expansion" of investments, i.e. prohibit discrimination *vis-à-vis* domestic investors and/or investors from third countries, subject to exceptions and reservations (sections 1.1.3 and 1.1.4 below).	It is an important policy choice to decide whether to extend the IIA to pre-establishment matters and, if so, to find a right balance between binding international commitments and domestic policy flexibility. The first step is to choose between the positive- and the negative-list approach to identifying industries in which the pre-establishment rights will be granted. The former offers selective liberalization by way of drawing up a "positive list" of industries in which investors will enjoy pre-establishment rights. Under the latter, investors benefit from pre-establishment commitments in all industries except in those that are explicitly excluded.
	1.1.3 Undertake pre-establishment commitments only with respect to sectors/industries specifically mentioned (*positive list*) or to all sectors/industries except those specifically excluded (*negative list*) or combining the two ("hybrid"). Country-specific reservations may carve out, as necessary, e.g.: - existing measures that provide preferential rights of establishment to domestic investors or investors from certain third countries (e.g. on the basis of preferential trade and investment agreements) - existing measures/laws that would otherwise be inconsistent with the newly concluded treaty (grandfathering) - sectors/industries where the Party wishes to retain full discretion on establishment, including future restrictive measures - specific procedures such as investment screening or an economic needs test (ENT).	
	1.1.4 Preserve additional policy flexibility on pre-establishment issues, with respect to "committed" (locked-in) sectors e.g.: - preserve the right of a Party to adopt new non-conforming measures in the future, as long as they do not "affect the overall level of commitments of that Party under the Agreement" - include a wide "catch-all" reservation into the schedule, e.g. that establishment is "subject to the requirement that no objection be raised, on reasons of national economy is made".	

Sections	Policy options for IIAs	Sustainable development (SD) implications
1.1.5	Reduce normative intensity of pre-establishment commitments e.g.: - postpone the entry into force of pre-establishment obligations until the date when the Parties agree on covered sectors/measures - agree to undertake negotiations on pre-establishment at a future date - exclude pre-establishment disciplines from dispute settlement provisions or subject them to State-State dispute settlement only - use "best efforts", as opposed to legally binding, language.	The negative-list approach is more demanding in terms of resources: it requires a thorough audit of existing domestic policies. In addition, under a negative-list approach and in the absence of specific reservations, a country commits to openness also in those sectors/activities, which, at the time an IIA is signed, do not yet exist or where the regulatory frameworks are still evolving. Generally, when aiming to preserve regulatory space, making commitments on a positive-list basis is considered to be safer. Properly managing a negative-list approach requires countries to have i) a sophisticated domestic regulatory regime and ii) sufficient institutional capacity for properly designing and negotiating the scheduling of liberalization commitments. In either case most IIAs include a list of reservations preserving specific non-conforming measures ("hybrid" approach).
1.1.6	Preserve policy flexibility on pre-establishment issues by carefully crafting relevant general provisions of the IIA, e.g.: - specifying the scope and coverage of the treaty (see section 2.3 of Part A) - including general and national security exceptions (see section 5 of Part A).	The need for reservations and «safety valves» is arguably greatest if a country opts for the negative list. From a SD perspective, it may be prudent to consider excluding certain sub-industries or grandfathering specific non-conforming measures, reserving the right to change the country's commitments under specified conditions or choose the right level of the normative intensity of commitments.
1.1.7	Provide that admission of investments is in accordance with domestic laws of the host State.	

UNCTAD's Investment Policy Framework for Sustainable Development

Policy options for IIAs

Part C. Special and Differential Treatment (SDT)

SDT provisions could be an option where Contracting Parties to an IIA have significantly different levels of development, especially when one of the Parties is a least-developed country. SDT presupposes that a treaty can be built asymmetrically, i.e. treaty obligations may differ between the Contracting Parties.

Sections		Policy options for IIAs	Sustainable development (SD) implications
1 **Asymmetrical obligations** ... enable imposition of less onerous obligations on a less developed Party	1.1.0	**Delayed implementation of obligations** Introduce a timetable for implementation of IIA commitments with longer time-frames for a less developed Party. Could be used for, e.g.: - pre-establishment obligations - national treatment - transfer of funds - performance requirements - transparency - investor-State dispute settlement.	SDT provisions give expression to the special needs and concerns of developing and particularly least-developed countries (LDCs). Largely absent from existing IIAs, this principle is expressed in numerous provisions of the WTO agreements and has found its way into other aspects of international law such as the international climate change framework. SDT may be necessary in order to ensure that a less developed Party to a treaty does not undertake obligations that would be too burdensome to comply with or contrary to its development strategy.
	1.1.1	**Reduced normative intensity** Replace binding obligations with best-endeavour obligations for a less developed Party. Could be used for, e.g.: - pre-establishment obligations - national treatment - performance requirements - transparency.	There are different ways to make an IIA asymmetrical and to reflect special needs of less developed Parties; moreover, several SDT options can be combined in the same treaty. For example, it can establish longer phase-in periods for pre-establishment obligations, country-specific carve-outs from the prohibition of performance requirements, best-endeavour obligations with respect to transparency, and account for the level of development in the FET provision.
	1.1.2	**Reservations** Include country-specific reservations from general obligations, e.g. carving out sensitive sectors, policy areas or enterprises of specific size (e.g. SMEs). Could be used for, e.g.: - pre-establishment obligations - national treatment - MFN treatment - performance requirements - personnel and staffing (senior management).	
	1.1.3	**Development-friendly interpretation** Promote interpretation of protection standards that takes into account States' different level of development. Could be used for, e.g.: - fair and equitable treatment - full protection and security - amount of compensation awarded.	
2 **Additional tools** ... encourage positive contributions by a more developed Party	2.1.0	**Technical assistance** Undertake a (best-endeavour) obligation to provide technical assistance to implement IIA obligations and facilitate FDI flows.	SDT can also manifest itself in special obligations for the more developed Contracting Party. These are meant to operationalize the IIA, so that it performs its FDI-promoting function and, if necessary, to help the less developed Party implement certain IIA obligations. Including such provisions in the treaty, even in a non-binding manner, would provide a mandate to the more developed partner to put in place relevant technical-assistance and promotion activities.
	2.1.1	**Investment promotion** Provide investment incentives to outward FDI such as investment guarantees.	

flexibilities for contracting parties are not mutually exclusive; rather, the combination of the two helps achieve a balanced agreement that meets the needs of different investment stakeholders. For example, an IIA can combine "strong" substantive protection (e.g. non-discrimination, capital transfer guarantees) with "strong" exceptions (e.g. national security exceptions or general exceptions to protect essential public policy objectives).[29]

The policy options presented in the IPFSD IIA-elements table are grounded in the Core Principles. For example, (i) the principle of investment protection directly manifests itself in IIA clauses on FET, non-discrimination, capital transfer, protection in case of expropriation or protection from strife; (ii) the principle of good governance is reflected, amongst others, in IIA clauses that aim at increasing host State's transparency regarding laws and regulations or in IIA clauses that foster transparency by the foreign investor vis-à-vis the host State; (iii) the right to regulate principle is reflected, amongst others, in IIA clauses stating that investments need to be in accordance with the host country's laws, allowing countries to lodge reservations (including for future policies); clarifying and circumscribing the content of indirect expropriation or general exceptions.

4. Implementation and institutional mechanisms for policy effectiveness

Implementation of IIAs at the national level entails:

- *Completing the ratification process.* This may vary from a few months to several years, depending on the countries involved and the concrete issues at stake. The distinction between the conclusion of an agreement and its entry into force is important, because the legal rights and obligations deriving from it do not become effective before the treaty has entered into force. The time lag between the conclusion of an IIA and its entry into force may therefore have implications, for both foreign investors and their host countries.

Capacity-building in developing countries is key to ensuring their effective engagement in IIAs.

- *Bringing national laws and practices into conformity with treaty commitments.* As with

any other international treaty, care needs to be taken that the international obligations arising from the IIA are properly translated into national laws and regulations, and depending on the scope of the IIA, e.g. with regard to transparency obligations, also into the administrative practices of the countries involved.

- *Disseminating information about IIA obligations.* Informing and training ministries, government agencies and local authorities on the implications of IIAs for their conduct in regulatory and administrative processes is important so as to avoid other arms of the government causing conflicts with treaty commitments and thus giving rise to investor grievances, which if unresolved could lead to arbitral disputes.

- *Preventing disputes,* including through ADR mechanisms. This may involve the establishment of adequate institutional mechanisms to prevent disputes from emerging and avoid the breach of contracts and treaties on the part of government agencies. This involves ensuring that the State and various government agencies take account of the legal obligations made under investment agreements when enacting laws and implementing policy measures, and establishing a system to identify more easily potential areas where disputes with investors can arise, and to respond to the disputes where and when they emerge.

- *Managing disputes* that may arise under IIAs. If dispute prevention efforts fail, States need to be prepared to engage effectively and efficiently in managing the disputes from beginning to end. This involves setting up the required mechanisms to take action in case of the receipt of a notice of arbitration, to handle the case, and ultimately to bring it to a conclusion, including possibly through settlement.

- *Establishing a review mechanism* to verify periodically the extent to which the IIA contributes to achieving expected results in terms of investment attraction and enhancing sustainable development – while keeping in mind that there is no mono-causal link between concluding an IIA and investment flows.

Moreover, because national and international investment policies must be considered in an integrated manner, and both need to evolve with a country's changing circumstances, countries have to assess continuously the suitability of their policy choices with regard to key elements of investment protection and promotion, updating model treaties and renegotiating existing IIAs.

Undertaking these implementation and follow-up efforts effectively and efficiently can be burdensome for developing countries, especially the least developed, because they often lack the required institutional capabilities or financial and human resources. Similarly, they often face challenges

when it comes to analyzing ex ante the scope of obligations into which they are entering when they conclude an IIA, and the economic and social implications of the commitments contained in IIAs.

This underlines the importance of capacity-building technical cooperation to help developing countries in assessing various policy options before entering into new agreements and subsequently to assist them in implementing their commitments. IIAs can include relevant provisions to this end, including setting up institutional frameworks under which the contracting parties (and, where appropriate and relevant, other IIA stakeholders such as investors or civil society) can review progress in the implementation of IIA commitments, with a view to maximizing their contribution to sustainable development. International organizations can also play an important capacity-building role.

F. THE WAY FORWARD

The IPFSD aims to provide a common language and point of reference for policymakers and investment stakeholders for the participative development of future investment policies.

A new generation of investment policies is emerging, pursuing a broader and more intricate development policy agenda within a framework that seeks to maintain a generally favourable investment climate. "New generation" investment policies recognize that investment is a primary driver of economic growth and development, and seek to give investment policy a more prominent place in development strategy. They recognize that investment must be responsible, as a prerequisite for inclusive and sustainable development. And in the design of "new generation" investment policies policymakers seek to address long-standing shortcomings of investment policy in a comprehensive manner in order to ensure policy effectiveness and build a stable investment climate.

This chapter has painted the contours of a new investment policy framework for sustainable development. The Core Principles set out the design criteria for investment policies. The national investment policy guidelines suggest how to ensure

integration of investment policy with development strategy, how to ensure policy coherence and design investment policies in support of sustainable development, and how to improve policy effectiveness. The policy options for key elements of IIAs provide guidance to IIA negotiators for the drafting of sustainable-development-friendly agreements; they form the first comprehensive overview of the myriad of options available to them in this respect.

In developing the IPFSD, UNCTAD has had the benefit of a significant body of existing work and experience on the topic. UNCTAD itself has carried out more than 30 investment policy reviews (IPRs) in developing countries over the years (box IV.4), analyzed in detail investment regulations in numerous countries for the purpose of investment facilitation (box IV.6), and produced many publications on best practices in investment policy (box IV.7), including in the *WIR* series. Other agencies have a similar track record, notably the OECD and the World Bank, various regional organizations, and a number of NGOs. In defining an IPFSD, this chapter has attempted to harness the best of existing work on investment policies, investment policy frameworks, guidelines and models, and to build on experience in the field in their implementation.

The IPFSD is not a negotiated text or an undertaking between States. It is an initiative by the UNCTAD secretariat, representing expert guidance for policymakers by an international organization, leaving national policymakers free to "adapt and adopt" as appropriate.

It is hoped that the IPFSD may serve as a key point of reference for policymakers in formulating national investment policies and in negotiating or reviewing IIAs. It may also serve as a reference for policymakers in areas as diverse as trade, competition, industrial policy, environmental policy, or any other field where investment plays an important role. The IPFSD can also serve as the basis for capacity-building on investment policy. And it may come to act as a point of convergence for international cooperation on investment issues.

In its current form the IPFSD has gone through numerous consultations, comprehensively and by individual parts, with expert academics and practitioners. It is UNCTAD's intention to provide a platform for further consultation and discussion with all investment stakeholders, including policymakers, the international development community, investors, business associations, labour unions, and relevant NGOs and interest groups. To allow for further improvements resulting from such consultations, the IPFSD has been designed as a "living document".

The dynamic nature of investment policymaking adds to the rationale for such an approach, in particular for the specific investment policy guidelines. The continuous need to respond to newly emerging challenges with regard to foreign investment makes it mandatory to review and, where necessary, modify these guidelines from time to time. Thus, from UNCTAD's perspective, while the IPFSD will serve to inform the investment policy debate and to guide technical assistance work in the field, new insights from that work will feed back into it.

The IPFSD thus provides a point of reference and a common language for debate and cooperation on national and international investment policies.

UNCTAD will add the infrastructure for such cooperation, not only through its numerous policy forums on investment, but also by providing a platform for "open sourcing" of best practice investment policies through its website, as a basis for the inclusive development of future investment policies with the participation of all.[30]

Notes

[1] Many successful developing countries maintained a significant level of government influence over the direction of economic growth and development throughout the period; see *Development-led globalization: Towards sustainable and inclusive development paths*, Report of the Secretary-General of UNCTAD to UNCTAD XIII.

[2] The G-20, in its 2010 Seoul declaration, asked international organizations (specifically, UNCTAD, WTO and OECD) to monitor the phenomenon of investment protectionism.

[3] See Sauvant, K.P. (2009). "FDI Protectionism Is on the Rise." *World Bank Policy Research Working Paper 5052.*

[4] For example, the World Bank's Guidelines on the Treatment of Foreign Direct Investment, the OECD's Policy Framework for Investment (PFI), and instruments developed by various regional organizations and NGOs.

[5] These include, inter alia, the UN Global Compact, the UN Guiding Principles on Business and Human Rights, the ILO Declaration on Fundamental Principles and Rights at Work, the IFC's Sustainability Framework and the OECD Guidelines for Multinational Enterprises.

[6] See ILO Global Employment Trends 2012, available on www.ilo.org.

[7] See, for example, "Promoting investment for development: Best practices in strengthening investment in basic infrastructure in developing countries," note by the UNCTAD secretariat to the Investment, Enterprise and Development Commission, May 2011, TD/B/C.II/14, www. unctad.org.

[8] Based on Doran, G. T. (1981). "There's a S.M.A.R.T. way to write management's goals and objectives." *Management Review*, 70 (11 AMA FORUM); 35-36.

[9] The universe of "core IIAs" principally consists of BITs and other agreements that contain provisions on investment, so-called "other IIAs". Examples of the latter include free trade agreements (FTAs) or economic partnership agreements (EPAs). As regards their substantive obligations, "other IIAs" usually fall into one of three categories: IIAs including obligations commonly found in BITs; agreements with limited investment-related provisions; and IIAs focusing on investment cooperation and/or providing for future negotiating mandates on investment. In addition to "core IIAs", numerous other legal instruments matter for foreign investment, including double taxation treaties.

[10] Examples include the interaction between IIAs and other bodies of international law or policy in the field of public health (e.g. the World Health Organization Framework Convention on Tobacco Control, WHO FCTC), environment (e.g. the Basel Convention on the Control of Transboundary Movements of Hazardous Wastes) or human rights (e.g. International Covenant on Economic, Social and Cultural Rights), to name a few. In the context

of ensuring coherence between investment protection and climate change, *WIR10* suggested a "multilateral declaration" clarifying that IIAs do not constrain climate change measures enacted in good faith.

[11] In some countries the existence of an IIA is a prerequisite for the granting of investment guarantees.

[12] This impact is generally stronger in the case of preferential trade and investment agreements than with regards to BITs. See "The Role of International Investment Agreements in Attracting Foreign Direct Investment to Developing Countries," UNCTAD Series on International Investment Policies for Development, December 2009; www.unctad.org. For a full discussion of FDI determinants, see *WIR98*.

[13] See also Skovgaard Poulsen, Lauge N. and Aisbett, Emma (2011) "When the Claim Hits: Bilateral Investment Treaties and Bounded Rational Learning." *Crawford School Research Paper No. 5.*

[14] As discussed in *WIR04*, interaction can be either autonomous-liberalization-led or IIA-driven, or anywhere in-between.

[15] Related are questions of forum-choice, double incorporation, dual liability and re-litigation of issues, all of which call for a careful consideration of how to manage the overlaps between agreements. See also Babette Ancery (2011), "Applying Provisions of Outside Trade Agreements in Investor-State Arbitration through the MFN-clause." *TDB*, 8 (3).

[16] This is in line with the traditional view of international law, as governing relations between its subjects, primarily between States. Accordingly, it is impossible for an international treaty to impose obligations on private actors (investors), which are not parties to the treaty (even though they are under the jurisdiction of the respective contracting parties).

[17] Article 13 "Investor Obligation" provides: "COMESA investors and their investments shall comply with all applicable domestic measures of the Member State in which their investment is made."

[18] In fact, in the course of the past century, international law has been moving away from the traditional, strict view towards including, where appropriate, non-State actors into its sphere. See, e.g., A. Bianchi (ed.) (2009), "Non-State Actors and International Law." (Ashgate, Dartmouth).

[19] Also the 2012 Revision of the International Chamber of Commerce (ICC) Guidelines for International Investment refer to investors' obligations to comply with the laws and regulations of the host State at all times and, in particular, to their obligation to comply with national and international labour laws, even where these are not effectively enforced by the host State.

[20] The aggregate amount of compensation sought by the three claimants constituting the majority shareholders of the former Yukos Oil Company in the ongoing arbitration proceedings against Russia. See *Hulley Enterprises Limited (Cyprus) v. The Russian Federation*, PCA Case No. AA 226; *Yukos Universal Limited (Isle of Man) v. The Russian Federation*, PCA Case No. AA 227; *Veteran Petroleum Limited (Cyprus) v. The Russian Federation*, PCA Case No. AA 228.

[21] *Ceskoslovenska Obchodni Banka (CSOB) v. The Slovak Republic,* ICSID Case No. ARB/97/4, Final Award, 29 December 2004. The case was brought by CSOB on the basis of consent to arbitration contained in the 1992 BIT between the Czech Republic and the Slovak Republic. The findings on liability and damages were based on the underlying contract and Czech law. For more information on ISDS consult http://www.unctad.org/iia-dbcases/cases.aspx.

[22] For details, see UNCTAD (2011) "Sovereign Debt Restructuring and International Investment Agreements." *IIA Issues Note, No.2,* www.unctad.org, *Abaclat and others v. Argentine Republic*, ICSID Case No. ARB/07/5, Decision on Jurisdiction and Admissibility, 4 August 2011.

[23] Nottage, Hunter (2003), Trade and Competition in the WTO: Pondering the Applicability of Special and Differential Treatment, Journal of International Economic Law, 6(1), p.28.

[24] Based on six categories as identified in WTO (2000) "Implementation of Special and Differential Treatment Provisions in WTO Agreements and Decisions," Note by Secretariat, WT/COMTD/W/77, 25 October 2000, available at www.wto.org. More recently, also the Doha Ministerial Declaration (2001) reaffirmed SDT as an integral part of the multilateral trade regime.

[25] COMESA Investment Agreement (2007), Article 14(3).

[26] Any comprehensive effort to reform the ISDS regime would also have to go beyond IIA clauses, and address other rules, including those for conducting international arbitrations (e.g. ICSID or UNCITRAL).

[27] Experience with ISDS has revealed numerous instances of unclear or ambiguous clauses that risk being interpreted in an unanticipated and broad manner. Therefore the table includes options to clarify. However, these clarifications should not be used by arbitrators to interpret earlier clauses that lack clarifications in broad and open-ended manner.

[28] Absence of ISDS – and hence of the possibility to be subject to financial liabilities arising from ISDS – may make it easier for countries to agree to certain standards of protections.

[29] Similarly, one can combine far-reaching liberalization or protection clauses with a possibility to lodge reservations (e.g. for pre- and post-establishment clauses, and for existing and future measures). See "Preserving Flexibility in IIAs: The Use of Reservations", UNCTAD Series on International Investment Policies for Development, June 2006; www.unctad.org.

[30] Interested stakeholders and experts are invited to provide feedback and suggestions through the dedicated UNCTAD IPFSD website, at www.unctad.org/DIAE/IPFSD.

REFERENCES

Baldwin-Edwards, Martin (2011). "Labour immigration and labour markets in the GCC countries: national patterns and trends". Research Paper, Kuwait Programme on Development, Governance and Globalisation in the Gulf States, Number 15, March.

British Private Equity and Venture Capital Association (2011). *Responsible Investment: A Guide for Private Equity & Venture Capital Firms*. London.

China, National Bureau of Statistics (2012). *China Statistical Yearbook 2011*. Beijing: China Statistical Press.

Deloitte (2011). "Fortresses and footholds: Emerging market growth strategies, practices, and outlook." Available at: www.deloitte.com.

FAO (Food and Agriculture Organization) (2011). *Land Grabbing: Case studies in 17 countries of Latin American and the Caribbean*. Available at: www.rlc.fao.org/es/prensa/noticias/estudio-de-la-fao-halla-intensos-procesos-de-concentracion-y-extranjerizacion-de-tierras-en-america-latina-y-el-caribe (accessed 13 June 2012).

ICC (International Chamber of Commerce) (2012). *Guidelines for International Investors*. Paris: ICC. Available at: www.iccwbo.org/Advocacy-Codes-and-Rules/Document-centre/2012/2012-ICC-Guidelines-for-International-Investment (accessed 13 June 2012).

ILO (International Labour Organization) (2012). *Global Employment Trends 2012*. Geneva: ILO.

International Energy Agency (2011). *World Energy Outlook 2011*. Paris: OECD/IEA.

IMF (International Monetary Fund) (2011). "Regional Economic Outlook, Middle East and Central Asia", October.

Kostyunina, G. (2012), "The impact of Russia's accession to WTO on FDI", paper prepared for *WIR12*.

OECD-UNCTAD (2011). "Report on G20 trade and investment measures" (6th Report October). Available at: http://unctad.org/en/Pages/DIAE/G-20/UNCTAD-OECD-reports.aspx.

OECD-UNCTAD (2012). "Report on G20 trade and investment measures" (7th Report, May). Available at: http://unctad.org/en/Pages/DIAE/G-20/UNCTAD-OECD-reports.aspx.

Peres, Wilson (2011). "Industrial policies in Latin America". United Nations University, World Institute for Development Economics Research (UNU-WIDER), Working Paper No. 2011/48, September.

PwC (2012). "15th Annual Global CEO Survey 2012." Available at: www.pwc.com.

Rodríguez, Carlos, Carmen Gómez and Jesús Ferreiro (2009). "A proposal to improve UNCTAD's FDI potential index". *Transnational Corporations*, 18(3): 85–113.

Samba Report Series (2010). "The GCC: increasingly diversified economies". Available atö www.samba.com.

UNCTAD (2010). "Denunciation of the ICSID Convention and BITs: Impact on Investor-State Claims". *IIA Issues Note*, No. 2. Available at: http://unctad.org/en/Docs/webdiaeia20106_en.pdf. (accessed 13 June 2012).

UNCTAD (2011a). "Global investment trends monitor". No. 5, January.

UNCTAD (2011b). *Foreign Direct Investment in LDCs: Lessons Learned from the Decade 2001-2010 and the Way Forward*. New York and Geneva: United Nations.

UNCTAD (2011c). "Promoting standards for responsible investment in value chains". Item 1. Report to the High-Level Development Working Group, September. New York and Geneva: United Nations.

UNCTAD (2011d). "Indicators for measuring and maximizing economic value added and job creation arising from private sector investment in value chains". Item 2. Report to the High-Level Development Working Group, September. New York and Geneva: United Nations.

UNCTAD (2011e). "Options for promoting responsible investment in agriculture". Report to the High-Level Development Working Group. June. New York and Geneva: United Nations.

UNCTAD (2011f). "Sovereign debt restructuring and international investment agreements", *IIA Issues Note*, No. 2. Available at: http://unctad.org/en/Docs/webdiaepcb2011d3_en.pdf. (accessed 13 June 2012).

UNCTAD (2011g). *Investment and Enterprise Responsibility Review: Analysis of investor and enterprise policies on corporate social responsibility*. New York and Geneva: United Nations.

UNCTAD (2012a). "Latest Developments in Investor-State Dispute Settlement". *IIA Issues Note*, No. 1. New York and Geneva: United Nations.

UNCTAD (2012b). "Corporate social responsibility in global value chains: evaluation and monitoring challenges for small and medium sized suppliers in developing countries" (forthcoming).

UN-DESA (2012) *World economic situation and prospects 2011: update as of mid-2012*. New York: United Nations.

United Nations (2011). *Manual on Statistics of International Trade in Services 2010 (MSITS 2010)*. Geneva, Luxembourg, Madrid, New York, Paris and Washington D.C.: UN, IMF, OECD, EuroStat, UNCTAD, UN-WTO, WTO.

United States Department of Commerce (2011). "Direct investment for 2007–2010 detailed historical-cost positions and related financial and income flows", *Survey of Current Business*, September: 50-56.

WIR98. *World Investment Report 1998: Trends and Determinants*. New York and Geneva: United Nations.

WIR00. *World Investment Report 2000: Cross-border Mergers and Acquisitions and Development*. New York and Geneva: United Nations.

WIR09. *World Investment Report 2009: Transnational Corporations, Agricultural Production and Development*. New York and Geneva: United Nations.

WIR10. *World Investment Report 2010: Investing in a Low-Carbon Economy*. New York and Geneva: United Nations.

WIR11. *World Investment Report 2011: Non-equity Modes of International Production and Development*. New York and Geneva: United Nations.

ANNEX TABLES

List of annex tables available on the UNCTAD website, www.unctad.org/wir

1. FDI inflows, by region and economy, 1990–2010
2. FDI outflows, by region and economy, 1990–2010
3. FDI inward stock, by region and economy, 1990–2010
4. FDI outward stock, by region and economy, 1990–2010
5. FDI inflows as a percentage of gross fixed capital formation, 1990–2010
6. FDI outflows as a percentage of gross fixed capital formation, 1990–2010
7. FDI inward stock as percentage of gross domestic products, by region and economy, 1990–2010
8. FDI outward stock as percentage of gross domestic products, by region and economy, 1990–2010
9. Value of cross-border M&A sales, by region/economy of seller, 1990–May 2011
10. Value of cross-border M&A purchases, by region/economy of purchaser, 1990–May 2011
11. Number of cross-border M&A sales, by region/economy of seller, 1990–May 2011
12. Number of cross-border M&A purchases, by region/economy of purchaser, 1990–May 2011
13. Value of cross-border M&A sales, by sector/industry, 1990–May 2011
14. Value of cross-border M&A purchases, by sector/industry, 1990–May 2011
15. Number of cross-border M&A sales, by sector/industry, 1990–May 2011
16. Number of cross-border M&A purchases, by sector/industry, 1990–May 2011
17. Cross-border M&A deals worth over $1 billion completed in 2010
18. Value of greenfield FDI projects, by source, 2003–April 2011
19. Value of greenfield FDI projects, by destination, 2003–April 2011
20. Value of greenfield FDI projects, by sector/industry, 2003–April 2011
21. Number of greenfield FDI projects, by source, 2003–April 2011
22. Number of greenfield FDI projects, by destination, 2003–April 2011
23. Number of greenfield FDI projects, by sector/industry, 2003–April 2011
24. Estimated world inward FDI stock, by sector and industry, 1990–2009
25. Estimated world outward FDI stock, by sector and industry, 1990–2009
26. Estimated world inward FDI flows, by sector and industry, 1990–1992 and 2007–2009
27. Estimated world outward FDI flows, by sector and industry, 1990–1992 and 2007–2009
28. Inward FDI Performance and Potential Index ranking, 1990–2010
29. The world's top 100 non-financial TNCs, ranked by foreign assets, 2010
30. The top 100 non-financial TNCs from developing and transition economies, ranked by foreign assets, 2010
31. The top 50 financial TNCs, ranked by Geographical Spread Index (GSI), 2010
32. Outward FDI projects by State-owned TNCs, by home region/economy, 2003-2010
33. Outward FDI projects by State-owned TNCs, by sector and industry, 2003-2010
34. Number of parent corporations and foreign affiliates, by region and economy, latest available year

Annex table I.1. FDI flows, by region and economy, 2006-2011
(Millions of dollars)

Region/economy	FDI inflows						FDI outflows					
	2006	2007	2008	2009	2010	2011	2006	2007	2008	2009	2010	2011
World	1 463 351	1 975 537	1 790 706	1 197 824	1 309 001	1 524 422	1 415 094	2 198 025	1 969 336	1 175 108	1 451 365	1 694 396
Developed economies	981 869	1 310 425	1 019 648	606 212	618 586	747 860	1 152 034	1 829 578	1 580 753	857 792	989 576	1 237 508
Europe	639 814	899 191	569 026	398 935	356 588	425 266	793 937	1 279 540	1 024 605	458 103	568 414	651 387
European Union	585 030	853 966	542 242	356 631	318 277	420 715	691 764	1 204 747	957 798	393 618	482 905	561 805
Austria	7 933	31 154	6 858	9 303	4 265	14 128	13 670	39 025	29 452	10 006	7 732	30 451
Belgium	58 893	93 429	193 950	61 744	81 190	89 142	50 685	80 127	221 023	9 205	55 709	70 706
Bulgaria	7 805	12 389	9 855	3 385	1 601	1 864	177	282	765	- 95	229	190
Cyprus	1 834	2 226	1 415	3 472	766	276	887	1 240	2 717	383	679	1 828
Czech Republic	5 463	10 444	6 451	2 927	6 141	5 405	1 468	1 620	4 323	949	1 167	1 152
Denmark	2 691	11 812	1 824	3 917	- 7 397	14 771	8 206	20 574	13 240	6 305	3 467	23 413
Estonia	1 797	2 716	1 729	1 839	1 540	257	1 107	1 747	1 112	1 549	133	- 1 458
Finland	7 652	12 451	- 1 144	398	6 733	54	4 805	7 203	9 297	4 917	10 471	5 417
France	71 848	96 221	64 184	24 219	30 638	40 945	110 673	164 310	155 047	107 130	76 867	90 146
Germany	55 626	80 208	8 109	24 156	46 860	40 402	118 701	170 617	72 758	75 391	109 321	54 368
Greece	5 355	2 111	4 499	2 436	373	1 823	4 045	5 246	2 418	2 055	979	1 788
Hungary	6 818	3 951	6 325	2 048	2 274	4 698	3 877	3 621	2 234	1 984	1 307	4 530
Ireland	- 5 542	24 707	- 16 453	25 960	26 330	13 102	15 324	21 146	18 949	26 616	17 802	- 2 148
Italy	42 581	43 849	- 10 835	20 077	9 178	29 059	43 797	96 231	67 000	21 275	32 655	47 210
Latvia	1 663	2 322	1 261	94	379	1 562	170	369	243	- 62	21	93
Lithuania	1 817	2 015	1 965	66	753	1 217	291	597	336	217	79	165
Luxembourg	31 837	- 28 260	11 216	22 408	9 211	17 530	7 747	73 350	11 759	7 547	15 123	11 741
Malta	1 838	805	802	746	1 063	539	30	14	291	114	57	21
Netherlands	13 978	119 383	4 549	36 042	- 8 966	17 129	71 175	55 606	68 334	28 180	55 217	31 867
Poland	19 603	23 561	14 839	12 932	8 858	15 139	8 883	5 405	4 414	4 699	5 487	5 860
Portugal	10 908	3 063	4 665	2 706	2 646	10 344	7 139	5 493	2 741	816	- 7 493	12 639
Romania	11 367	9 921	13 909	4 844	2 940	2 670	423	279	274	- 88	- 20	32
Slovakia	4 693	3 581	4 687	- 6	526	2 143	511	600	530	904	327	490
Slovenia	644	1 514	1 947	- 653	359	999	862	1 802	1 440	260	- 212	112
Spain	30 802	64 264	76 993	10 407	40 761	29 476	104 248	137 052	74 717	13 070	38 341	37 256
Sweden	28 941	27 737	37 153	10 023	- 1 347	12 091	26 593	38 806	31 326	25 908	17 956	26 850
United Kingdom	156 186	196 390	91 489	71 140	50 604	53 949	86 271	272 384	161 056	44 381	39 502	107 086
Other developed Europe	54 783	45 225	26 784	42 303	38 311	4 551	102 173	74 793	66 808	64 485	85 509	89 582
Gibraltar	137[a]	165[a]	159[a]	172[a]	165[a]	166[a]	-	-	-	-	-	-
Iceland	3 843	6 824	917	86	246	1 013	5 533	10 186	- 4 209	2 292	- 2 357	- 29
Norway	7 085	5 800	10 564	13 403	17 519	3 569	20 816	13 588	25 683	34 400	23 086	19 999
Switzerland	43 718	32 435	15 144	28 642	20 381	- 196	75 824	51 020	45 333	27 793	64 780	69 612
North America	297 430	330 604	363 543	165 010	221 318	267 869	270 434	451 244	388 090	308 620	342 984	446 225
Canada	60 294	114 652	57 177	21 406	23 413	40 932	46 214	57 726	79 794	41 665	38 585	49 569
United States	237 136	215 952	306 366	143 604	197 905	226 937	224 220	393 518	308 296	266 955	304 399	396 656
Other developed countries	44 626	80 631	87 079	42 268	40 680	54 725	87 663	98 794	168 058	91 069	78 178	139 896
Australia	31 050	45 535	47 218	26 554	35 556	41 317	25 409	16 857	33 618	16 693	12 791	19 999
Bermuda	261	617	173	- 70	231	424	579	105	403	21	- 33	- 310
Israel	15 296	8 798	10 875	4 607	5 510	11 374	11 228	4 581	5 616	693	8 567	2 998
Japan	- 6 507	22 550	24 426	11 938	- 1 252	- 1 758	50 264	73 548	128 019	74 699	56 263	114 353
New Zealand	4 526	3 131	4 388	- 761	636	3 369	182	3 703	402	- 1 037	591	2 856
Developing economies	427 163	574 311	650 017	519 225	616 661	684 399	239 336	316 863	328 121	268 476	400 144	383 754
Africa	36 783	51 479	57 842	52 645	43 122	42 652	8 225	9 322	7 896	3 169	7 027	3 512
North Africa	23 194	23 936	23 114	18 224	15 709	7 686	1 142	5 560	8 752	2 588	4 847	1 753
Algeria	1 795	1 662	2 594	2 746	2 264	2 571	35	295	318	215	220	534
Egypt	10 043	11 578	9 495	6 712	6 386	- 483	148	665	1 920	571	1 176	626
Libya	2 064	3 850	3 180	3 310	1 909	-	474	3 947	5 888	1 165	2 722	233
Morocco	2 449	2 805	2 487	1 952	1 574	2 519	445	622	485	470	589	247
Sudan	3 534	2 426	2 601	1 816	2 064	1 936	7	11	98	89	66	84[a]
Tunisia	3 308	1 616	2 759	1 688	1 513	1 143	33	20	42	77	74	28
Other Africa	13 589	27 543	34 727	34 421	27 413	34 966	7 083	3 763	- 856	581	2 180	1 760
West Africa	7 037	9 555	12 617	13 461	11 825	16 100	669	- 475	- 398	- 967	- 421	- 281
Benin	53	255	170	134	177	118	- 2	- 6	- 4	31	- 18	3[a]
Burkina Faso	34	344	238	101	35	7	1	0	8	8	- 4	4[a]
Cape Verde	131	190	209	119	111	93		0	- 0	0	0	0
Côte d' Ivoire	319	427	446	377	339	344	-	-	-	- 9	25	8[a]
Gambia	71	76	70	40	37	36	-	-	-	-	-	-
Ghana	636	855	1 220	1 685	2 527	3 222	-	-	9	7	8	8[a]
Guinea	125	386	382	141	101	1 211	-	-	126			5
Guinea-Bissau	17	19	6	18	33	19[a]	0	- 0	- 0	- 3	6	1[a]
Liberia	108	132	284	218	450	508	346	363	382	364	369	372[a]
Mali	83	73	180	748	406	178	1	7	1	- 1	7	2[a]
Mauritania	155	139	343	- 3	131	45	5	4	4	4	4	4[a]
Niger	51	129	340	791	940	1 014	- 1	8	24	59	60	48[a]
Nigeria	4 898	6 087	8 249	8 650	6 099	8 915	322	- 875	- 1 058	- 1 542	- 923	- 824

/...

Annex table I.1. FDI flows, by region and economy, 2006-2011 (continued)
(Millions of dollars)

Region/economy	FDI inflows						FDI outflows					
	2006	2007	2008	2009	2010	2011	2006	2007	2008	2009	2010	2011
Saint Helena	0	0	-	-	-	-	-	-	-	-	-	-
Senegal	220	297	398	320	266	286	10	25	126	77	2	66[a]
Sierra Leone	59	97	58	74	87	49	-	-	-	-	5	-
Togo	77	49	24	49	86	54[a]	- 14	- 1	- 16	37	37	20[a]
Central Africa	2 759	5 892	4 180	6 223	9 501	8 533	80	83	104	- 19	52	104
Burundi	0	1	4	0	1	2[a]	-	0	1	-	-	-
Cameroon	16	191	- 24	668	354	360	- 48	- 6	- 47	- 141	- 36	- 75[a]
Central African Republic	35	57	117	121	92	109	-	-	-	-	-	-
Chad	- 279	- 69	234	1 105	1 940	1 855	-	-	-	-	-	-
Congo	1 925	2 275	2 526	1 862	2 209	2 931	-	-	-	-	-	-
Congo, Democratic Republic of	256	1 808	1 727	664	2 939	1 687	18	14	54	35	7	91
Equatorial Guinea	470	1 243	- 794	1 636	1 369	737[a]	-	-	-	-	-	-
Gabon	268	269	209	33	531	728	106	59	96	87	81	88[a]
Rwanda	31	82	103	119	42	106	-	13	-	-	-	-
São Tomé and Principe	38	36	79	16	25	18	3	3	0	0	0	0[a]
East Africa	2 394	4 020	4 183	3 786	3 682	3 959	42	112	109	89	133	106
Comoros	1	8	5	14	4	7	-	-	-	-	-	-
Djibouti	108	195	229	100	27	78	-	-	-	-	-	-
Eritrea	0	- 0	- 0	0	56	19[a]	-	-	-	-	-	-
Ethiopia	545	222	109	221	288	206[a]	-	-	-	-	-	-
Kenya	51	729	96	116	178	335	24	36	44	46	2	9
Madagascar	295	773	1 169	1 066	860	907	-	-	-	-	-	-
Mauritius	105	339	383	248	430	273	10	58	52	37	129	89
Mayotte	0	-	-	-	-	-	-	-	-	-	-	-
Seychelles	146	239	130	118	160	144	8	18	13	5	6	8
Somalia	96	141	87	108	112	102[a]	-	-	-	-	-	-
Uganda	644	792	729	842	544	792	-	-	-	-	- 3	-
United Republic of Tanzania	403	582	1 247	953	1 023	1 095	-	-	-	-	-	-
Southern Africa	1 400	8 075	13 748	10 951	2 406	6 374	6 292	4 043	- 670	1 478	2 416	1 830
Angola	- 38	- 893	1 679	2 205	- 3 227	- 5 586	191	912	2 570	7	1 340	1 300
Botswana	486	495	528	968	559	587	50	51	- 91	48	3	4
Lesotho	89	97	56	48	55	52[a]	-	-	-	-	-	-
Malawi	72	92	71	55	58	56[a]	-	-	- 19	-	-	-
Mozambique	154	427	592	893	989	2 093	0	- 0	- 0	- 3	1	- 3
Namibia	387	733	720	552	712	900	- 12	3	5	- 3	5	- 3
South Africa	- 527	5 695	9 006	5 365	1 228	5 807	6 063	2 966	- 3 134	1 151	- 76	- 635
Swaziland	121	37	106	66	136	95	- 1	23	- 8	7	4	4
Zambia	616	1 324	939	695	1 729	1 982	-	86	-	270	1 095	1 150
Zimbabwe	40	69	52	105	166	387	0	3	8	-	43	14
Asia	290 907	349 412	380 360	315 238	384 063	423 157	151 400	228 154	223 116	210 925	273 033	280 478
East and South-East Asia	195 867	236 606	235 506	206 591	294 124	335 533	114 006	174 016	165 446	176 636	242 980	239 892
East Asia	131 829	151 004	185 253	159 183	201 364	218 974	85 402	114 411	133 192	143 639	198 809	180 002
China	72 715	83 521	108 312	95 000	114 734	123 985	21 160	22 469	52 150	56 530	68 811	65 117
Hong Kong, China	45 060	54 341	59 621	52 394	71 069	83 156	44 979	61 081	50 581	63 991	95 396	81 607
Korea, Democratic People's Republic of	- 105	67	44	2	38	55[a]	-	-	-	-	-	-
Korea, Republic of	4 881	2 628	8 409	7 501	8 511	4 661[b]	11 175	19 720	20 251	17 197	23 278	20 355
Macao, China	1 608	2 305	2 591	858	2 828	4 365[a]	636	23	- 83	- 11	- 312	62[a]
Mongolia	245	373	845	624	1 691	4 715	54	13	6	54	62	94
Taiwan Province of China	7 424	7 769	5 432	2 805	2 492	- 1 962	7 399	11 107	10 287	5 877	11 574	12 766
South-East Asia	64 038	85 603	50 254	47 408	92 760	116 559	28 604	59 605	32 255	32 997	44 171	59 890
Brunei Darussalam	434	260	330	371	626	1 208	17	- 7	16	9	6	10
Cambodia	483	867	815	539	783	892	8	1	20	19	21	24
Indonesia	4 914	6 928	9 318	4 877	13 771	18 906	2 726	4 675	5 900	2 249	2 664	7 771
Lao People's Democratic Republic	187	324	228	319	333	450[a]	39	1	- 75	1	6[a]	7[a]
Malaysia	6 060	8 595	7 172	1 453	9 103	11 966	6 021	11 314	14 965	7 784	13 329	15 258
Myanmar	428	715	976	963	450	850[a]	-	-	-	-	-	-
Philippines	2 921	2 916	1 544	1 963	1 298	1 262	103	3 536	259	359	616	9
Singapore	36 700	46 930	11 798	24 418	48 637	64 003	18 637	36 897	6 812	17 704	21 215	25 227
Thailand	9 501	11 359	8 455	4 854	9 733	9 572	968	3 003	4 057	4 172	5 415	10 634
Timor-Leste	8	9	40	50	27	20[a]	-	-	-	-	-	-
Viet Nam	2 400	6 700	9 579	7 600	8 000	7 430	85	184	300	700	900	950
South Asia	27 919	34 695	52 869	42 370	31 746	38 942	14 812	20 070	19 756	16 403	13 605	15 234
Afghanistan	238	189	94	76	211	83	-	-	-	-	-	-

/...

Annex table I.1. FDI flows, by region and economy, 2006-2011 (continued)
(Millions of dollars)

Region/economy	FDI inflows						FDI outflows					
	2006	2007	2008	2009	2010	2011	2006	2007	2008	2009	2010	2011
Bangladesh	792	666	1 086	700	913	1 136	4	21	9	29	15	9
Bhutan	72	3	7	18	16	14[a]	-	-	-	-	-	-
India	20 328	25 506	43 406	35 596	24 159	31 554	14 285	19 594	19 257	15 927	13 151	14 752
Iran, Islamic Republic of	1 647	2 005	1 909	3 048	3 648	4 150	386	302	380	356	346[a]	360[a]
Maldives	95	126	174	152	212	282	-	-	-	-	-	-
Nepal	- 7	6	1	39	87	95	-	-	-	-	-	-
Pakistan	4 273	5 590	5 438	2 338	2 022	1 327	109	98	49	71	47	62
Sri Lanka	480	603	752	404	478	300[a]	29	55	62	20	46	50[a]
West Asia	67 121	78 112	91 985	66 276	58 193	48 682	22 582	34 068	37 913	17 886	16 448	25 353
Bahrain	2 915	1 756	1 794	257	156	781	980	1 669	1 620	- 1 791	334	894
Iraq	383	972	1 856	1 598	1 396	1 617[a]	305	8	34	72	125	77[a]
Jordan	3 544	2 622	2 826	2 413	1 651	1 469	- 138	48	13	72	28	31
Kuwait	121	112	- 6	1 114	319	399	8 211	9 784	9 091	8 582	5 065	8 711
Lebanon	3 132	3 376	4 333	4 804	4 280	3 200[a]	875	848	987	1 126	487	900[a]
Oman	1 597	3 332	2 952	1 508	1 142	788	276	- 36	585	109	1 012	572
Palestinian Territory	19	28	52	301	180	214	125	- 8	- 8	- 15	77	- 20
Qatar	3 500	4 700	3 779	8 125	4 670	- 87	127	5 160	3 658	3 215	1 863	6 027
Saudi Arabia	17 140	22 821	38 151	32 100	28 105	16 400	- 39	- 135	3 498	2 177	3 907	3 442
Syrian Arab Republic	659	1 242	1 467	1 514	1 850	1 059[a]	- 11	2	2	- 3	0[a]	- 0[a]
Turkey	20 185	22 047	19 504	8 411	9 038	15 876	924	2 106	2 549	1 553	1 464	2 464
United Arab Emirates	12 806	14 187	13 724	4 003	5 500	7 679	10 892	14 568	15 820	2 723	2 015	2 178
Yemen	1 121	917	1 555	129	- 93	- 713	56	54	66	66	70[a]	77[a]
Latin America and the Caribbean	98 175	172 281	209 517	149 402	187 401	216 988	79 670	79 345	97 013	54 305	119 908	99 653
South and Central America	69 463	110 700	127 694	77 080	117 207	149 367	43 645	25 687	38 364	12 658	47 213	32 146
South America	43 480	71 787	92 820	56 323	90 357	121 472	35 493	14 526	35 149	3 255	31 201	20 848
Argentina	5 537	6 473	9 726	4 017	7 055	7 243	2 439	1 504	1 391	712	965	1 488
Bolivia, Plurinational State of	281	366	513	423	643	859	3	4	5	- 3	- 29	-
Brazil	18 822	34 585	45 058	25 949	48 506	66 660	28 202	7 067	20 457	- 10 084	11 588	- 1 029
Chile	7 426	12 572	15 518	12 887	15 373	17 299	2 212	4 852	9 151	7 233	9 231	11 822
Colombia	6 656	9 049	10 620	7 137	6 899	13 234	1 098	913	2 254	3 088	6 562	8 289
Ecuador	271	194	1 006	321	158	568	8	- 8	8	36	12	18[a]
Falkland Islands (Malvinas)	- 0	-	-	-	-	-	-	-	-	-	-	-
Guyana	102	152	178	164	154	165[a]	-	-	-	-	-	-
Paraguay	95	202	209	94	228	303	7	7	8	8	- 4	-
Peru	3 467	5 491	6 924	6 431	8 455	8 233	-	66	736	411	266	113
Suriname	- 163	- 247	- 231	- 93	- 612	- 585	-	-	-	-	-	- 12
Uruguay	1 493	1 329	2 106	1 529	2 289	2 191	- 1	89	- 11	16	- 60	- 15
Venezuela, Bolivarian Republic of	- 508	1 620	1 195	- 2 536	1 209	5 302	1 524	33	1 150	1 838	2 671	173
Central America	25 984	38 913	34 874	20 757	26 849	27 895	8 152	11 161	3 215	9 404	16 012	11 298
Belize	109	143	170	109	97	94	1	1	3	0	1	1
Costa Rica	1 469	1 896	2 078	1 347	1 466	2 104	98	263	6	7	25	56
El Salvador	241	1 551	903	366	117	386	26	- 95	- 80	-	-	-
Guatemala	592	745	754	600	806	985	40	25	16	26	24	17
Honduras	669	928	1 006	523	797	1 014	- 1	- 1	1	- 1	1	- 7
Mexico	20 119	31 492	27 140	16 119	20 709	19 554	5 758	8 256	1 157	7 019	13 570	8 946
Nicaragua	287	382	626	434	508	968	21	9	16	15	14	15
Panama	2 498	1 777	2 196	1 259	2 350	2 790	2 209	2 704	2 095	2 336	2 377	2 269[a]
Caribbean	28 712	61 581	81 823	72 322	70 194	67 622	36 025	53 658	58 650	41 647	72 696	67 507
Anguilla	142	119	99	37	25	11	-	-	-	-	-	-
Antigua and Barbuda	359	338	174	81	97	59	-	-	-	-	-	-
Aruba	220	- 474	14	- 33	160	544	- 13	40	3	2	3	3
Bahamas	1 492	1 623	1 512	873	1 142	1 533	333	459	410	216	149	524
Barbados	342	476	464	247	290	334[a]	44	82	- 6	- 56	- 54	- 39[a]
British Virgin Islands	7 549[a]	31 764[a]	51 722[a]	46 503[a]	49 058[a]	53 717[a]	27 185[a]	43 668[a]	44 118[a]	35 143[a]	58 717[a]	62 507[a]
Cayman Islands	14 963[a]	23 218[a]	19 634[a]	20 426[a]	15 875[a]	7 408[a]	8 013[a]	9 303[a]	13 377[a]	6 311[a]	13 857[a]	4 456[a]
Cuba	26[a]	64[a]	24[a]	24[a]	86[a]	110[a]	- 2[a]	-	-	-	-	-
Curaçao	-	106	147	55	89	69	-	7	1	- 5	- 15	13
Dominica	26	40	57	41	24	25	-	-	-	-	-	-
Dominican Republic	1 085	1 667	2 870	2 165	1 896	2 371	- 61	- 17	- 19	- 32	- 23	- 25[a]
Grenada	90	157	142	103	60	40	-	-	-	-	-	-
Haiti	160	75	30	38	150	181	-	-	-	-	-	-
Jamaica	882	867	1 437	541	228	242[a]	85	115	76	61	58	62
Montserrat	4	7	13	3	3	3	-	-	-	-	-	-
Netherlands Antilles[c]	- 22	-	-	-	-	-	57	-	-	-	-	-
Saint Kitts and Nevis	110	134	178	131	120	142	-	-	-	-	-	-

Annex table I.1. FDI flows, by region and economy, 2006-2011 (concluded)
(Millions of dollars)

Region/economy	FDI inflows						FDI outflows					
	2006	2007	2008	2009	2010	2011	2006	2007	2008	2009	2010	2011
Saint Lucia	234	272	161	146	110	76	-	-	-	-	-	-
Saint Vincent and the Grenadines	109	130	159	97	103	135	-	-	-	-	-	-
Sint Maarten	-	72	86	40	33	- 48	-	- 4	- 16	- 1	- 3	- 1
Trinidad and Tobago	883	830	2 801	709	549	574	370	0	700	-	-	-
Turks and Caicos Islands	58[a]	97[a]	99[a]	95[a]	97[a]	97[a]	14[a]	5[a]	6[a]	9[a]	7[a]	7[a]
Oceania	1 298	1 139	2 298	1 940	2 075	1 602	40	41	96	77	176	110
Cook Islands	3	- 0	1	1	1	1[a]	0	-	-	-	-	-
Fiji	370	376	354	137	195	204	1	- 6	- 8	3	6	- 3
French Polynesia	31	58	14	10	95	40[a]	10	14	30	8	89	42[a]
Kiribati	1	1	3	3	4	4[a]	0	0	1	0	0	1[a]
Marshall Islands	6[a]	12[a]	6[a]	8[a]	9[a]	7[a]	- 8	-	-	-	-	-
Micronesia, Federated States of	1[a]	17[a]	6[a]	8[a]	10[a]	8[a]	-	-	-	-	-	-
Nauru	- 0[a]	1[a]	1[a]	1[a]	1[a]	1[a]	-	-	-	-	-	-
New Caledonia	749	417	1 746	1 182	1 439	1 415[a]	31	7	64	58	76	65[a]
Niue	-	-	-	-	-	-	- 2	4	2	- 0	-	1[a]
Palau	1[a]	3[a]	2[a]	2[a]	2[a]	2[a]	-	-	-	-	-	-
Papua New Guinea	- 7	96	- 30	423	29	- 309	1	8	- 0	4	0	1
Samoa	22	7	49	10	1	12	-	-	-	- 1	-	- 1
Solomon Islands	34	64	95	120	238	146	5	12	4	3	2	4
Tonga	11	29	6	0	9	10	1	2	2	0	2	1
Tuvalu	5[a]	0[a]	2[a]	2[a]	2[a]	2[a]	-	-	-	-	-	-
Vanuatu	72	57	44	32	41	58	1	1	1	1	1	1
Wallis and Futuna Islands	0	1	1	1	1	1[a]	-	-	-	-	-	-
Transition economies	54 318	90 800	121 041	72 386	73 755	92 163	23 724	51 583	60 462	48 840	61 644	73 135
South-East Europe	9 658	12 541	12 657	8 289	3 974	6 650	396	1 451	1 896	1 385	119	295
Albania	324	659	974	996	1 051	1 031	10	24	81	36	6	42
Bosnia and Herzegovina	555	1 819	1 002	251	230	435	4	28	17	6	42	20
Croatia	3 468	4 997	6 180	3 355	394	1 494	261	296	1 421	1 234	- 150	44
Serbia	4 256	3 439	2 955	1 959	1 329	2 709	88	947	283	52	189	170
Montenegro	622	934	960	1 527	760	558	33	157	108	46	29	17
The former Yugoslav Republic of Macedonia	433	693	586	201	211	422	0	- 1	- 14	11	2	2
CIS	43 491	76 509	106 820	63 439	68 966	84 539	23 344	50 057	58 420	47 474	61 390	72 694
Armenia	453	699	935	778	570	525	3	- 2	10	53	8	78
Azerbaijan	- 584	- 4 749	14	473	563	1 465	705	286	556	326	232	533
Belarus	354	1 805	2 181	1 884	1 403	3 986	3	15	31	102	50	57
Kazakhstan	6 278	11 119	14 322	13 243	10 768	12 910	- 385	3 153	1 204	3 159	7 837	4 530
Kyrgyzstan	182	208	377	189	438	694	- 0	- 1	- 0	- 0	- 0	- 0
Moldova, Republic of	258	541	711	145	197	274	- 1	17	16	7	4	21
Russian Federation	29 701	55 073	75 002	36 500	43 288	52 878	23 151	45 916	55 594	43 665	52 523	67 283
Tajikistan	339	360	376	16	- 15	11	-	-	-	-	-	-
Turkmenistan	731	856	1 277	4 553	3 631	3 186[a]	-	-	-	-	-	-
Ukraine	5 604	9 891	10 913	4 816	6 495	7 207	- 133	673	1 010	162	736	192
Uzbekistan	174	705	711	842	1 628	1 403[a]	-	-	-	-	-	-
Georgia	1 170	1 750	1 564	658	814	975	- 16	76	147	- 19	135	146
Memorandum												
Least developed countries (LDCs)[d]	11 739	15 237	18 497	18 342	16 899	15 011	679	1 529	3 381	1 095	3 091	3 270
Landlocked developing countries (LLDCs)[e]	11 943	15 637	25 011	28 017	28 191	34 837	476	3 668	1 639	4 008	9 323	6 492
Small island developing states (SIDS)[f]	5 566	6 477	8 640	4 431	4 231	4 142	855	752	1 244	275	299	647

Source: UNCTAD, FDI/TNC database (www.unctad.org/fdistatistics).

[a]   Estimates.

[b]   This figure does not include reinvested earnings ($7 209 million), according to the Ministry of Knowledge Economy of the Republic of Korea.

[c]   This economy dissolved on 10 October 2010.

[d]   Least developed countries include: Afghanistan, Angola, Bangladesh, Benin, Bhutan, Burkina Faso, Burundi, Cambodia, Central African Republic, Chad, Comoros, Democratic Republic of the Congo, Djibouti, Equatorial Guinea, Eritrea, Ethiopia, Gambia, Guinea, Guinea-Bissau, Haiti, Kiribati, Lao People's Democratic Republic, Lesotho, Liberia, Madagascar, Malawi, Mali, Mauritania, Mozambique, Myanmar, Nepal, Niger, Rwanda, Samoa, São Tomé and Principe, Senegal, Sierra Leone, Solomon Islands, Somalia, Sudan, Timor-Leste, Togo, Tuvalu, Uganda, United Republic of Tanzania, Vanuatu, Yemen and Zambia.

[e]   Landlocked developing countries include: Afghanistan, Armenia, Azerbaijan, Bhutan, the Plurinational State of Bolivia, Botswana, Burkina Faso, Burundi, Central African Republic, Chad, Ethiopia, Kazakhstan, Kyrgyzstan, Lao People's Democratic Republic, Lesotho, The former Yugoslav Republic of Macedonia, Malawi, Mali, Republic of Moldova, Mongolia, Nepal, Niger, Paraguay, Rwanda, Swaziland, Tajikistan, Turkmenistan, Uganda, Uzbekistan, Zambia and Zimbabwe.

[f]   Small island developing countries include: Antigua and Barbuda, Bahamas, Barbados, Cape Verde, Comoros, Dominica, Fiji, Grenada, Jamaica, Kiribati, Maldives, Marshall Islands, Mauritius, Federated States of Micronesia, Nauru, Palau, Papua New Guinea, Saint Kitts and Nevis, Saint Lucia, Saint Vincent and the Grenadines, Samoa, São Tomé and Principe, Seychelles, Solomon Islands, Timor-Leste, Tonga, Trinidad and Tobago, Tuvalu and Vanuatu.

Annex table I.2. FDI stock, by region and economy, 1990, 2000, 2011
(Millions of dollars)

Region/economy	FDI inward stock			FDI outward stock		
	1990	2000	2011	1990	2000	2011
World	2 081 147	7 450 022	20 438 199	2 092 927	7 952 878	21 168 489
Developed economies	1 563 939	5 653 715	13 055 903	1 946 833	7 074 435	17 055 964
Europe	808 866	2 442 937	8 081 422	885 707	3 750 671	10 443 870
European Union	761 820	2 323 505	7 275 622	808 661	3 482 534	9 198 832
Austria	10 972	31 165	148 799	4 747	24 821	199 261
Belgium	..	..	957 836	..	..	944 056
Belgium and Luxembourg	58 388	195 219	-	40 636	179 773	-
Bulgaria	112	2 704	47 653	124	34	1 697
Cyprus	..[a,b]	2 846	16 398	8	557	7 850
Czech Republic	1 363	21 644	125 245	..	738	15 470
Denmark	9 192	73 574	152 847[a]	7 342	73 100	231 325[a]
Estonia	..	2 645	16 727	..	259	4 740
Finland	5 132	24 273	82 962	11 227	52 109	138 843
France	97 814	390 953	963 792	112 441	925 925	1 372 676
Germany	111 231	271 613	713 706[a]	151 581	541 866	1 441 611[a]
Greece	5 681	14 113	27 433	2 882	6 094	42 938
Hungary	570	22 870	84 447	159	1 280	23 756
Ireland	37 989	127 089	243 484	14 942	27 925	324 226
Italy	59 998	122 533	332 664	60 184	169 957	512 201
Latvia	..	2 084	12 109	..	23	887
Lithuania	..	2 334	13 921	..	29	2 014
Luxembourg	..	..	114 617[a]	..	..	129 482[a]
Malta	465	2 263	16 706[a]	..	193	1 491[a]
Netherlands	68 701	243 733	589 051	105 088	305 461	943 086
Poland	109	34 227	197 538	95	1 018	50 044
Portugal	10 571	32 043	109 034	900	19 794	68 051
Romania	..	6 953	70 328	66	136	1 487
Slovakia	282	4 762	51 293	..	379	4 210
Slovenia	1 643	2 893	15 145	560	768	7 142
Spain	65 916	156 348	634 532	15 652	129 194	640 312
Sweden	12 636	93 995	338 484	50 720	123 256	358 886
United Kingdom	203 905	438 631	1 198 870	229 307	897 845	1 731 095
Other developed Europe	47 045	119 432	805 800	77 047	268 137	1 245 038
Gibraltar	263[a]	642[a]	2 069[a]	-	-	-
Iceland	147	1 720	48 752	75	1 951	45 603
Norway	12 391	30 265	171 524[a]	10 884	34 026	207 469[a]
Switzerland	34 245	86 804	583 455	66 087	232 161	991 966
North America	652 444	2 995 951	4 104 361	816 569	2 931 653	5 170 379
Canada	112 843	212 716	595 002	84 807	237 639	670 417
United States	539 601	2 783 235	3 509 359	731 762	2 694 014	4 499 962
Other developed countries	102 629	214 827	870 120	244 556	392 111	1 441 715
Australia	80 364	118 858	499 663	37 505	95 979	385 470
Bermuda	-	265	3 985	-	108	2 859
Israel	4 476	20 426	66 768	1 188	9 091	71 589
Japan	9 850	50 322	225 787	201 441	278 442	962 790
New Zealand	7 938	24 957	73 917	4 422	8 491	19 007
Developing economies	517 200	1 735 488	6 625 032	146 094	857 107	3 705 410
Africa	60 553	153 553	569 559	20 798	44 729	126 281
North Africa	23 962	45 590	210 487	1 836	3 199	27 505
Algeria	1 561[a]	3 379[a]	21 781[a]	183[a]	205a	2 174[a]
Egypt	11 043[a]	19 955	72 612	163[a]	655	6 074
Libya	678[a]	471[a]	16 334[a]	1 321[a]	1 903a	16 848[a]
Morocco	3 011[a]	8 842[a]	46 300[a]	155[a]	402a	2 098[a]
Sudan	55[a]	1 398[a]	22 047[a]	-	-	-
Tunisia	7 615	11 545	31 414	15	33	310
Other Africa	36 591	107 963	359 072	18 962	41 530	98 777
West Africa	14 013	33 061	110 395	2 202	6 471	11 812
Benin	..[a,b]	213	968[a]	2[a]	11	37[a]
Burkina Faso	39[a]	28	350[a]	4[a]	0	11[a]
Cape Verde	4[a]	192[a]	1 232	-	-	1
Côte d' Ivoire	975[a]	2 483	6 408[a]	6[a]	9	98[a]
Gambia	157[a]	216[a]	703[a]	-	-	-
Ghana	319[a]	1 605[a]	12 320[a]	-	-	-
Guinea	69[a]	263[a]	2 927[a]	-	7a	144[a]
Guinea-Bissau	8[a]	38[a]	175[a]	-	-	6[a]
Liberia	2 732[a]	3 247[a]	5 465[a]	846[a]	2 188	5 086[a]
Mali	229[a]	132	2 253[a]	22[a]	1	19[a]
Mauritania	59[a]	146[a]	2 407[a]	3[a]	4a	35[a]
Niger	286[a]	45	3 123[a]	54[a]	1	54[a]

/...

Annex table I.2. FDI stock, by region and economy, 1990, 2000, 2011 (continued)
(Millions of dollars)

Region/economy	FDI inward stock			FDI outward stock		
	1990	2000	2011	1990	2000	2011
Nigeria	8 539[a]	23 786[a]	69 242	1 219[a]	4 144a	5 865
Senegal	258[a]	295	1 912[a]	47[a]	117a	316[a]
Sierra Leone	243[a]	284[a]	313[a]	-	-	-
Togo	268[a]	87	598[a]	-	..b	141[a]
Central Africa	3 686	5 492	48 164	372	648	779
Burundi	30[a]	47[a]	7[a]	0[a]	2a	1[a]
Cameroon	1 044[a]	1 600[a]	4 497[a]	150[a]	254a	..a,b
Central African Republic	95[a]	104[a]	548	18[a]	43a	43[a]
Chad	128[a]	336[a]	7 249[a]	37[a]	70a	70[a]
Congo	575[a]	1 889[a]	18 127[a]	-	-	-
Congo, Democratic Republic of	546[a]	617	5 590	-	-	-
Equatorial Guinea	25[a]	1 060[a]	8 785[a]	0[a]	..a,b	3[a]
Gabon	1 208[a]	..a,b	2 526[a]	167[a]	280a	750[a]
Rwanda	33[a]	55	583	-	-	13
São Tomé and Principe	0[a]	11[a]	252[a]	-	-	-
East Africa	1 701	7 202	33 054	734	1 204	3 468
Comoros	17[a]	21[a]	62[a]	-	-	-
Djibouti	13[a]	40	956	-	-	-
Eritrea	0[a]	337[a]	456[a]	-	-	-
Ethiopia	124[a]	941[a]	4 412[a]	-	-	-
Kenya	668[a]	931[a]	2 618[a]	668[a]	931a	2 618[a]
Madagascar	107[a]	141	5 359[a]	1[a]	10a	6[a]
Mauritius	168[a]	683[a]	2 583[a]	1[a]	132a	592[a]
Seychelles	213	515	1 745[a]	64	130	255[a]
Somalia	..a,b	4[a]	668[a]	-	-	-
Uganda	6[a]	807	6 367	-	-	..b
United Republic of Tanzania	388[a]	2 781	7 825	-	-	-
Southern Africa	17 191	62 208	167 460	15 653	33 208	82 718
Angola	1 024[a]	7 978	6 273[a]	1[a]	2	6 150[a]
Botswana	1 309	1 827	1 088	447	517	386
Lesotho	83[a]	330	1 181[a]	0[a]	2	2[a]
Malawi	228[a]	358	939[a]	-	..a,b	24[a]
Mozambique	25	1 249	7 404	2[a]	1	2
Namibia	2 047	1 276	4 670	80	45	29
South Africa	9 207	43 451	129 890	15 004	32 325	72 285
Swaziland	336	536	881[a]	38	87	82[a]
Zambia	2 655[a]	3 966	12 932	-	-	3 448
Zimbabwe	277[a]	1 238[a]	2 201[a]	80[a]	234a	310[a]
Asia	342 937	1 071 917	3 990 731	67 600	606 860	2 572 705
East and South-East Asia	304 948	982 395	3 144 429	58 505	588 852	2 282 625
East Asia	240 645	716 103	2 066 984	49 032	504 301	1 786 921
China	20 691[a]	193 348[a]	711 802[a]	4 455[a]	27 768a	365 981[a]
Hong Kong, China	201 653[a]	455 469	1 138 365	11 920[a]	388 380	1 045 920
Korea, Democratic People's Republic of	572[a]	1 044[a]	1 530[a]	-	-	-
Korea, Republic of	5 186	43 738	131 708[a]	2 301[a]	21 497	159 339[a]
Macao, China	2 809[a]	2 801[a]	17 991[a]	-	-	744[a]
Mongolia	0[a]	182[a]	9 435	-	-	1 875
Taiwan Province of China	9 735[a]	19 521	56 154	30 356[a]	66 655	213 062
South-East Asia	64 303	266 292	1 077 445	9 472	84 551	495 704
Brunei Darussalam	33[a]	3 868	12 452	0[a]	512	691
Cambodia	38[a]	1 580	6 850	..	193	377
Indonesia	8 732[a]	25 060[a]	173 064[a]	86[a]	6 940a	9 502[a]
Lao People's Democratic Republic	13[a]	588[a]	2 521[a]	1[a]	26a	6[a]
Malaysia	10 318	52 747[a]	114 555	753	15 878a	106 217
Myanmar	281[a]	3 211[a]	9 123[a]	-	-	-
Philippines	4 528[a]	18 156[a]	27 581[a]	406[a]	2 044a	6 590[a]
Singapore	30 468	110 570	518 625[a]	7 808	56 755	339 095[a]
Thailand	8 242	29 915	139 735[a]	418	2 203	33 226[a]
Timor-Leste	-	-	161[a]	-	-	-
Viet Nam	1 650[a]	20 596[a]	72 778[a]	-	-	-
South Asia	6 795	29 834	270 890	422	2 949	116 141
Afghanistan	12[a]	17[a]	1 475[a]	-	-	-
Bangladesh	477[a]	2 162	6 166	45[a]	69	107
Bhutan	2[a]	4[a]	177[a]	-	-	-
India	1 657	16 339	201 724	124	1 733	111 257
Iran, Islamic Republic of	2 039[a]	2 597[a]	32 443	0[a]	572a	2 915[a]
Maldives	25[a]	128[a]	1 372[a]	-	-	-
Nepal	12[a]	72[a]	348[a]	-	-	-
Pakistan	1 892[a]	6 919	21 876	245[a]	489	1 432

/...

Annex table I.2. FDI stock, by region and economy, 1990, 2000, 2011 (continued)
(Millions of dollars)

Region/economy	FDI inward stock			FDI outward stock		
	1990	2000	2011	1990	2000	2011
Sri Lanka	679[a]	1 596	5 308[a]	8[a]	86	430[a]
West Asia	31 194	59 688	575 412	8 674	15 059	173 939
Bahrain	552	5 906	15 935	719	1 752	8 776
Iraq	..[a,b]	..[a,b]	9 601[a]	-	-	-
Jordan	1 368[a]	3 135	23 368	158[a]	44	504
Kuwait	37[a]	608	10 765	3 662[a]	1 677	22 059
Lebanon	53[a]	4 988	40 645	43[a]	586	7 550
Oman	1 723[a]	2 577[a]	15 005[a]	590[a]	611a	3 507[a]
Palestinian Territory	-	647[a]	2 389[a]	-	..[a,b]	221[a]
Qatar	63[a]	1 912[a]	30 477[a]	-	74a	18 572[a]
Saudi Arabia	15 193[a]	17 577	186 850[a]	2 328[a]	5 285a	29 970[a]
Syrian Arab Republic	154[a]	1 244	10 323[a]	4[a]	107a	418[a]
Turkey	11 150[a]	19 209	140 305	1 150[a]	3 668	24 034
United Arab Emirates	751[a]	1 069[a]	85 406[a]	14[a]	1 938a	57 738[a]
Yemen	180[a]	843[a]	4 344[a]	5[a]	12a	589[a]
Latin America and the Caribbean	111 377	507 388	2 048 101	57 645	205 269	1 005 859
South and Central America	103 311	428 931	1 529 944	56 014	115 170	505 102
South America	74 815	308 951	1 157 477	49 346	96 041	357 793
Argentina	9 085[a]	67 601	95 148	6 057[a]	21 141	31 329[a]
Bolivia, Plurinational State of	1 026[a]	5 188	7 728	7[a]	29	8
Brazil	37 143	122 250	669 670	41 044[a]	51 946a	202 586
Chile	16 107[a]	45 753	158 102	154[a]	11 154	68 974
Colombia	3 500	11 157	95 668	402	2 989	31 119
Ecuador	1 626	6 337	12 380	18[a]	247a	342[a]
Falkland Islands (Malvinas)	0[a]	58[a]	75[a]	-	-	-
Guyana	45[a]	756[a]	1 905[a]	-	1a	2[a]
Paraguay	418[a]	1 221	3 371	134[a]	214	238
Peru	1 330	11 062	51 208	122	505	3 099
Uruguay	671[a]	2 088	17 021[a]	186[a]	138	289[a]
Venezuela, Bolivarian Republic of	3 865	35 480	45 200	1 221	7 676	19 808
Central America	28 496	119 980	372 467	6 668	19 129	147 309
Belize	89[a]	301	1 336	20[a]	43	51
Costa Rica	1 324[a]	2 709	16 340	44[a]	86	704
El Salvador	212[a]	1 973	8 141	56[a]	104	6
Guatemala	1 734	3 420	7 709	-	93	399
Honduras	293	1 392	7 808	-	-	49
Mexico	22 424	101 996	302 309	2 672[a]	8 273	112 088
Nicaragua	145[a]	1 414	5 666	-	22a	184
Panama	2 275	6 775	23 159	3 876[a]	10 507a	33 828[a]
Caribbean	8 066	78 457	518 157	1 630	90 099	500 757
Anguilla	11[a]	231[a]	980[a]	-	-	-
Antigua and Barbuda	290[a]	596[a]	2 336[a]	-	-	-
Aruba	145[a]	1 161	4 297	-	675	682
Bahamas	586[a]	3 278[a]	14 965[a]	-	452a	3 061[a]
Barbados	171	308	2 374[a]	23	41	20[a]
British Virgin Islands	126[a]	32 093[a]	288 987[a]	875[a]	67 132a	401 468[a]
Cayman Islands	1 749[a]	25 585[a]	148 037[a]	648[a]	20 788a	93 112[a]
Cuba	2[a]	74[a]	427[a]	-	-	-
Curaçao	-	-	596	-	-	45
Dominica	66[a]	272[a]	600[a]	-	-	-
Dominican Republic	572[a]	1 673	17 103[a]	-	-	-
Grenada	70[a]	346[a]	1 274[a]	-	-	-
Haiti	149[a]	95	784[a]	-	2a	2[a]
Jamaica	790[a]	3 317[a]	11 097[a]	42[a]	709a	238[a]
Montserrat	40[a]	83[a]	127[a]	-	-	-
Netherlands Antilles[c]	408[a]	277	-	21[a]	6	-
Saint Kitts and Nevis	160[a]	484[a]	1 693[a]	-	-	-
Saint Lucia	316[a]	802[a]	2 173[a]	-	-	-
Saint Vincent and the Grenadines	48[a]	499[a]	1 449[a]	-	-	-
Sint Maarten	-	-	208	-	-	9
Trinidad and Tobago	2 365[a]	7 280[a]	17 998[a]	21[a]	293a	2 119[a]
Turks and Caicos Islands	2[a]	4[a]	654[a]	-	-	-
Oceania	2 333	2 630	16 641	51	249	565
Cook Islands	14[a]	34[a]	42[a]	-	-	-
Fiji	284[a]	356	2 456[a]	25[a]	39	38[a]
French Polynesia	69[a]	139[a]	450[a]	-	-	238[a]
Kiribati	-	-	23[a]	-	-	4[a]
New Caledonia	70[a]	67[a]	7 315[a]	-	-	-
Niue	-	0[a]	7[a]	-	-	-

/...

Annex table I.2. FDI stock, by region and economy, 1990, 2000, 2011 (concluded)
(Millions of dollars)

Region/economy	FDI inward stock			FDI outward stock		
	1990	2000	2011	1990	2000	2011
Palau	-	97[a]	131[a]	-	-	-
Papua New Guinea	1 582[a]	935	4 567	26[a]	210a	226[a]
Samoa	9[a]	53[a]	60[a]	-	-	2[a]
Solomon Islands	-	106[a]	869	-	-	33
Tokelau	-	0[a]	1[a]	-	-	-
Tonga	1[a]	15[a]	98[a]	-	-	-
Tuvalu	-	..[a,b]	37[a]	-	-	-
Vanuatu	-	61[a]	584	-	-	23
Transition economies	..	60 820	757 264	..	21 337	407 115
South-East Europe	..	5 682	75 706	..	840	9 330
Albania	..	247	4 701[a]	..	-	202[a]
Bosnia and Herzegovina	..	1 083[a]	6 719[a]	..	-	153[a]
Croatia	..	2 796	30 883	..	824	4 529
Serbia	..	1 017[a]	22 872	..	-	3 972
Montenegro	..	-	5 803	..	-	379
The former Yugoslav Republic of Macedonia	..	540	4 728[a]	..	16	95[a]
CIS	..	54 375	672 253	..	20 407	397 043
Armenia	9[a]	513	5 046	..	..	163
Azerbaijan	..	3 735	9 113	..	1	6 323
Belarus	..	1 306	12 987	..	24	284
Kazakhstan	..	10 078	93 624	..	16	19 924
Kyrgyzstan	..	432	1 274	..	33	2
Moldova, Republic of	..	449	3 163	..	23	88
Russian Federation	..	32 204	457 474	..	20 141	362 101
Tajikistan	..	136	993	..	-	-
Turkmenistan	..	949[a]	16 627[a]	..	-	-
Ukraine	..	3 875	65 192[a]	..	170	8 158[a]
Uzbekistan	..	698[a]	6 761[a]	..	-	-
Georgia	..	762	9 305	..	89	742
Memorandum						
Least developed countries (LDCs)[d]	10 929	36 367	154 611	1 089	2 746	16 751
Landlocked developing countries (LLDCs)[e]	7 349	35 552	210 498	844	1 311	33 182
Small island developing states (SIDS)[f]	7 166	20 356	72 192	202	2 007	6 614

Source: UNCTAD, FDI/TNC database (www.unctad.org/fdistatistics).

[a]   Estimates.

[b]   Negative stock value. However, this value is included in the regional and global total.

[c]   This economy dissolved on 10 October 2010.

[d]   Least developed countries include: Afghanistan, Angola, Bangladesh, Benin, Bhutan, Burkina Faso, Burundi, Cambodia, Central African Republic, Chad, Comoros, Democratic Republic of the Congo, Djibouti, Equatorial Guinea, Eritrea, Ethiopia, Gambia, Guinea, Guinea-Bissau, Haiti, Kiribati, Lao People's Democratic Republic, Lesotho, Liberia, Madagascar, Malawi, Mali, Mauritania, Mozambique, Myanmar, Nepal, Niger, Rwanda, Samoa, São Tomé and Principe, Senegal, Sierra Leone, Solomon Islands, Somalia, Sudan, Timor-Leste, Togo, Tuvalu, Uganda, United Republic of Tanzania, Vanuatu, Yemen and Zambia.

[e]   Landlocked developing countries include: Afghanistan, Armenia, Azerbaijan, Bhutan, the Plurinational State of Bolivia, Botswana, Burkina Faso, Burundi, Central African Republic, Chad, Ethiopia, Kazakhstan, Kyrgyzstan, Lao People's Democratic Republic, Lesotho, the former Yugoslav Republic of Macedonia, Malawi, Mali, Republic of Moldova, Mongolia, Nepal, Niger, Paraguay, Rwanda, Swaziland, Republic of Tajikistan, Turkmenistan, Uganda, Uzbekistan, Zambia and Zimbabwe.

[f]   Small island developing countries include: Antigua and Barbuda, Bahamas, Barbados, Cape Verde, Comoros, Dominica, Fiji, Grenada, Jamaica, Kiribati, Maldives, Marshall Islands, Mauritius, Federated States of Micronesia, Nauru, Palau, Papua New Guinea, Saint Kitts and Nevis, Saint Lucia, Saint Vincent and the Grenadines, Samoa, São Tomé and Principe, Seychelles, Solomon Islands, Timor-Leste, Tonga, Trinidad and Tobago, Tuvalu and Vanuatu.

Annex table I.3. Value of cross-border M&As, by region/economy of seller/purchaser, 2005–2011

(Millions of dollars)

Region/economy	Net sales[a]							Net purchases[b]						
	2005	2006	2007	2008	2009	2010	2011	2005	2006	2007	2008	2009	2010	2011
World	462 253	625 320	1 022 725	706 543	249 732	344 029	525 881	462 253	625 320	1 022 725	706 543	249 732	344 029	525 881
Developed economies	403 731	527 152	891 896	581 394	203 530	257 152	409 691	359 551	497 324	841 714	568 041	160 785	223 726	400 929
Europe	316 891	350 740	559 082	273 301	133 871	124 973	200 363	233 937	300 382	568 988	358 981	102 709	41 943	145 542
European Union	304 740	333 337	527 718	251 169	116 226	115 974	172 257	210 111	260 680	537 890	306 734	89 694	25 960	117 050
Austria	1 713	1 145	9 661	1 327	1 797	432	6 928	3 871	6 985	4 720	3 049	3 345	1 523	3 627
Belgium	4 277	1 794	961	2 491	12 089	9 444	3 920	4 067	3 640	8 258	30 146	- 9 638	222	7 757
Bulgaria	2 551	807	971	227	151	24	- 96	-	-	5	7	2	19	-
Cyprus	24	294	1 343	- 909	52	680	780	52	1 274	775	1 725	1 395	- 39	3 903
Czech Republic	6 196	1 154	107	5 169	2 669	- 457	725	579	812	846	34	1 608	14	26
Denmark	12 093	11 235	5 761	6 095	1 651	1 448	7 695	11 921	2 078	3 226	2 841	3 198	- 3 427	252
Estonia	82	3	- 57	110	28	3	239	16	179	-	4	- 0	4	-
Finland	2 923	1 321	8 313	1 153	508	324	973	2 720	2 169	- 1 128	13 179	653	391	3 303
France	25 172	19 423	28 207	4 590	724	3 837	24 325	58 255	41 030	78 451	56 806	41 565	6 117	31 804
Germany	47 501	41 388	44 091	31 911	12 790	8 507	12 709	4 677	16 427	58 795	61 340	24 313	6 848	4 801
Greece	872	7 309	723	6 903	477	- 819	1 205	1 159	5 238	1 495	2 697	386	520	79
Hungary	2 470	2 337	721	1 559	1 853	213	1 714	415	1 522	1	41	0	799	17
Ireland	725	2 731	811	2 892	1 712	2 127	2 181	3 375	10 176	6 677	3 693	- 526	5 101	- 6 018
Italy	40 445	25 760	23 630	- 2 377	1 109	6 329	13 450	23 565	6 887	55 880	21 358	17 505	- 6 193	4 176
Latvia	9	11	47	195	109	72	2	-	-	4	3	- 30	40	- 3
Lithuania	61	97	35	98	20	462	386	-	-	30	31	-	4	4
Luxembourg	7 989	35 005	7 339	- 3 570	444	5 446	9 393	6 847	15 539	22 631	8 109	3 382	431	- 20 751
Malta	12	517	- 86	-	13	315	-	-	115	-	- 25	-	235	13
Netherlands	21 326	25 560	162 770	- 8 156	17 988	4 113	14 031	3 140	51 304	- 3 268	53 668	- 3 273	20 112	19 750
Poland	1 487	773	728	966	776	1 063	10 043	586	194	128	432	117	292	511
Portugal	1 648	537	1 715	- 1 279	504	2 208	911	- 1 612	644	4 023	1 164	1 236	- 8 965	2 404
Romania	1 851	5 324	1 926	993	314	148	88	-	-	-	4	7	24	-
Slovakia	117	194	50	136	13	-	0	493	- 142	-	-	-	-	- 18
Slovenia	148	15	57	418	-	332	51	47	29	74	320	251	- 50	- 10
Spain	21 217	7 951	51 686	33 708	32 173	8 669	17 298	24 162	71 481	40 893	- 14 654	- 1 278	1 367	11 579
Sweden	7 892	15 228	4 563	18 770	1 098	221	7 616	11 606	3 199	32 390	6 108	9 024	796	- 4 032
United Kingdom	93 940	125 421	171 646	147 748	25 164	60 833	35 691	50 170	19 900	222 984	54 653	- 3 546	- 227	53 876
Other developed Europe	12 150	17 403	31 363	22 132	17 645	8 999	28 106	23 826	39 702	31 099	52 247	13 015	15 983	28 493
Andorra	- 433	1 174	-	-	-	-	-	-	-	-	-	-	-	166
Faeroes	-	-	-	0	-	85	-	-	-	-	-	-	-	-
Gibraltar	4	-	50	212	-	-	-	13	404	116	1	253	8	1 757
Guernsey	-	-	31	17	260	171	25	667	1 424	1 144	556	4 001	8 246	2 963
Iceland	12	39	- 227	-	-	14	-	3 714	2 171	4 664	737	- 317	- 221	- 446
Isle of Man	606	-	221	35	66	157	- 217	489	990	720	319	136	850	- 740
Jersey	32	254	816	251	414	81	74	- 1 561	96	814	- 829	844	1 244	5 900
Liechtenstein	-	-	-	-	-	-	-	-	154	270	-	1	-	-
Monaco	-	-	437	-	-	-	30	- 455	- 13	-	-	100	100	16
Norway	4 568	4 289	7 831	14 997	1 630	7 171	8 567	6 994	9 465	10 641	6 102	611	- 3 940	1 415
Switzerland	7 361	11 647	22 206	6 620	15 275	1 321	19 627	13 966	25 010	12 729	45 362	7 385	9 696	17 463
North America	79 865	165 591	265 866	262 698	51 475	97 914	164 365	94 088	138 576	226 646	114 314	40 477	118 147	170 425
Canada	12 464	37 841	100 888	35 253	11 389	14 917	30 263	8 000	20 848	46 751	44 141	16 718	30 794	40 215
United States	67 401	127 750	164 978	227 445	40 085	82 996	134 103	86 088	117 729	179 895	70 173	23 760	87 353	130 210
Other developed countries	6 975	10 821	66 948	45 395	18 185	34 265	44 963	31 525	58 366	46 080	94 747	17 598	63 636	84 962
Australia	2 070	10 508	44 222	33 530	22 206	26 866	35 460	26 602	31 949	43 439	18 454	- 2 981	15 851	6 868
Bermuda	1 613	1 083	1 424	850	820	- 405	60	400	503	- 40 691	4 507	3 248	5 701	2 290
Israel	1 223	8 061	684	1 363	803	1 147	3 663	403	9 747	8 408	11 316	167	5 863	8 086
Japan	662	- 11 683	16 538	9 251	- 5 771	6 895	4 991	5 012	16 966	30 346	56 379	17 440	31 183	62 687
New Zealand	1 407	2 853	4 081	401	126	- 238	788	- 892	- 799	4 578	4 092	- 275	5 037	5 031
Developing economies	63 801	89 163	100 381	104 812	39 077	82 378	83 220	68 680	114 922	144 830	105 849	73 975	98 149	103 615
Africa	8 685	11 181	8 076	21 193	5 140	8 072	7 205	14 494	15 913	9 891	8 216	2 702	3 309	4 812
North Africa	3 351	6 773	2 182	16 283	1 475	1 141	1 353	12 892	5 633	1 401	4 665	1 004	1 471	17
Algeria	-	18	-	82	-	-	-	-	-	- 47	-	-	-	-
Egypt	1 478	2 976	1 713	15 895	993	195	609	12 892	5 633	1 448	4 613	76	1 092	-
Libya	-	1	200	307	145	91	20	-	-	-	51	601	377	-
Morocco	1 438	133	269	- 125	333	846	274	-	-	-	-	324	-	17
Sudan	390	1 332	-	-	-	-	450	-	-	-	-	-	-	-
Tunisia	46	2 313	-	122	4	9	-	-	-	-	-	3	2	-
Other Africa	5 334	4 408	5 894	4 910	3 665	6 931	5 853	1 603	10 279	8 490	3 551	1 697	1 838	4 795
Angola	175	1	-	- 475	- 471	1 300	-	-	-	- 60	-	-	-	-
Botswana	-	57	1	-	50	-	20	88	-	-	3	-	-	-
Burkina Faso	-	289	-	20	-	-	-	-	-	-	-	-	-	-
Cameroon	-	-	-	1	-	-	0	-	-	-	-	-	-	-
Cape Verde	-	-	-	4	-	-	-	-	-	-	-	-	-	-
Congo	13	20	-	435	-	-	-	-	-	-	-	-	-	-
Congo, Democratic Republic of	-	-	-	-	5	175	-	-	-	- 45	-	-	-	-
Equatorial Guinea	-	-	-	- 2 200	-	-	-	-	-	-	-	-	-	-

/...

Annex table I.3. Value of cross-border M&As, by region/economy of seller/purchaser, 2005–2011 (continued)

(Millions of dollars)

Region/economy	Net sales[a]							Net purchases[b]						
	2005	2006	2007	2008	2009	2010	2011	2005	2006	2007	2008	2009	2010	2011
Eritrea	-	-	-	-	-	12	- 254	-	-	-	-	-	-	-
Ethiopia	-	-	-	-	-	-	146	-	-	-	-	-	-	-
Gabon	-	-	82	-	-	-	-	-	-	- 16	-	-	-	-
Ghana	-	3	122	900	0	-	- 3	-	-	-	-	-	1	-
Guinea	0	2	-	-	-	-	-	-	-	-	-	-	-	-
Kenya	32	2	396	-	-	9	19	12	-	-	18	-	-	- 3
Liberia	-	-	-	-	-	587	-	-	-	-	-	-	-	-
Madagascar	-	1	-	-	-	-	-	-	-	-	-	-	-	-
Malawi	-	-	5	-	0	0	-	-	-	-	-	-	-	-
Mali	-	1	-	-	-	-	-	-	-	-	-	-	-	-
Mauritania	-	-	375	-	-	-	-	-	-	-	-	-	-	-
Mauritius	- 25	268	-	26	27	203	6	- 265	232	89	206	191	- 50	268
Mozambique	-	34	2	-	-	35	27	-	-	-	-	-	-	-
Namibia	7	181	2	15	59	104	40	-	-	-	-	-	-	-
Niger	-	-	-	-	-	-	3	-	-	-	-	-	-	-
Nigeria	25	4 883	490	- 597	- 241	664	539	-	-	-	418	-	-	4
Rwanda	-	-	-	6	-	-	-	-	-	-	-	-	-	-
Senegal	-	-	-	-	-	- 457	-	22	-	-	-	-	-	-
Seychelles	-	-	89	49	-	19	-	115	-	0	66	-	5	- 78
Sierra Leone	-	-	31	40	-	13	52	-	-	-	-	-	-	-
South Africa	5 092	- 1 336	4 301	6 676	4 215	3 934	5 228	1 604	10 046	8 541	2 817	1 491	1 600	4 252
Swaziland	-	-	-	-	-	-	-	-	-	-	-	-	6	-
Togo	-	-	-	-	-	-	-	-	-	-	20	-	-	353
Uganda	-	-	-	1	-	-	-	-	-	-	-	-	257	-
United Republic of Tanzania	-	-	-	-	2	60	0	-	-	-	-	-	18	-
Zambia	8	4	-	1	11	272	-	29	-	25	-	16	2	-
Zimbabwe	7	-	0	7	6	-	27	- 0	1	- 44	1	-	-	-
Asia	40 537	65 250	71 423	68 909	38 291	36 873	55 302	44 023	70 792	94 469	94 398	67 310	79 013	80 179
East and South-East Asia	26 441	34 936	43 451	39 968	28 654	26 417	32 715	22 164	28 696	25 270	58 810	40 176	67 609	67 966
East Asia	20 998	25 456	23 390	17 226	15 741	16 972	12 575	12 597	21 163	- 667	39 888	35 851	53 879	50 403
China	7 207	11 298	9 332	5 375	10 898	6 306	11 176	3 653	12 090	- 2 282	37 941	21 490	29 578	34 355
Hong Kong, China	5 449	9 106	7 102	8 707	3 028	12 182	1 028	8 195	8 003	- 7 980	- 1 048	7 461	14 806	11 293
Korea, Republic of	5 165	- 161	46	1 194	1 956	- 2 012	2 466	194	1 057	8 646	3 882	6 951	9 949	4 109
Macao, China	67	413	133	593	- 57	33	34	0	-	-	0	- 580	52	-
Mongolia	-	2	7	-	344	65	88	-	-	-	106	- 24	-	-
Taiwan Province of China	3 110	4 798	6 770	1 356	- 429	399	- 2 216	554	14	949	- 993	552	- 506	645
South-East Asia	5 443	9 480	20 061	22 743	12 913	9 445	20 139	9 567	7 533	25 936	18 922	4 325	13 730	17 563
Brunei Darussalam	-	0	0	-	3	-	-	-	112	-	-	10	-	-
Cambodia	-	9	6	30	- 336	5	50	-	-	-	-	-	-	0
Indonesia	6 171	388	1 706	2 070	1 332	1 672	6 467	290	- 85	826	913	- 2 590	256	449
Lao People's Democratic Republic	-	-	-	-	-	110	5	-	-	-	-	-	-	-
Malaysia	1 141	2 509	6 976	2 781	354	3 443	4 517	1 946	2 664	3 654	9 751	3 277	2 432	3 909
Myanmar	-	-	- 1	-	- 0	-	-	-	- 1 010	-	-	-	-	-
Philippines	- 5 180	- 134	1 165	2 621	1 291	- 270	2 586	1 829	190	- 2 514	- 174	- 7	19	466
Singapore	3 933	2 908	7 426	14 240	9 693	3 941	4 484	5 706	5 566	23 916	6 992	2 762	8 233	7 743
Thailand	- 632	3 771	2 372	142	346	443	570	- 203	88	54	1 416	872	2 731	4 996
Timor-Leste	-	-	-	-	-	-	-	-	-	-	-	-	-	-
Viet Nam	10	29	412	859	230	101	1 460	-	8	-	25	-	59	-
South Asia	738	7 883	5 371	12 654	6 094	5 569	12 875	1 877	6 745	29 096	13 488	291	26 682	6 078
Bangladesh	-	330	4	-	9	10	0	-	-	-	-	-	1	-
India	526	4 424	4 405	10 427	6 049	5 550	12 577	1 877	6 715	29 083	13 482	291	26 698	6 072
Iran, Islamic Republic of	-	-	-	695	-	-	-	-	-	-	-	-	-	-
Maldives	-	-	-	3	-	-	-	-	-	-	-	-	- 3	-
Nepal	-	- 15	-	13	-	-	4	-	-	-	-	-	-	-
Pakistan	207	3 139	956	1 147	-	- 0	247	-	30	-	-	-	- 13	-
Sri Lanka	5	4	6	370	36	9	47	-	-	12	6	-	-	6
West Asia	13 358	22 431	22 602	16 287	3 543	4 887	9 713	19 983	35 350	40 103	22 099	26 843	- 15 278	6 136
Bahrain	85	- 410	190	178	-	452	30	4 514	4 275	1 002	4 497	323	- 3 362	- 2 740
Iraq	-	-	-	34	-	-	717	-	-	33	-	-	-	-
Jordan	89	750	440	773	108	- 103	391	-	4	45	322	-	- 34	37
Kuwait	-	13	3 963	496	- 55	463	16	725	1 345	1 416	2 147	124	- 10 810	2 033
Lebanon	236	5 948	- 153	108	-	642	-	103	716	210	- 233	283	0	834
Oman	116	1	621	10	-	386	-	6	5	79	601	893	- 529	172
Qatar	-	-	-	124	298	13	28	352	127	5 160	6 029	10 266	590	- 833
Saudi Arabia	-	21	125	102	42	164	629	6 603	5 405	15 780	1 442	121	706	- 17

/...

Annex table I.3. Value of cross-border M&As, by region/economy of seller/purchaser, 2005–2011 (continued)

(Millions of dollars)

Region/economy	Net sales[a]							Net purchases[b]						
	2005	2006	2007	2008	2009	2010	2011	2005	2006	2007	2008	2009	2010	2011
Syrian Arab Republic	-	-	-	-	-	41	-	-	-	-	-	-	-	-
Turkey	12 771	15 340	16 415	13 238	2 849	2 053	7 348	199	356	767	1 313	-	- 38	908
United Arab Emirates	61	53	856	1 225	300	756	554	7 481	23 117	15 611	5 983	14 831	- 1 803	5 741
Yemen	-	716	144	-	-	20	-	-	-	-	-	-	-	-
Latin America and the Caribbean	14 563	12 768	20 648	15 452	- 4 358	28 414	20 689	10 013	28 064	40 195	2 466	3 740	15 831	18 659
South America	8 427	4 503	13 697	8 121	- 5 342	17 045	16 271	2 513	19 923	13 152	4 765	3 104	12 900	10 145
Argentina	358	344	877	- 3 283	111	3 458	- 246	- 173	160	569	274	- 77	499	102
Bolivia, Plurinational State of	-	- 39	- 77	24	-	- 18	-	-	-	-	-	-	-	-
Brazil	2 993	2 637	6 539	7 568	- 1 369	8 857	15 422	2 505	18 629	10 785	5 243	2 501	8 465	5 540
Chile	- 779	447	1 480	3 234	829	353	574	- 80	431	466	- 88	55	642	1 083
Colombia	5 775	1 319	4 303	- 57	- 1 633	- 1 255	- 884	258	697	1 384	16	211	3 210	4 314
Ecuador	-	21	29	0	6	357	167	-	-	-	0	-	-	40
Guyana	-	-	3	1	1	-	3	-	-	-	-	-	-	0
Paraguay	-	-	10	4	- 60	- 1	0	-	-	-	-	-	-	-
Peru	55	53	1 135	293	38	687	488	3	6	195	679	416	77	321
Uruguay	0	164	157	8	3	448	747	-	-	-	-	-	7	13
Venezuela, Bolivarian Republic of	26	- 443	- 760	329	- 3 268	4 158	-	-	-	- 248	- 1 358	- 2	-	- 1 268
Central America	3 903	2 898	4 889	2 899	153	8 854	1 210	3 140	3 699	17 452	- 1 053	3 434	2 909	4 853
Belize	-	-	-	0	-	1	-	-	4	- 43	-	2	-	-
Costa Rica	59	294	- 34	405	-	5	17	-	97	642	-	-	-	-
El Salvador	441	173	835	-	30	43	103	15	370	-	-	-	-	-
Guatemala	10	- 2	5	145	-	650	-	1	317	140	-	-	-	-
Honduras	-	-	140	-	-	1	23	-	-	-	-	-	-	-
Mexico	2 899	874	3 717	2 304	104	7 990	1 231	3 036	2 750	18 226	- 463	3 247	2 892	4 390
Nicaragua	-	2	-	-	- 1	-	71	-	-	-	-	-	-	-
Panama	493	1 557	226	44	20	164	- 235	88	160	- 1 512	- 591	185	17	462
Caribbean	2 232	5 367	2 061	4 432	832	2 516	3 208	4 359	4 442	9 592	- 1 245	- 2 799	22	3 661
Anguilla	-	-	-	-	-	-	-	71	- 1	-	30	-	- 10	3
Antigua and Barbuda	160	85	1	-	-	-	-	-	-	-	-	-	-	-
Aruba	1	468	-	-	-	-	-	-	-	-	-	-	-	-
Bahamas	-	3 027	-	41	-	82	212	- 146	- 411	2 693	537	11	112	- 350
Barbados	-	999	1	207	-	328	-	166	-	3	3	-	-	-
British Virgin Islands	524	19	559	980	242	432	631	2 086	2 900	5 017	- 1 635	- 1 579	- 774	1 481
Cayman Islands	449	49	-	969	-	84	- 105	1 800	1 563	2 047	2 079	- 1 237	743	1 152
Dominican Republic	-	427	42	-	0	1	39	-	-	93	- 25	-	31	-
Haiti	-	-	-	-	1	59	-	-	-	-	-	-	-	-
Jamaica	- 0	67	595	-	-	-	9	1	158	3	13	28	1	-
Netherlands Antilles[c]	43	10	-	-	2	19	235	- 20	350	-	-	- 30	- 156	38
Puerto Rico	1 085	216	862	-	587	1 037	1 214	512	- 216	- 261	- 2 454	13	77	202
Saint Kitts and Nevis	-	-	-	-	-	-	-	-	-	-	-	-	- 0	-
Saint Vincent and the Grenadines	-	-	-	-	-	-	-	- 1	-	-	-	-	-	-
Trinidad and Tobago	- 30	-	-	2 236	-	-	973	- 129	97	- 2	207	- 10	-	- 15
US Virgin Islands	-	-	-	-	-	473	-	21	-	-	-	4	-	1 150
Oceania	16	- 36	234	- 742	4	9 019	23	150	154	275	770	224	- 4	- 35
Cook Islands	-	-	-	-	-	-	-	-	-	-	-	50	-	-
Fiji	1	-	12	2	-	1	-	-	-	-	-	-	-	-
French Polynesia	-	-	-	-	-	-	-	-	-	-	-	1	-	-
Guam	-	72	-	-	-	-	-	150	-	-	-	-	-	-
Marshall Islands	-	-	45	-	-	-	-	-	-	-	-	0	-	- 35
Nauru	-	-	-	-	-	-	-	- 3	-	-	-	172	-	-
New Caledonia	-	- 100	-	-	-	-	-	3	-	-	-	-	-	-
Niue	6	-	-	-	-	-	-	-	-	-	-	-	-	-
Norfolk Island	-	-	-	-	-	-	-	-	90	-	-	-	-	-
Papua New Guinea	9	7	160	- 758	0	9 018	5	-	-	275	1 051	-	- 4	-
Samoa	-	- 18	3	13	-	-	-	-	64	-	- 324	-	-	-
Solomon Islands	-	-	14	-	-	-	19	-	-	-	-	-	-	-
Tuvalu	-	-	-	-	-	-	-	-	-	-	43	-	-	-
Vanuatu	-	3	-	-	4	-	-	-	-	-	-	-	-	-
Transition economies	- 5 279	9 005	30 448	20 337	7 125	4 499	32 970	6 188	2 940	21 729	20 167	7 432	5 693	13 510
South-East Europe	955	3 942	2 192	767	529	266	1 460	- 654	- 2 092	1 039	- 4	- 167	325	51
Albania	7	41	164	3	146	-	-	-	-	-	-	-	-	-
Bosnia and Herzegovina	21	79	1 022	2	8	-	-	-	-	-	-	-	-	-
Croatia	360	2 530	674	204	-	201	92	- 125	3	-	2	8	325	-
Montenegro	-	7	0	-	362	-	-	-	-	4	-	-	-	-

/...

Annex table I.3. Value of cross-border M&As, by region/economy of seller/purchaser, 2005–2011 (concluded)
(Millions of dollars)

Region/economy	Net sales[a]							Net purchases[b]						
	2005	2006	2007	2008	2009	2010	2011	2005	2006	2007	2008	2009	2010	2011
Serbia	-	582	280	501	10	19	1 340	-	- 1 898	860	- 7	- 174	-	51
Serbia and Montenegro	549	419	-	-	3	-	-	-	-	-	-	-	-	-
The former Yugoslav Republic of Macedonia	0	280	53	57	-	46	27	-	-	-	-	-	-	-
Yugoslavia (former)	17	5	-	-	-	-	-	- 529	- 198	175	-	-	-	-
CIS	- 6 466	4 949	28 203	19 466	6 581	4 203	31 510	6 842	5 032	20 691	20 171	7 599	5 368	13 270
Armenia	4	-	423	204	30	-	26	-	-	-	-	-	-	-
Azerbaijan	-	-	-	2	-	0	-	-	-	-	519	-	-	2
Belarus	4	-	2 500	16	-	649	10	-	-	-	-	-	-	-
Kazakhstan	1 474	- 1 751	727	- 242	1 322	101	293	430	1 503	1 833	2 047	-	1 462	8 081
Kyrgyzstan	155	-	179	-	-	44	72	-	-	-	-	-	-	-
Moldova, Republic of	-	10	24	4	-	-	- 9	-	-	-	-	-	-	-
Russian Federation	- 14 547	6 319	22 529	13 507	5 079	3 085	29 705	6 029	3 507	18 598	16 634	7 599	3 866	5 084
Tajikistan	12	-	5	-	-	-	14	-	-	-	-	-	-	-
Turkmenistan	47	-	-	-	-	-	-	-	-	-	-	-	-	-
Ukraine	6 386	261	1 816	5 933	147	322	1 400	383	23	260	972	-	40	103
Uzbekistan	-	110	-	42	4	1	-	-	-	-	-	-	-	-
Georgia	232	115	53	104	14	30	-	-	-	-	-	-	- 0	188
Unspecified	-	-	-	-	-	-	-	27 835	10 134	14 452	12 486	7 540	16 461	7 827
Memorandum														
Least developed countries[d]	573	2 688	584	- 2 552	- 774	2 201	504	51	- 946	- 80	- 261	16	277	353
Landlocked developing countries[e]	1 707	- 1 052	1 357	144	1 708	621	716	546	1 504	1 814	2 676	- 8	1 727	8 083
Small island developing states[f]	115	4 438	920	1 824	31	9 650	1 223	- 263	141	3 061	1 803	393	60	- 210

Source: UNCTAD cross-border M&A database (www.unctad.org/fdistatistics).

[a] Net sales by the region/economy of the immediate acquired company.

[b] Net purchases by region/economy of the ultimate acquiring company.

[c] This economy dissolved on 10 October 2010.

[d] Least developed countries include Afghanistan, Angola, Bangladesh, Benin, Bhutan, Burkina Faso, Burundi, Cambodia, the Central African Republic, Chad, the Comoros, the Democratic Republic of the Congo, Djibouti, Equatorial Guinea, Eritrea, Ethiopia, the Gambia, Guinea, Guinea-Bissau, Haiti, Kiribati, the Lao People's Democratic Republic, Lesotho, Liberia, Madagascar, Malawi, Mali, Mauritania, Mozambique, Myanmar, Nepal, Niger, Rwanda, Samoa, São Tomé and Principe, Senegal, Sierra Leone, Solomon Islands, Somalia, Sudan, Timor-Leste, Togo, Tuvalu, Uganda, the United Republic of Tanzania, Vanuatu, Yemen and Zambia.

[e] Landlocked developing countries include Afghanistan, Armenia, Azerbaijan, Bhutan, the Plurinational State of Bolivia, Botswana, Burkina Faso, Burundi, the Central African Republic, Chad, Ethiopia, Kazakhstan, Kyrgyzstan, the Lao People's Democratic Republic, Lesotho, the former Yugoslav Republic of Macedonia, Malawi, Mali, the Republic of Moldova, Mongolia, Nepal, Niger, Paraguay, Rwanda, Swaziland, the Republic of Tajikistan, Turkmenistan, Uganda, Uzbekistan, Zambia and Zimbabwe.

[f] Small island developing countries include Antigua and Barbuda, the Bahamas, Barbados, Cape Verde, the Comoros, Dominica, Fiji, Grenada, Jamaica, Kiribati, Maldives, Marshall Islands, Mauritius, the Federated States of Micronesia, Nauru, Palau, Papua New Guinea, Saint Kitts and Nevis, Saint Lucia, Saint Vincent and the Grenadines, Samoa, São Tomé and Principe, Seychelles, Solomon Islands, Timor-Leste, Tonga, Trinidad and Tobago, Tuvalu and Vanuatu.

Note: Cross-border M&A sales and purchases are calculated on a net basis as follows: Net cross-border M&A sales in a host economy = Sales of companies in the host economy to foreign TNCs (-) Sales of foreign affiliates in the host economy; Net cross-border M&A purchases by a home economy = Purchases of companies abroad by home-based TNCs (-) Sales of foreign affiliates of home-based TNCs. The data cover only those deals that involved an acquisition of an equity stake of more than 10 per cent.

Annex table I.4. Number of cross-border M&As, by region/economy of seller/purchaser, 2005–2011
(Number of deals)

Region / economy	Net sales[a]							Net purchases[b]						
	2005	2006	2007	2008	2009	2010	2011	2005	2006	2007	2008	2009	2010	2011
World	5 004	5 747	7 018	6 425	4 239	5 484	5 769	5 004	5 747	7 018	6 425	4 239	5 484	5 769
Developed economies	3 805	4 326	5 187	4 603	2 920	3 668	3 995	3 741	4 446	5 443	4 732	2 666	3 713	4 179
Europe	2 271	2 531	2 955	2 619	1 476	1 961	2 298	2 109	2 519	3 117	2 853	1 522	2 032	2 093
European Union	2 108	2 354	2 717	2 419	1 344	1 796	2 093	1 828	2 216	2 782	2 548	1 328	1 759	1 848
Austria	57	44	48	30	19	30	40	62	77	104	75	42	35	36
Belgium	64	87	81	86	50	80	62	49	63	77	61	15	19	38
Bulgaria	29	29	30	28	14	5	2	1	2	2	6	3	3	3
Cyprus	-	5	17	32	22	23	27	3	23	21	46	160	280	149
Czech Republic	31	53	54	72	29	24	58	7	14	12	10	6	11	14
Denmark	90	90	89	75	39	87	68	112	85	82	102	43	45	30
Estonia	13	10	13	19	5	8	9	3	8	10	4	-	2	11
Finland	53	68	91	52	25	38	61	56	66	66	109	32	57	66
France	222	224	232	178	101	152	187	253	265	404	381	191	226	252
Germany	374	426	434	337	169	186	313	226	229	264	286	196	137	255
Greece	9	11	9	13	15	1	8	13	20	17	27	7	1	5
Hungary	20	46	27	26	8	19	16	8	13	14	10	5	2	-
Ireland	42	49	76	62	41	37	38	48	94	128	82	32	30	40
Italy	118	111	140	150	85	112	124	52	59	121	119	45	50	52
Latvia	14	10	17	14	4	16	11	1	1	4	- 1	-	4	1
Lithuania	14	18	17	18	4	7	17	3	2	2	7	2	5	5
Luxembourg	11	12	20	10	10	13	21	26	39	42	53	34	33	33
Malta	3	3	2	-	4	2	2	1	1	1	1	4	4	3
Netherlands	126	88	163	116	74	105	140	91	146	173	221	104	169	142
Poland	44	49	55	43	48	58	46	15	8	30	28	3	21	15
Portugal	37	29	32	11	15	14	15	10	16	25	36	20	17	4
Romania	41	44	48	38	18	16	19	-	1	- 1	7	3	6	-
Slovakia	13	12	15	14	6	6	6	2	2	1	7	2	5	3
Slovenia	5	7	8	6	2	3	2	6	7	6	4	4	5	- 2
Spain	81	148	162	193	147	151	161	82	109	156	106	50	64	38
Sweden	115	144	148	164	73	112	118	154	185	207	161	94	177	199
United Kingdom	482	537	689	632	317	491	522	544	681	814	600	231	351	456
Other developed Europe	163	177	238	200	132	165	205	281	303	335	305	194	273	245
Andorra	- 1	1	-	-	-	-	-	-	1	-	1	1	1	7
Faeroes	1	-	-	1	-	1	-	-	-	1	-	-	1	-
Gibraltar	2	1	2	1	- 1	-	-	1	3	3	1	3	1	3
Guernsey	-	2	6	3	6	5	3	5	14	21	20	11	29	12
Iceland	5	3	1	-	-	3	1	47	50	38	4	- 11	- 16	- 3
Isle of Man	7	4	3	4	3	4	2	11	14	25	5	3	14	- 2
Jersey	3	3	7	6	4	7	2	4	18	28	13	8	22	22
Liechtenstein	-	2	1	-	-	1	-	-	1	1	1	3	-	1
Monaco	1	-	4	1	-	2	2	- 1	- 1	-	2	2	2	2
Norway	78	81	93	86	53	89	88	82	84	93	84	41	52	42
San Marino	-	-	-	-	1	-	-	1	-	-	-	-	-	-
Switzerland	67	80	121	98	66	53	107	131	119	125	174	133	167	161
North America	1 200	1 380	1 717	1 491	1 013	1 234	1 278	1 234	1 458	1 667	1 436	888	1 315	1 614
Canada	252	324	420	374	303	349	329	337	395	426	351	306	424	467
United States	948	1 056	1 297	1 117	710	885	949	897	1 063	1 241	1 085	582	891	1 147
Other developed countries	334	415	515	493	431	473	419	398	469	659	443	256	366	472
Australia	180	229	252	306	283	309	287	209	246	363	153	58	108	133
Bermuda	6	8	7	8	5	8	3	11	8	28	31	9	7	22
Greenland	-	-	-	-	-	-	1	-	1	-	-	-	-	-
Israel	25	35	31	30	16	25	29	38	49	59	42	22	34	28
Japan	44	57	106	99	85	99	52	126	137	161	185	160	198	265
New Zealand	79	86	119	50	42	32	47	14	28	48	32	7	19	24
Developing economies	1 062	1 219	1 552	1 501	975	1 323	1 458	765	839	1 047	1 011	746	1 084	1 012
Africa	72	107	116	106	58	79	129	54	53	60	47	56	63	37
North Africa	21	25	20	23	15	14	21	6	16	11	8	14	14	5
Algeria	2	5	2	4	1	-	-	-	1	- 1	-	-	1	-
Egypt	11	14	9	11	3	9	13	4	14	8	6	5	9	2
Libya	2	1	1	1	2	2	1	1	-	2	1	3	3	-
Morocco	- 1	1	4	2	7	-	6	1	1	2	1	3	-	1
Sudan	3	2	1	1	-	-	1	-	-	-	-	-	-	-
Tunisia	4	2	3	4	2	3	-	-	-	-	-	3	1	2
Other Africa	51	82	96	83	43	65	108	48	37	49	39	42	49	32
Angola	1	2	1	-	-	1	-	-	-	- 1	-	-	-	-
Benin	-	-	-	-	-	-	1	-	-	-	-	-	-	-
Botswana	1	1	4	1	1	1	3	1	- 1	-	3	1	1	-
Burkina Faso	-	1	-	2	-	1	-	-	-	-	-	-	-	-

/...

Annex table I.4. Number of cross-border M&As, by region/economy of seller/purchaser, 2005–2011 (continued)

(Number of deals)

Region / economy	Net sales[a]							Net purchases[b]						
	2005	2006	2007	2008	2009	2010	2011	2005	2006	2007	2008	2009	2010	2011
Burundi	-	1	-	1	-	-	-	-	-	-	-	-	-	-
Cameroon	1	1	-	2	-	- 1	1	-	-	-	-	-	-	-
Cape Verde	1	-	-	1	-	-	-	-	-	-	-	-	-	-
Chad	-	-	-	-	-	-	-	-	-	-	-	-	-	1
Congo	1	4	-	1	1	1	-	-	-	-	-	-	-	-
Congo, Democratic Republic of	-	-	2	-	2	1	-	-	-	- 2	-	-	-	- 1
Côte d' Ivoire	-	-	-	1	-	-	-	-	- 1	-	-	-	-	1
Djibouti	-	-	-	-	-	-	1	-	-	-	-	-	-	-
Equatorial Guinea	-	-	-	- 1	-	-	-	-	-	-	-	-	-	-
Eritrea	-	-	-	-	-	1	- 1	-	- 1	-	-	-	-	-
Ethiopia	-	-	1	-	-	-	2	-	-	-	-	-	-	-
Gabon	-	1	3	2	-	-	-	-	-	- 1	-	-	-	-
Gambia	1	-	-	-	-	-	-	-	-	-	-	-	-	-
Ghana	1	2	5	3	2	-	-	-	-	-	-	-	1	-
Guinea	1	1	-	-	-	-	-	-	-	-	-	-	-	-
Kenya	3	2	2	5	-	2	6	2	4	4	3	1	2	3
Liberia	-	1	-	-	-	3	1	-	-	-	-	-	-	-
Madagascar	-	3	-	1	-	-	-	-	-	-	-	-	-	-
Malawi	-	-	2	-	1	1	-	-	-	-	-	-	-	-
Mali	-	2	1	-	-	-	1	-	-	-	-	-	-	-
Mauritania	-	-	1	-	-	-	-	-	-	-	-	-	-	-
Mauritius	3	4	2	5	5	9	7	14	12	6	6	10	5	3
Mozambique	-	5	2	-	-	4	6	-	-	-	-	-	- 1	-
Namibia	2	2	7	2	3	2	2	-	-	-	-	1	-	-
Niger	-	-	-	-	-	-	1	-	-	-	-	- 1	-	1
Nigeria	2	5	1	-	- 2	3	9	2	- 1	1	4	1	-	1
Reunion	-	-	-	1	-	1	-	-	-	-	-	-	-	-
Rwanda	-	1	3	2	-	-	1	-	-	-	-	-	-	-
Senegal	1	-	1	1	-	- 1	-	1	-	-	-	-	-	-
Seychelles	-	-	2	1	-	1	-	3	-	2	- 1	- 1	4	1
Sierra Leone	-	-	1	3	-	1	1	-	-	-	-	-	-	-
South Africa	24	34	41	37	22	27	58	26	22	38	22	29	33	21
Swaziland	1	-	2	-	-	-	-	-	-	-	-	-	1	-
Togo	-	-	-	-	-	-	2	- 1	-	-	2	-	-	1
Uganda	2	2	5	3	1	1	1	-	-	1	-	-	1	-
United Republic of Tanzania	-	4	2	2	3	1	1	-	-	-	-	-	1	-
Zambia	3	3	-	5	2	4	3	1	1	1	-	1	1	-
Zimbabwe	2	-	5	2	2	1	1	- 1	2	-	-	1	-	-
Asia	832	854	999	1 011	693	829	893	630	649	809	813	565	825	797
East and South-East Asia	674	629	724	715	504	600	626	465	421	504	481	435	617	612
East Asia	408	396	430	403	279	341	322	190	190	226	252	266	351	383
China	217	224	232	236	142	155	151	45	38	61	69	97	150	143
Hong Kong, China	138	119	144	93	67	108	72	117	118	116	110	88	121	146
Korea, Democratic People's Republic of	-	1	-	-	-	-	-	-	-	-	-	-	-	-
Korea, Republic of	25	17	19	37	59	46	68	17	30	39	50	57	57	80
Macao, China	7	6	5	-	-	1	1	1	1	-	1	- 1	2	1
Mongolia	1	1	3	2	5	8	16	-	-	-	1	-	-	-
Taiwan Province of China	20	28	27	35	6	23	14	10	3	10	21	25	21	13
South-East Asia	266	233	294	312	225	259	304	275	231	278	229	169	266	229
Brunei Darussalam	-	5	2	-	2	2	-	-	1	-	-	2	1	-
Cambodia	2	3	3	1	2	1	2	-	-	-	-	-	-	1
Indonesia	30	24	40	54	35	62	81	5	1	5	11	9	11	11
Lao People's Democratic Republic	2	-	-	- 1	-	1	2	-	-	-	-	-	- 1	-
Malaysia	92	67	91	80	75	60	44	120	117	123	113	63	89	60
Myanmar	-	-	- 1	-	- 1	-	-	-	- 1	-	-	-	-	-
Philippines	13	5	11	18	3	11	24	8	2	10	9	4	3	10
Singapore	96	91	103	89	62	74	86	134	100	129	78	74	139	124
Thailand	29	36	31	41	12	16	29	10	9	11	17	16	21	22
Timor-Leste	-	-	-	-	-	-	-	-	-	-	-	-	-	-
Viet Nam	2	2	14	30	35	32	36	- 2	2	-	1	1	3	1
South Asia	101	139	159	158	112	123	145	99	137	176	166	57	144	101
Afghanistan	-	-	-	-	-	-	-	1	-	- 1	-	-	-	-
Bangladesh	1	1	1	1	1	2	1	-	-	-	-	-	3	-
India	94	130	147	136	104	115	131	98	134	175	163	56	141	99
Iran, Islamic Republic of	-	-	-	3	-	-	1	-	-	-	-	-	- 1	-
Maldives	1	-	-	2	-	1	-	-	-	-	-	-	- 1	-
Nepal	-	- 1	-	1	-	-	3	-	-	-	-	-	-	-

Annex table I.4. Number of cross-border M&As, by region/economy of seller/purchaser, 2005–2011
(continued)
(Number of deals)

Region / economy	Net sales[a]							Net purchases[b]						
	2005	2006	2007	2008	2009	2010	2011	2005	2006	2007	2008	2009	2010	2011
Pakistan	5	7	7	10	- 1	- 1	4	-	1	-	1	1	-	-
Sri Lanka	-	2	4	5	8	6	5	-	2	2	2	-	1	2
West Asia	57	86	116	138	77	106	122	66	91	129	166	73	64	84
Bahrain	3	2	6	9	3	3	1	8	14	15	28	3	8	13
Iraq	4	-	-	2	2	-	4	-	-	1	-	-	-	-
Jordan	4	9	4	8	12	4	6	3	4	3	2	1	-	2
Kuwait	-	1	4	14	2	13	7	11	6	19	23	7	6	12
Lebanon	3	2	- 1	2	-	3	1	2	2	3	1	5	6	4
Oman	1	2	9	2	2	2	-	1	4	2	7	5	7	1
Qatar	-	-	2	2	2	-	2	4	1	8	19	9	6	5
Saudi Arabia	1	5	10	12	8	12	17	8	14	10	13	3	10	6
Syrian Arab Republic	-	-	-	-	2	2	-	-	-	-	-	-	-	1
Turkey	29	51	63	60	31	46	53	7	4	12	5	4	2	9
United Arab Emirates	12	13	18	27	13	20	31	22	42	56	68	36	18	31
Yemen	-	1	1	-	-	1	-	-	-	-	-	-	1	-
Latin America and the Caribbean	147	250	425	378	221	408	431	80	132	174	146	116	196	178
South America	77	135	265	266	130	257	305	24	39	67	63	37	98	106
Argentina	5	40	43	44	11	44	52	-	3	- 1	3	-	6	13
Bolivia, Plurinational State of	1	-	2	2	-	- 1	1	-	-	1	-	1	-	-
Brazil	37	54	126	116	44	114	125	15	20	35	50	19	37	31
Chile	9	14	20	31	29	21	37	3	7	13	1	3	24	22
Colombia	13	13	26	30	22	37	43	3	4	16	2	8	15	16
Ecuador	1	6	9	2	7	9	6	-	1	-	1	-	2	1
Falkland Islands (Malvinas)	1	-	-	-	-	-	-	1	-	-	-	-	-	-
Guyana	-	1	1	1	1	1	4	-	-	-	-	-	-	1
Paraguay	-	-	2	5	- 1	2	2	-	-	-	-	1	-	1
Peru	3	8	30	28	24	29	26	-	2	1	6	4	13	15
Suriname	-	-	1	-	-	-	1	-	-	-	-	-	-	-
Uruguay	2	-	6	4	3	6	6	2	-	-	-	-	1	2
Venezuela, Bolivarian Republic of	5	- 1	- 1	3	- 10	- 5	2	-	2	2	-	1	-	4
Central America	37	79	97	64	39	86	65	27	42	38	19	34	31	33
Belize	-	-	-	1	1	1	1	- 2	1	- 1	1	5	11	2
Costa Rica	3	2	2	7	3	4	7	2	3	3	2	- 1	-	4
El Salvador	4	4	5	-	3	5	1	1	13	-	-	-	-	1
Guatemala	2	-	3	4	2	2	1	5	9	3	1	3	-	-
Honduras	1	1	2	-	-	1	2	-	-	-	-	-	-	1
Mexico	23	67	75	46	26	59	38	17	14	28	16	22	13	24
Nicaragua	1	2	1	-	- 1	4	5	-	-	-	-	-	-	-
Panama	3	3	9	6	5	10	10	4	2	5	- 1	5	7	1
Caribbean	33	36	63	48	52	65	61	29	51	69	64	45	67	39
Anguilla	-	-	-	-	-	-	1	2	-	-	1	-	- 1	1
Antigua and Barbuda	6	1	1	-	-	-	-	1	2	-	2	- 1	-	-
Aruba	1	3	-	-	-	-	-	-	-	-	-	-	-	-
Bahamas	1	-	2	4	1	4	2	1	1	1	4	2	5	3
Barbados	-	1	2	-	-	1	-	6	3	9	4	1	- 1	- 2
British Virgin Islands	10	8	20	25	39	42	33	3	9	19	20	21	37	23
Cayman Islands	4	4	5	12	3	3	5	5	19	35	37	17	13	7
Cuba	-	-	-	-	-	-	-	-	-	-	-	1	-	-
Dominican Republic	-	2	6	1	3	3	1	-	1	1	- 1	-	5	-
Guadeloupe	-	-	-	-	-	-	1	-	-	-	-	-	-	-
Haiti	-	2	-	-	1	2	-	-	-	-	-	-	-	-
Jamaica	1	3	13	1	-	-	1	3	6	4	-	6	1	- 1
Martinique	-	-	-	2	-	1	1	-	-	1	-	-	1	1
Netherlands Antilles[c]	5	5	1	-	3	2	1	-	3	-	-	- 1	4	6
Puerto Rico	4	6	9	1	-	5	10	7	5	-	- 4	-	5	2
Saint Kitts and Nevis	-	-	-	-	-	-	-	-	-	-	-	-	-	- 1
Saint Lucia	1	-	1	-	-	-	-	-	-	-	-	-	-	-
Saint Vincent and the Grenadines	-	-	-	-	-	-	-	- 1	-	-	-	-	-	-
Trinidad and Tobago	1	1	1	2	2	-	6	1	-	- 1	1	- 3	- 2	- 2
US Virgin Islands	- 1	-	1	-	-	2	-	1	1	-	-	2	-	2
Oceania	11	8	12	6	3	7	5	1	5	4	5	9	-	-
Cook Islands	-	-	-	-	-	-	-	-	-	-	-	2	-	-
Fiji	3	1	1	3	-	1	-	-	-	- 1	1	-	-	-
French Polynesia	-	1	1	-	- 1	-	-	-	2	1	-	2	-	-
Guam	-	2	-	-	-	-	-	1	-	-	-	-	-	-
Marshall Islands	-	-	1	-	1	1	-	-	-	1	-	3	-	- 1
Nauru	-	-	-	-	-	-	-	- 1	-	-	-	1	-	-

/...

Annex table I.4. Number of cross-border M&As, by region/economy of seller/purchaser, 2005–2011 (concluded)

(Number of deals)

Region / economy	Net sales[a]							Net purchases[b]						
	2005	2006	2007	2008	2009	2010	2011	2005	2006	2007	2008	2009	2010	2011
New Caledonia	1	- 1	-	-	-	-	2	1	1	-	-	-	1	-
Niue	2	-	-	-	-	-	-	-	-	-	-	-	-	-
Norfolk Island	-	-	-	-	-	-	-	-	1	1	-	-	-	-
Northern Mariana Islands	1	-	1	-	-	1	-	-	-	-	-	-	-	-
Papua New Guinea	4	3	3	1	1	3	2	-	-	2	2	1	- 1	-
Samoa	-	1	3	1	1	-	-	-	1	-	1	-	-	1
Solomon Islands	-	-	1	-	-	-	1	-	-	-	-	-	-	-
Tonga	-	-	1	1	-	-	-	-	-	-	-	-	-	-
Tuvalu	-	-	-	-	-	-	-	-	-	-	-	1	-	-
Vanuatu	-	1	-	-	1	-	-	-	-	-	-	-	-	-
Transition economies	137	202	279	321	343	493	316	51	62	102	123	70	80	78
South-East Europe	30	39	73	46	17	18	25	- 9	- 2	9	4	-	3	2
Albania	1	1	4	6	2	-	-	-	-	-	-	-	-	-
Bosnia and Herzegovina	6	9	8	4	2	1	2	-	-	-	1	-	1	1
Croatia	7	8	18	12	2	11	8	1	2	6	3	1	1	1
Montenegro	-	1	2	-	3	1	1	-	-	1	-	-	-	-
Serbia	-	4	21	20	7	4	10	-	4	2	-	- 1	1	-
Serbia and Montenegro	14	10	-	2	1	-	-	-	-	-	-	-	-	-
The former Yugoslav Republic of Macedonia	1	5	20	2	-	1	4	-	-	-	-	-	-	-
Yugoslavia (former)	1	1	-	-	-	-	-	- 10	- 8	-	-	-	-	-
CIS	102	156	197	271	327	472	291	60	64	92	119	70	78	75
Armenia	3	2	5	4	3	-	3	-	-	-	-	-	-	-
Azerbaijan	-	-	1	3	2	3	-	-	-	-	-	1	-	1
Belarus	1	1	7	4	-	10	8	-	1	1	-	-	2	-
Kazakhstan	6	2	9	6	12	12	5	9	4	11	6	- 1	- 1	4
Kyrgyzstan	3	2	5	-	1	3	4	-	-	-	-	-	-	-
Moldova, Republic of	1	5	2	6	-	-	2	-	-	-	1	-	-	-
Russian Federation	66	101	118	181	185	357	227	45	54	70	108	65	72	62
Tajikistan	1	-	3	-	-	-	1	-	-	-	-	-	-	-
Turkmenistan	2	-	1	-	-	-	-	-	-	-	-	-	-	-
Ukraine	19	37	43	63	122	86	40	6	4	10	4	5	5	8
Uzbekistan	-	6	3	4	2	1	1	-	1	-	-	-	-	-
Georgia	5	7	9	4	- 1	3	-	-	-	1	-	-	- 1	1
Unspecified	-	-	-	-	1	-	-	447	400	426	559	757	607	500
Memorandum														
Least developed countries[d]	17	36	31	23	14	25	31	2	-	- 2	4	-	5	4
Landlocked developing countries[e]	30	33	79	50	31	39	57	11	7	13	11	3	2	8
Small island developing states[f]	22	16	34	22	12	21	18	27	25	23	21	19	10	1

Source: UNCTAD cross-border M&A database (www.unctad.org/fdistatistics).

[a] Net sales by the region/economy of the immediate acquired company.

[b] Net purchases by region/economy of the ultimate acquiring company.

[c] This economy dissolved on 10 October 2010.

[d] Least developed countries include Afghanistan, Angola, Bangladesh, Benin, Bhutan, Burkina Faso, Burundi, Cambodia, the Central African Republic, Chad, Comoros, Democratic Republic of the Congo, Djibouti, Equatorial Guinea, Eritrea, Ethiopia, the Gambia, Guinea, Guinea-Bissau, Haiti, Kiribati, the Lao People's Democratic Republic, Lesotho, Liberia, Madagascar, Malawi, Mali, Mauritania, Mozambique, Myanmar, Nepal, Niger, Rwanda, Samoa, São Tomé and Principe, Senegal, Sierra Leone, Solomon Islands, Somalia, Sudan, Timor-Leste, Togo, Tuvalu, Uganda, the United Republic of Tanzania, Vanuatu, Yemen and Zambia.

[e] Landlocked developing countries include Afghanistan, Armenia, Azerbaijan, Bhutan, the Plurinational State of Bolivia, Botswana, Burkina Faso, Burundi, the Central African Republic, Chad, Ethiopia, Kazakhstan, Kyrgyzstan, the Lao People's Democratic Republic, Lesotho, the former Yugoslav Republic of Macedonia, Malawi, Mali, the Republic of Moldova, Mongolia, Nepal, Niger, Paraguay, Rwanda, Swaziland, the Republic of Tajikistan, Turkmenistan, Uganda, Uzbekistan, Zambia and Zimbabwe.

[f] Small island developing countries include Antigua and Barbuda, the Bahamas, Barbados, Cape Verde, the Comoros, Dominica, Fiji, Grenada, Jamaica, Kiribati, Maldives, the Marshall Islands, Mauritius, the Federated States of Micronesia, Nauru, Palau, Papua New Guinea, Saint Kitts and Nevis, Saint Lucia, Saint Vincent and the Grenadines, Samoa, São Tomé and Principe, Seychelles, Solomon Islands, Timor-Leste, Tonga, Trinidad and Tobago, Tuvalu and Vanuatu.

Note: Cross-border M&A sales and purchases are calculated on a net basis as follows: Net cross-border M&A sales in a host economy = Sales of companies in the host economy to foreign TNCs (-) Sales of foreign affiliates in the host economy; Net cross-border M&A purchases by a home economy = Purchases of companies abroad by home-based TNCs (-) Sales of foreign affiliates of home-based TNCs. The data cover only those deals that involved an acquisition of an equity stake of more than 10 per cent.

Annex table I.5. Value of cross-border M&As, by sector/industry, 2005–2011
(Millions of dollars)

Sector/industry	Net sales[a]							Net purchases[b]						
	2005	2006	2007	2008	2009	2010	2011	2005	2006	2007	2008	2009	2010	2011
Total	462 253	625 320	1 022 725	706 543	249 732	344 029	525 881	462 253	625 320	1 022 725	706 543	249 732	344 029	525 881
Primary	17 145	43 093	74 013	90 201	48 092	76 475	124 475	2 816	32 650	95 021	53 131	29 097	61 717	63 005
Agriculture, hunting, forestry and fisheries	7 499	- 152	2 422	2 898	1 033	5 576	1 635	85	2 856	887	4 240	1 476	514	- 69
Mining, quarrying and petroleum	9 647	43 245	71 591	87 303	47 059	70 899	122 840	2 731	29 794	94 134	48 891	27 622	61 203	63 074
Manufacturing	147 527	212 998	336 584	326 114	76 080	131 843	200 165	118 804	163 847	218 661	244 667	37 632	121 031	208 610
Food, beverages and tobacco	37 047	6 736	49 950	131 855	9 636	37 911	43 578	17 763	3 124	36 280	54 667	- 804	33 964	27 393
Textiles, clothing and leather	1 818	1 799	8 494	2 112	410	976	2 130	3 266	809	- 1 220	- 189	537	3 708	3 077
Wood and wood products	333	1 922	5 568	3 166	821	- 248	2 268	- 524	1 660	4 728	- 251	536	8 457	3 596
Publishing and printing	4 933	24 386	5 543	4 658	66	4 977	1 802	3 882	7 783	843	8 228	- 130	519	2 825
Coke, petroleum products and nuclear fuel	- 77	2 005	2 663	3 086	2 214	2 584	- 472	820	5 429	7 691	- 3 244	- 1 096	- 6 967	213
Chemicals and chemical products	31 709	48 035	116 736	73 563	32 559	31 774	76 426	29 069	35 192	89 397	71 293	28 861	43 987	87 749
Rubber and plastic products	2 639	6 577	7 281	1 200	15	5 974	2 379	684	5 409	658	- 235	- 197	169	1 505
Non-metallic mineral products	11 281	6 166	37 800	28 944	118	3 575	1 522	17 534	6 370	16 613	23 053	- 260	4 766	1 332
Metals and metal products	20 371	46 312	69 740	14 215	- 2 953	2 668	6 574	15 255	47 613	44 241	20 695	1 433	2 777	18 969
Machinery and equipment	1 467	17 664	20 108	15 060	2 431	7 933	14 381	6 421	14 890	- 37 504	7 868	2 635	6 027	12 728
Electrical and electronic equipment	11 938	35 305	24 483	14 151	17 763	13 592	27 564	8 305	27 908	33 644	32 401	1 880	6 096	19 514
Precision instruments	11 339	7 064	- 17 184	23 059	4 105	12 121	11 354	9 102	9 118	19 339	19 176	4 428	10 180	17 763
Motor vehicles and other transport equipment	8 524	7 475	3 099	11 608	8 753	7 437	5 370	5 827	- 2 031	3 795	10 254	- 480	6 808	9 493
Other manufacturing	4 205	1 552	2 305	- 565	141	570	5 290	1 400	574	158	951	290	539	2 455
Services	297 581	369 228	612 128	290 228	125 561	135 711	201 241	340 634	428 822	709 043	408 746	183 003	161 282	254 266
Electricity, gas and water	40 158	1 402	103 005	48 969	61 627	- 1 577	24 984	25 274	- 18 197	50 150	25 270	47 613	- 18 352	11 602
Construction	4 319	9 955	12 994	2 452	10 391	7 034	3 131	3 683	3 372	10 222	- 5 220	- 1 704	- 1 361	- 1 298
Trade	15 946	11 512	41 307	17 458	3 658	14 042	22 038	406	4 241	7 422	19 766	3 360	8 410	7 976
Hotels and restaurants	3 273	14 476	9 438	3 499	1 422	5 367	4 162	- 779	- 164	- 8 357	3 702	673	988	688
Transport, storage and communications	75 783	113 915	66 328	34 325	15 912	15 345	35 734	49 802	87 466	45 574	48 088	12 187	14 629	45 125
Finance	53 912	107 951	249 314	73 630	9 535	31 285	37 096	224 103	316 920	548 901	311 409	110 555	126 066	149 221
Business services	84 366	80 978	102 231	100 701	17 167	45 591	45 127	42 487	47 087	50 893	57 088	17 652	27 104	31 968
Public administration and defense	324	- 111	29	30	110	63	257	- 9 201	- 15 477	- 17 058	- 46 337	- 8 202	- 1 293	- 184
Education	1 474	- 429	860	1 048	559	1 676	702	1 112	122	42	155	51	111	408
Health and social services	2 293	10 624	8 140	2 222	1 123	9 238	2 310	- 2 247	506	9 493	- 176	40	3 824	648
Community, social and personal service activities	15 627	17 060	15 625	1 002	3 434	5 566	6 846	5 524	1 798	9 263	- 5 270	87	7 009	1 324
Other services	105	1 896	2 856	4 893	624	2 080	18 853	471	1 148	2 497	270	692	- 5 853	6 788

Source: UNCTAD, cross-border M&A database (www.unctad.org/fdistatistics).

[a] Net sales in the industry of the acquired company.

[b] Net purchases by the industry of the acquiring company.

Note: Cross-border M&A sales and purchases are calculated on a net basis as follows: Net cross-border M&As sales by sector/industry = Sales of companies in the industry of the acquired company to foreign TNCs (-) Sales of foreign affiliates in the industry of the acquired company; Net cross-border M&A purchases by sector/industry = Purchases of companies abroad by home-based TNCs, in the industry of the acquiring company (-) Sales of foreign affiliates of home-based TNCs, in the industry of the acquiring company. The data cover only those deals that involved an acquisition of an equity stake of more than 10 per cent.

Annex table I.6. Number of cross-border M&As, by sector/industry, 2005–2011
(Number of deals)

Sector/industry	Net sales[a]							Net purchases[b]						
	2005	2006	2007	2008	2009	2010	2011	2005	2006	2007	2008	2009	2010	2011
Total	5 004	5 747	7 018	6 425	4 239	5 484	5 769	5 004	5 747	7 018	6 425	4 239	5 484	5 769
Primary	265	413	485	486	433	595	603	199	288	350	296	221	362	383
Agriculture, hunting, forestry and fisheries	38	39	64	59	63	72	73	24	34	35	40	28	42	45
Mining, quarrying and petroleum	227	374	421	427	370	523	530	175	254	315	256	193	320	338
Manufacturing	1 522	1 688	1 993	1 976	1 153	1 523	1 613	1 367	1 523	1 872	1 850	909	1 315	1 490
Food, beverages and tobacco	158	130	213	220	109	168	217	147	110	237	180	71	125	145
Textiles, clothing and leather	41	62	56	64	39	53	50	20	39	36	22	26	42	40
Wood and wood products	40	75	78	49	26	51	73	25	37	58	52	10	43	60
Publishing and printing	96	97	90	60	37	36	51	105	110	100	72	20	37	63
Coke, petroleum products and nuclear fuel	9	21	14	20	16	18	11	9	10	16	11	4	-	- 6
Chemicals and chemical products	321	275	325	316	225	319	288	252	231	266	323	191	284	261
Rubber and plastic products	38	55	66	63	35	50	37	51	49	60	41	25	30	51
Non-metallic mineral products	76	91	130	91	22	47	34	79	102	110	92	16	24	26
Metals and metal products	146	155	218	199	95	126	155	133	162	205	224	87	140	132
Machinery and equipment	160	187	228	265	134	174	199	124	166	195	247	127	168	221
Electrical and electronic equipment	167	257	266	309	203	205	219	162	254	255	259	144	182	238
Precision instruments	148	152	155	184	109	140	134	140	159	164	203	91	120	147
Motor vehicles and other transport equipment	78	84	86	95	74	87	87	77	49	122	88	60	79	67
Other manufacturing	44	47	68	41	29	49	58	43	45	48	36	37	41	45
Services	3 217	3 646	4 539	3 962	2 653	3 366	3 553	3 438	3 936	4 796	4 279	3 109	3 807	3 896
Electricity, gas and water	97	110	135	159	130	169	147	61	75	92	155	98	65	85
Construction	99	118	149	114	96	131	113	44	55	83	73	48	57	60
Trade	441	425	588	590	324	458	486	276	354	374	352	198	270	361
Hotels and restaurants	49	101	134	123	77	111	73	14	24	56	60	26	39	39
Transport, storage and communications	351	352	436	343	211	298	292	285	304	346	260	169	221	257
Finance	484	531	712	563	458	557	518	1 492	1 661	2 121	1 887	1 728	1 925	1 653
Business services	1 402	1 651	1 972	1 681	1 109	1 329	1 573	1 188	1 331	1 545	1 305	816	1 026	1 240
Public administration and defense	10	7	10	8	13	2	13	- 81	- 84	- 77	- 72	- 86	12	- 2
Education	22	22	19	43	30	23	41	22	12	12	22	15	17	24
Health and social services	85	85	124	95	59	113	113	35	39	69	52	22	72	73
Community, social and personal service activities	149	178	197	177	116	115	127	75	111	123	127	50	70	85
Other services	28	66	63	66	30	60	57	27	54	52	58	25	33	21

Source: UNCTAD, cross-border M&A database (www.unctad.org/fdistatistics).

[a] Net sales in the industry of the acquired company.

[b] Net purchases by the industry of the acquiring company.

Note: Cross-border M&A sales and purchases are calculated on a net basis as follows: Net cross-border M&As sales by sector/industry = Sales of companies in the industry of the acquired company to foreign TNCs (-) Sales of foreign affiliates in the industry of the acquired company; Net cross-border M&A purchases by sector/industry = Purchases of companies abroad by home-based TNCs, in the industry of the acquiring company (-) Sales of foreign affiliates of home-based TNCs, in the industry of the acquiring company. The data cover only those deals that involved an acquisition of an equity stake of more than 10 per cent.

Annex table I.7. Cross-border M&A deals worth over $3 billion completed in 2011

Rank	Value ($ billion)	Acquired company	Industry of the acquired company	Host economy[a]	Acquiring company	Home economy[a]	Industry of the acquiring company	Shares acquired
1	25.1	GDF Suez Energy	Natural gas transmission	Belgium	International Power PLC	United Kingdom	Electric services	100
2	22.4	Weather Investments Srl	Telephone communications, except radiotelephone	Italy	VimpelCom Ltd	Netherlands	Radiotelephone communications	100
3	21.2	Genzyme Corp	Biological products, except diagnostic substances	United States	Sanofi-Aventis SA	France	Pharmaceutical preparations	100
4	13.7	Nycomed International Management GmbH	Pharmaceutical preparations	Switzerland	Takeda Pharmaceutical Co Ltd	Japan	Pharmaceutical preparations	100
5	11.8	Petrohawk Energy Corp	Crude petroleum and natural gas	United States	BHP Billiton PLC	United Kingdom	Steel works, blast furnaces, and rolling mills	100
6	10.8	Foster's Group Ltd	Malt beverages	Australia	SABMiller Beverage Investments Pty Ltd	Australia	Investors, nec*	100
7	9.4	Centro Properties Group	Land subdividers and developers, except cemeteries	United States	BRE Retail Holdings Inc	United States	Real estate investment trusts	100
8	9.0	Reliance Industries Ltd	Crude petroleum and natural gas	India	BP PLC	United Kingdom	Oil and gas field exploration services	30
9	8.5	Skype Global Sarl	Prepackaged software	Luxembourg	Microsoft Corp	United States	Prepackaged software	100
10	7.8	Morgan Stanley	Offices of bank holding companies	United States	Mitsubishi UFJ Financial Group Inc	Japan	Banks	22
11	7.4	Equinox Minerals Ltd	Copper ores	Australia	Barrick Canada Inc	Canada	Gold ores	98
12	7.3	Pride International Inc	Drilling oil and gas wells	United States	Ensco PLC	United Kingdom	Drilling oil and gas wells	100
13	7.2	Danisco A/S	Food preparations, nec*	Denmark	DuPont Denmark Holding ApS	Denmark	Offices of holding companies, nec*	100
14	7.1	AXA Asia Pacific Holdings Ltd	Life insurance	Australia	AMP Ltd	Australia	Investment advice	54
15	6.6	Polkomtel SA	Radiotelephone communications	Poland	Spartan Capital Holdings Sp zoo	Poland	Investment offices, nec*	100
16	6.5	Central Networks PLC	Electric services	United Kingdom	PPL Corp	United States	Electric services	100
17	6.3	Cephalon Inc	Pharmaceutical preparations	United States	Teva Pharmaceutical Industries Ltd	Israel	Pharmaceutical preparations	100
18	6.3	Chrysler Financial Corp	Personal credit institutions	United States	TD Bank NA	United States	National commercial banks	100
19	6.3	OAO "Polyus Zoloto"	Gold ores	Russian Federation	KazakhGold Group Ltd	Kazakhstan	Gold ores	73
20	6.0	AXA Asia Pacific Holdings Ltd	Life insurance	Australia	AMP Ltd	Australia	Investment advice	46
21	5.6	Bank Zachodni WBK SA	Banks	Poland	Banco Santander SA	Spain	Banks	96
22	5.5	Vivo Participacoes SA	Radiotelephone communications	Brazil	Telecommunicacoes de Sao Paulo SA	Brazil	Telephone communications, except radiotelephone	100
23	5.5	OAO "Polimetall"	Gold ores	Russian Federation	PMTL Holding Ltd	Jersey	Offices of holding companies, nec*	83
24	5.4	Anglo American Sur SA	Copper ores	Chile	Mitsubishi Corp	Japan	Chemicals and chemical preparations, nec*	25
25	5.1	Kinetic Concepts Inc	Surgical and medical instruments and apparatus	United States	Chiron Holdings Inc	United States	Investment offices, nec*	100
26	5.0	Cia Espanola de Petroleos SA	Crude petroleum and natural gas	Spain	International Petroleum Investment Co	United Arab Emirates	Investors, nec*	49
27	4.9	Macarthur Coal Ltd	Coal mining services	Australia	PEAMCoal Pty Ltd	Australia	Investment offices, nec*	100
28	4.9	Vale SA-Aluminum Operations	Iron ores	Brazil	Norsk Hydro ASA	Norway	Crude petroleum and natural gas	100
29	4.9	Shell International Petroleum Co Ltd	Industrial organic chemicals, nec*	Brazil	Cosan SA Industria e Comercio	Brazil	Petroleum and petroleum products wholesalers, nec*	100
30	4.8	AIG Star Life Insurance Co Ltd	Life insurance	Japan	Prudential Financial Inc	United States	Life insurance	100
31	4.8	Chesapeake Energy Corp.	Crude petroleum and natural gas	United States	BHP Billiton Ltd	Australia	Copper ores	100
32	4.7	Tognum AG	Internal combustion engines, nec*	Germany	Engine Holding GmbH	Germany	Investors, nec*	98
33	4.7	Nuon NV	Electric services	Netherlands	Vattenfall AB	Sweden	Electric services	15
34	4.6	Rhodia SA	Manmade organic fibers, except cellulosic	France	Solvay SA	Belgium	Plastics materials and synthetic resins	100
35	4.5	Porsche Holding GmbH	Automobiles and other motor vehicles	Austria	Volkswagen AG	Germany	Motor vehicles and passenger car bodies	100
36	4.5	Cairn India Ltd	Crude petroleum and natural gas	India	Vedanta Resources PLC	United Kingdom	Copper ores	30
37	4.5	Musketeer GmbH	Cable and other pay television services	Germany	UPC Germany HoldCo 2 GmbH	Germany	Offices of holding companies, nec*	100
38	4.4	Consolidated Thompson Iron Mines Ltd	Iron ores	Canada	Cliffs Natural Resources Inc	United States	Iron ores	100
39	4.2	OAO "Pervaya Gruzovaya Kompaniya"	Railroads, line-haul operating	Russian Federation	OOO "Nezavisimaya Transportnaya Kompaniya"	Russian Federation	Courier services, except by air	75
40	4.1	Marshall & Ilsley Corp.	National commercial banks	United States	Bank of Montreal	Canada	Banks	100
41	4.0	OAO "Novatek"	Crude petroleum and natural gas	Russian Federation	Total SA	France	Crude petroleum and natural gas	12
42	3.9	Riverdale Mining Ltd	Bituminous coal and lignite surface mining	Australia	Rio Tinto PLC	United Kingdom	Gold ores	100
43	3.9	Baldor Electric Co	Motors and generators	United States	ABB Ltd	Switzerland	Switchgear, switchboard equip	90
44	3.8	Alberto-Culver Co	Perfumes, cosmetics, and other toilet preparations	United States	Unilever PLC	United Kingdom	Food preparations, nec*	100
45	3.8	Northumbrian Water Group PLC	Water supply	United Kingdom	UK Water(2011)Ltd	United Kingdom	Investment offices, nec*	100
46	3.8	Turkiye Garanti Bankasi AS	Banks	Turkey	Banco Bilbao Vizcaya Argentaria SA	Spain	Banks	19
47	3.8	OAO "Vimm-Bill'-Dann Produkty Pitaniya"	Fluid milk	Russian Federation	Pepsi-Cola (Bermuda) Ltd	Bermuda	Bottled and canned soft drinks and carbonated waters	66

/...

Annex table I.7. Cross-border M&A deals worth over $3 billion completed in 2011 (concluded)

Rank	Value ($ billion)	Acquired company	Industry of the acquired company	Host economy[a]	Acquiring company	Home economy[a]	Industry of the acquiring company	Shares acquired
48	3.8	Universal Studios Holding III Corp	Television broadcasting stations	United States	General Electric Co	United States	Power, distribution, and specialty transformers	62
49	3.6	ING Groep NV	Insurance agents, brokers, and service	Mexico	Investor Group	Colombia	Investors, nec*	100
50	3.6	Parmalat SpA	Fluid milk	Italy	Investor Group	France	Investors, nec*	52
51	3.6	Talecris Biotherapeutics Holdings Corp	Pharmaceutical preparations	United States	Grifols SA	Spain	Pharmaceutical preparations	100
52	3.5	EMI Group PLC	Services allied to motion picture production	United Kingdom	Citigroup Inc	United States	National commercial banks	100
53	3.5	Phadia AB	Surgical and medical instruments and apparatus	Sweden	Thermo Fisher Scientific Inc	United States	Measuring and controlling devices	100
54	3.5	Frac Tech Holdings LLC	Oil and gas field services, nec*	United States	Investor Group	Singapore	Investors, nec*	70
55	3.4	Securitas Direct AB	Security systems services	Sweden	Investor Group	United States	Investors, nec*	100
56	3.3	Hutchison Essar Ltd	Telephone communications, except radiotelephone	India	Vodafone Group PLC	United Kingdom	Radiotelephone communications	22
57	3.3	GDF Suez SA	Electric services	France	China Investment Corp.	China	Management investment offices, open-end	30
58	3.2	Converteam Group SAS	Motors and generators	France	GE Energy	United States	Turbines and turbine generator sets	90
59	3.1	Distribuidora Internacional de Alimentacion SA	Grocery stores	Spain	Shareholders	France	Investors, nec*	100
60	3.1	Peregrino Project,Campos Basin	Crude petroleum and natural gas	Brazil	Sinochem Group	China	Crude petroleum and natural gas	40
61	3.0	SPIE SA	Electrical work	France	Investor Group	United States	Investors, nec*	100
62	3.0	Global Crossing Ltd	Telephone communications, except radiotelephone	Bermuda	Level 3 Communications Inc	United States	Telephone communications, except radiotelephone	100

Source: UNCTAD, cross-border M&A database (www.unctad.org/fdistatistics).

[a] Immediate country.

Note: As long as the ultimate host economy is different from the ultimate home economy, M&A deals that were undertaken within the same economy are still considered cross-border M&As.

*nec: not elsewhere classified.

Annex table I.8. Value of greenfield FDI projects, by source/destination, 2005–2011
(Millions of dollars)

Partner region/economy	World as destination							World as source						
	2005	2006	2007	2008	2009	2010	2011	2005	2006	2007	2008	2009	2010	2011
	By source							By destination						
World	754 910	989 581	1 015 738	1 634 445	1 051 581	904 572	904 267	754 910	989 581	1 015 738	1 634 445	1 051 581	904 572	904 267
Developed countries	556 165	682 052	707 083	1 158 675	754 286	643 504	643 490	227 335	341 045	326 894	500 831	322 951	300 648	276 430
Europe	283 395	382 083	448 394	656 225	453 182	390 052	358 571	152 523	231 878	234 898	342 018	203 207	169 146	171 000
European Union	265 649	353 310	407 715	602 953	420 083	358 467	331 944	148 967	228 029	229 275	332 341	197 220	162 541	167 295
Austria	9 438	18 330	14 784	24 308	10 057	9 309	8 158	3 616	2 096	3 166	3 028	1 717	2 289	4 123
Belgium	3 615	3 854	7 332	14 420	8 872	5 729	5 928	4 690	4 936	10 519	10 797	3 796	6 060	3 121
Bulgaria	116	84	81	258	30	147	121	4 387	19 330	7 695	11 422	4 780	4 780	5 300
Cyprus	349	368	393	249	856	536	4 379	126	390	465	629	249	720	385
Czech Republic	819	1 584	5 159	4 582	1 686	2 200	1 939	5 098	7 677	7 491	5 684	4 575	7 733	4 910
Denmark	9 445	4 589	7 342	14 861	10 169	4 635	8 275	1 663	1 697	2 047	1 968	2 195	457	780
Estonia	708	1 131	2 656	556	188	1 088	352	2 032	954	840	1 481	1 260	947	883
Finland	9 062	9 889	13 189	11 139	3 660	4 351	5 804	1 485	1 797	1 269	2 415	1 208	1 661	2 180
France	34 215	50 280	57 751	92 633	66 125	52 956	49 747	11 486	18 554	19 435	24 349	11 410	9 140	10 569
Germany	56 251	74 440	79 609	103 347	75 729	71 884	70 841	13 464	18 028	18 562	36 871	20 039	17 108	15 325
Greece	1 208	2 309	1 700	5 553	1 802	1 300	1 448	915	1 706	5 096	5 278	2 090	1 123	2 372
Hungary	2 412	1 067	2 914	4 956	3 389	431	1 135	7 850	8 784	9 550	9 003	4 665	7 566	3 212
Ireland	4 144	9 347	8 998	18 164	15 015	5 698	4 674	9 224	6 575	4 680	8 265	4 948	4 487	7 020
Italy	16 875	16 390	26 973	44 945	30 168	23 545	23 117	8 054	11 710	11 915	14 513	10 501	11 366	5 623
Latvia	322	1 001	284	660	761	821	279	1 623	3 248	717	2 550	828	965	717
Lithuania	1 083	3 387	303	723	305	252	158	1 448	1 306	1 485	1 518	1 232	1 558	7 285
Luxembourg	2 183	11 847	11 373	13 635	10 904	6 865	9 422	89	228	685	431	759	731	290
Malta	132	7	68	212	773	12	40	154	880	299	395	467	300	174
Netherlands	27 974	36 857	25 810	40 821	32 825	20 612	17 452	4 176	4 942	5 828	9 438	9 459	10 959	5 620
Poland	613	1 292	2 999	2 968	1 235	2 656	924	14 243	15 651	22 803	35 208	14 548	11 446	12 620
Portugal	1 153	1 815	4 522	11 159	7 180	5 015	2 124	1 005	4 381	10 945	7 763	4 932	2 665	1 701
Romania	152	152	150	4 257	131	708	128	11 469	19 251	21 959	32 596	15 019	7 774	16 188
Slovakia	10	296	474	135	393	1 314	277	9 108	11 557	5 485	3 350	5 382	4 242	5 676
Slovenia	812	1 811	683	1 658	586	536	356	476	657	1 037	612	282	748	658
Spain	12 666	27 752	37 632	49 628	41 724	40 477	29 225	10 382	21 157	23 589	31 572	15 993	16 372	11 343
Sweden	9 992	12 141	11 949	22 527	15 502	14 928	13 775	3 059	7 037	4 391	2 982	2 879	2 364	3 081
United Kingdom	59 901	61 290	82 586	114 598	80 018	80 461	71 865	17 641	33 500	27 321	68 224	52 008	26 983	36 140
Other developed Europe	17 746	28 773	40 679	53 273	33 099	31 585	26 627	3 556	3 848	5 623	9 676	5 988	6 605	3 704
Iceland	432	3 980	1 545	568	123	633	433	2	186	53	1 077	-	705	203
Liechtenstein	74	101	74	110	132	111	59	30	-	131	8	-	9	-
Norway	6 831	4 437	11 867	13 223	10 619	5 433	6 619	1 853	915	795	3 200	2 334	2 236	830
Switzerland	10 410	20 256	27 193	39 371	22 225	25 408	19 516	1 671	2 747	4 644	5 391	3 654	3 655	2 672
North America	200 924	186 441	156 384	351 292	205 010	166 171	189 443	53 458	54 174	58 725	114 580	87 613	82 058	84 546
Canada	45 599	15 351	16 562	80 315	30 930	20 006	31 729	17 056	15 507	8 632	20 541	14 084	18 913	27 197
United States	155 324	171 089	139 821	270 977	174 079	146 165	157 714	36 402	38 666	50 094	94 039	73 529	63 145	57 349
Other developed countries	71 846	113 529	102 305	151 158	96 094	87 282	95 476	21 355	54 993	33 271	44 233	32 131	49 444	20 884
Australia	16 065	18 158	18 974	31 952	18 422	12 433	14 575	9 109	37 695	22 828	30 062	19 990	41 186	12 137
Bermuda	916	1 309	4 123	4 000	8 116	1 572	1 198	34	23	48	-	1	165	6
Greenland	24	-	214	35	-	-	-	-	-	-	-	-	457	-
Israel	3 066	10 250	4 347	16 025	2 755	6 618	3 179	4 757	914	457	853	3 333	856	697
Japan	51 635	83 141	74 110	98 536	65 798	65 888	75 551	6 375	14 599	7 762	11 287	8 240	6 400	6 089
New Zealand	140	671	537	611	1 004	770	972	1 081	1 762	2 177	2 030	568	380	1 956
Developing economies	171 033	287 371	283 969	442 158	277 061	239 492	242 811	462 111	587 234	600 709	1 007 585	670 185	547 991	568 376
Africa	4 911	7 347	8 497	16 467	15 279	16 662	16 551	89 673	106 123	95 396	230 542	95 274	88 918	82 315
North Africa	2 301	3 799	4 439	7 109	2 396	3 295	745	42 780	71 111	54 901	112 454	41 499	26 535	13 660
Algeria	-	30	60	2 522	16	-	130	15 113	11 243	13 771	21 506	2 380	1 716	1 127
Egypt	2 081	3 534	3 680	3 498	1 828	3 190	76	14 392	28 032	13 480	20 456	20 678	14 154	6 244
Libya	30	-	-	-	19	-	-	5 631	20 992	4 061	23 056	1 689	1 858	49
Morocco	147	81	50	619	393	58	87	4 442	6 614	5 113	18 925	6 189	4 217	4 344
South Sudan	-	-	-	-	-	-	-	19	578	19	1 181	54	139	235
Sudan	-	9	42	-	-	-	432	1 661	639	-	1 612	2 025	2 440	58
Tunisia	43	144	609	471	140	47	21	1 523	3 012	18 458	25 718	8 484	2 010	1 602
Other Africa	2 610	3 548	4 057	9 357	12 883	13 367	15 806	46 894	35 012	40 495	118 088	53 774	62 384	68 655
Angola	-	-	39	78	-	494	-	580	2 675	8 138	11 204	5 542	1 148	312
Benin	-	-	-	-	-	-	-	-	-	-	9	-	14	46
Botswana	-	108	-	-	11	9	138	183	909	344	2 220	349	660	492
Burkina Faso	-	-	-	-	-	-	-	549	-	9	281	272	479	165
Burundi	-	-	-	-	-	-	-	-	-	-	19	47	25	41
Cameroon	9	-	-	-	19	-	-	900	799	2 460	351	1 155	5 289	4 272
Cape Verde	-	-	-	-	-	-	-	-	-	9	128	-	38	62
Central African Republic	-	-	-	-	-	-	-	-	-	361			-	-
Chad	-	-	-	-	-	-	-	-	-	-	1 819	402	-	135
Comoros	-	-	-	-	-	-	-	-	-	9	9	-	-	7
Congo	-	-	-	-	-	-	-	-	-	198	9	1 281	-	37
Congo, Democratic Republic of	-	-	-	161	-	7	-	2 800	1 880	1 238	3 294	43	1 238	2 242
Côte d'Ivoire	28	9	-	13	10	19	-	829	359	71	372	131	261	937
Djibouti	-	-	-	-	-	-	-	300	521	5	1 555	1 245	1 255	-
Equatorial Guinea	-	-	-	-	-	-	-	-	110	-	6	3 119	9	1 881

/...

Annex table I.8. Value of greenfield FDI projects, by source/destination, 2005–2011 (continued)
(Millions of dollars)

Partner region/economy	World as destination (By source)							World as source (By destination)						
	2005	2006	2007	2008	2009	2010	2011	2005	2006	2007	2008	2009	2010	2011
Eritrea	-	-	-	3	-	-	-	1 088	30	-	-	-	-	-
Ethiopia	-	-	-	18	12	-	-	20	1 508	2 389	762	321	290	630
Gabon	-	-	-	-	-	-	9	2 227	1 727	328	5 118	927	1 231	219
Gambia	-	-	-	-	-	-	-	351	83	9	31	31	405	26
Ghana	-	-	-	-	7	15	51	4 939	1 240	141	4 918	7 059	2 654	6 077
Guinea	-	-	-	-	-	-	-	58	304	-	-	61	1 411	548
Guinea-Bissau	-	-	-	-	-	-	-	-	-	361	-	19	-	-
Kenya	39	82	19	596	222	3 893	421	275	174	332	549	3 716	1 382	2 855
Lesotho	-	-	-	-	-	-	-	-	-	51	16	28	51	710
Liberia	-	-	-	-	-	-	-	909	-	-	2 600	821	4 591	287
Madagascar	-	27	-	-	-	-	-	381	246	3 335	1 325	365	-	140
Malawi	-	-	-	9	9	-	-	-	-	-	19	713	314	454
Mali	-	-	-	19	10	19	9	657	401	-	172	59	13	0
Mauritania	-	-	-	-	-	-	-	1 177	579	37	272	-	59	279
Mauritius	2	-	38	307	1 809	2 642	3 287	78	15	481	317	147	71	1 749
Mozambique	-	-	-	-	-	-	-	-	637	2 100	12 100	1 539	3 278	9 971
Namibia	-	23	-	23	-	-	-	961	32	473	1 907	1 519	390	832
Niger	-	-	-	-	-	-	-	-	1	-	3 319	-	100	277
Nigeria	23	465	202	2 517	659	1 020	1 046	19 005	11 074	4 213	36 134	7 978	14 080	4 445
Reunion	-	-	-	-	-	-	-	-	13	-	-	-	-	-
Rwanda	-	-	-	-	26	-	-	19	-	283	252	312	1 839	779
São Tomé and Principe	-	-	-	-	-	-	-	9	-	2	351	-	-	-
Senegal	-	-	-	-	-	-	10	25	1 262	3 008	1 281	548	883	69
Seychelles	-	-	-	-	-	-	-	81	-	1 425	130	1	121	9
Sierra Leone	-	-	-	-	-	-	-	583	280	-	73	260	230	153
Somalia	-	-	-	-	-	-	-	-	351	-	361	-	59	-
South Africa	2 469	2 834	3 693	4 841	9 820	5 146	10 592	3 658	5 085	5 247	13 533	7 695	6 805	12 410
Swaziland	-	-	-	-	-	-	-	179	-	-	23	12	-	646
Togo	9	-	49	94	142	34	214	-	323	351	146	26	-	-
Uganda	30	-	9	40	28	9	-	69	373	291	3 057	2 147	8 505	2 466
United Republic of Tanzania	-	-	9	9	57	49	27	1 700	294	317	2 492	623	1 077	3 806
Zambia	-	-	-	-	9	-	-	2 240	1 596	422	4 576	2 375	1 376	2 366
Zimbabwe	-	-	-	629	34	10	-	65	133	2 057	979	889	754	5 825
Asia	148 419	270 277	261 931	401 980	243 819	201 061	205 253	286 216	407 885	428 518	626 449	447 272	336 680	344 093
East and South-East Asia	75 301	92 053	148 290	168 200	130 890	143 094	125 466	160 105	208 468	290 952	338 091	264 717	213 770	206 924
East Asia	56 327	65 095	100 992	114 753	90 451	106 899	97 077	112 212	143 676	159 404	155 649	135 543	119 264	119 816
China	10 009	17 490	32 765	51 477	30 512	32 880	39 718	93 917	127 325	110 419	130 518	116 765	98 406	100 696
Hong Kong, China	7 434	12 390	19 814	16 986	17 468	8 238	13 024	4 533	5 168	4 742	7 164	9 074	8 187	7 008
Korea, Democratic People's Republic of	-	-	-	-	-	-	-	-	236	560	533	228	-	59
Korea, Republic of	25 599	24 935	29 623	34 785	30 596	37 485	32 439	8 262	7 314	9 129	11 828	4 583	3 601	7 037
Macao, China	-	-	-	2	-	-	-	459	126	4 899	909	310	282	430
Mongolia	-	-	-	-	-	150	-	1 500	216	448	330	302	1 608	183
Taiwan Province of China	13 284	10 280	18 789	11 503	11 875	28 147	11 896	3 540	3 291	29 206	4 367	4 280	7 179	4 403
South-East Asia	18 974	26 958	47 298	53 447	40 438	36 195	28 389	47 893	64 792	131 547	182 441	129 174	94 506	87 108
Brunei Darussalam	15	-	-	77	-	-	2	133	-	721	435	470	156	7 669
Cambodia	-	-	-	51	149	-	-	248	1 240	261	3 581	3 895	1 759	2 365
Indonesia	4 502	800	1 824	393	1 043	415	5 037	13 294	14 351	20 512	41 929	31 271	13 740	24 031
Lao People's Democratic Republic	-	-	-	192	-	-	-	490	567	1 371	1 151	2 118	335	980
Malaysia	6 410	5 806	25 583	19 988	14 904	21 319	4 140	4 294	5 242	10 306	24 054	13 753	15 541	13 621
Myanmar	-	-	20	-	-	-	84	2	299	1 378	1 434	1 889	449	667
Philippines	214	367	1 550	563	1 410	1 782	257	3 845	5 322	19 517	15 800	9 719	4 645	2 902
Singapore	6 358	12 125	14 526	21 444	12 985	8 631	12 844	7 165	14 160	23 722	13 995	12 940	16 960	20 384
Thailand	907	3 092	3 149	7 936	8 298	3 128	4 385	6 134	5 592	7 427	15 122	7 678	8 641	4 117
Timor-Leste	-	-	-	-	-	-	-	10	-	-	-	-	1 000	-
Viet Nam	568	4 768	647	2 804	1 651	920	1 643	12 280	18 018	46 333	64 942	45 442	31 280	10 372
South Asia	14 212	38 499	31 886	43 644	30 196	20 777	35 593	48 060	112 160	68 232	97 542	77 147	62 899	68 019
Afghanistan	-	5	-	-	-	-	8	181	36	6	269	2 978	634	305
Bangladesh	209	56	-	72	37	103	109	1 653	703	170	860	645	2 720	490
Bhutan	-	-	-	-	-	-	-	-	-	74	-	135	83	86
India	12 906	31 650	25 679	40 792	24 308	19 912	34 621	30 240	86 147	54 002	80 588	57 170	51 956	58 273
Iran, Islamic Republic of	301	889	6 137	1 531	5 743	535	515	1 381	1 100	8 217	6 911	9 133	3 034	1 812
Maldives	-	-	-	-	-	-	-	-	1 029	206	462	453	2 162	1 012
Nepal	-	-	-	2	-	6	31	-	110	3	740	295	340	128
Pakistan	367	130	40	1 220	42	153	227	14 159	22 086	4 939	6 390	3 955	1 255	2 397
Sri Lanka	429	5 769	29	27	66	68	82	445	875	689	1 323	2 383	714	3 515

/...

Annex table I.8. Value of greenfield FDI projects, by source/destination, 2005–2011 (continued)
(Millions of dollars)

Partner region/economy	World as destination							World as source						
	2005	2006	2007	2008	2009	2010	2011	2005	2006	2007	2008	2009	2010	2011
	By source							By destination						
West Asia	58 907	139 725	81 755	190 137	82 733	37 190	44 194	78 051	87 256	69 334	190 817	105 408	60 011	69 151
Bahrain	8 580	21 934	8 995	21 015	14 771	1 162	1 019	1 972	5 911	834	8 050	2 036	1 997	3 899
Iraq	82	-	42	-	20	-	48	1 464	8 334	474	28 482	12 849	5 486	10 590
Jordan	162	164	244	2 627	1 650	591	52	2 121	4 770	1 250	12 882	2 506	2 824	3 250
Kuwait	9 314	17 519	4 444	16 108	4 585	2 850	4 502	581	1 922	373	2 256	987	673	491
Lebanon	904	5 493	596	6 706	561	226	223	864	2 060	428	1 292	1 772	1 632	609
Oman	-	-	87	84	3 110	39	158	2 791	3 209	1 794	10 954	5 608	4 248	8 043
Palestinian Territory	-	300	-	-	-	-	-	-	76	52	1 050	16	15	-
Qatar	195	1 682	2 472	10 072	13 663	2 891	13 044	11 674	5 388	1 368	19 006	21 524	6 334	4 341
Saudi Arabia	6 568	6 787	2 089	13 980	6 105	1 441	5 027	7 227	20 205	26 630	42 318	14 860	10 332	14 722
Syrian Arab Republic	-	-	-	326	59	-	193	18 580	2 535	3 354	6 052	3 379	2 165	1 315
Turkey	3 703	1 941	2 399	4 464	4 068	4 031	4 937	4 569	14 568	14 655	17 120	23 859	10 417	10 299
United Arab Emirates	29 400	83 905	60 387	114 705	34 142	23 958	14 991	24 233	17 947	17 776	37 422	15 052	12 869	11 581
Yemen	-	-	-	49	-	2	-	1 976	332	347	3 933	961	1 019	11
Latin America and the Caribbean	17 703	9 130	13 541	23 636	17 942	21 754	20 655	86 172	72 642	72 561	144 298	125 461	120 113	138 680
South America	16 428	7 106	9 925	20 896	14 540	18 710	10 467	69 753	49 324	43 230	95 925	88 828	92 507	104 718
Argentina	50	918	628	470	1 118	1 284	905	3 146	10 665	6 403	7 193	9 217	7 112	12 416
Bolivia, Plurinational State of	-	-	-	-	-	-	-	343	2 444	1 449	789	1 947	797	305
Brazil	3 232	3 632	5 771	15 773	10 236	10 431	4 583	35 783	15 459	18 988	46 994	44 515	44 007	62 916
Chile	1 012	476	2 256	855	1 758	2 564	1 558	5 349	4 365	3 093	9 360	13 596	8 374	13 808
Colombia	-	53	139	500	102	3 390	1 020	2 718	2 458	3 985	9 781	2 945	10 614	8 616
Ecuador	10	34	89	67	330	166	60	3 066	1 065	518	511	348	132	475
Guyana	-	-	-	-	-	-	-	563	412	10	1 000	12	160	15
Paraguay	-	-	-	-	-	-	-	9	-	607	378	83	3 873	108
Peru	5	8	315	17	108	25	380	7 083	6 908	2 974	11 259	14 331	11 956	4 074
Suriname	-	-	-	-	-	-	-	-	-	-	101	-	-	384
Uruguay	-	-	25	3	49	3	5	501	2 413	2 910	4 381	504	750	1 030
Venezuela, Bolivarian Republic of	12 120	1 985	702	3 211	840	847	1 956	11 190	3 135	2 293	4 179	1 331	4 732	571
Central America	512	1 757	2 883	1 196	2 459	2 869	9 752	10 128	19 231	26 812	41 333	32 910	19 895	25 518
Belize	-	-	-	-	-	-	5	-	-	-	-	3	5	-
Costa Rica	3	-	95	6	45	63	10	746	796	2 161	582	2 427	1 981	3 364
El Salvador	-	-	102	-	281	147	20	78	765	355	562	716	276	462
Guatemala	42	-	79	58	131	86	125	357	67	982	905	1 330	963	209
Honduras	18	57	61	-	-	-	-	163	59	951	1 089	126	226	551
Mexico	429	1 682	2 447	990	1 923	2 101	9 431	7 598	16 863	19 055	34 896	25 040	14 679	18 644
Nicaragua	-	-	54	67	-	251	-	81	163	62	185	877	280	274
Panama	20	18	47	75	80	220	161	1 106	518	3 248	3 114	2 391	1 485	2 013
Caribbean	763	267	733	1 544	944	175	436	6 291	4 088	2 519	7 039	3 723	7 712	8 445
Antigua and Barbuda	-	-	-	-	-	-	-	-	-	-	82	-	-	-
Aruba	-	-	-	-	-	-	-	790	-	-	64	-	6	25
Bahamas	390	5	19	18	42	-	2	52	-	18	61	5	64	333
Barbados	-	-	2	-	-	5	26	-	-	-	-	29	137	303
Cayman Islands	311	57	166	554	853	52	243	51	66	36	326	104	253	349
Cuba	-	-	-	77	-	-	21	915	450	127	2 703	1 015	6 067	465
Dominican Republic	10	-	498	-	30	25	-	1 496	827	749	2 044	1 399	330	5 143
Grenada	-	-	-	-	-	-	-	-	-	3	-	-	5	5
Guadeloupe	-	-	-	-	-	-	-	-	25	-	267	-	-	25
Haiti	-	-	-	-	-	9	-	34	164	-	2	110	59	376
Jamaica	-	205	2	889	17	33	127	260	369	29	317	41	23	491
Martinique	-	-	-	-	-	13	-	-	25	35	-	6	-	-
Puerto Rico	-	-	20	6	4	36	18	454	621	713	739	716	570	752
Saint Lucia	18	-	-	-	-	-	-	-	-	12	-	3	144	64
Saint Vincent and the Grenadines	-	-	-	-	-	-	-	34	-	-	-	-	-	-
Trinidad and Tobago	34	1	26	-	-	3	-	2 208	1 542	797	372	296	22	114
Turks and Caicos Islands	-	-	-	-	-	-	-	-	-	-	64	-	34	-
Oceania	-	618	-	76	20	16	351	49	584	4 234	6 296	2 179	2 279	3 287
Fiji	-	-	-	-	2	8	-	-	228	206	117	339	-	179
French Polynesia	-	-	-	-	10	-	-	-	-	-	-	-	108	-
Micronesia, Federated States of	-	18	-	-	-	-	-	-	98	-	-	-	-	-
New Caledonia	-	-	-	-	-	-	202	42	-	3 800	3 200	22	-	8
Papua New Guinea	-	-	-	73	-	8	149	8	259	228	2 438	1 786	1 944	3 050
Samoa	-	600	-	2	-	-	-	-	-	-	500	-	-	-
Solomon Islands	-	-	-	-	8	-	-	-	-	-	42	32	228	51

/...

Annex table I.8. Value of greenfield FDI projects, by source/destination, 2005–2011 (concluded)

(Millions of dollars)

Partner region/economy	World as destination							World as source						
	2005	2006	2007	2008	2009	2010	2011	2005	2006	2007	2008	2009	2010	2011
	By source							By destination						
Transition economies	27 711	20 157	24 686	33 612	20 235	21 575	17 967	65 463	61 302	88 135	126 029	58 445	55 934	59 461
South-East Europe	485	486	2 940	3 920	472	1 556	307	5 473	8 662	14 303	21 362	8 178	7 638	9 261
Albania	-	-	-	-	-	105	-	668	2 346	4 454	3 505	124	68	488
Bosnia and Herzegovina	64	-	-	7	-	16	2	2 243	643	2 623	1 993	1 368	283	1 252
Croatia	421	314	2 909	3 261	146	1 071	105	1 080	600	1 795	3 194	1 707	2 397	1 788
Montenegro	-	-	-	-	-	7	-	-	344	1 794	851	120	380	436
Serbia	-	173	31	651	314	356	150	1 181	3 270	3 131	9 197	4 095	4 040	4 341
The former Yugoslav Republic of Macedonia	-	-	-	-	12	1	49	302	1 460	505	2 622	763	470	956
CIS	27 226	19 671	21 746	29 610	19 714	19 964	17 485	58 825	51 660	72 496	101 852	45 868	47 279	48 209
Armenia	45	2	-	51	-	9	83	452	366	2 463	690	1 003	265	805
Azerbaijan	260	75	4 307	1 223	3 779	580	435	1 611	953	2 002	2 921	1 980	701	1 289
Belarus	47	157	76	1 323	391	2 091	127	887	923	531	2 477	1 134	1 888	1 268
Kazakhstan	461	230	66	379	706	600	383	3 152	4 176	4 251	20 468	1 949	2 536	7 993
Kyrgyzstan	4	-	-	60	30	-	-	179	81	3 362	539	50	-	358
Moldova, Republic of	-	-	-	557	-	-	0	451	130	162	163	488	301	320
Russian Federation	26 125	16 134	15 454	23 280	13 096	15 466	15 503	42 137	39 271	50 144	61 607	31 298	34 658	22 522
Tajikistan	-	-	-	82	10	-	-	1 157	43	327	226	570	3	1 076
Turkmenistan	-	-	-	-	-	-	-	12	11	1 051	3 974	1 433	458	1 926
Ukraine	284	3 073	1 842	2 656	1 703	1 218	954	7 276	4 972	7 185	7 686	4 546	4 061	3 092
Uzbekistan	-	-	-	-	-	-	-	1 513	734	1 017	1 101	1 418	2 408	7 560
Georgia	-	-	-	82	49	56	174	1 165	980	1 336	2 816	4 398	1 017	1 991
Memorandum														
Least developed countries[a]	248	697	168	798	487	732	923	19 767	17 617	26 251	65 523	36 001	39 714	33 304
Landlocked developing countries[b]	801	420	4 383	3 259	4 675	1 394	1 137	15 332	16 323	25 233	53 874	25 437	29 217	39 360
Small island developing states[c]	444	829	87	1 290	1 877	2 698	3 591	2 739	3 539	3 425	5 325	3 132	5 957	7 429

Source: UNCTAD, based on information from the Financial Times Ltd, fDi Markets (www.fDimarkets.com).

[a] Least developed countries include Afghanistan, Angola, Bangladesh, Benin, Bhutan, Burkina Faso, Burundi, Cambodia, the Central African Republic, Chad, the Comoros, the Democratic Republic of the Congo, Djibouti, Equatorial Guinea, Eritrea, Ethiopia, the Gambia, Guinea, Guinea-Bissau, Haiti, Kiribati, the Lao People's Democratic Republic, Lesotho, Liberia, Madagascar, Malawi, Mali, Mauritania, Mozambique, Myanmar, Nepal, Niger, Rwanda, Samoa, São Tomé and Principe, Senegal, Sierra Leone, Solomon Islands, Somalia, Sudan, Timor-Leste, Togo, Tuvalu, Uganda, the United Republic of Tanzania, Vanuatu, Yemen and Zambia.

[b] Landlocked developing countries include Afghanistan, Armenia, Azerbaijan, Bhutan, the Plurinational State of Bolivia, Botswana, Burkina Faso, Burundi, the Central African Republic, Chad, Ethiopia, Kazakhstan, Kyrgyzstan, the Lao People's Democratic Republic, Lesotho, the former Yugoslav Republic of Macedonia, Malawi, Mali, the Republic of Moldova, Mongolia, Nepal, Niger, Paraguay, Rwanda, Swaziland, the Republic of Tajikistan, Turkmenistan, Uganda, Uzbekistan, Zambia and Zimbabwe.

[c] Small island developing countries include Antigua and Barbuda, the Bahamas, Barbados, Cape Verde, the Comoros, Dominica, Fiji, Grenada, Jamaica, Kiribati, Maldives, the Marshall Islands, Mauritius, the Federated States of Micronesia, Nauru, Palau, Papua New Guinea, Saint Kitts and Nevis, Saint Lucia, Saint Vincent and the Grenadines, Samoa, São Tomé and Principe, Seychelles, Solomon Islands, Timor-Leste, Tonga, Trinidad and Tobago, Tuvalu and Vanuatu.

Note: Data refer to estimated amounts of capital investment.

Annex table I.9. Number of greenfield FDI projects, by source/destination, 2005–2011

Partner region/economy	World as destination							World as source						
	2005	2006	2007	2008	2009	2010	2011	2005	2006	2007	2008	2009	2010	2011
	By source							By destination						
World	10 874	12 868	13 065	17 307	14 763	15 131	15 638	10 874	12 868	13 065	17 307	14 763	15 131	15 638
Developed countries	9 329	10 778	11 010	14 203	12 140	12 309	12 715	5 293	6 417	6 732	7 934	6 923	7 435	7 287
Europe	5 097	6 188	6 784	8 499	7 480	7 390	7 331	4 174	5 073	5 163	6 070	4 843	4 999	4 704
European Union	4 753	5 725	6 296	7 771	6 884	6 740	6 733	4 072	4 937	4 962	5 833	4 668	4 840	4 541
Austria	223	258	256	294	211	234	192	107	91	111	114	74	87	105
Belgium	133	153	199	225	145	151	143	164	136	216	184	111	147	101
Bulgaria	6	6	7	13	4	12	6	136	290	154	157	108	126	94
Cyprus	5	12	8	10	17	23	20	5	17	8	18	10	17	9
Czech Republic	22	42	33	54	12	39	39	154	190	155	152	129	187	167
Denmark	159	145	142	191	215	141	163	78	71	68	68	37	36	38
Estonia	25	44	41	27	15	11	17	64	56	32	44	26	27	29
Finland	188	197	186	214	138	139	140	36	46	41	40	25	43	76
France	656	736	944	1 109	1 013	853	806	508	602	605	724	429	390	335
Germany	1 053	1 299	1 347	1 541	1 384	1 420	1 465	291	383	469	744	715	784	611
Greece	39	65	64	78	28	28	34	31	31	41	51	43	26	36
Hungary	12	22	30	30	23	21	25	204	251	222	159	114	153	151
Ireland	77	108	110	151	173	159	184	192	144	119	184	177	190	228
Italy	339	315	372	533	465	418	371	143	162	202	253	181	203	142
Latvia	13	25	15	19	9	18	12	85	111	33	53	29	23	20
Lithuania	54	66	13	19	12	16	9	76	60	48	51	35	43	39
Luxembourg	27	37	102	96	89	90	139	3	15	27	20	16	29	18
Malta	4	3	3	4	3	4	3	9	12	9	9	17	15	13
Netherlands	249	376	328	489	430	429	405	120	147	142	181	167	160	201
Poland	29	41	48	48	40	48	34	274	347	360	407	246	313	301
Portugal	24	30	69	104	65	71	62	34	61	85	84	58	57	36
Romania	13	13	13	29	13	14	8	265	389	389	368	212	232	248
Slovakia	1	4	2	7	2	7	5	120	119	109	89	63	102	91
Slovenia	42	49	27	31	20	23	24	20	24	23	24	12	26	18
Spain	220	282	519	658	654	641	598	179	321	471	595	410	413	341
Sweden	277	295	314	356	328	346	313	106	127	89	91	101	70	76
United Kingdom	863	1 102	1 104	1 441	1 376	1 384	1 516	668	734	734	969	1 123	941	1 017
Other developed Europe	344	463	488	728	596	650	598	102	136	201	237	175	159	163
Iceland	14	31	27	12	4	9	13	1	5	1	3	-	4	2
Liechtenstein	4	4	3	7	4	6	4	1	-	2	1	-	2	-
Norway	92	104	84	124	117	101	117	20	23	25	47	33	32	31
Switzerland	234	324	374	585	471	534	464	80	108	173	186	142	121	130
North America	3 186	3 421	3 198	4 083	3 469	3 610	3 991	826	973	1 122	1 316	1 579	1 847	2 036
Canada	413	258	288	356	347	317	445	213	187	181	238	272	329	325
United States	2 773	3 163	2 910	3 727	3 122	3 293	3 546	613	786	941	1 078	1 307	1 518	1 711
Other developed countries	1 046	1 169	1 028	1 621	1 191	1 309	1 393	293	371	447	548	501	589	547
Australia	146	146	149	214	175	181	221	123	145	199	253	267	338	320
Bermuda	24	44	43	66	52	41	27	1	2	4	-	1	2	1
Greenland	1	-	1	1	-	-	-	-	-	-	-	-	2	-
Israel	55	101	66	122	67	84	72	23	34	21	44	23	30	40
Japan	807	851	746	1 187	856	963	1 020	127	166	196	216	179	190	137
New Zealand	13	27	23	31	41	40	53	19	24	27	35	31	27	49
Developing economies	1 365	1 866	1 859	2 793	2 377	2 548	2 678	4 657	5 644	5 495	8 135	6 970	6 761	7 469
Africa	73	94	73	207	188	164	215	460	474	418	899	747	674	859
North Africa	24	30	19	46	39	34	19	212	207	202	379	270	224	234
Algeria	-	1	2	3	1	-	3	47	51	34	77	32	20	25
Egypt	13	19	10	24	14	25	6	48	58	55	88	108	75	51
Libya	1	-	-	-	2	-	-	15	12	21	43	17	17	5
Morocco	4	5	3	5	14	4	5	58	48	59	99	49	55	93
South Sudan	-	-	-	-	-	-	-	2	3	2	6	6	4	15
Sudan	-	1	1	-	-	-	2	8	8	-	7	6	·5	5
Tunisia	6	4	3	14	8	5	3	34	27	31	59	52	48	40
Other Africa	49	64	54	161	149	130	196	248	267	216	520	477	450	625
Angola	-	-	2	4	-	4	-	17	18	27	49	54	45	37
Benin	-	-	-	-	-	-	-	-	-	-	1	-	1	1
Botswana	-	4	-	-	2	1	13	5	4	7	17	13	8	14
Burkina Faso	-	-	-	-	-	-	-	3	-	1	2	1	3	4
Burundi	-	-	-	-	-	-	-	-	-	-	2	5	3	3
Cameroon	1	-	-	-	2	-	-	1	1	1	3	8	3	9
Cape Verde	-	-	-	-	-	-	-	-	-	1	2	-	4	1
Central African Republic	-	-	-	-	-	-	-	-	-	2	-	-	-	-
Chad	-	-	-	-	-	-	-	-	-	-	1	2	-	3
Comoros	-	-	-	-	-	-	-	-	-	1	1	-	-	1
Congo	-	-	-	-	-	-	-	-	-	1	1	3	-	2
Congo, Democratic Republic of	-	-	-	2	-	1	-	10	8	5	15	5	9	12
Côte d'Ivoire	3	1	-	2	2	2	-	2	2	2	5	8	9	4
Djibouti	-	-	-	-	-	-	-	1	2	1	3	2	3	-
Equatorial Guinea	-	-	-	-	-	-	-	-	3	-	1	2	2	6
Eritrea	-	-	-	1	-	-	-	4	1	-	-	-	-	-

/...

Annex table I.9. Number of greenfield FDI projects, by source/destination, 2005–2011 (continued)

Partner region/economy	World as destination							World as source						
	2005	2006	2007	2008	2009	2010	2011	2005	2006	2007	2008	2009	2010	2011
	By source							By destination						
Ethiopia	-	-	-	2	1	-	-	1	3	10	10	8	8	20
Gabon	-	-	-	-	-	-	1	4	3	3	6	4	5	3
Gambia	-	-	-	-	-	-	-	1	2	1	3	3	3	1
Ghana	-	-	-	-	1	2	5	17	17	5	20	27	25	46
Guinea	-	-	-	-	-	-	-	2	3	-	-	2	3	4
Guinea-Bissau	-	-	-	-	-	-	-	-	-	2	-	2	-	-
Kenya	4	4	2	25	26	19	20	13	12	9	23	29	34	58
Lesotho	-	-	-	-	-	-	-	-	-	1	1	1	1	4
Liberia	-	-	-	-	-	-	-	2	-	-	1	5	6	3
Madagascar	-	2	-	-	-	-	-	4	3	3	4	3	-	2
Malawi	-	-	-	1	1	-	-	-	-	-	2	4	4	5
Mali	-	-	-	2	2	2	1	3	3	-	2	1	3	1
Mauritania	-	-	-	-	-	-	-	3	4	2	1	-	4	2
Mauritius	1	-	2	5	8	10	12	5	2	4	15	6	6	6
Mozambique	-	-	-	-	-	-	-	-	5	6	24	10	15	26
Namibia	-	1	-	1	-	-	-	7	5	6	14	11	6	14
Niger	-	-	-	-	-	-	-	-	1	-	2	-	1	2
Nigeria	3	7	6	27	24	13	18	37	25	21	46	43	37	50
Reunion	-	-	-	-	-	-	-	-	1	-	-	-	-	-
Rwanda	-	-	-	-	1	-	-	2	-	9	12	26	6	14
São Tomé and Principe	-	-	-	-	-	-	-	1	-	1	1	-	-	-
Senegal	-	-	-	-	-	-	1	3	5	4	9	11	9	6
Seychelles	-	-	-	-	-	-	-	3	-	3	2	1	1	1
Sierra Leone	-	-	-	-	-	-	-	1	2	-	5	1	2	1
Somalia	-	-	-	-	-	-	-	-	1	-	2	-	1	-
South Africa	35	45	34	68	57	66	107	61	90	56	125	116	104	159
Swaziland	-	-	-	-	-	-	-	2	-	-	3	1	-	9
Togo	1	-	6	10	11	4	15	-	1	1	1	1	-	-
Uganda	1	-	1	3	3	1	-	6	15	7	42	17	22	15
United Republic of Tanzania	-	-	1	1	4	3	3	11	7	6	19	12	25	35
Zambia	-	-	-	-	1	-	-	14	14	5	17	16	15	29
Zimbabwe	-	-	-	7	3	2	-	2	4	2	5	13	14	12
Asia	1 202	1 640	1 545	2 343	1 951	2 097	2 192	3 606	4 515	4 189	5 982	4 947	4 839	5 135
East and South-East Asia	747	877	997	1 352	1 198	1 226	1 199	2 384	2 682	2 745	3 696	3 020	3 003	3 048
East Asia	542	617	733	917	849	937	918	1 660	1 830	1 673	2 102	1 686	1 789	1 896
China	131	127	223	282	340	357	407	1 314	1 476	1 328	1 624	1 195	1 344	1 409
Hong Kong, China	118	134	132	176	143	127	143	133	179	168	255	283	222	236
Korea, Democratic People's Republic of	-	-	-	-	-	-	-	-	2	5	4	1	-	2
Korea, Republic of	200	227	230	290	225	263	213	124	93	84	100	104	118	130
Macao, China	-	-	-	1	-	-	-	10	7	13	16	9	7	8
Mongolia	-	-	-	-	-	1	-	8	3	8	8	3	9	5
Taiwan Province of China	93	129	148	168	141	189	155	71	70	67	95	91	89	106
South-East Asia	205	260	264	435	349	289	281	724	852	1 072	1 594	1 334	1 214	1 152
Brunei Darussalam	2	-	-	1	-	-	1	4	-	6	4	8	4	6
Cambodia	-	-	-	1	6	-	-	6	5	10	35	32	36	37
Indonesia	9	5	9	5	10	14	4	77	103	88	140	121	128	150
Lao People's Democratic Republic	-	-	-	2	-	-	-	8	8	11	21	16	12	13
Malaysia	72	78	81	134	112	77	74	97	140	176	222	166	193	188
Myanmar	-	-	1	-	-	-	3	1	2	3	6	5	5	11
Philippines	6	10	28	19	15	23	9	68	62	100	144	121	96	74
Singapore	85	114	99	188	124	106	113	161	210	267	327	327	348	364
Thailand	19	36	31	49	55	40	52	128	118	131	334	281	212	137
Timor-Leste	-	-	-	-	-	-	-	1	-	-	-	-	1	-
Viet Nam	12	17	15	36	27	29	25	173	204	280	361	257	179	172
South Asia	215	323	231	397	308	418	457	707	1 095	804	1 129	868	892	1 045
Afghanistan	-	1	-	-	-	-	1	5	3	1	2	6	9	3
Bangladesh	4	3	-	3	2	6	6	7	12	5	15	18	33	18
Bhutan	-	-	-	-	-	-	-	-	2	-	-	2	2	3
India	193	303	219	375	281	384	426	603	1 020	733	1 023	761	774	932
Iran, Islamic Republic of	7	7	7	9	17	13	2	10	10	17	21	16	11	6
Maldives	-	-	-	-	-	-	-	-	5	2	4	3	10	5
Nepal	-	-	-	1	-	3	2	-	2	1	12	4	5	5
Pakistan	6	4	4	6	5	9	17	70	28	30	29	35	20	29
Sri Lanka	5	5	1	3	3	3	3	12	13	15	23	23	28	44
West Asia	240	440	317	594	445	453	536	515	738	640	1 157	1 059	944	1 042
Bahrain	4	12	11	36	31	15	25	29	51	35	69	73	57	70
Iraq	1	-	1	-	1	-	2	9	6	3	22	26	48	32
Jordan	6	12	7	14	14	10	6	25	35	20	35	27	47	31
Kuwait	18	47	29	82	40	30	55	11	23	12	30	28	33	30
Lebanon	13	21	9	12	6	19	8	12	19	11	9	28	31	27
Oman	-	-	4	6	3	4	4	13	38	17	56	42	40	68
Palestinian Territory	-	1	-	-	-	-	-	-	5	4	2	1	1	-
Qatar	10	20	10	49	22	19	41	23	45	36	83	86	67	85
Saudi Arabia	20	61	55	56	32	38	68	60	95	59	110	144	119	162

Annex table I.9. Number of greenfield FDI projects, by source/destination, 2005–2011 (continued)

Partner region/economy	World as destination							World as source						
	2005	2006	2007	2008	2009	2010	2011	2005	2006	2007	2008	2009	2010	2011
	By source							By destination						
Syrian Arab Republic	-	-	-	2	1	-	3	26	18	17	29	24	22	15
Turkey	66	51	37	64	63	103	67	70	93	104	178	162	150	151
United Arab Emirates	102	215	154	269	232	214	257	234	307	317	524	413	323	369
Yemen	-	-	-	4	-	1	-	3	3	5	10	5	6	2
Latin America and the Caribbean	90	130	241	240	234	285	266	589	651	885	1 242	1 267	1 241	1 465
South America	69	97	156	185	157	183	183	374	377	498	689	709	794	974
Argentina	3	19	31	17	22	23	20	41	59	116	130	116	119	154
Bolivia, Plurinational State of	-	-	-	-	-	-	-	2	9	4	3	14	6	3
Brazil	34	40	67	103	63	76	87	172	167	165	268	289	366	507
Chile	17	17	29	35	37	52	45	39	44	32	72	113	59	70
Colombia	-	2	10	13	6	13	16	49	37	91	90	64	123	127
Ecuador	1	1	3	2	12	5	1	4	5	8	10	6	7	12
Guyana	-	-	-	-	-	-	-	3	3	1	1	1	2	2
Paraguay	-	-	-	-	-	-	-	2	-	2	4	3	9	4
Peru	2	1	5	3	5	2	2	29	28	44	67	78	60	61
Suriname	-	-	-	-	-	-	-	-	-	-	2	-	-	1
Uruguay	-	-	1	1	2	1	1	8	9	22	17	8	23	25
Venezuela, Bolivarian Republic of	12	17	10	11	10	11	11	25	16	13	25	17	20	8
Central America	14	24	65	40	61	83	65	178	237	344	481	502	385	418
Belize	-	-	-	-	-	-	1	-	-	-	-	1	1	-
Costa Rica	1	-	7	2	5	5	2	14	23	41	22	69	43	41
El Salvador	-	-	2	-	5	2	1	4	5	9	13	19	13	17
Guatemala	1	-	5	4	7	5	3	3	3	16	19	20	14	12
Honduras	1	2	2	-	-	-	-	3	2	11	11	7	9	12
Mexico	10	21	44	28	37	54	52	144	197	235	373	330	252	280
Nicaragua	-	-	2	2	-	7	-	2	3	5	8	8	10	13
Panama	1	1	3	4	7	10	6	8	4	27	35	48	43	43
Caribbean	7	9	20	15	16	19	18	37	37	43	72	56	62	73
Antigua and Barbuda	-	-	-	-	-	-	-	-	-	-	2	-	-	-
Aruba	-	-	-	-	-	-	-	1	-	-	1	-	1	2
Bahamas	1	1	3	1	1	-	1	2	-	1	3	2	1	6
Barbados	-	-	1	-	-	1	2	-	-	-	-	1	2	3
Cayman Islands	3	3	6	7	9	7	9	1	2	2	7	4	5	3
Cuba	-	-	-	1	-	-	1	5	1	2	7	12	8	5
Dominican Republic	1	-	3	-	2	2	-	9	10	10	18	13	10	17
Grenada	-	-	-	-	-	-	-	-	-	1	-	-	1	2
Guadeloupe	-	-	-	-	-	-	-	-	1	-	1	-	-	2
Haiti	-	-	-	-	-	1	-	1	2	-	1	2	1	3
Jamaica	-	4	1	5	2	4	4	2	2	2	5	3	2	6
Martinique	-	-	-	-	-	1	-	-	1	2	-	1	-	-
Puerto Rico	-	-	4	1	2	2	1	9	13	18	21	16	26	20
Saint Kitts and Nevis	-	-	-	-	-	-	-	-	-	-	-	-	-	-
Saint Lucia	1	-	-	-	-	-	-	-	-	1	-	1	2	1
Saint Vincent and the Grenadines	-	-	-	-	-	-	-	1	-	-	-	-	-	-
Trinidad and Tobago	1	1	2	-	-	1	-	6	5	4	5	1	2	3
Turks and Caicos Islands	-	-	-	-	-	-	-	-	-	-	1	-	1	-
Oceania	-	2	-	3	4	2	5	2	4	3	12	9	7	10
Fiji	-	-	-	-	1	1	-	-	1	1	3	2	-	5
French Polynesia	-	-	-	-	1	-	-	-	-	-	-	-	1	-
Micronesia, Federated States of	-	1	-	-	-	-	-	-	1	-	-	-	-	-
New Caledonia	-	-	-	-	-	-	1	1	-	1	1	1	-	1
Papua New Guinea	-	-	-	2	-	1	4	1	2	1	6	5	5	3
Samoa	-	1	-	1	-	-	-	-	-	-	1	-	-	-
Solomon Islands	-	-	-	-	2	-	-	-	-	-	1	1	1	1
Transition economies	180	224	196	311	246	274	245	924	807	838	1 238	870	935	882
South-East Europe	8	14	9	33	22	33	23	149	143	168	240	143	180	228
Albania	-	-	-	-	-	1	-	13	11	8	16	7	6	7
Bosnia and Herzegovina	2	-	-	1	-	2	2	27	19	25	27	20	21	29
Croatia	6	7	7	17	9	14	9	45	39	32	41	35	46	51
Montenegro	-	-	-	-	-	1	-	-	3	5	14	1	10	6
Serbia	-	7	2	15	8	13	8	54	44	88	116	62	83	110
The former Yugoslav Republic of Macedonia	-	-	-	-	5	2	4	10	27	10	26	18	14	25
CIS	172	210	187	276	221	238	219	764	645	646	944	696	724	624
Armenia	2	1	-	3	-	2	2	12	8	9	23	24	8	21
Azerbaijan	4	2	10	21	20	17	11	20	15	18	44	46	25	23
Belarus	2	7	14	8	9	19	10	11	18	20	30	26	41	31
Kazakhstan	12	5	2	8	10	9	9	31	26	37	63	47	35	51
Kyrgyzstan	1	-	-	1	1	-	-	4	4	4	7	2	-	5
Moldova, Republic of	-	-	-	1	-	-	1	13	6	13	6	9	13	12
Russian Federation	135	159	137	199	151	163	161	525	413	416	601	411	464	383
Tajikistan	-	-	-	3	2	-	-	7	3	4	4	6	1	4
Turkmenistan	-	-	-	-	-	-	-	1	1	5	11	10	7	9
Ukraine	16	36	24	32	28	28	25	126	133	109	135	94	116	69

Annex table I.9. Number of greenfield FDI projects, by source/destination, 2005–2011 (concluded)

Partner region/economy	World as destination							World as source						
	2005	2006	2007	2008	2009	2010	2011	2005	2006	2007	2008	2009	2010	2011
	By source							By destination						
Uzbekistan	-	-	-	-	-	-	-	14	18	11	20	21	14	16
Georgia	-	-	-	2	3	3	3	11	19	24	54	31	31	30
Memorandum														
Least developed countries[a]	6	8	12	38	34	26	34	129	148	131	344	291	310	338
Landlocked developing countries[b]	20	13	13	55	52	40	44	175	179	182	372	339	257	337
Small island developing states[c]	4	8	9	14	14	18	23	22	18	23	51	26	38	44

Source: UNCTAD, based on information from the Financial Times Ltd, fDi Markets (www.fDimarkets.com).

[a] Least developed countries include Afghanistan, Angola, Bangladesh, Benin, Bhutan, Burkina Faso, Burundi, Cambodia, the Central African Republic, Chad, the Comoros, the Democratic Republic of the Congo, Djibouti, Equatorial Guinea, Eritrea, Ethiopia, the Gambia, Guinea, Guinea-Bissau, Haiti, Kiribati, the Lao People's Democratic Republic, Lesotho, Liberia, Madagascar, Malawi, Mali, Mauritania, Mozambique, Myanmar, Nepal, Niger, Rwanda, Samoa, São Tomé and Principe, Senegal, Sierra Leone, Solomon Islands, Somalia, Sudan, Timor-Leste, Togo, Tuvalu, Uganda, the United Republic of Tanzania, Vanuatu, Yemen and Zambia.

[b] Landlocked developing countries include Afghanistan, Armenia, Azerbaijan, Bhutan, the Plurinational State of Bolivia, Botswana, Burkina Faso, Burundi, the Central African Republic, Chad, Ethiopia, Kazakhstan, Kyrgyzstan, the Lao People's Democratic Republic, Lesotho, the former Yugoslav Republic of Macedonia, Malawi, Mali, the Republic of Moldova, Mongolia, Nepal, Niger, Paraguay, Rwanda, Swaziland, the Republic of Tajikistan, Turkmenistan, Uganda, Uzbekistan, Zambia and Zimbabwe.

[c] Small island developing countries include Antigua and Barbuda, the Bahamas, Barbados, Cape Verde, the Comoros, Dominica, Fiji, Grenada, Jamaica, Kiribati, Maldives, the Marshall Islands, Mauritius, the Federated States of Micronesia, Nauru, Palau, Papua New Guinea, Saint Kitts and Nevis, Saint Lucia, Saint Vincent and the Grenadines, Samoa, São Tomé and Principe, Seychelles, Solomon Islands, Timor-Leste, Tonga, Trinidad and Tobago, Tuvalu and Vanuatu.

Annex table I.10. FDI Contribution Index, rankings and indicator quartiles, 2009
(Quartile rankings for shares of each indicator in economy totals)

Rank	Region/economy	FDI Contribution Index Indicators by Quartile							Memorandum item:
		Value added	Employment	Exports	Tax revenue	Wages and salaries	R&D expenditures	Capital expenditures	FDI inward stock/GDP
1	Hungary	1	1	1	1	1	1	1	1
2	Belgium	..	1	1	1	1	..	1	1
3	Czech Republic	1	1	1	1	1	1	1	1
4	Romania	1	1	1	..	1	2	1	2
5	Hong Kong, China	1	1	1	1	1	1	1	1
6	Poland	1	1	1	1	1	2	1	2
7	Malaysia	1	2	2	1	..	..	1	2
8	Estonia	1	1	..	2	1	3	2	1
9	Bolivia, Plurinational State of	2	2	..	..	2	..	1	3
10	Colombia	2	4	2	1	2	1	2	3
11	Switzerland	1	3	1	2	2	1	2	1
12	Sweden	2	1	1	4	1	..	2	1
13	Singapore	3	2	2	1	1	3	1	1
14	Finland	3	1	2	2	3	1	1	3
15	United Kingdom	2	1	3	2	2	1	2	2
16	Thailand	1	3	3	..	2	..	1	2
17	Ireland	1	1	1	3	4	..	..	1
18	South Africa	2	3	2	1	2	2	2	3
19	Cambodia	3	1	..	..	2	..	3	2
20	Panama	2	2	1	..	1	4	2	1
21	Morocco	1	2	..	..	2	4	1	2
22	Portugal	4	2	2	2	1	3	1	2
23	Trinidad and Tobago	1	3	..	..	4	..	1	1
24	Kazakhstan	1	4	..	..	4	..	1	2
25	Costa Rica	1	4	2	3	1	..	2	2
26	Netherlands	2	2	..	3	2	2	3	1
27	Dominican Republic	3	4	1	1	..	..	2	3
28	Brazil	3	3	2	2	3	2	2	3
29	Norway	2	1	4	1	3	4	1	2
30	Germany	3	2	3	4	1	1	2	4
31	Slovenia	4	2	1	..	3	..	1	3
32	Italy	3	3	3	2	2	1	3	4
33	Denmark	2	1	4	2	2	3	2	2
34	Croatia	1	4	..	..	2	3	2	2
35	Bosnia and Herzegovina	1	4	..	..	2	..	3	2
36	Honduras	1	4	..	2	1	..	4	2
37	Argentina	2	2	3	..	2	3	1	4
38	Cyprus	4	3	..	..	1	..	2	1
39	France	3	2	2	3	2	2	3	3
40	Austria	2	1	2	3	3	3	3	3
41	Canada	3	2	1	3	3	3	2	3
42	Ukraine	1	3	..	..	3	3	2	2
43	United Arab Emirates	1	3	4	..	1	..	4	3
44	Lithuania	2	2	..	..	3	2	4	3
45	Indonesia	3	3	4	..	1	1	3	4
46	Bulgaria	2	2	..	..	2	..	4	1
47	Peru	2	4	3	1	2	..	2	3
48	Latvia	2	1	..	..	3	..	4	2
49	Egypt	3	2	4	2	4	3	1	3

/...

Annex table I.10. FDI Contribution Index, rankings and indicator quartiles,2009 (concluded)
(Quartile rankings for shares of each indicator in economy totals)

Rank	Region/economy	FDI Contribution Index Indicators by Quartile							Memorandum item:
		Value added	Employment	Exports	Tax revenue	Wages and salaries	R&D expenditures	Capital expenditures	FDI inward stock/GDP
50	Australia	3	2	3	3	3	3	2	3
51	Jamaica	2	4	..	..	1	..	3	1
52	Ecuador	3	3	3	..	..	1	3	4
53	Chile	2	4	3	2	3	4	1	1
54	Guatemala	4	2	..	..	3	..	3	4
55	Uruguay	2	4	..	..	1	4	3	3
56	New Zealand	3	1	4	3	3	4	3	2
57	Spain	3	3	3	4	2	2	3	2
58	Sri Lanka	3	1	..	..	3	..	4	4
59	China	4	2	1	4	4	2	4	4
60	Philippines	3	4	3	2	3	..	3	4
61	India	4	3	3	3	3	2	4	4
62	Mexico	4	2	2	4	3	2	3	3
63	Luxembourg	1	1	4	4	4	..	4	1
64	Israel	4	3	2	4	4	1	3	3
65	Turkey	3	3	4	3	2	4	3	4
66	Russian Federation	3	4	4	4	3	3	2	3
67	Greece	4	3	3	3	3	4	4	4
68	Barbados	2	4	4	3	4	..	4	1
69	Taiwan Province of China	4	1	4	4	4	4	3	4
70	United States	4	3	2	4	4	4	3	4
71	Venezuela, Bolivarian Republic of	4	4	..	..	4	..	4	4
72	Korea, Republic of	4	3	4	4	4	4	4	4
73	Japan	4	4	3	4	4	4	4	4
74	Kenya	4	3	..	..	4	..	4	4
75	Algeria	4	4	..	..	4	..	4	4
76	Saudi Arabia	4	4	4	..	4	..	4	3
77	Paraguay	4	4	..	..	4	..	4	4
78	Bahamas	4	4	..	..	4	..	4	1
79	Bermuda	4	..	4	..	4	..	4	1

Source: UNCTAD; for further information on data and methodology, see www.unctad.org/diae.

Annex table III.1. List of IIAs, as of mid-June 2012[a]

Economies and territories	BITs	Other IIAs[b]	Total
Afghanistan	3	3	6
Albania	42	6	48
Algeria	47	6	53
Angola	8	7	15
Anguilla	-	1	1
Antigua and Barbuda	2	10	12
Argentina	58	16	74
Armenia	36	2	38
Aruba	-	1	1
Australia	23	17	40
Austria	64	64	128
Azerbaijan	44	3	47
Bahamas	1	7	8
Bahrain	30	12	42
Bangladesh	30	4	34
Barbados	10	10	20
Belarus	58	3	61
Belgium[c]	93	64	157
Belize	7	9	16
Benin	14	6	20
Bermuda	-	1	1
Bolivia, Plurinational State of	22	15	37
Bosnia and Herzegovina	39	4	43
Botswana	8	6	14
Brazil	14	17	31
British Virgin Islands	-	1	1
Brunei Darussalam	8	19	27
Bulgaria	68	62	130
Burkina Faso	14	7	21
Burundi	7	8	15
Cambodia	21	16	37
Cameroon	16	5	21
Canada	29	21	50
Cape Verde	9	5	14
Cayman Islands	-	2	2
Central African Republic	4	4	8
Chad	14	4	18
Chile	51	26	77
China	128	16	144
Colombia	7	18	25
Comoros	6	8	14
Congo	12	5	17
Democratic Republic of the Congo	15	8	23
Cook Islands	-	2	2
Costa Rica	21	15	36
Côte d'Ivoire	10	6	16
Croatia	58	5	63
Cuba	58	3	61
Cyprus	27	61	88
Czech Republic	79	64	143
Denmark	55	64	119
Djibouti	7	9	16
Dominica	2	10	12

/...

Annex table III.1. List of IIAs, as of mid-June 2012ᵃ (continued)

Economies and territories	BITs	Other IIAsᵇ	Total
Dominican Republic	15	6	21
Ecuador	18	12	30
Egypt	100	15	115
El Salvador	22	11	33
Equatorial Guinea	8	4	12
Eritrea	4	4	8
Estonia	27	63	90
Ethiopia	29	5	34
Fiji	-	3	3
Finland	71	64	135
France	101	64	165
Gabon	12	6	18
Gambia	13	6	19
Georgia	29	4	33
Germany	136	64	200
Ghana	26	6	32
Greece	43	64	107
Grenada	2	9	11
Guatemala	17	13	30
Guinea	19	6	25
Guinea-Bissau	2	7	9
Guyana	8	10	18
Haiti	6	4	10
Honduras	11	11	22
Hong Kong, China	15	4	19
Hungary	58	64	122
Iceland	9	31	40
India	83	14	97
Indonesia	63	17	80
Iran, Islamic Republic of	60	1	61
Iraq	4	6	10
Ireland	-	64	64
Israel	37	5	42
Italy	93	64	157
Jamaica	16	10	26
Japan	18	21	39
Jordan	52	10	62
Kazakhstan	42	5	47
Kenya	12	8	20
Kiribati	-	2	2
Korea, Democratic People's Republic of	24	-	24
Korea, Republic of	90	16	106
Kuwait	59	13	72
Kyrgyzstan	28	5	33
Lao People's Democratic Republic	23	14	37
Latvia	44	62	106
Lebanon	50	8	58
Lesotho	3	7	10
Liberia	4	6	10
Libya	32	10	42
Liechtenstein	-	26	26
Lithuania	52	62	114
Luxembourgᶜ	93	64	157

/...

Annex table III.1. List of IIAs, as of mid-June 2012ᵃ (continued)

Economies and territories	BITs	Other IIAsᵇ	Total
Macao, China	2	2	4
Madagascar	9	8	17
Malawi	6	8	14
Malaysia	67	23	90
Mali	17	7	24
Malta	22	61	83
Mauritania	19	5	24
Mauritius	36	9	45
Mexico	28	19	47
Moldova, Republic of	39	2	41
Monaco	1	0	1
Mongolia	43	3	46
Montenegro	18	3	21
Montserrat	-	5	5
Morocco	62	7	69
Mozambique	24	6	30
Myanmar	6	12	18
Namibia	13	6	19
Nepal	6	3	9
Netherlands	98	64	162
New Caledonia	-	1	1
New Zealand	5	14	19
Nicaragua	18	12	30
Niger	5	7	12
Nigeria	22	6	28
Norway	15	30	45
Oman	33	11	44
Pakistan	46	7	53
Palestinian Territory	2	6	8
Panama	23	10	33
Papua New Guinea	6	4	10
Paraguay	24	15	39
Peru	32	29	61
Philippines	35	16	51
Poland	62	64	126
Portugal	55	64	119
Qatar	49	11	60
Romania	82	63	145
Russian Federation	71	4	75
Rwanda	6	8	14
Saint Kitts and Nevis	-	10	10
Saint Lucia	2	10	12
Saint Vincent and the Grenadines	2	10	12
Samoa	-	2	2
San Marino	7	0	7
São Tomé and Principe	1	3	4
Saudi Arabia	22	12	34
Senegal	24	7	31
Serbia	49	3	52
Seychelles	7	8	15
Sierra Leone	3	6	9
Singapore	41	29	70

/...

Annex table III.1. List of IIAs, as of mid-June 2012ᵃ (concluded)

Economies and territories	BITs	Other IIAsᵇ	Total
Slovakia	54	64	118
Slovenia	38	62	100
Solomon Islands	-	2	2
Somalia	2	6	8
South Africa	46	9	55
Spain	76	64	140
Sri Lanka	28	5	33
Sudan	27	11	38
Suriname	3	7	10
Swaziland	5	9	14
Sweden	70	64	134
Switzerland	118	32	150
Syrian Arab Republic	41	6	47
Taiwan Province of China	23	4	27
Tajikistan	31	4	35
Thailand	39	23	62
The former Yugoslav Republic of Macedonia	37	5	42
Timor-Leste	3	0	3
Togo	4	6	10
Tonga	1	2	3
Trinidad and Tobago	12	10	22
Tunisia	54	9	63
Turkey	84	21	105
Turkmenistan	23	5	28
Tuvalu	-	2	2
Uganda	15	9	24
Ukraine	66	5	71
United Arab Emirates	39	11	50
United Kingdom	104	64	168
United Republic of Tanzania	15	7	22
United States	47	63	110
Uruguay	30	17	47
Uzbekistan	49	4	53
Vanuatu	2	2	4
Venezuela, Bolivarian Republic of	28	7	35
Viet Nam	59	20	79
Yemen	37	7	44
Zambia	12	9	21
Zimbabwe	30	9	39

Source: UNCTAD, based on IIA database.

ᵃ This includes not only agreements that are signed and entered into force, but also agreements where negotiations are only concluded. Note that the numbers of BITs and "other IIAs" in this table do not add up to the total number of BITs and "other IIAs" as stated in the text, because some economies/territories have concluded agreements with entities that are not listed in this table. Note also that because of ongoing reporting by member States and the resulting retroactive adjustments to the UNCTAD database, the data differ from those reported in *WIR11*.
ᵇ These numbers include agreements concluded by economies as members of a regional integration organization.
ᶜ BITs concluded by the Belgo-Luxembourg Economic Union.

WORLD INVESTMENT REPORT PAST ISSUES

WIR 2011: Non-Equity Modes of International Production and Development

WIR 2010: Investing in a Low-carbon Economy

WIR 2009: Transnational Corporations, Agricultural Production and Development

WIR 2008: Transnational Corporations and the Infrastructure Challenge

WIR 2007: Transnational Corporations, Extractive Industries and Development

WIR 2006: FDI from Developing and Transition Economies: Implications for Development

WIR 2005: Transnational Corporations and the Internationalization of R&D

WIR 2004: The Shift Towards Services

WIR 2003: FDI Policies for Development: National and International Perspectives

WIR 2002: Transnational Corporations and Export Competitiveness

WIR 2001: Promoting Linkages

WIR 2000: Cross-border Mergers and Acquisitions and Development

WIR 1999: Foreign Direct Investment and the Challenge of Development

WIR 1998: Trends and Determinants

WIR 1997: Transnational Corporations, Market Structure and Competition Policy

WIR 1996: Investment, Trade and International Policy Arrangements

WIR 1995: Transnational Corporations and Competitiveness

WIR 1994: Transnational Corporations, Employment and the Workplace

WIR 1993: Transnational Corporations and Integrated International Production

WIR 1992: Transnational Corporations as Engines of Growth

WIR 1991: The Triad in Foreign Direct Investment

All downloadable at www.unctad.org/wir

SELECTED UNCTAD PUBLICATION SERIES
ON TNCs AND FDI

World Investment Report
www.unctad.org/wir

FDI Statistics
www.unctad.org/fdistatistics

World Investment Prospects Survey
www.unctad.org/wips

Global Investment Trends Monitor
www.unctad.org/diae

Investment Policy Monitor
www.unctad.org/iia

Issues in International Investment Agreements: I and II (Sequels)
www.unctad.org/iia

International Investment Policies for Development
www.unctad.org/iia

Investment Advisory Series A and B
www.unctad.org/diae

Investment Policy Reviews
www.unctad.org/ipr

Current Series on FDI and Development
www.unctad.org/diae

Transnational Corporations Journal
www.unctad.org/tnc

HOW TO OBTAIN THE PUBLICATIONS

The sales publications may be purchased from distributors of United Nations publications throughout the world. They may also be obtained by contacting:

United Nations Publications Customer Service
c/o National Book Network
15200 NBN Way
PO Box 190
Blue Ridge Summit, PA 17214
email: unpublications@nbnbooks.com

https://unp.un.org/

For further information on the work on foreign direct investment and transnational corporations, please address inquiries to:

Division on Investment and Enterprise
United Nations Conference on Trade and Development
Palais des Nations, Room E-10052
CH-1211 Geneva 10 Switzerland

Telephone: +41 22 917 4533
Fax: +41 22 917 0498
web: www.unctad.org/diae